"It is indeed a great honor for me that a book about my theology consisting of contributions by a large group of Roman Catholic theologians is published. And it is an expression of generosity and openness that I have been asked to write an answer to some of the criticisms made by the contributors. I did this reply with the same joy about a fruitful dialogue with which I read the articles. One thing I learned in doing so is the necessity that we learn more about each other's thought, the classical as well as the contemporary. Much misunderstanding on both sides could be prevented by such better information. A dialogue, done in 'listening love,' can be a tool of providence and a channel of the divine Spirit."

Paul Tillich

PAUL TILLICH
IN CATHOLIC THOUGHT

REVISED EDITION

EDITORS
Thomas F. O'Meara, O.P.
Donald M. Weisser, O.P.

FOREWORD BY
J. Heywood Thomas

AN AFTERWORD BY
Paul Tillich

IMAGE BOOKS
A Division of Doubleday & Company, Inc.
Garden City, New York

Image Books edition 1969
by special arrangement with The Priory Press

Image Books edition published September 1969

D. M. Weisser, "Paul Tillich: A Roman Catholic Appreciation." Reprinted from *Christian Advocate*, February 10,
1966. Copyright © 1966 by The Methodist Publishing
House.

"Christology as Symbol" is reprinted, with some omissions,
from *Paul Tillich and the Christian Message* by George
H. Tavard. Copyright © 1962 George H. Tavard. Used by
permission of Charles Scribner's Sons.

Dedicated
to the memory of

GUSTAVE WEIGEL, S.J.

J. HEYWOOD THOMAS

Foreword

It is ironic that the person hailed as America's greatest theologian and philosopher is not an American. Paul Tillich, as Father Schepers aptly puts it in his essay in this volume, "is essentially a *European* theologian, who happens to be living and writing in the United States." This struck me forcibly when I heard him lecture in New York. There was a sense of tradition in his thinking which was quite un-American. In a way his thinking is distinctly classical. It is not only that he has drunk deeply of the classical springs which have always refreshed the European scholar so that his "New World" is the glory of the old, but rather that the essence of classicism as an intellectual movement is at the core of his theology. There are times when one feels that his outlook is quite simply Platonic (or at least Plotinian), and he once remarked to me that the trouble with me was that I was too Aristotelian in my logic whereas he was more Platonic. Also, there is a classicism apparent in the etymological approach that he favors in his theological method, as if language itself were something that obeyed clearly-formulated laws. But, though a European indeed, Tillich strikes the British reader as a very foreign author. It is likely, I think, that his theological system will exert a more powerful influence on American theology than on British theology, and this is precisely because it is a system and as such foreign to British theology. In Britain there is a long and powerful tradition of empiricism (the dominant movement in philosophy since Locke), and consequently the British theologian regards systematic constructions with a very sceptical eye.

That such a standpoint can contribute a much-needed critique of Tillich's theology is obvious; but for this very reason the criticism is likely to be ignored by Tillich himself and those who have made him the leader of a school of theology. It is, therefore, very encouraging to see the interest taken in Tillich's theology by Catholic theologians who clearly have no a priori objection to a systematic construction. Not only Catholic students of theology but, indeed, all students of theology are indebted to the late Father Weigel for pioneering Catholic interest in Tillich, and all who read his essays in this volume will feel that American theology has lost one of its brightest stars. His article, "Contemporaneous Protestantism and Paul Tillich," published in 1950,[1] was, to the best of my knowledge, the first serious attempt by a Catholic theologian to indicate the significant work done in theology by Tillich. The editors of this volume have shown their appreciation of Father Weigel's contribution to contemporary theological discussion by choosing his excellent paper on Tillich's theological significance as the opening item in this collection. Seldom has any thinker had so sympathetic and understanding a critic to introduce his work. Indeed, complete fairness is characteristic of all Catholic criticism of Tillich, and this makes the criticism all the more valuable.

One of the most exciting features of this volume of criticism is the very real ecumenical spirit it displays. Father Tavard's paper on Christ as the answer to existential anguish shows openness and readiness not only to relearn what Catholicism has taught, but an equal readiness to learn emphases which Catholicism needs to teach. Father Schepers, too, is prepared to admit that Tillich has something to teach Catholicism about how Catholicity is to be realized today. In this Father Schepers does not try to suggest that Tillich is a Catholic *malgré lui*, but states Tillich's disagreement with Catholicism clearly and emphatically, so that the very real similarities and agreements may be the more clearly understood. Father McLean again shows how close Tillich comes to Catholicism, whilst clearly indicating the points of difference. These are of fundamental importance to the student of

[1] See *Theological Studies*, 11 (1950), 177–202.

Tillich's theology, and one of the most significant is what might be called the essentially Protestant character of Tillich's theology as a *free* creation. This is a point which is made in various ways. Father Tavard speaks of the negative character of the Protestant principle which Tillich can be said to enunciate, and he voices the doubt whether Tillich has not diluted the Church's message. Both Father Weigel and Father McLean express the suspicion that Tillich's system is not theology, but phenomenological discourse about theological terms. This is the central issue in Tillich's theology, and I have argued elsewhere that it will not do to pose the question as a problem of correlating philosophy and theology. The question is, rather, whether Tillich has reinterpreted the Christian doctrines he set out to expound, so that what we have is no longer recognizable as Christian doctrine. Only the clear asking and answering of this question can help theology. As Father Kiesling says, we must judge Tillich's theology "on the basis of his intention, the *sense* of the totality of his words, and the correspondence of that sense with reality." Now here we reach the fundamental division in theology between those who imagine that they have some direct access to the reality and those who feel that they see through a glass darkly. But nothing is gained by making the issues muddled. Making the issues clear is itself a contribution to that great dialogue which we hope Christendom will witness in this century. Certainly the papers in this volume make one very hopeful of such a flowering of mutual understanding between the divided branches of the Christian Church. The concern for that truth of faith which is, in Kierkegaard's words, "infinite subjectivity," the desire to uphold the biblical revelation, and the appreciation of the urgent need of theology in the modern world to communicate the faith which has set us free—all of these reassure those who have tended to feel that the Second Vatican Council cannot really bring about cooperation and closer relations.

One other feature which I think recommends this book is that it discusses some of the points which Tillich often stresses but never explains. I will mention but one of these at the moment: the theory of symbolism that he offers.

As I have remarked in my *Paul Tillich: An Appraisal*,[2] Tillich's formulations of his doctrine of symbolism are always vague, and we are never told how symbols participate in the reality they symbolize, whereas signs have no such relation with that to which they point. Two papers by Father Weigel which are included here deal with this problem. The first is the paper already referred to, "The Theological Significance of Paul Tillich," where Father Weigel elicited from Tillich the claim that he means by symbols what St. Thomas meant by analogy. The other paper is "Myth, Symbol, and Analogy," which is very valuable because it contains clear and precise interpretation of the vague phrase employed by Tillich—"participate in the reality of." It is significant that Father Weigel did not go on to argue that, if this was so, then Tillich could not mean by symbol what St. Thomas meant by analogy; but he probably considered this unnecessary in view of the fact that he had said more than once that Tillich's doctrine of analogy was not sufficiently radical.[3] The identification of "Symbol"—Tillich uses it with "analogy"—understood by St. Thomas is taken up again and discussed in some detail by Father McLean in his paper, "Symbol and Analogy: Tillich and Thomas." It seems to me that the charges of subjectivism and relativism which he makes against Tillich are charges which Tillich will find it hard to refute. These papers are valuable not only as elucidations of what Tillich is in fact saying but also as contributions to the theological debate which he has started.

In conclusion I may say that I regard it an honour to contribute the Foreword to this volume for two reasons—first because it is the work of theologians whom I respect greatly, and secondly because the kindness thus shown to me is a token of the ecumenical character of contemporary theology.

J.H.T.

Faculty of Theology, University of Manchester

2 (Philadelphia: The Westminster Press, 1963), p. 194.

3 See "The Theological Significance of Paul Tillich," *Gregorianum*, 37 (1956), 43 (see below, p. 32); "Recent Protestant Theology," *Theological Studies*, 14 (1953), 583.

Acknowledgments

The Editors gratefully acknowledge the kindness of the authors, editors, and publishers who have granted permission to reprint the following material:

Donald M. Weisser, O.P., "Paul Tillich: A Roman Catholic Appreciation," *Christian Advocate*, 10 (1966), 7–8. Gustave Weigel, S.J., "The Theological Significance of Paul Tillich," *Gregorianum*, 37 (1956), 34–54. Edward O'Connor, C.S.C., "Paul Tillich: An Impression," *Thought*, 30 (1955–56), 507–24. George F. McLean, O.M.I., "Paul Tillich's Existential Philosophy of Protestantism," *The Thomist*, 28 (1964), 1–50. George H. Tavard, "The Protestant Principle and the Theological System of Paul Tillich," translated from the French by Joachim Culotta, O.P., *Revue des sciences philosophiques et théologiques*, 46 (1962), 242–53. Kenelm Foster, O.P., "Paul Tillich and St. Thomas," *Blackfriars*, 41 (1960), 306–13.

Avery Dulles, S.J., "Paul Tillich and the Bible," *Theological Studies*, 17 (1956), 345–67. George F. McLean, O.M.I., "Symbol and Analogy: Tillich and Thomas," *Revue de l'Université de Ottawa*, 28 (1958), 193*–233*. Gustave Weigel, S.J., "Myth, Symbol, and Analogy," *Religion and Culture: Essays in Honor of Paul Tillich*, edited by Walter Leibrecht (New York: Harper & Brothers, 1959), pp. 120–30. Erich Przywara, S.J., "Christian Root-Terms: Kerygma, Mysterium, Kairos, Oikonomia," translated by Calvin Schrag, *Religion and Culture: Essays in Honor of Paul Tillich*, edited by Walter Leibrecht (New York: Harper & Brothers, 1959), pp. 113–19.

George H. Tavard, "Christology as Symbol," from his *Paul Tillich and the Christian Message* (New York: Charles Scribner's Sons, 1962), pp. 52–81, with some omissions. George H. Tavard, "Christ as the Answer to Existential Anguish," reprinted from *Continuum*, 4 (1966), 3–13.

CONTENTS

Abbreviations

This listing contains the abbreviations used for the principal writings of Paul Tillich in English.

BRSUR   *Biblical Religion and the Search for Ultimate Reality*. Chicago: University of Chicago Press, 1955.

CB   *The Courage to Be*. New Haven: Yale University Press, 1955. Yale paperbound edition, 1959.

CEWR   *Christianity and the Encounter of the World Religions*. New York: Columbia University Press, 1963.

DF   *Dynamics of Faith*. New York: Harper and Brothers, 1957. Also available as a Harper Torchbook.

IH   *The Interpretation of History*. Translated by N. A. Rasetski and Elsa L. Talmay. New York: Charles Scribner's Sons, 1936.

LPJ   *Love, Power, and Justice*. New York: Oxford University Press, 1954. Galaxy paperbound edition, Oxford University Press, 1960.

NB   *The New Being*. New York: Charles Scribner's Sons, 1955. Also available as a Scribner Library paperback.

PE   *The Protestant Era*. Translated by James Luther Adams. Chicago: University of Chicago Press,

1948. Abridged edition available as a Phoenix paperback, University of Chicago Press.

RS   *The Religious Situation*. Translated by H. Richard Niebuhr. New York: Henry Holt, 1932. Meridian paperback edition, 1956.

SF   *The Shaking of the Foundations*. New York: Charles Scribner's Sons, 1948. Also available as a Scribner Library paperback.

ST, I,   *Systematic Theology*. In three volumes. Chicago: University of Chicago Press, 1951, 1957, 1963.
    II,
    III

TC   *Theology of Culture*. Edited by Robert C. Kimball. New York: Oxford University Press, 1959.

*   *   *

Mention should also be made of the following works by Dr. Tillich which are not cited in this collection:

The Eternal Now. New York: Charles Scribner's Sons, 1963.
Morality and Beyond. Volume Nine of *Religious Perspectives*, edited by Ruth Nanda Anshen. New York: Harper and Row, 1965.
Ultimate Concern. New York: Harper and Row, 1965.
Protestant Theology in the Nineteenth and Twentieth Century. New York: Harper and Row, 1967.
A History of Christian Thought. New York: Harper and Row, 1968.

*   *   *

A full bibliography of Paul Tillich, from 1910–58, compiled by Peter H. John, can be found in *Religion and Culture: Essays in Honor of Paul Tillich*, edited by Walter Leibrecht. New York: Harper and Brothers, 1959. Pp. 367–96.

Introduction

For an anniversary celebration the editors of *Time* magazine wanted a theologian to speak about "The Human Condition." They asked Paul Tillich.

This eminent Protestant scholar was an apt choice, for behind decades of study, teaching, and preaching, it has been man's existential condition, the relationship of present time to past events which has given direction to the thought of Paul Tillich.

On August 20, 1886, Paul Tillich was born in Starzeddell, Kreis Guben, a small industrial town in Prussia. His mother, Mathilde Dürselen Tillich, had come from the Rhineland of West Germany, and his father, Johannes, was a minister of the Prussian Territorial Church. When Paul was four, the Tillich family moved to Schönfliess-Neumark, where his father had been called to become superintendent of the diocese, an office "with functions similar to those of a bishop, but on a smaller scale."[1]

During his early years, life in the parish house was balanced with occasional trips to Berlin, where his father had lived as a young man, and by vacations to the Baltic seaside.

---

[1] Paul Tillich, "Autobiographical Reflections," *The Theology of Paul Tillich*, C. W. Kegley and R. W. Bretall, editors (New York: Macmillan, 1952), p. 4. These "reflections," together with those in the introductions to *IH* and *PE*, provide us with fairly full biographical detail. Because Tillich attempts in these sketches "to give an account of how my ideas have grown from my life" (*IH*, p. 3), they form in themselves a valuable introduction to his thought.

And from his twelfth to his fourteenth year, Paul was away from home as a boarder in Königsberg-Neumark, a pupil at the *Gymnasium*, where Greek and Latin formed the core of his education. He sees in the varied impressions gathered during these years a partial explanation for his special relationship to nature, a relationship "expressed in a predominantly aesthetic-meditative attitude to nature."[2] He also finds here a reason for the great emotional influence which Schelling's philosophy of nature had on him—"although I was well aware that this philosophy was scientifically impossible."[3] Coupled with this romanticism was a revolutionary motive, actively stemming from his inception in the *Gymnasium*. Here he shared in the animosity toward the upper social classes, among whom were his parents. Despite the closeness and love of his family life, he found himself reacting to the authoritarian attitude of his conservative Lutheran father and to the moral rigidity of his mother. Even now, Paul Tillich sees in the balance of these two motives, the romantic and the revolutionary, the basic problem of his life and thought.

While still young, Tillich began reading history of philosophy, and he acquired a fundamental acquaintance with Kant, Fichte, Hegel, and Schelling. Schelling became the particular object of his study in the coming years, during which, too, Tillich first discovered Kierkegaard. In 1904, after completing his humanistic studies in a Berlin *Gymnasium*, he matriculated in the theological faculty of the university there. The following year he was first at Tübingen and then at the University of Halle until 1907, when he returned to Berlin. His Doctorate in Philosophy was won from the University of Breslau in 1911, and his Licentiate in Theology from Halle in 1912. In this latter year Paul Tillich was ordained a minister in the Evangelical Church of the province of Brandenberg.

After two years as an assistant pastor in various places, he entered the German Army as a chaplain and was sent to the

2 Tillich, "Autobiographical Reflections," Kegley and Bretall, *op. cit.*, p. 4.
3 *Loc. cit.*

Western Front. When the war was over, Tillich returned to academic life, now as *Privatdozent* of theology in the University of Berlin (1919–24). Here he lectured on the relation of religion to politics, art, philosophy, depth psychology, and sociology, presenting his students with what he has termed a "theology of culture." A lecture on "The Theology of Culture," delivered in 1919, made Paul Tillich famous in Europe overnight.[4]

Two significant events mark 1924. In that year he married Hannah Werner; from their marriage have come two children, a daughter, Erdmuthe, and a son, René Stephen. A professorship was available at Marburg; against his own wishes, Tillich accepted the position. There he encountered for the first time the "radical effects of neo-orthodox theology on theological students,"[5] and existentialism.[6] In 1925, at Marburg, he set to work on *Systematic Theology*, the first volume of which was not to appear for another quarter century. Subsequently, he held teaching posts at Dresden, Leipzig, and Frankfurt-am-Main.

From its rise, Tillich was an outspoken critic of Nazism. As a result, when Hitler became chancellor, Tillich was immediately dismissed from his university position. This was in 1933, when the weakness of German Protestantism in the face of a totalitarian government brought him to consider entering the Catholic Church. The only two choices, he remarked, seemed to be "Christian or heathen Catholicism, the Roman Church or national heathenism in Protestant garb."[7] But the German Protestant Church rallied.

At the age of forty-seven, in the latter half of 1933, Paul Tillich accepted an invitation extended by Reinhold Niebuhr to come to Union Theological Seminary. Tillich and his fam-

---

[4] Walter Leibrecht, "The Life and Mind of Paul Tillich," *Religion and Culture: Essays in Honor of Paul Tillich*, Walter Leibrecht, editor (New York: Harper, 1959), p. 7.

[5] Tillich, "Autobiographical Reflections," Kegley and Bretall, *op. cit.*, p. 14.

[6] See T. F. O'Meara, O.P., "Tillich and Heidegger: A Structural Relationship," *Harvard Theological Review*, 61 (1968), 249–61.

[7] *IH*, pp. 24–25.

ily arrived in New York on November 4, 1933. It was, of course, not easy to begin life anew in the United States. The atmosphere at Union, however, was stimulating: "If New York is the bridge between the continents, Union Seminary is the lane of that bridge, on which the churches of the world move."[8] Tillich rose quickly to a position of prominence on the American theological scene. Through his regular seminary courses, his sermons and special lectures throughout the country, through his many books and myriad articles, through his position on the editorial boards of such periodicals as *Pastoral Psychology* and *Daedalus*, all permeated by the warmth and dynamism of his personality and the depth of his religious commitment, he influenced countless students of Protestant theology. Nor has he been forgotten in Europe. Several times since the end of World War II he has returned to teach in the foremost German universities. In 1956, he was presented with the Grosse Verdienstkreuz, highest service award of the West German Republic. His complete works are in the course of publication in German. Moreover, considerable interest in Tillich's thought has been shown by Japanese scholars; in the summer of 1960, he was guest lecturer of the Japan Committee for Intellectual Interchange, visiting leading universities throughout the country. As recently as the autumn of 1963, he lectured in the Theological Faculty of the University of Zurich.

Upon his retirement from Union Theological Seminary in 1955, Tillich was invited to join the faculty of Harvard Divinity School, where he continued to work and teach until after his seventy-fifth birthday. From September of 1962, he was professor of theology at the University of Chicago. In November of 1965 during his last year as John Nuveen Professor of Theology, Paul Tillich died. His influence upon students, now a broader group due to the conciliar changes within Roman Catholicism and due to their growing appreciation of his theology, was as significant as ever. Visits to the Far East and joint efforts with scholars such as Mircea

[8] Tillich, "Autobiographical Reflections," Kegley and Bretall, *op. cit.*, p. 17.

Eliade had broadened his theology, making it even more fruitful and stimulating. Tillich is buried, by choice, at New Harmony, Indiana. This is a remarkable place in the heartland of the American continent near Vincennes. Millenarianism, German pietism, scientific utopianism, progressive education have all rested for a while in the beautiful early nineteenth-century buildings there, coming and going, intangibly catalytic in the broader streams of American life and thought.

The following pages represent an appraisal by contemporary Catholic theologians of Dr. Tillich's theology. The viewpoint and impression cannot help but be from a single position. However, this collection should be of interest to Protestants as well as Catholics: to Protestants concerned with contemporary theology in its now necessarily ecumenical dimension; and to Catholics who are intent upon learning what Protestant theology is saying today. The volume is not a total and thorough examination of Dr. Tillich's theology, but a collection of essays. These studies, arranged in an order somewhat similar to his theological system, touch upon the fundamental areas of his thought: the nature of revelation and theology; its relationship to human thought; Jesus Christ; the Church and the Christian. The purpose of the volume is not, ultimately, critical; its purpose is to explore the truth and relevance of a theologian's understanding of Christianity and the causes for his success in forming our contemporary scene. The Catholic who is being introduced to the theology of Paul Tillich should realize he is being introduced through an examination of this or that part, and through criticism. Whether each and every apparent difference is really a disagreement is not yet certain; the dialogue is not finished.

Yet, this is a time of discussion. Tillich has written that a Christian theology which is not able to enter into creative dialogue with other theologies "misses a world-historical occasion and remains provincial. . . . There is a *kairos*, a moment full of potentialities, in Protestant-Catholic relations."

Paul Tillich's theology, along with the Protestant trends and heritage he represents, raises two questions for the Catholic. First, it often appears to Catholics that Protestant theology is too much the thought of a single man and too little the respectful examination of the deposit of faith. The Catholic faith retains a basic and substantial permanence whether it is explained by John Damascene or Thomas Aquinas. In contrast, how radically different is Barth from Tillich, Cullmann from Harnack. Still, this impression is not complete. No one labors successfully without beginning where others have stopped. Paul Tillich is the heir of German philosophical and theological trends from the past century and beyond. The precision of systematic thought, the rebirth of ontology, existentialism, the "ambiguity of the human condition" in this century of war and science, the unrewarding quest for the historical Jesus—these currents fashioned Paul Tillich. Secondly, the reader from a more traditional theological background will be respectful of Tillich's struggle to make Christ meaningful to our culture, but will wonder at the changes made in Christianity. In short, what continuity can Tillich have with the theological past? Is his separation of our century from the century of revelation and inspiration too severe?

The answer to both of these questions lies in the problem of the evolution of dogma, the transmission of a special Word of God through history and time. At the beginning of our century it was the studied decision of the Catholic Church's magisterium that traditional dogmatic statements were not simply symbols or temporary projected formulae. Our understanding of the revelation of God through Christ can improve in extension and comprehension, but it cannot contradict or totally replace the substantial and universal understanding which the *Ecclesia* possesses at any point as it passes through time. Tillich's view of the content and form of divine revelation is quite different; it allows Protestant theology to change more extensively. Tillich's ultimate theological principle seems to be a protest against man's setting up idols of infallible creed, certain dogma, and efficacious sacrament. If this principle is the origin of Protestant theology, its goal is relevance for the man who stands before the preacher and teacher. Modern man should not be tied down to a "religion" formulated for an almost different creature. The present point in mankind's religious and cultural evolution determines this theologian's Christ more than an event in the past.

Tillich speaks of *the theological circle,* and this concept is important for the development of dogma. The theologian, he observes, cannot look upon theology with a purely abstract, disinterested phenomenology. He must be committed. He must be within the theological circle, having made an existential decision which places him in the situation of faith. Aquinas, in a similar manner, explained theology as the scientific exploration of a group of first principles which are the Christian faith. Science cannot exist without principles, and so theology demands its principles, faith. The difference between the Catholic theologian's point of view and that of Tillich (along with his associates and predecessors) can be described in terms of how the evolution of Christian doctrine influences the theological circle.

The theological circle (which is the circle of faith) offers to the traditional theologian something limited but also something infinite. There are limits to the correct human expression of Christian revelation, and beyond these limits man leaves the light. To the intellectual and specific stability of man there corresponds a basic stability in the Word of God. Formulae may change, understanding may deepen, but the promise of a permanent Spirit residing in the Church precludes the emergence in time of falsehood from truth, irrelevance from salvation. The limitation of the theological circle from the Catholic viewpoint is obvious. What is problematic for the Catholic faith is the indefinite depth and height which is contained in the Word of God. No dogma, no culture, no theological system can exhaust Christ or his revelation. Without substantially changing, revelation offers itself to the Church to be explored. In the night of faith under the inspiration of the Spirit, every level of the Christian community is enabled to increase its understanding of the revelation made once in history. Hence, while the deposit of faith, the life of the Church, and the means of salvation remain the same, there is always the challenge to relate to contemporary man and to fathom "the depths of the wisdom of God."

From the theological point of view of Paul Tillich, the theological circle owns broader, more flexible dimensions. The circle's limits are themselves changing; time passes and a new circle has evolved with new dimensions. Revelation, as Tillich describes it, is changed by every historical medium and recipient touching it. Therefore, the entire commitment of the Christian faith is radically, if not quite totally, evolving. Tillich is not unrelated to the past, to the first century of our era, but the circle of faith within which he stands today has modified itself frequently, especially since the Reformation and in the last two centuries. Today's result is naturally different from its beginning. The goal, however, is the same: New Being (not always grace, religion, or church) must be given to a world in need of salvation. What these words now mean and how they are to be enacted is answered by each generation. This answer traces the new theological circle for the next theologian to enter.

Tillich's ideas and terms are new and, as he wishes, contemporary. The judgment of right and wrong in relation to Catholic theology should be made only after the meaning behind the words is explored. The newness of terminology should not be a cause of fear. Dr. Tillich's desire to be relevant, his prominence, and his respect for coherence should lead us to expect that he has something to offer anyone interested in shepherding the space age. The Catholic reader may recall that Paul Tillich spoke as today's theologian before many eminent gatherings because he has worked for the present and the future. The tragedy of being out of touch with man and his life can never prevail over the revelation of Christ. But irrelevance is a perennial threat to theologians.

PART ONE

Paul Tillich and His Theological System

Theology, as a function of the Christian church, must serve the needs of the church. A theological system is supposed to satisfy two basic needs: the statement of the truth of the Christian message and the interpretation of this truth for every new generation. Theology moves back and forth between two poles, the eternal truth of its foundation and the temporal situation in which the eternal truth must be received.

Systematic Theology, **I**

I

DONALD M. WEISSER, O.P.

Paul Tillich:
A Roman Catholic Appreciation

A few years ago Paul Tillich celebrated New Year's Eve in Rome at the residence of a well-known German cardinal. For several hours their discussion centered on the progress of Dr. Tillich's own work and of the work then being carried on by the Second Vatican Council. By the end of the evening a new year was under way. As Tillich was saying good-bye to his host, the cardinal grasped his hand and said, "Tonight I have learned many things. But best of all I have learned that our hopes—yours and mine—for the Church are the same."

As Tillich told me this story, I couldn't help thinking for just a moment of Martin Luther standing before Cardinal Cajetan centuries before. And I thought that perhaps something more than just another year had begun. I had gone to see Paul Tillich in his Swift Hall offices at the University of Chicago to invite him to contribute a reply to the appraisals and criticisms contained in a number of essays on his theology. The essays were all by Roman Catholics. At that time Father Thomas O'Meara and I were involved in the process of gathering them into a volume, and we felt that the value and usefulness of our collection would be greatly increased if Professor Tillich would agree to conclude the book with his own reflections. He did agree and was in fact most enthused about the idea. His "Afterword," completed some months later while recuperating from a serious illness, ended with a conviction typical not only of Tillich's approach to the ecumenical task at hand but of his whole life's encounter with the oikoumene: "A dialogue," he said, "done in 'listening love' can be a tool of providence and a channel of the divine Spirit."

But Paul Tillich will never be accused of lowest-common-denominator theology for the sake of ecumenics. He would have agreed with Karl Barth that honest and profitable exchange between the churches and their theologians is possible only where there is "genuine dogmatic intolerance." Particularly intolerant, in this sense, was Tillich's frequent challenge in the name of the Protestant principle. Tillich did not identify this principle with organized or institutional Protestantism, but rather he saw it as the judge of all religious and cultural reality including Protestant.

This principle derived nominally from the historic sixteenth-century protest against dominant Catholicism, and it still functions as an assertion against any absolutizing of relative reality. It protests every attempt to confound the finite and conditioned with the one unconditioned. In the name of the Protestant principle Tillich protested often and vigorously against much of Roman Catholic doctrine. Catholic theologians reading Tillich's works are not, of course, always able to agree with him, but they do find him a constantly stimulating and thoroughly contemporary ecumenical partner.

I would like to indicate in a broad and general way a few areas and aspects of Tillich's theologizing which I and other Roman Catholics have found particularly provocative and rewarding. They are by no means meant to exhaust Tillich's significance for Catholicism.

SYNTHESIS. In the judgment of the late Father Gustave Weigel, the man who initiated Catholic interest in Tillich, the latter's fundamental importance lies in the fact that he constructed an all-embracing synthesis of Protestant doctrine and thought. His theology is able to gather all the elements of Protestant thought from the Reformation to the present and to incorporate and reemphasize those elements of "Catholic substance" latent in Protestant belief. Tillich's theology is above all open. He recognized the need, especially toward the end of his life, to lay new stress on Catholic sub-

stance because he saw in the present time a kairos, "a moment full of potentialities in Protestant-Catholic relations."

To speak of this late emphasis, however, is not to forget
the fact that as early as 1941, Tillich wrote with sympathetic
perception of the "Permanent Significance of Roman Catholicism for Protestants."[1] Tillich's vigorous use of philosophical insights, his interest in the fine arts, in depth psychology,
in the history of culture, his encounter with the thought of
the Far East, particularly after his 1960 guest lectureship in
Japan, all of these could be synthesized in his broad theological view.[2]

Yet despite his wide-ranging interest, all of which found
welcome reception in the boundary-line situation of Paul
Tillich, his work remains decisively Protestant in conception
and execution. We should not forget that it was precisely because of his openness and receptivity that Paul Tillich was
called upon more than once to speak not only for Protestantism but for Christianity before secular gatherings.

APOLOGETIC. The word "apologetic" still sounds a defensive note in Catholic ears. Apologetics, especially as it
developed around the turn of the present century, was centered on the Church and on divine revelation and was
often conceived in exclusively juridical terms. It busily defended them in no uncertain terms against all kinds of heretical comers: modernists, liberals, secularists, and of course
Protestants. This effort impresses the contemporary reader as
trying to build up an impregnable wall around the Church,
a wall before which every foe must fall. One really wonders
why they didn't.

On the other hand, apologetic theology as developed by
Paul Tillich is concerned with tearing down walls, not build-
ing them up. Tillich, like the great theologians of the past,
is not afraid of the world. He welcomes it as the situation in which the Son of God became incarnate and as the

[1] Paul Tillich, "The Permanent Significance of Roman Catholicism for Protestants," *Dialog*, 1 (1962), 24–25.
[2] See Paul Tillich, *CEWR*.

situation in which His good news of salvation must be proclaimed today.

Tillich has reminded us that Christians by the fact of their Christianity have not been set over against the world. The message of Christ is not something like a stone for Christians to throw at the hardened hearts of men from a new vantage point. Such apartheid in the name of Christ is a betrayal of His appearance among us, and theologians should beware. Their task in its ecclesial dimension, and apart from which theology has no reason to exist, is twofold: to state the truth of the Christian message and to interpret it in and for every situation.

What is it that Tillich means by "situation"? He is quite clear that he is not referring primarily to the varying psychological and sociological conditions of individuals or groups. These will be of paramount importance to the preacher. Although the theologian will not be unconcerned with such conditions, the precise situation which he addresses and in which he participates is rather contemporary man's understanding and interpretation of his own existence.

Man expresses this self-understanding in the various cultural forms such as art, science, politics. These are expressions of how man understands himself. The theologian's work will not be complete if he chooses to ignore this understanding. He must on the contrary have the courage to enter into it and respond in Christ. If the Christian message cannot be interpreted for modern man in terms he understands, in a manner that is fully meaningful to him as he is, then where is its power?

METHOD.   Tillich constructs his theology using what he calls the method of correlation. This method requires theology to cohere with the data of the history of revelation, to be logically consistent throughout, and to be relevant to the concerns of today's man. Whatever we may wish to say about Tillich's own use of this method in the structuring of his theological system, we should not fail to recognize that the methodology itself is not a new invention but one always operative, as Father Weigel has said, in the theological enterprise. It was a principle for Aquinas as much as for Tillich.

FAITH. Roman Catholic theologians have, until quite recently, become accustomed to placing considerable stress on the intellectual element in the act of faith. As a result faith has sometimes appeared as little more than the assent of the mind to a series of revealed propositions. But faith's terminating object can never be a set of propositions. It is rather able to rest only in the ultimate reality which is God Himself known through propositions but never totally grasped in them. Paul Tillich reminds us that faith is the "state of being ultimately concerned." Faith commands not just man's intellect or his will or his emotions, but it demands the total surrender of the whole man. Tillich's reflections on the nature of faith and the act of faith can be richly rewarding and corrective for Catholics who have forgotten the full meaning of faith.

These four areas of Tillich's thought have been singled out to show that there is much community of interest between his theology and the contemporary renewal of Roman Catholic theology. Clearly, Catholics learned and are learning from Tillich, and this dialogue points to the increasingly ecumenical nature of all Christian theology.

II

GUSTAVE WEIGEL, S.J.

The Theological Significance
of Paul Tillich

In our time the Atlantic Ocean is only a slight barrier between Europe and the Americas. Yet, as a symbol of intellectual separation it is more eloquent. This does not mean that the world-views are specifically different, but it does mean that the Americas cannot be considered as mere subsumptions of Europe. A greater category than Europe must be used to indicate the union, and the greater classification is the West.

The contributions of the Americas to the theological tradition of the West have not been startling and they have usually been not too significant local modifications of European ideas. This was discouragingly true for the American Catholic theologians, either of the northern or southern hemisphere, and it was only less true for the Protestant divines.

In Paul Tillich this condition has ended. His early academic career was set against the German scene; but since 1933 he has been in America. Professor Tillich, however, is a Westerner rather than a European or an American. His native soil was Europe, and he has returned to England and to the Continent frequently since he originally left Germany. His home, nevertheless, is America and he has learned much from the new country of which he is a citizen.

This man is most significant for theology in the contemporary West. It can be maintained without rashness that he is the most impressive figure in today's Protestant theology, which is distinguished by many great names both in

Europe and America. It is high time that Catholic theologians knew Tillich's work better and studied it more.

Professor Tillich is almost eighty years old and his theology has been evolving during the last forty years. His later works clarify earlier positions and every new article or volume helps the reader to understand better the achievements and orientation Tillich adopted years ago. He makes progress by deepening his own thought and rendering it clearer to himself and others.

The Importance of Tillich

Wherein lies the importance of Tillich? In the fact that he has made an all-embracing system of Protestant thought and doctrine. This synthesis is not merely a free construction involving the rejection of some unloved tendencies. He is really bringing together all the elements of Protestant thinking, from the days of the reformers to our own time. What is more, this synthesis takes into consideration the Catholic elements which are latent in Protestant belief, though often unrecognized. A unified rational synthesis of the diverse and seemingly contradictory stands and tenets of the Reform tradition in its life of four centuries is a major event. Has anyone ever attempted it before? Others produce a personal synthesis, leaving out of it the elements of Protestantism which are not congenial to them. But Tillich has the courage and the knowledge to bring in all the movements of Protestant reality, past and present.

Secondly, Tillich has achieved his system in the only way it could be realized. He takes an ontological approach to his task. He knows history well, but in his theology he deliberately follows the light of ontology. This is undoubtedly a new note in recent Protestant theology. Tillich's ontology is neither Platonic nor Scholastic; it is existentialist, but it is a formal ontology and it is chosen deliberately and consciously.

Thirdly, Tillich is original. He is indebted to many theologians: Kähler, Barth, Niebuhr and others. However, he is not the follower of any one man. He embraces positions which are typical of other theologians, but his stand is bigger and frequently not to the taste of the theologians whose thought he has absorbed.

Professor Tillich lectures often and publishes much. Much of his earlier work is not too significant for our time, though it is significant enough in the evolution of Tillich's vision. Instead of offering an historical conspectus of the growth of Tillich's theology, it seems more profitable to construct an outline of his thought as it exists at the moment. Given such an outline, any theologian will be able to see, at least roughly, where Tillich is going and what doctrines are implied in order to put flesh and blood on the skeleton.

Tillich's Conception of Theology

As a logical beginning we must explain Tillich's conception of theology. In the first volume of his *Systematic Theology* the author thoroughly, clearly, and with profundity explains his notion of the divine discipline. The thing which must be stressed is his positive doctrine that theology is the rational effort to unite humanly and organically the data of revelation. Now this seemingly obvious formula is not at all obvious. Revelation for Tillich is God's self-manifestation to man. This manifestation is through existentialist encounter and it is immediate. God is presented to us under two aspects. First of all, God ontologically is the ground of being, the *prius* of all thought and reality, the unconditioned "no-thing" to which all things must be referred. Concerning this God we can think and express ourselves only symbolically, for human conceptions are utterly inept to deal with this primal matrix of reality. Concepts can and must be used by the theologian, but they must be used in a "method of correlation." This method demands that the doctrine cohere with the data of the history of revelation, be consistent logically with all the rest of theology, be relevant definitively to all man's concerns as these derive from his total and actual experience.

Secondly, on the phenomenological side, God is the object of man's ultimate concern—not really the object but rather the first subject. What concerns man ultimately, that is divine and that is the exclusive phenomenological norm for theology. Where reality is considered in obedience to concerns less than ultimate, we have no theology and whatever is said in terms of ultimate human concern is *eo ipso* theology. (It is not necessarily good theology, but it belongs to the theological plane of human thought.)

There is a negative consequence of this positive ultimate theological principle. In line with Barth's thinking, but not identical with it, natural theology for Tillich is an unhappy delusion, for it is a complex of fallacious reasonings. The attempt to prove the "existence" of God or the immortality of the soul involves a logical impossibility. This radical stand of Professor Tillich does not mean that he denies all value to past efforts engaged in the formulation of natural theology. All such formulation is really a vital witness of man to the ultimate which he has discovered existentially, aconceptually, in his encounter with the self-revealing God. The concepts used in the testimony about the revelation are not achievements of the divine but only existentialist pointers to the ground of being which is man's ultimate concern. We have in this doctrine a transformation of the Thomistic *analogia entis,* which was studied carefully and seriously by Professor Tillich.

On last analysis, God is reached existentially, aconceptually, and immediately by man. But that is hardly the full statement of the matter. Man is a creature of history and community, so that God's self-revelation is made socially and in history through progressive stages. The fuller revelation of God demands a *kairos,* an apt historical moment, in which the reality of God is experienced in a peculiar way. Consequently, Tillich does not refer immediately to man's personal and individual experience of God for his theological construction. Individual experience is only a sharing in the continuous solidarity of the corporate human achievement of God. Individual experience is a carrier of total human experience; so, individual experience is a medium but not the source for theological investigation. The specific content of historically progressive revelation, carried by experiencing persons, is given to us in three ways: first, in the Scriptures; secondly, in the continuous life of the Church; thirdly, in the cultural postulates of communities. These are the three sources from which the theologian derives the data relevant to what concerns man ultimately.

However, these three sources can be further reduced. The Bible, in its composition and in its transmission, did not and does not exist in a void. It is mediated to men by the living community which accepts the Bible. This is the living Church, which is conditioned by the human culture in which it exists. Hence, we can say that the three sources of theology can be described by the simpler formula: the biblical message in its assimilation by the living, historical Church.

Briefly then, theology is man's intellectual quest for the real under its formal and specifying dimension of relevancy to the ultimate ground of being; or put phenomenologically, the real in terms of ultimate human concern. This is the criterion, or what Catholic theology calls the formal object. Since the ground of being can only be known in revelation which is a human experience of the ultimate, experience is the carrier or medium of theophany. Here the theologian will find his data. However, it is not human experience in individual isolation which genuinely manifests the revelation, but rather the collective experience of the human family in its historical continuity. This then indicates the methodological norm of the theologian, the method of correlation. The sources of theology, Scripture and Tradition, guide and limit the theological enterprise.

Tillich makes one important addition. The methodological norm, which is formal, leads the theologian to the climactic biblical message of New Being in Christ. That is the content or matter of the revelatory tidings. Hence, the ultimate material norm of theology is the consideration of man as the New Being.

It might be well to point out here what was already stated in the beginning of our study. Tillich organically recapitulates all previous Protestant positions. In his conception of revelation and theology we find the inwardness so stressed by Luther and Calvin, and their biblical preoccupations are preserved. We are also offered the later Protestant corrective, namely the theological relevance of the continuous Church and of history. We are given the antirationalism which was the heart of pietism and Schleiermacher's sentimentalism. We have the recognition of the legitimacy of contributions from historical-criticism and even empiricism. Finally, we feel the pull of existentialism in drawing all these elements together.

What is perhaps more interesting is the way Tillich fuses mysticism and nominalism. Sheer encounter is, after a fashion, mystical, for knowledge is attained with no content expressible by concepts. From the point of view of categorization, the knowledge is declared to be without content. Yet, the experience is significant. It is a mode of perceiving reality anew; conceptually nothing has been added. Universal concepts, the inevitable elements of judgments, are constructs which are adequate for the work of rendering our contacts with the world luminous. They do not discover the structure of the real, but instead give reality a structure. They are, therefore, useless in man's achievement of the transcendental, but still useful for the purposes of communicating to men the stimulus whereby the transcendental can be existentially achieved. This is a brilliant fusion of all recent epistemologies: positivism, phenomenology, ontologism, and existentialism. Nor are Scholastic insights ignored. In Tillich, Kant and St. Thomas walk in friendship.

God Is Suprapersonal

Is God personal in this theology? Tillich considers the question to be a pseudoquestion. God is suprapersonal. He cannot be called properly either personal or impersonal. Such categories are finite and natural and therefore useless in a discussion of the reality of God, though symbolically the divinity should be described as personal; for only such description makes God significant for man's ultimate concern. However, such a description is only a pointer to the numinous, not a statement about his inner reality. Is God triune? He is if we mean that the human preoccupations with power, justice, and love have their ultimate answer in the one ground of being. However, the Trinity is not a metaphysical statement concerning God, but only a phenomenological statement about man in terms of his ultimate concern which drives him to meet his last ground in mortal and sinful anxiety.

This encounter is, epistemologically, a peculiar thing, though historically quite common. It is not natural in the sense that it conforms to the structure of judgment whereby we luminously synthesize the events which make up the finite order. Nor is it an elevation of man into the order of divine reality. This latter notion, absolutely basic in the Catholic notion of the supernatural, is rejected by Tillich as blasphemous and absurd unless taken symbolically. Man reaches God because man is hounded by anxiety. This anguish has three drives: death, which must overcome the inevitable; guilt, which witnesses man's estrangement from the being he would be; scepticism, which hopelessly seeks for an ultimate truth whereby his existence can become meaningful. When fear of death, guilt, and scepticism attack man in their most formidable and final strength, man sees that it *is he* who fears, so that extreme fear itself affirms existence and therefore meaning and justification. In the ground of being there is power, meaning, justice, and love. This is the self-revelation of being-itself, which is another Tillichian word for God. The phenomenal subject who is a finite, guilt-ridden man is thus shown to be rooted in an ontological subject greater than he. Man's being (which really means his existence) is a participation of an existence inconceivably transcending the phenomenal subject. The recognition of this truth is not essential knowledge, that is, through conceptual categories. It is an existential awareness. It carries with it no essential content. It is the same conceptualized world seen in a new light, with a new dimension. The ultimate subject, the ground of existence, is not contemplated; it is only existentially apperceived as illuminating the being of man. This experience is totally grasping, but not a bizarre transport.

Is this the God of theism? No, this is the God above and below theism. The God of theism can and should be doubted, and in that doubt, through existential reflection, the God beyond theism reveals himself.

Is not this solipsistic subjectivism? No, for the existentialist reflection can only be produced by a *kairos*, an historical moment which by its structure is social, and in history and society spontaneously induces the reflection. True, nature alone can lead man to revelation, but it is a man conditioned by culture. The more usual ways toward revelation involve more than a consideration of nature. Some men come to it by moral endeavor which, because of the human situation, is never truly successful but only ambiguous. Some men meet revelation in social history either by immediate contact with a man who has achieved revelation or by the recorded witness to revelation which is the Bible. The majority find it in the life of the Church which is a concrete community under the impact of the Bible message.

Conception of the Bible

Here we have the newer Protestant conception of the Bible. Its propositions are not the revelation which is carried only by experience, original or dependent. In the Scriptures witness is given to the original experience, which as a stimulus excites a similar experience in others who thus depend on the revelation of others. Hence, the Scriptures are pointers whereby the reader can be led to the encounter with the self-revealing God. The Bible considered as a collection of propositions can be called revelation only in an improper sense; for revelation is always an existential experience.

How can I know that revelation is authentic? By its signs. True revelation is recognized by its miraculous epiphenomenon. Only a miracle is the guarantee that a determined experience is revelatory. This sounds like the doctrine of the First Vatican Council, but it is quite different really. Tillich does not believe in miracles in the sense that they are physical events outside the natural configurations of process.

All things in history conform to the universal structures for
events, the "natural law." An acceptable meaning for the
word miracle is "sign-event"; for the coming of revelation is
divine and therefore wonderful, i.e., ecstatically impressive.
In the revelatory experience three things take place. First, a
mystery is unveiled. This means that something ineffable, in-
conceivable, is perceived without conceptual content. Secondly, the event in which the mystery became unveiled is
God-produced and thus wonderful. Thirdly, the wonder produced in man is ecstatic though not in the sense that it is
an abnormal mental state. "Ecstasy is the miracle of the
mind and . . . miracle is the ecstasy of the reality. . . ."[1]

The Data of Doctrine

All that we have stated so far belongs to the propaedeutic of
theology. It does not offer us a doctrine, but only the loci
and rules for the formulation of doctrine. The data of doctrine Tillich derives according to the principles already cited.
The teaching of the Scripture, insofar as it has impact on
the continuous life of the Church, made manifest in the
perennial vital tradition, is datum. Consequently, Tillich sincerely and enthusiastically holds the Apostles' and Nicene
Creeds. He believes in God the Father, Creator of heaven and
earth. He believes in Jesus Christ as the only Son of God.
He believes in the Holy Ghost as proceeding from the
Father and the Son. He believes in the holy Catholic Church.
He even has no difficulty in believing in the assumption of
the Virgin Mary. However, here is the rub. He believes that
these are symbolic statements. Literally understood, they are
for Tillich non-sense or blasphemy.

It is this capacity for affirmation and negation which makes
Tillich simultaneously fascinating and frightening. Everything is affirmed and yet everything is denied. This fact does
not escape Professor Tillich, and he considers it the proper
use of the theory of analogy, which is the only way in which

[1] *ST*, I, p. 117.

we can speak of the divine, the exclusive object-subject of theology. Analogy affirms and denies, and only in and through analogy can we speak seriously and significantly of God.

Perhaps it would not be too fantastic to say that, for Tillich, this affirmation-situation is the Catholic-Protestant structure of Christian thought. Catholicism affirms, and it stays loyal to the revelatory data by its affirmations. Protestantism denies the rationalistic or literal meanings of the Catholic formulae, lest they become idolatrous.

Conception of Protestantism

This becomes clearer in Tillich's conception of Protestantism. He does not identify it with the Protestant churches. They live off the essence of the Protestant principle; but that principle does not owe its reality to the Protestant churches which might well disappear without destroying the vitality of the principle. Tillich is inclined to believe that the Protestant Era, the historical age when the Protestant churches were a highly significant factor in the evolution of Christianity, is coming to an end. However, should this be so, it would not mean the end of Protestantism, which is essentially the prophetic principle which lies at the very heart of the Christian vision. It would only mean that the historical manifestation of the Protestant principle would be different than in our day. The Protestant principle is a protest, a protest in the name of the Lord God against all idolatry. It protests not only against the Roman Catholic Church but against the Protestant churches as well. The protest is loyalty to the revealing God, so that the believer will tolerate nothing to take the place of his definitive and unique lordship: nothing at all; whether it be the society of the Church or the letter of the Bible or the insights of philosophers or the formulae of churchmen and divines.

This loyalty, which expresses itself in protest, is the soul of Christianity. It makes man theonomous, which as a Tillichian term means that man follows only God as achieved in the encounter of revelation unveiling the ground of being. This

God and he alone is the first and last definitive norm for the believer. Hence, the theonomous man is distinguished from the autonomous man who finds his ultimate norm of life and action in himself as revealed by experience and reason. Such a man is a humanist who subscribes to the old principle that man is the measure of all. The theonomous man is also distinguished from the heteronomous man who puts his norm in something finite outside himself because it claims ultimate authority. For Tillich heteronomy is the danger inherent in Catholicism, though he admits that theonomy is possible within its framework, so that the Protestant protest is not really excluded by Catholicism.

The Essence of Christianity

What is the essence of Christianity, which from what has been said must not be identified adequately either with Catholicism or Protestantism? It is New Being. This term is the pure essence of Tillich's theology. For a Catholic reader the term can be puzzling. It inescapably brings up the doctrine of Paul, from which the term is borrowed, and it also suggests Thomistic ontology. Of course Tillich wishes the term to be both Pauline and ontological, but the ontology is not Thomistic. It is existentialist. There is no pretense of giving us a system of categories, abstract and strictly rational. Existentialist ontology is vibrant, living, and immediately relevant to the anguish of existence. To be means to exist; to exist means to live; to live means to feel the drives, pushes, and pulls which define the human situation.

This is why Tillich's ontology sounds so familiar and yet so strange to Catholic theologians. Their ontology is calmer and less involved with the emotions and feelings of the harassed mortal who thinks. This is why the Tillichian doctrine of analogy is like and unlike that of St. Thomas. Tillich, from the existentialist point of view, reduces Thomistic analogy to the only value it can have in an existentialist scheme. It is the device of symbolic expression where the proposition has no rational content. It is yet significant, for it acts as a pointer to the ultimate existent which is grasped in existentialist awareness that prescinds from the limitations implied in all category systems. The subject-object achieved can only be affirmed, but the categories unavoidably used in the affirmation are ignored in everything they mean beyond their pointing potentiality. It is not that the categories are not used seriously, so that any or every concept could be used. Concretely certain terms and certain things, given concrete peoples in concrete cultures, not only have rational content but by reason of the union of content with existentialist apperception go beyond content when they are used. Thus, Tillich says the Virgin Mary is an important symbol for Catholics, but it has lost all symbolic power for the generality of Protestantism.[2]

What is the New Being? In this term God, Jesus, and the Church come together. In this term the Scriptures give the essence of their message. In the explanation of this term Christian theology has its function.

What does the term have to say about God? It does not say but rather supposes that beneath and over the reality of natural phenomenon stands the matrix of reality, unseen but yet revealed, meaningful though no human word can express that meaning, real with the ultimate reality incomprehensible according to the categories men construct for the ordering of their lives and for the visions of the real which impinges on their awareness through direct impact. This is the living God. He is beyond theism, which wishes to reduce God to the categories of ordinary human discourse. Such a reduction perhaps destroys God, though its intention is innocent, since it only tries to render more effective the pointing potential of terms and concepts. Is God personal? Is God infinite? Is God the cause of things? These questions are for Tillich unreal questions, because they are the illogical quest for a logical God. God transcends logic, and logic is helpless to achieve him. All that can be said is that God is the ultimate ground of being, and thus man's ultimate concern. Being is reached through concern; and concern,

2 See *ST*, I, p. 128.

though subjective, reveals being. Being, in consequence, is
what is relevant to human existence: not because human existence produces being, but because being is meaningless except in terms of human existence.

Jesus as the Christ

Where does Jesus Christ fit into this scheme? He is the definite answer to the divine-human question. This must be
understood correctly. The man Jesus of Nazareth is not the
answer. He was a man like all others, with their defects, virtues, shortcomings, and aspirations. To declare him to be
God is blasphemy and idolatry. However, with him and in
him came the revelation of God rendered definitively luminous in the minds of Christ's disciples who saw in the man
Jesus, Jesus as the Christ. It is Jesus as the Christ who definitively reveals God to the world. It is Jesus as the Christ
who saves men by showing them man's true response to God.
In Jesus as the Christ, man rises to the God-dimension of
reality, and is thus a New Being. In the passion and death
of Jesus, God's acceptance of Jesus and Jesus' acceptance of
God unite. Jesus the Christ was the Son of God in power, and
he was the incarnation of the wisdom of God.

Because Jesus as the Christ accepted life even when it up-
set all his own desires and schemes, he rose above the threatening anxieties of human existence. He died indeed, but his
existence was in God; and in consequence, he rose from the
dead; and all who join themselves to him in his faith, who
trust in God when trust itself seems meaningless, become
one with him in New Being. This being transcends the finitude of the human situation, ever exposed to inevitable
death, loveless loneliness, and meaningless search. In the abiding God who is power, justice, and love, man is transfused
with life, community, and meaning. This is the resurrected
life of Jesus, which is not a physical thing but a new mode
of existence. The natural has not been annihilated; it has
only become absorbed into its ultimate meaning. The old
categories have not been superseded; they have only taken on

a new dimension which cannot be imagined or categorically expressed. The new dimension adds no content to the old; it only puts the old in a fuller context.

The recognition of Jesus as the Christ was the experience of the first Christians. They expressed their recognition in the books we call the New Testament. These books had to be set into the background of the Old Testament, which is the history of human encounter with God as it was experienced in one people. The combination of Old and New Testaments revealed God and his Christ to men, and the impact of that book as a witness on men produced the Church. The book is not the revelation. It points to it, and each man and each generation, under the pointing prod of the Bible as delivered by the Church, can meet God just as the first Christians did. Revelation is always to the individual, but it is never individualistic, since it is a function of social stimulus. Christ lives in the Church, and outside of the Church he cannot be found.

Needless to say, in this scheme the Church is not to be identified with any group calling itself the Church. The Church is the social carrier of the Christ revelation; it is the transhistorical fellowship of New Beings. The Church is indifferent and condescending to this or that form of polity or structure. Its dogmas are not expressions of philosophical or historical truth, but only efficient pointers to God, who can only be met in encounter. Liturgy and sacraments are perfectly proper to the Church because by them man is effectively guided to God, though this is not achieved by magical automatism. Liturgy and sacraments open the door to encounter, and insofar as they are conducive to this end, they are valid and legitimate elements of the Church's life. Obviously, they are not to be taken as holy in themselves. Hence, Tillich can at once justify and correct the Protestant objection to sacramental liturgy. It is justified because it is a protest against the materialization of the divine; and it is corrected because the use of sacrament as a symbolic stimulus for the God-encounter is declared legitimate. However, sacrament and cult are subject to the law of their purpose. Once the concrete symbols lose their symbolic power, they must be dropped, because of themselves they are not holy. They are reductively holy if they lead existential awareness to the holy; otherwise they have no holiness at all. Hence, Mariology is valid enough in the Catholic tradition because it still has stimulating power in the Catholic framework. But in the Protestant setting it has little meaning or utility.

What is Christian life? It is New Being. This means that man, hemmed in by the absolute meaninglessness of existence as seen in its phenomenological dimension, threatened by inevitable nonbeing because of death, solitary in his estrangement from all things by his individuality, accepts in love and trust the unseen meaning, the abiding existence, and the love which lie at the heart of existence beyond its phenomenological dimension. This is the eschatological aspect of Christianity. This is salvation, produced by faith (i.e., trust) alone. The Christian dogmas of heaven, hell, final resurrection, are not statements concerning physical situations. They are eschatological pointers to New Being; and eschatology means the overcoming of the limited historical consideration of man. Eschatology is the consideration of man beyond history, not the promise of a new history.

Can a morality be erected on this scheme? It can, but it will have a structure not immediately visible in the usual codes of Christianity. The overriding principle, absolute and universal, will be the law of love. Man in love, *agape*, surrenders himself to God the unseen. He seeks not himself autonomously. This love engenders humility; for it is not the affirmation of the phenomenal subject, the little "I," but the recognition that the little, passing, limited "I" is embedded in the true I Who Am. This same love of God sees all men embedded in God as manifestations of his power, justice, and love; and consequently there is a respect and felt solidarity for all men.

Beyond these universal, ever valid principles nothing will be absolute. A detailed moral code perennially applicable to all men in all times and in all places is impossible, even though the great Christian principles will help to produce and criticize the concrete codes framed in concrete communities. On the plane of daily life, moral relativism will be inevitable, and the resulting ambiguity will always manifest man's abiding sinfulness, because of which he can never glory, and because of which he must take refuge from his sinfulness in divine acceptance achieved by faith alone.

Critique of a System

This scheme of Paul Tillich's thought is made from the point of view of a Catholic who by that fact cannot be totally sympathetic with the ideas expressed. This lack of total sympathy means that some distortion of the thought cannot be avoided. However, there has been sympathy enough to make substantial objectivity possible. Another limitation distorts this report. Professor Tillich's thought is vast; his erudition, amazing; his breadth, dazzling. A few pages cannot do anything but injustice to his great vision. He is rigorously systematic in his thinking, and therefore he can be presented schematically; but a scheme is like a skeleton and it includes so little of the living reality.

Recognizing these limitations, candor yet demands that the uneasiness with which his thought was achieved be also explained. The brilliance of the Tillichian synthesis cannot soothe the disturbance caused by his theology. It is a great synthesis of Protestantism, better than anything this reporter knows. Everything in the winding history of Protestantism is included and given a place. Justification through faith alone, primacy of the Scriptures, free interpretation, rational criticism, pietistic arationalism, reconstructionism, existentialism—all are kept and fused together into a coherent whole. Needless to say, few if any Protestants will accept completely the Tillichian synthesis, but he has shown what Protestantism, through evolution, now is. Some Protestants keep some of the elements of Protestant development, rejecting others, but Tillich has the courage and capacity to see and take them all consistently.

The first feeling of uneasiness the Catholic experiences on reading Tillich is that his supernaturalism (a term he does not like) is, on ultimate reduction, purest naturalism. He rejects natural theology on principle, but his whole theology is not only a natural theology, but more ominously a naturalistic theology. The final chapter of his *The Courage To Be* can have a depressing effect, for it seems to equate God with the basic energy at work in the universe, but interpreted in terms of human concern. Of course, the book cited is a phenomenology of the human search for God and not a theology. However, the question a Catholic asks is this: Does the theology of Tillich add anything to his phenomenology, or is it only the phenomenology written theologically? One reluctantly feels that the theology does nothing to correct the phenomenology.

It is Tillich's epistemology which proves unsettling. It is a mélange of Kant, positivism, and existentialism. Meaningful knowledge is reduced to empirically founded statements. All other knowledge is either merely formal or symbolic. Unlike Kant, Tillich believes in ontology, but the ontology in which he believes is existentialist. Being means existence, and since existence is experienced meaningfully only by human beings, being can be understood only in terms of human concern. It is not that human concern drives man to ontology, but rather that ontology is the ultimate expression of that concern. In Tillich we never leave the realm of human concern, in spite of the fact that that concern is a dynamism to lead us beyond itself. If this is the role of ontology, then it follows logically that all ontological statement is symbolic. It cannot say anything except concern, and all of its seemingly transpersonal statements are only and necessarily witnesses to human concern, saying nothing which adds content to what man experiences objectively. This, I submit, is not ontology, but rather its betrayal.

Tillich lays himself open to the charge that he has called man's imperious compulsion to exist the ultimate justification of a stoic acceptance of death, solitude, and meaninglessness. Existence is evidently bigger than any existence, and my existence is only one instance of absolute existence. Transcendental existence, therefore, precedes me, goes vigorously through me, and stretches indefinitely beyond me. This existence is called God, the ultimate objective formulation of my felt compulsion to exist. Of course, it is not logical to call it unjust, meaningless, and heartless; for justice, power, meaning, and love are themselves intelligible only as reductive to existence. Accept existence, therefore, and make the most of it, or, in religious terms, serve the Lord in gladness. In an enthusiastic surrender to the imperious thrust of existence, the black shadows of death, isolation, and meaninglessness lose their terrifying aspects, and we live contentedly and creatively.

I do not believe that this really summarizes the thought of Tillich. I do think that such a construction of his thought has warrant in his expressions. The piety so patent in his work prevents the acceptance of the construction as a valid indication of Professor Tillich's world-view. His works give the unescapable impression that he is teaching something deeper and better than an acosmic pantheism touchingly expressed in terms of misery and hope.

If this impression be valid, then the Catholic theologian is faced with a genuine problem. There will be Catholics who will read the works of Tillich and then promptly dismiss him as a naturalist or even an atheist who speaks in biblical terms linked together by a shallow ontology. There will be others who will feel his fascination, but will be mystified because of the freshness of the approach and the original twists given to old terms so that their content is not too precisely clear.

To those who see in Tillich nothing but an existentialist naturalist it can only be said that they have missed the fearful drive which lies at the heart of his teaching. To those who are mystified it might be well to point out the cause of the mystification.

Tillich's ultimate guide is not his formal ontology; rather, he leans on an epistemology which he has slowly molded in his own mind over the years. This epistemology, like any epistemology, has implicit metaphysical roots. Tillich has the undoubtedly sincere intention of constructing theologically the Christian kerygma. He believes wholeheartedly in that kerygma. He believes that it is the ultimate answer for the problems of our time, if it can be theologically constructed on the principle of correlation. That principle, as he explains it, means adherence to the data, consistency in its reconstruction, and relevance to contemporaneous man. Now this principle also worked in St. Thomas, and no Catholic theologian is totally ignorant of it. A Catholic theologian, perhaps more than any other, is scrupulously preoccupied in being true to the data of revelation. This was so even in Origen who speculated only where he felt that the data were silent. It was true of the Scholastics who were passionately interested in the logical consistency of their doctrine. It was true of St. Robert Bellarmine who was anxious to offer a theology relevant to the Protestants and Catholics of his time. The Tillichian principle of correlation is not a new discovery but only an urgent exhortation to use efficiently the principle always functioning in the theological enterprise, though it often functions with less than desirable energy.

What needs clarification in Tillich's thought is the role of symbolism. He himself thinks that it explains the problem touched by the Thomistic doctrine of analogy. It seems clear to a Catholic reader that Tillich's conception of analogy is inadequate. Let us see why.

First of all, he has identified being with existence, *sensu negante*. Secondly, he supposes that class-concepts have meaningful content only for extrapersonal reality as achieved in ordinary human experience. Beyond such an empirical context class-concepts can only be pointers. Thirdly, he recognizes a form of knowledge which gives dimension but not content. The expression of such knowledge is symbolism. Fourthly, the knowledge which gives dimension is an awareness achieved in the autoperception of existence at the point of its ultimate ground. In consequence, he sees God in his own existence, not because God is identified with the finite subject, but because the finite subject is rooted in an infinite subject who can be known only as a subject and never as an object. Fifthly, existential awareness is specifically different from the conceptual achievement of empirical objects. This latter knowledge is "natural," i.e., it achieves "nature." The deepest awareness of existence, since it does not give us "nature," can be called supernatural, at least in the sense that it is not "natural." Lastly, though reason is inevitable in all thinking, yet true reasoning, or what Aristotle would call the syllogism, can only use univocal terms. An analogous term cannot enter into a syllogism; and when it does we have a fallacy and not a true reasoning.

With such an epistemology Tillich's brilliant scheme becomes inevitable for a man who has the talent, learning, and courage of Tillich. However, in the light of the Thomistic doctrine of analogy, it is evident that a very different scheme can and should be built. St. Thomas does not believe that analogical terms need be excluded from the syllogism. They can be admitted; but when they are, they only give analogous conclusions. Secondly, an analogous term, when applied beyond nature, is not empty of content. Its content is only of a different order than the content denoted by the same term when applied to nature. But between nature and what is beyond nature there is an objective proportion, so that an equivalence, though not an equality, exists. Two halves are not four quarters, but they are equivalent for the construction of a whole. They are proportional, which means that they are analogous. We have content, not merely pointings. Mathematics, reasoning in its purity, lovingly deals with proportions, and so it is rather willful to say that reasoning demands univocal terms exclusively. Aristotle's rejection of the analogous term in the syllogism was a needless restriction of the inferential rationale in order to make it simple; and Aquinas rejected the restriction because it was needless—and too simple.

The absolute divorce which the existentialists make between subject and object is also willful. Subject and object are different points of view; they are not different things. Subject and object are both *things*, existentialist howls to the contrary notwithstanding. A thing does not mean something dead beyond subjectivity. A thing just means a reality, which can be living or nonliving, subject or object. It is an analogous term. To call God a "no-thing" can have a good sense because it attempts to affirm the transcendence of God; but it would be a blasphemous contradiction to make it mean that God is not a thing. God *is a thing*; he is the first thing and the thing because of which all other things are.

Thing does not say finitude or relativity, though it can have these meanings when referred to a finite and relative subject or object. It depends on what thing we are talking about. Any subject can be considered objectively, and I do no violence to the subject by considering it as an object. Any object in some sense is a subject; for any object has its own dynamism, which makes it, from the viewpoint of action, a subject. *Actiones sunt suppositorum.* To reduce the use of subject to living, free, awareful subjects is again a willful restriction of the meaning of the word. And the existentialists do it all the time. The vulgar truth that the interior view of a reality or thing is different from its exterior view hardly warrants the exaggerations of the typical existentialism of our day. It still remains true that I can consider the same thing from the inside and from the outside. Just because the inside view shows up whole phases of the reality which cannot be perceived nor even communicated adequately on the outside, subject and object are not put in different universes of discourse. Existentialism saw that more could be said for a human subject than objective classification allows. That valid insight does not imply that objective classification is false or bad. It only means that it does not tell the whole story.

Thomistic analogy overcomes all existential aporiae, for it is truly transcendental. It dominates the subjective-objective dichotomy and is not dominated by it. I can make statements concerning God which have conceptual content, but the content is proportional, not univocal. These are valid positive statements, even though they contain an element of negation. We deny the negative aspects of the category which, after all, was framed originally to take care of reality limited by negation. When I deny the negation, I have God.

But what have I got when I have denied the negative aspect of a category? Does it not lose all of its definiteness by the very process? By no means. No category is purely negative. Pure nothing is not, nor can it be conceived. There is in all finite reality the basis of the recognition of reality which of itself does not say finitude. *Omnia cognoscentia cognoscunt implicite Deum in quolibet cognito.*[3]

---

[3] St. Thomas Aquinas, *De veritate*, q. 22, a. 2 ad 1.

Thomas does not need Tillich's kindly justification of Thomistic analogy by reducing it to symbolism. Rather, Thomas finds some justification for Tillich's symbolism because it is a weak pointer to solid, inevitable, ontological analogy. Thomistic analogy does not give us a comprehensive grasp of God, but, given human limitations, it gives us an adequate intellection of God. Analogy does not define God; for, as St. Thomas says, he cannot be defined: *Patet quod [Deus] non habet genus, neque differentias, neque est definitio ipsius.*[4] But this lack does not mean that he is not understood at all. The understanding is imperfect and proportional. We know that God exists; we cannot know clearly and precisely what he is.

Tillich's apparent naturalism can be understood in the light of Thomistic analogy, and if it is, then Tillich's work can be extremely useful to Catholic theologians. It can be objected that Tillich explicitly rejects Thomistic analogy. This is true, but it is also true that he can consistently take all of the doctrine of St. Thomas, and he certainly does take much of it. He is anxious to admit Thomistic doctrine on Tillichian terms, and the terms are perhaps more generous in Tillich than in any other contemporaneous Protestant theologian. Our age has conditioned Professor Tillich. Where Thomas clung to the affirmatives in the paradoxical grasp of God, Tillich stresses the negative. The difference is more profound than this superficial generalization seems to indicate, but the generalization has the pragmatic value of making Tillich genuinely relevant to the Catholic theological enterprise.

Professor Tillich Replies

To give the readers of this report a guarantee of its substantial fidelity to the thought of Professor Tillich, it was submitted to his criticism. With his wonted kindness he read the study and made the following observations: "Thank you very much for your kindness in sending me the manuscript of your excellent article about my theological system. As you

[4] *Summa theologiae,* I, q. 3, a. 5.

know, I am always pleased to read your interpretation and criticism of my thought. This is also true of the present manuscript. It is a confirmation of my doctrine that interpretation can never be repetition. It must always be something new, created by the encounter of the text with the mind of the interpreter. This is even the case when the author becomes his own interpreter. Out of what he had in mind when he wrote his earlier texts and the categories of understanding which are in his mind at the moment he interprets himself, he creates a new thing. In dealing with my texts you have created something above the text written by a Protestant theologian and above your own Thomistic categories of understanding. This is as it should be, and the result is extremely positive.

"Since, however, you allow me to reply to some of your criticisms, I shall gratefully use the occasion and discuss two points made in your critical section. The first one is the question of ontology. I certainly do not identify (as Heidegger in his earlier period *seemed* to do) being with existence. My whole system is based on the distinction of essential and existential being. My doctrine concerning God, in good Scholastic tradition asserts that for God the difference between essence and existence is invalid. He is 'being-itself' or, in a metaphorical expression, the 'power of being.' As such he cannot be called a 'thing'—even if the term 'thing' covers not only objects but subjects as well. For *a* thing is always an event *within* the universe of events, but God is the creative ground of all events, of every 'thing.' A God who is less than this is an idol, even though a theistic idol. The 'God above the God of theism,' of whom I speak in the last chapter of *The Courage To Be*, is the protest against this most refined form of idolatry. My thinking is not naturalistic. Naturalism and supernaturalism provoke each other and should be removed together. Protestant theologians have criticized me on the grounds that the 'God above God' is mystical. This is certainly nearer to the truth, but it is hardly a subject of Catholic criticism. With respect to my ontological thought generally, I want to state that it is much less influenced by existentialism than by Aristotle and Schelling. It is my doctrine concerning man in which the influence of existentialism is important.

"The second point of your criticism to which I wish to reply concerns my doctrine of symbolic knowledge. One of the things I always forbid my students to say is 'only a symbol.' This bad phrase is rooted in the confusion of sign and symbol. Signs point to something different in which they do not participate at all. Symbols participate in the power of what they symbolize. This is—if I understand Thomas and your interpretation of his thought rightly—the positive or proportional element in the *analogia entis* on which you insist. Such an insistence lies clearly in the line of my doctrine concerning God and of my use of metaphors like 'ground of being' and 'power of being' for God. If God is the creative ground of everything that has being, everything insofar as it is must express something knowable about God. In this I fully agree with Aquinas. Every symbol—if it is an adequate and not demonic symbol—says something positively true about God. He is not the 'ineffable' simply and unconditionally; but on the basis of his ineffability much can and must be said about him. It is not true that in the finite-infinite proportion there is no difference between the kinds of the finite which enter into this proportion. There is a profound difference between the proportion: stone—the infinite, and the proportion: man—the infinite. This difference is the basis of the possibility whereby God is manifest according to his innermost nature in man but not in a stone. I am grateful to you because your incisive criticism enables me to clarify my doctrine on the symbolic knowledge of God.

"Nevertheless, I believe you are right when you say that my understanding of *analogia* is more negative-protesting than positive-affirming. I am more worried about the idolic character of traditional theology and popular beliefs about God than you are. But I am grateful and glad that this Catholic-Protestant dialogue has been made possible by your kindness."

III

EDWARD D. O'CONNOR, C.S.C.

Paul Tillich: An Impression

In May, 1955, Paul Tillich gave a series of lectures at Indiana University on "Schelling's Positive Philosophy as an Anticipation of Existentialism." Tillich proved to be an excellent lecturer. Without ever stooping to entertainment or having recourse to rhetoric to help carry the load of the discourse, but single-mindedly intent upon his subject, he captured and held attention by the sheer interest of his message, and earned an enthusiastic applause.

A greater contrast with British playfulness or French brilliance could hardly be imagined than his workmanlike German seriousness. Though not a big man physically, he has a strong voice and a grave manner, which lend authority to him and importance to his subject—an impression to which his silvering gray hair and not unpleasant German accent contribute. He is master of his material, which he chooses judiciously—abstaining from all display of erudition—and arranges intelligibly. By making his points decisively, and moving ahead without tarrying, he is able, though speaking slowly, to say a great deal in a short time. There is assurance, even (when he is answering questions and speaking impromptu) a trace of a swagger in his manner; but at the same time there is an attractive modesty in his objectivity which carefully avoids any dogmatism or undue persuasion. In an unobtrusive way he is attentive to the pedagogical needs of the listener: he keeps the line of thought always clearly in view, skillfully arranges to approach difficult problems from the point of easiest access, and prefaces his discussions of them with discreet introductions that give a beginner his bearings without wearying those already acquainted with the material.

The single flaw of which one gradually became aware as the lectures progressed was an occasional disconcerting shift of perspective, joined to a failure sometimes to reach the fundamental issue of a question; but this pertains more to his thought than to his style, and we shall return to it below.

Tillich dealt principally with the turning point in Schelling's philosophy constituted by his *Essay on Human Liberty*, by which, from having been chiefly a "philosopher of identity" or of essence, he became the pioneer of existentialism. Since his youth, Tillich has been a serious student of Schelling, and has probably been influenced by him more than by any other thinker.

But it is not our purpose here to discuss Tillich's interpretation of Schelling; it is Tillich himself that we are interested in. We will try to discern some of the characteristic traits that will help to situate this important landmark among modern Protestant thinkers, and help to orientate a Catholic appraisal of him. We are not, of course, undertaking to give a balanced survey of his thought, but only to pick out some of its more noteworthy features. For this purpose, the chief significance of the lectures on Schelling lay in remarks and concepts often quite incidental to the main line of thought.[1]

Tillich's Ideal of Autonomy

One of the chief inspirations of Tillich's life and thought has been the ideal of "autonomy." This is quite plain from the autobiographical sketch which Tillich prefixed to the English translation of some of his essays, entitled, *The Interpretation*

---

[1] Quotations given without reference are from the as yet unpublished Schelling lectures; but where possible we have drawn our texts from other works of Tillich already in print. [Father O'Connor's essay was written in 1955.—Editors.]

of History. In the important chapter, "On the Boundary between Heteronomy and Autonomy," he declares:

From earliest times I was opposed to the most potent system of religious heteronomy, Roman Catholicism, with a protest which was at once both Protestant and autonomous. This protest was not directed and does not direct itself, in spite of theological contrasts, to the dogmatic values or the liturgical forms of the Catholic system, but is concerned with its heteronomous character, with the assertion of a dogmatic authority, which is valid even when subjection to it is only external.[2]

But it must be understood clearly that the autonomy which Tillich aspires to is not an absolute one—this he explicitly rejects—but rather "a *theonomy*, that is, an autonomy filled with religion."[3] His goal seems to be to exclude all human authority from religious matters, in favor of a direct relationship between God and the individual; to eliminate the intervention of other men between the soul and God. "The immediacy of God," writes Father Weigel, "is at the heart of Tillich's theology as it was of Luther's. With this doctrine of immediacy rides a corollary—the corruptive influence of all things finite, and God's incapacity to unite the finite, the limited, the imperfect, to himself to make of it a carrier of divinity."[4]

The rejection of all intermediaries between God and man is the mainspring of Lutheran spirituality, and has become in our time perhaps the principal motivation of non-Catholic objection to the Church generally. A sense of the inviolability of the mind's freedom of thought, which is more acute today perhaps than ever before, protests instinctively and vehemently against the attempt of any man or group of men to impose beliefs on others; and that divine authority should be invoked to justify such an attempt only intensifies the resentment. In protesting not so much against the particular

[2] *IH*, pp. 24–25.
[3] *Ibid.*, p. 24.
[4] "Contemporaneous Protestantism and Paul Tillich," *Theological Studies*, 11 (1950), 177–202.

doctrines of the Church as against her claim to teach them with authority, Tillich is the spokesman of countless numbers of our contemporaries.[5] We will try to discover the sense and motivation of this antiauthoritarian inclination, and, while never minimizing the claim to authority which the Church undeniably makes, we will seek for any indication furnished by Tillich's theology as to how this claim may be made intelligible to minds formed in the outlooks and biases of the present age.

From the outset, it must be realized clearly that Tillich's antiauthoritarianism is not based primarily on historical or scriptural arguments. Indeed, not much of Tillich's thought is.[6] He has made it quite clear that he has little confidence in the possibility of attaining historical certitude about details of Christ's life and work, and he is inclined to regard positive historical inquiry as inconsequential or irrelevant in properly religious questions. He says:

> The foundation of Christian belief is not the historical Jesus, but the biblical picture of Christ. The criterion of human thought and action is not the constantly changing and artificial product of historical research, but the picture of Christ as it is rooted in ecclesiastical belief and human experience.[7]

It is not, therefore, historical or exegetical research which is the basis of Tillich's objection to the Church's claim to

[5] Cf. the remark of Walter M. Horton in his essay, "Tillich's Role in Contemporary Theology": "Robert Hutchins, at the University of Chicago, did not hesitate to surround himself with neo-Thomist advisers; but many of his faculty fled further into chaotic autonomy rather than risk involvement in Catholic authoritarianism" (C. Kegley and R. Bretall, editors, *The Theology of Paul Tillich* [New York: Macmillan, 1952], p. 45). The same note recurs almost monotonously in the essays on Catholicism from the pens of Protestants and other non-Catholics, which appear in our periodicals from time to time.

[6] On this matter see R. Niebuhr's essay, "Biblical Thought and Ontological Speculation in Tillich's Theology," Kegley and Bretall, *ibid.*, pp. 216–27.

[7] *IH*, p. 34.

divine authority, but the very notion itself of such a claim being made by a human institution. For Tillich, this is "demonry."

> The dogmatism of religions . . . is established in the fact that a portion of human-religious reality is garbed in the unconditioned validity of the divine. Such a reality, like a book, person, a community, an institution, or doctrine, claims absolute authority and lays claim to submission of every kind of reality, life, and doctrine; for no other claim can exist beside the unconditioned claim of the divine. But that this claim is established by a finite, historical reality, is the root of all heteronomy and of all demonry. For the demonic is something finite, something limited, which puts on infinite unlimited dignity.[8]

The question of authority and autonomy was not introduced by Tillich in the Schelling conferences, except for the remark, incidental but quite typical, that, in contrast with what occurs in Catholicism, where a predetermined philosophy is imparted to seminarians, candidates for the Protestant ministry in Schelling's time were encouraged to think *autonomously*. Nevertheless, these conferences brought out several ideas which shed considerable light on Tillich's position. The first is that of the divine transcendence.

The notion of God recurred frequently in the Schelling lectures, even though the matter under consideration was the world and the life of man; and while Tillich did not stop to discuss his own or Schelling's concept of God, the one point that became obvious as the lectures proceeded was his profound respect for God's transcendence. This constant attitude was perhaps more impressive than the explicit statements to be found in his writings. It is this strong sense of the divine transcendence, we believe, that constitutes the chief speculative basis for Tillich's and many other men's opposition to the authority claimed by the Church.

For a Catholic apologist to disregard this mentality, as he hastens into the fray armed with manifold arguments to establish the Church's credentials, would be a grave blunder. Perhaps there is room to inquire whether Tillich's "rev-

[8] *Ibid.*, p. 26.

erence" for God is altogether authentic; but it may not be discounted altogether. Generically, at least, it surely represents a genuine perception of a divine truth, and this is what it is important to recognize. In our overeagerness to defend the participation in divine attributes, which we maintain that Christian institutions enjoy, and in our familiarity with the visible sacraments by which God permits us to encounter him, we Catholics sometimes lose the humble abasement and reverence for God which these institutions presuppose, and the sense of mystery, which is capital in a due appreciation of them. The case of a man like Tillich can usefully serve to recall to us our shortcomings in this regard. Furthermore, we need to take care not to prejudice our attempts to lead all men to the "knowledge of the Truth" by inconsiderately offending a genuine sense of the Truth which they already have.

The authority of the Church need not be presented in such a way as to be opposed to the divine transcendence. On the contrary, in a true view of things, it is based on it, for it is not in virtue of any human excellence of hers nor in the sense of a dependence of God on her (not thus does God "need men"), but solely in virtue of an absolutely free choice by which God assumes her for his use that the Church has divine authority. It is only because God utterly transcends the Church that he can confer on it a function that surpasses its nature; only because he is by nature indifferent to the employment of any or all of his creatures can he, with entire freedom, select that which he pleases and use it as he sees fit.

Another reason for Tillich's opposition to an authoritative Church is that he finds repugnant the very notion of a divine choice, of God's selection of a particular institution for a special function not conferred on all. This at least is the implication of his assertion that, "in face of the unconditioned, or, religiously speaking, of the Majesty of God, there is no preferred sphere, there are no persons, Scriptures, communities, institutions that are holy in themselves. . . ."[9]

[9] *Ibid.*, p. 52. These lines were written in regard to holiness rather than authority; but they seem to apply equally to the latter, which is what we are primarily concerned with here.

That "the Lord who made heaven and earth" should be in a special sense "the God of Israel," that the universal Father should have a predilection for the offspring of Abraham, and should give his blessing "out of Sion" is a mystery that has baffled many other minds besides Tillich's. St. Paul was obliged to consider it, and—significantly—he resolved it by an appeal to the sovereign independence of God, who, like the potter, makes, from the same mass of clay, one vessel for noble and one for ignoble use (see Rom. 9:21).

Tillich, however, will not admit divine preferences. Is this because of a more basic position in his philosophy of freedom? In his conferences, he represented Schelling as conceiving of freedom as the possibility of good or evil, the possibility of contradicting one's own essence. In the free act, the being "affirms itself by denying itself." Man is able to be free because he is a union of two principles, a "dark" principle of power and vitality, and a principle of "light," that is, of meaning or rationality. Their separation is sin, and freedom is ultimately the power of this separation.

If freedom be so conceived, we must conclude that it does not exist in God. It is true that the above conception does not represent Tillich's personal view,[10] and he does not deny that God is free. Perhaps, however, some of the implications of Schelling's concept influence him in his rejection of the notion of a "divine preference." If so, this influence is exerted in a direction counter to the principal dynamism of Tillich's thought and his entire life, which, in their quest for autonomy, are inspired by a deep appreciation of the high dignity of freedom. He is denying to God the very autonomy he vindicates for man!

---

[10] He has a much superior presentation of the concept of freedom in PE, Chapter VIII, "The Idea and the Ideal of Personality," where he says, e.g., "to be free means to have power over one's self, not to be bound to one's given nature. . . . Freedom is the power of transcending one's own given nature . . ." (pp. 115, 116). The latter definition is repeated in the essay, "Freedom in the Period of Transformation," in R. N. Anshen's *Freedom: Its Meaning* (New York: Harcourt, Brace, 1940), p. 123; cf. p. 124.

In any event, what is to this writer's mind significant is that, elsewhere in the Schelling conferences, Tillich envisaged the possibility of a special divine communication made to privileged individuals. It is precisely in such terms, according to him, that Schelling explained the case of "ethical and aesthetic geniuses," i.e., saints and artists. In reinterpreting in his own idiom the views of Schelling, Tillich found nothing repugnant in them, but rather embraced them sympathetically. Could the question not be asked, then, if particular individuals can be privileged with divine inspiration, why is there any intrinsic objection to an analogous privilege being bestowed on a community, that is, the Church, and particularly attached to certain offices in that Church?[11]

But of all the notions developed by Tillich in his Schelling lectures, that which might best serve to make the notion of ecclesiastical authority intelligible is the view which Tillich seems to have derived from Schelling that the knowledge of God is a kind of grace.[12] Man cannot come to the knowledge of God, he avers, by mere rational reflection. The reason Tillich takes this position lies in his respect for the divine transcendence, to which we have already alluded. He quoted with approval the lines of Schelling, "There is no knowledge of God in which he is only object. Either he cannot be known at all, or he is both subject and object of our knowledge at the same time." It is only by a participation in God, transcending the distinction between subject and object, that man can know God. The saint (or just man, or "ethical genius") and the artist ("aesthetic genius") are to be described in terms of *God present*. This divine presence is for Tillich a *grace*, a

---

[11] There must be no question, of course, of holiness or authority or any other divine prerogatives possessed by the Church in herself, as a creature, i.e., anterior to the free divine act instituting her; nor of any superior qualities in certain elite creatures which attract to themselves God's preference; but only of a divine choice by which God associates with himself in sovereign freedom one creature rather than another in his salvific work.

[12] Tillich did not expressly call the knowledge of God a grace; but from the way he associated these two notions, he plainly intended that the one be regarded as an example of the other.

"status which cannot be produced willfully, but is given and either accepted or not."

It must not be imagined that Tillich's concept of grace coincides with that found in Catholic theology; and obviously his views on the knowledge of God would not be altogether acceptable there. But the significant point is that he recognizes the existence of a knowledge of God which is unattainable by mere reason and can be had only by a free gift from God to man.[13] This furnishes the precise perspective in which the doctrinal authority of the Church is best made intelligible. For, in the total pattern of divine beneficence to mankind, the Church figures only among the concrete conditions according to which, *de facto*, the divine gift is made. Her role is essentially instrumental, as channel through which a communication passes. For a rationalist, admitting no truth which reason cannot attain for itself, the magisterium will necessarily appear as a usurpation; but anyone who acknowledges a truth that can come only as a gift from heaven[14] has at least the basis for understanding the Church's magisterial function (and, by analogy, her other authoritative functions), even though he does not believe in it. And he must admit that the gift can be received only on the Giver's terms: that is, in the way and according to the conditions under which he sees fit to bestow it, whether or not the reason for his way of acting be understood.

If the preceding interpretations are just, it would seem that the essential notions necessary for an acceptance of the Church's authority, particularly in doctrinal questions, are already admitted in Tillich's theology. Granted a knowledge of God that can only be received by his gracious gift, and the possibility of a special union with God on the part of partic-

[13] The expression, "free gift from God to man," is no doubt more congenial to traditional Christian belief than to Tillich's theology of the "ground of being." Nevertheless, if Tillich admits the concept of divine communications to privileged individuals, he cannot reject this expression radically and on principle.

[14] It should not be supposed that Tillich admits a "divine revelation" in the traditional sense; but the issues raised by this difficulty are beyond the scope of the present essay.

ular individuals, there does not seem to be any room left for a very fundamental objection to the concept of certain individuals divinely charged with a mediative office regarding others. The only logical basis for rejecting the Church's claim to authority would seem to be the argument based on historico-scriptural considerations, that, *de facto*, the Church was never so constituted. But, as we have already mentioned, this argument does not figure importantly in Tillich's theology, and it does not appear to us to be the true basis of his "protest."

Basis of Tillich's Protest

This basis, we strongly suspect, is not theoretical but practical. To see this, one must bear in mind that Tillich once seriously considered joining the Church, "when, in 1933, prior to the resurgence of German Protestantism, the alternative seemed to confront me, between either Christian or heathen Catholicism, the Roman Church or national heathenism in Protestant garb."[15] Elsewhere he declares that "the Catholic Church has a great attraction for the man of our day"; and he explains:

The Catholic Church . . . has manifestly been able to preserve a genuine spiritual substance that continues to exist, although it is encased within an ever hardening crust. But whenever the hardness and crust are broken through and the substance becomes visible, it exercises a peculiar fascination; then we see what was once the life-substance and inheritance of us all and what we have now lost, and a deep yearning awakens in us for the departed youth of our culture.[16]

What kept Tillich out of the Church was precisely its assertion of authority, as he himself declares in the passage already cited[17] in which he says that it was against the

15 *IH*, p. 25.
16 *PE*, p. 194.
17 At fn. 2 above, p. 58.

Church's "assertion of dogmatic authority," more than any-thing else, that he protested. He says also: "The man who enjoys autonomy—however feeble and empty it may be—has experienced something that he cannot easily surrender, even if he wished to respond to the appeal of the Catholic Church."[18]

But protest against the Church's "authoritarianism" is only one manifestation of Tillich's lifelong effort for autonomy in many areas.

It was only in severe struggles that it was possible for me to break through to the affirmation of mental and moral autonomy. My father's authority, which was at once personal and intellectual, and which, because of his position in the Church, coincided for me with the religious authority of rev-elation, made every manifestation of autonomous thinking a piece of religious daring, and involved the critique of author-ity in a sense of guilt . . . every step in theological, ethical, and political criticism encountered inhibitions, which often could be overcome only after conflicts lasting for years.[19]

He makes it clear, as has been mentioned already, that it was not pure autonomy he wanted, but "an autonomy filled with religion." Then he goes on to remark, with reference to the return to "heteronomy," that is, authoritarianism, that was being manifested in Europe at the time of his writing (1936):

If the trend of events in Europe is currently quite doubt-lessly under the sign of a return to old and new heteronomies, that can awaken only passionate protest in me, even when I realize the fated inevitability of this development. An autonomy won in hard struggle cannot be surrendered so

[18] PE, p. 195. He continues: "This 'something' which unites the Protestants and those who live in secular autonomy must be examined and understood. Upon it depends the religious and also the intellectual integrity of our day. . . . It is the awareness of the human boundary-situation or of the ultimate threat to human ex-istence that prevents the modern man from surrendering to heter-onomy."

[19] IH, p. 22.

readily as an autonomy that had always been accepted as matter-of-course. Whoever has once broken determinedly with the taboos of the most sacred authorities cannot subject himself to a new heteronomy, whether religious or political.[20]

Finally, he observes that "the struggle between autonomy and heteronomy returns on a higher plane in Protestantism. Precisely in the protest against the Protestant orthodoxy (even its moderate form of the nineteenth century) I had won my way through to autonomy."[21]

Was this campaign a genuine crusade for liberty, as he represents it, or mere rebelliousness? Doubtless it would be an oversimplification to regard it as exclusively one or the other. We cannot avoid the suspicion, however, that there is profound significance in a line that occurs in the first of the three passages just cited: "The immemorial experience of mankind, that new knowledge can be won only through breaking a taboo, that all autonomous thinking is accompanied by a consciousness of guilt, has been a fundamental experience of my life."[22] How are we to interpret this guilt which Tillich has experienced in his "struggle for autonomy"? That the mind which dares to think differently from others often experiences fearfulness and uncertainty, at times even tormenting doubt about its surest perceptions, cannot be denied; but this is not a sense of guilt. That social pressures can engender a pseudoguilt in the soul of a man who quite justifiably breaks with unreasonable taboos, must also be admitted; but we submit that this explanation is not so universally valid as certain naturalistic psychologies suppose. The sensation of guilt is normally the valid protest against evil of an inner faculty which, in an obscure, intuitive way, is more loyal to the truth than the conscious reason by which man justifies to himself the course he has taken. And even when it accompanies—and annoys!—what is to all evidence a genuinely creative thought or a rightly independent decision,

[20] *Ibid.*, p. 24.
[21] *Ibid.*, p. 25.
[22] *Ibid.*, p. 23.

it is often a true sign of some element of disorder, some
trace of pride or immoderation, in an act that is otherwise
good.

A Crisis of Conscience

To attempt to estimate the degree to which these general
considerations apply to the individual case in question would
be improper here, and at best could only be conjecture. Let
us merely observe that Tillich's constant preoccupation with
defining and defending "the Protestant principle" has every
sign of being an *apologia pro vita sua*; while the incessant
return of his thoughts to Catholicism, and especially the not
quite controlled bitterness which breaks out in each reference
to its "heteronomy" or authoritarianism (he manifests no
comparable bitterness over the grave injustice done him by
Nazism), could be readily understood as an attempt to justify
his refusal to submit to it.

In any event, we are interested in Tillich chiefly insofar as
he appears to be representative of a crisis of conscience which
seems to us to be among the most acute and widespread in
our time. Whether or not the foregoing remarks apply to
Tillich personally—and we apologize sincerely if there is any
injustice in them—we are convinced that they have a wide
application elsewhere. Countless tortured souls experience a
strong attraction toward the Church, but recoil from the
sacrifice of submission to its authority. Entrance to the
Heavenly Jerusalem is gained only by passing through the
lowly gate of submission, and many will not bow their heads.
Submission to authority is humiliating, and never so much
as when that authority, vested in human beings, asserts its
right not merely to direct our acts, but even to guide our
thinking. Even the conviction that this authority derives from
God Incarnate who declared, "He that hears you hears me,"
and that it is reinforced by the "Spirit of Truth," while making submission to the authority reasonable, does not eliminate
the humiliation of it, which is, on the contrary, intensified

by the obligation to give a kind of divine reverence to a human person.

And yet, even in virtue of the theology of Paul Tillich, the meaning and usefulness of this humiliation can be understood. Because of the transcendence of God, humility is an indispensable attitude in the creature who would draw near to him. This is the great lesson of the Old Testament for which Tillich has expressed a particular preference.[23] Moses must take off his sandals when he steps on holy ground. And, humility purifies the mind, thereby qualifying it for the vision of truths to which it would otherwise be blind.

Theoretically, the soul should perhaps be capable by itself of assuming an attitude of utter humility in its interior relations with God. In fact, however, the human soul is inclined to "put its center in itself," and lose its "unity with the Ultimate Being"—to adopt Tillich's own terminology in characterizing the sin which is pride. And, in practice, there is no lesson so efficacious for interior submission to the invisible God as the humiliating realism of subjection to visible men. This, at least, is the wisdom of the saints, who learned even to love humiliations, once they had experienced their fruitfulness. In this light, the humiliation entailed in receiving the divine Truth through the intermediary of a human magisterium appears not just as a sacrifice, an unavoidable price, but as a preparation contributing positively to the fuller reception of that Truth.[24]

Tillich's Philosophical Mentality

One of the most striking characteristics of Professor Tillich's thought is its metaphysical tone. He raises metaphysical ques-

---

[23] See *ibid.*, p. 33.

[24] The notion of humility is not alien to Tillich's thought; in fact, he seems to cherish this virtue as characteristically Protestant. But the act of humility, which consists in submission to authority, that is, to the divine authority incarnate in the Church, he is loath to admit.

tions constantly, treats all problems in metaphysical language, and has a vast acquaintance with metaphysical literature. But although he has been judged by others "a real contributor to the present-day revival of metaphysical inquiry,"[25] we submit that Tillich is more at home on the phenomenological level of the history of philosophy than in the depths of ontological mystery. We think it is no exaggeration to say that his writing abounds with instances of obvious disregard for fundamental distinctions between the orders of being—as between the substantial and accidental, between the real and the ideal orders —while attending only to relatively external resemblances and dissemblances.

Adequately to substantiate such a judgment, it would be necessary to make a detailed study of typical notions drawn from Tillich's works. Such an undertaking would be tedious, and most of the examples, although significant, would be trivial. Therefore, we will be content here to offer only indications, and leave to others to decide from the direct reading of the author whether this appraisal is correct.

One example that comes readily to mind is Tillich's use and conception of *symbols*. In a letter to Father Weigel he declares:

> Usually I speak of symbolic knowledge and mean with it exactly what St. Thomas means with *analogia entis*. The reason I used symbol more than analogy is a methodological difference between St. Thomas and myself. I would agree with him that every knowledge of God has analogical character, but I do not agree with him that it is possible to develop a natural theology on this basis.[26]

But it is patent from Tillich's writings that he does not mean by *symbol* what St. Thomas means by *analogy*, and this is precisely the reason why it is no basis for a natural theology.

Symbol and analogy[27] are not the same thing; two beings

---

[25] John H. Randall, Jr., "The Ontology of Paul Tillich," Kegley and Bretall, *op. cit.*, p. 161.

[26] *Theological Studies*, 11 (1950), 201.

[27] We are considering, of course, only the analogy of "proper proportionality," which is analogy in the strictest sense, and the only sense relevant here.

are analogous by reason of an "essence" which is realized properly, even though differently, in both of them; hence, there is adequate objective basis for making the same predication of them both. But we *freely* take one being to symbolize another because of some likeness or association between them, which is not, however, by itself sufficient reason for a common predication: that is why the symbol is often erected by an act of the will.[28] Tillich is entirely right in preferring the term "symbol" to "analogy," for it is symbols that he is dealing with, precisely insofar as these are distinct from analogies; and the fact that he thinks that there is nothing more in analogy than in symbol is a convincing sign that he is not thinking on a truly ontological level, but on a more imaginative level, where the two can no longer be distinguished.

Tillich writes in his autobiography:

The difficulties I experienced in coming to terms with reality transported me at an early age into the life of phantasy. For some years, certain imaginative worlds constituted true reality for me, into which I withdrew as often as possible from the external reality not taken seriously by me. That was the time from my fourteenth to my seventeenth year of age. At the end of that period the romantic imagination was ultimately transmuted into the philosophical imagination, which ever since has stayed by me, for good and ill.[29]

Perhaps what Tillich has actually done has been, to a degree at least, to substitute imagination for philosophy. This is not to deny the stimulating and valuable insights with which his works teem, but only to declare that they pertain to an order of thought much more concrete and imaginative than the genuinely metaphysical. They are not sufficiently abstracted from the concrete for the latter; not fully resolved

[28] Note the significance in this regard of the following line taken from the Introduction to Tillich's autobiography: "When I received the invitation to give an account of how my ideas have grown from my life, it came to me that the concept of border line *might be the fitting symbol* of the whole of my personal and intellectual development" (*IH*, p. 3; italics the author's).

[29] *IH*, p. 13.

into terms of being proper. Tillich is like a painter considering in a landscape its superficial coloring and visible forms,
and disregarding the structural factors that concern the en-
gineer or the geologist.

If he is a painter, then he is, like many modern philosophers, an impressionist. The cosmos is not transferred to his
canvas by a one-to-one correspondence between the elements
of pigment and the elements of the reality being portrayed,
but only by an over-all likeness of impression. In such a style,
inconsistency, contradiction, and even a limited amount of
nonsense is tolerable, for the elements are intended to
counterbalance one another in the total picture, rather than
to say anything in isolation from one another. In the same
way, green and yellow and red strokes are tolerable in an
impressionistic rendering of a solid blue sky; all that matters
is the total blend. To stop, therefore, and inquire as to
the sense of each statement or the precise reference of terms
in such a writer is to read him in a spirit alien to that
in which he writes; and this is the danger to which a scholas-
tically trained mind is particularly liable in reading Paul
Tillich. Nevertheless, there are limits which may not rightly
be exceeded even in the freedom of this literary genre, and
it may well be questioned whether it has any place in philosophy or theology.

Perhaps a clue to Tillich's philosophical mentality can be
found in a remark made during one of the Schelling lectures:
"Philosophy must be dramatic." From his explanation, it was
evident that by *philosophy* he meant the *history of philosophy*, or even better the recounting of this history; for he
conceives the history of philosophy as a perpetual conflict
between opposite tendencies, such as essentialism and existentialism, monism and pluralism, with the predominance
passing back and forth from one to the other in a series of
dramatic crises. What is significant in this otherwise commonplace attitude is the unconscious (but so much the more
meaningful!) identification of philosophy and the history of
philosophy (paralleled several times in the same lectures by
an analogous identification of religion and the history of religions), and the fact that it is especially the dramatic charac-

ter of the history of philosophy that Tillich finds interesting. ("This is what makes it fascinating," he remarked.)

That is to say, what interests him in the ideas and philosophies of the past, is not their essential, fundamental truths, so much as accidental traits of resemblance among them and the historical role they have played in the drama of man's pursuit of wisdom. His account of the progressive establishment of contact between the mind and the world, from Kant through Fichte, leading up to the extreme essentialism of Schelling's younger days, and then the sudden breakthrough of the vanguard of existentialism in Schelling's discovery of the meaning of liberty, had the character of a dramatic build-up and denouement, or a journalistic battle report, more than that of a deep-seeing philosophical scrutiny of the notions and changes involved. In other words, he has less the attitude of a passionate seeker for truth than that of a spectator engrossed in following the fortunes of other seekers. He is not so much a "philosopher," that is, a lover of wisdom, as a lover of philosophies, or better, a man with a *taste* for philosophies.

Conclusion

The preceding criticism of Tillich amounts to this, that he does not attain a truly metaphysical depth. His thought has been, we may say, seduced by the multiplicity and variety of forms appearing in the history of philosophy, and thereby distracted from the still, penetrating contemplation necessary to attain in any serious degree the meaning of being-itself. This is one of the commonest intellectual maladies today, but one with which the medievals were well acquainted when they declared that detachment from things of sense is an indispensable requisite to the pursuit of wisdom (a principle which Tillich himself evidently had in mind, and approved of, in some interesting observations he made about the necessity of both detachment and engagement for the attainment of truth).

This brings us to the profound connection which we suspect may exist between this unmetaphysical quality of Tillich's thought and the hostility toward authority pointed out in the first part of this essay. The human mind's congenital weakness for being ensnared by the superficial and phenomenal, the multiple and accidental, in short, the sensible and all that polarizes around the sensible, is a malady requiring a strong medicine. To be rendered apt for the attainment of wisdom, to be able to penetrate through externals to essences and to being, the human mind needs to be cured—purified and strengthened.

St. Augustine, who was more keenly aware of this than anyone else in the early Christian tradition, prescribed as a remedy the submission to authority involved in Christian faith: "The soiled mind is not able to adhere to the Truth. . . . In order for the man who is not qualified (*idoneus*) to see the Truth to become qualified, and permit himself to be purified, authority is at hand."[30]

St. Augustine did not say that submission to authority replaces the vision of the Truth, but that, by purifying the mind, it makes this vision possible, whereas before it was not. It is, perhaps, paradoxical that, for the mind suffering under an excessive dominion of the visible world, St. Augustine should prescribe a new and voluntary submission to creatures as the means of attaining freedom, and thereby wisdom. Paul Tillich's autonomy might seem to be the more natural and direct route. But St. Augustine spoke from experience; he knew the deceptive impossibility of the direct route for the human soul which is existentially incapable of attaining the fulfillment of its essential aspirations. The tradition of authentic Christian spirituality has confirmed his judgment many times.[31] The humility of submission purifies

---

[30] *De utilitate credendi*, xvi, 34.

[31] The Truth which St. Augustine and Christian spirituality in general are concerned with attaining is not primarily that of metaphysics; nevertheless, the latter also demands of those who pursue it a certain purification of the intelligence, to which the renouncements prescribed by Christian spirituality can contribute more efficaciously, perhaps, than is commonly acknowledged.

the soul, releases it from the chains of sense that weigh it down, and lets it fly free. The pride and exaltation of a direct assault upon spiritual heights, on the other hand, only strengthen the bondage that is being fought against.

The principal error of the Protestant tradition, of which Paul Tillich is here an authentic representative, is this: It has sought to rise too directly, and in so doing, has only fastened itself all the more firmly to the ground. Its own attitude has prevented it from attaining those very spiritual goals of which it spoke eloquently, and often quite truly, and in the name of which it crusaded. The feebleness of Protestant thought in the realm of metaphysics, which has been a constant in its tradition from Luther to Tillich (although in such different ways: for Luther mistrusted philosophy, while Tillich cultivates it), is only the inevitable consequence of the most characteristic Protestant position; and the spiritual freedom to which Tillich aspires can be obtained only by the sacrifice of some of the autonomy he insists on.

IV

GEORGE F. McLEAN, O.M.I.

Paul Tillich's Existential
Philosophy of Protestantism

In recent years the Christian community has been blessed
with an increasingly urgent sense of the unity of Christ's
Church. This has created a special interest in Protestant theology and led to an ever increasing number of irenically
oriented studies. Such work has contributed much by pointing
to the authentically Christian content of Protestant theologies, from the discussion of which one might hope for an
improved unity of belief.

There remained, nevertheless, an important reservation to
a fully sympathetic and fruitful dialogue, for it was observed
that true ecumenism can be expected as a result of discussions, such as those on justification, only when the meaning
attached to such terms as God, creature, sin, and New Being,
has been, if not agreed upon, at least understood.[1] Most
fundamentally, this demanded an appreciation of the philosophical position which stood as their presuppositions or pre-
determinants; and there lay a new level of divergence. Among
Protestant thinkers these positions were generally those of
recent philosophies reflective of man's contemporary dilemma,
whereas among Catholic thinkers they were of a more traditional philosophy reflective of the rich insights of classical

---

[1] See Juan Alfaro, S.J., "Justificacion Barthiana y Justificacion
Catolica," *Gregorianum*, 39 (1958), 757–69; Henri de Lubac, S.J.,
"Zum katholischen Dialog mit Karl Barth," *Dokumente*, 14 (1958),
448–54.

philosophy. With the opening of Vatican II, however, this difference more than ever before has been shown to be one of complementarity rather than competition. "The Council," said Pope Paul VI, "will build a bridge toward the contemporary world. . . . The Church looks at the world . . . with the sincere intention . . . not of condemning it but of strengthening and saving it." In this project the Protestant philosophical insight into man's contemporary religious dilemma becomes an indispensable element in any solution, and does so in a way which opens a dimension of ecumenism sufficiently profound to contribute to all others.

For this reason the study of the basic religious philosophy of America's foremost Protestant theologian, Dr. Paul Tillich, takes on a special importance. His thought is contemporary, reflecting the modern dichotomy of subject and object in the manner of the existentialist movement. It is also Protestant, stressing the corruption of man and his distance from the Creator. The investigation of these facets of Tillich's philosophy will proceed by three stages. First, it will consider his evaluation of the nature and extent of the elements of individuation and participation in relation to previous forms of Christianity. Then it will analyze his conciliation of these two aspects in a philosophy which is religious, Protestant, and contemporary. Finally, it will evaluate his contributions both in themselves and in relation to Catholicism.

It can be hoped that the study of this recent adaptation of Protestantism to the contemporary scene will shed light on two matters of great interest and urgency. One is the nature of the religious problem expressed in present-day thought. The other is the nature of the religious system which can answer these demands. Both contributions should be of assistance to all in understanding that faith which was given for all days even unto the consummation of the world.

Norms for Religious Philosophies

Paul Tillich is much concerned with the relation between
subject and object. His concern extends from its contemporary
modality to its fundamental nature. There has been a general
consensus of opinion that the great tragedy of recent times
has been the subjection of man to the objects he produces.
Man is seen to be reduced to the state of an impersonal
object.[2] We will be able to follow the analysis of this
contemporary situation more completely below. For now, it
is sufficient to note that it is a pressing manifestation of the
fundamental polar relation of self and world, subject and
object. Tillich considers this to be the basic ontological structure because it is the presupposition of ontological investigation, without itself being able to be deduced from any prior
unity. Idealism has been no more successful in deriving the
object from the subject than earlier naturalisms have been
in reducing the subject to the state of a physical object. The
polarity of the self-world or subject-object structure is then
something which "cannot be derived. It must be accepted."[3]

The polar relation of these elements assumes delicate
nuances according to the nature of the reality under consideration. This provides a very sensitive norm for evaluating
any system of thought. The strength and weaknesses of a
philosophy will appear clearly from the degree of its success
in conciliating the twin poles of subject and object in its
own area. Tillich applies this norm in the form of the polar
notions of individualization and participation to various types

[2] See *TC*, pp. 91–94.
[3] *ST*, I, p. 174; cf. "Participation and Knowledge, Problems of an
Ontology of Cognition," *Sociologica*, Vol. I of *Frankfurter Beiträge
zur Soziologie*, Theodor W. Adorno and Walter Dirks, editors (Stuttgart: Europäische Verlagsanstalt, 1955): "Being, insofar as it is an
object of asking presupposes the subject-object structure of reality"
(p. 201).

of religious thought.[4] A study of his evaluation will provide an insight into his requirements for an authentic religion and reveal what elements of Protestant and Catholic thought he would retain in his own contemporary religious philosophy.

While neither of the polar notions can be fully realized without the other, individualization will be analyzed first. This element is implied in the constitution of every being as a self and points to the fact that it is particular and indivisible. As particular, the self maintains an identity separate from all else and opposite anything which might be related to it. As indivisible it maintains its identity by retaining the integrity of its own self center much as a mathematical point resists partition.[5] One can hear the traditional definition of the individual in these notions. He does fail to extend this to the temporal order making self-affirmation something unique, unrepeatable, and irreplaceable. The infinite value of every human soul is a consequence of its "ontological self-affirmation as an indivisible, unexchangeable self."[6]

While this individuality is an indispensable element in reality, it is a grave error to consider it without the polar element of participation. An exclusive insistence on the particular and unrepeatable brings with it the nominalistic breakdown in the philosophy of essence.[7] This breakdown, in turn, becomes the source of a number of philosophical positions which have had great influence on religious ideas. One of the more important of the nominalistic consequences is the position that "only the individual has ontological reality; universals are verbal signs which point to similarities between individual things."[8] Another is the attribution of an element of indeterminacy to the divine and of radical contingency to finite beings. The epistemological expression of

---

[4] This is developed at length in *CTB*.

[5] See *ST*, I, pp. 170, 174–75; "Participation and Knowledge," *art. cit.*, 201.

[6] *CTB*, p. 87.

[7] See *ibid.*, p. 129.

[8] *ST*, I, pp. 73, 97, 177.

this nominalistic ontology is referred to by Max Scheler as controlling knowledge. In this the object is transformed into a completely conditioned and calculable "thing" to be studied with detached analysis by the methods of empiricism and positivism. In the ethical sphere it follows that the determination of ends is outside the competency of this knowledge, which restricts itself to the consideration of means and receives the ends from nonrational sources such as positive tradition or arbitrary decision. These are the nominalistic results of a development of individuation without its polar element of participation.

Concerning the relationship of medieval nominalism to Protestantism Tillich is particularly circumspect. He has written some of the strongest contemporary passages on the inevitability of the ontological question for the theologian. Nevertheless, he proceeds to detach the reformers from their philosophical background and to make their religious experience the sole determinant of their system.[9] In this he manifests a decidedly different understanding of the Protestant phenomenon than Louis Bouyer, who has recently written that "the reformers no more invented this strange and despairing universe than they had been brought up in, Scholasticism in its decadence."[10] Certainly, Luther's famous *"Sum enim Occamicae factionis"* must be given progressively less weight as he gradually dissociated himself from many of their positions. However, through such men as Biel, Trutfetter, and Paltz, he had been well introduced to the contemporary Occamist school, and it is not surprising to find him retaining much of its basic philosophical orientation.[11]

If Tillich is slow to point to this fundamental connection of Luther with nominalism, he does not fail to appreciate the particular stress laid on individualization by the reformer

[9] See *ibid.*, p. 21; cf. *TC*, p. 19.

[10] Louis Bouyer, *The Spirit and Forms of Protestantism*, trans. A. V. Littledale (Westminster: Newman Press, 1956), p. 153. This would be in general agreement with the work of H. Denifle, O.P., and the research of Catholic scholars since.

[11] Cf. fn. 130 below.

and especially by the theologians who followed him. But for Luther an immediate implication of this stress, and one so important that it alone would suffice to guarantee the purity of Christianity, was the rejection of an analogous, internal reality by which man supernaturally participates in the divine. In its place he substituted the mere imputation of the divine. This was something which Occam had considered possible but insufficient to fulfill the requirements of faith.[12] A related expression of this accent on individualization is the development of the notion of personal guilt, in the Protestant concept of the Fall, into that of the total depravity of man's nature. This implies that the power of communion with God has been not only weakened but lost. The result is that "man is separated from God, and he has no freedom of return."[13] It is true that these elements of individualization and guilt call for the notion of forgiveness as an element of participation. However, historical Protestantism has never managed to integrate these two elements. This integration was impeded for a century and a half by the way in which Calvinism and sectarianism stressed "the unconditional character of the divine judgment and the free character of God's forgiveness."[14] For this led to a separation between man and religious truth similar to that between an abstract subject and object. When at last there was a return to emphasis on personal guilt and perfection it only proved to be a step toward rationalism and romanticism in which the person was attributed such independent dignity that the content of his reason or of his person lost all notion of participation in the divine. Thus it has gone with the various Protestant concep-

[12] Martin Luther, *Vorlesung über den Römerbrief*, 1515–16, *die Scholien*, J. Ficker, editor (Leipzig: Dieterich, 1925): *"Bonitas Dei facit nos bonos et opera nostra bona; quia non essent in se bona, nisi quia Deus reputat ea bona. . . . Perversa itaque est definitio virtutis apud Aristotelem, quod ipsa nos perficit et opus eius laudabile reddit"* (p. 221). For a variant interpretation of this point and suggestions for further research see Paul Vignaux, "Sur Luther et Ockham," *Franziskanische Studien*, 32 (1950), 20–30.

[13] *ST*, I, p. 258.

[14] *CTB*, p. 132; cf. *ibid.*, pp. 114–18.

tions of man. An historical background of nominalism gave it an excessive individuation from which it has never managed to free itself.

The insufficiency of this thought is realized by Tillich. He considers pure nominalism to be untenable because its radical individualism renders impossible the mutual participation of the knower and the known.[15] Thus, the various forms of Protestant thought which have emphasized individualization almost exclusively tended by that very fact to cut themselves off from all meaningful contact with the divine. He feels that a mitigated, but none the less dangerous, form of this had already tainted the Catholic theology of St. Thomas when it made of God an object for us as subjects. In logical predication this cannot be avoided. The error of Catholic and much orthodox Protestant theology on this point is seen to be its failure to reject the ontological implication by which God's holiness is negated, and he becomes an object beside the subject, merely one being among others.[16] Much Catholic thought on the supernatural is criticized in this light.

At no time has the exaggerated stress on individualization appeared as inadequate as it has in the contemporary context of meaninglessness. Neo-Protestantism, built on biblical criticism and the Ritschlian theological synthesis of modern naturalism and historicism, has been shattered. Its social foundations were destroyed by Marx, its moral grounds by Nietzsche, and its religious basis by Kierkegaard.[17] The question is no longer which values are true or how God speaks to us as individuals. Instead, God has been pronounced dead "and with him the whole system of values and meanings in which one lived."[18] Thus, the import of the traditional

[15] See *ST*, I, p. 177. In the ontological realm such radical individualization would remove all basis for the category of relation. The foundations of religion would thus be destroyed.

[16] See *ibid.*, pp. 172–73, 272.

[17] See Paul Tillich, "The Present Theological Situation in the Light of the Continental European Development," *Theology Today*, 6 (1949), 299–302.

[18] *CTB*, pp. 142, 152–53.

Protestant accentuation on the meaning of the individual, his sin and forgiveness, is lost because the contemporary question concerns the very possibility of meaning itself. The problem which faces a present-day religious philosophy is that of finding the divine through nonbeing in its most radical form, the anxiety of doubt and meaninglessness.

Given this problem of individualization in the contemporary situation, we may now turn to its polar element of participation. Despite the history of its exaggerations, individualization remains indispensable, for it provides the terms of the relation of man to God. But in order to have a basis for the relationship, the corresponding element of participation must also be introduced. Participation points to "an element of identity in that which is different or of a togetherness of that which is separated. Whether it is the identity of the same enterprise, or the identity of the same universal or the same whole, of which one is a part, in each case participation implies identity."[19]

The task of this element is twofold. First, it gives meaning and content to the individual, keeping it from being an empty form. It is then an essential perfection, proportionate to the being and its act. Thus, when the individual is on the level of person, participation has the perfect form of communion. Secondly, participation provides the basis in reality for unity with God by expressing the presence of the divine. No religion can be without this without being reduced to a secular movement of political, educational, or scientific activism.[20] It is the relationship to the divine which is expressed by the notion of participation.

Tillich is certain that all religions have some form of this element of participation because there could be no real religion without it. However, he considers the notion of the presence of the divine to be developed in a special degree by Catholicism. This is expressed in two ways. One is the

[19] Tillich, "Participation and Knowledge," *art. cit.*, 201–2. He terms the system which stresses participation mystical realism.

[20] See Paul Tillich, "The Permanent Significance of the Catholic Church for Protestantism," *Protestant Digest* (1941), 25–29.

Catholic retention, even after original sin, of the integrity of human nature with its powers of reason and free will. Man thus remains the *imago Dei* and retains some power to return to God.[21] In order to appreciate this aspect proper to Catholicism, it is not necessary to accept the possible Pelagian implications of Tillich's statement of the Catholic position. It is sufficient simply to note the difference between the Council of Trent, Session VI, Chapter 1, and Luther's notions of the total depravity of human nature, man's incapacity to do good, and forensic justification.[22]

Another Catholic expression of the presence of the divine is its notion of sacrament. For Tillich, "any revelatory experience transforms the medium of revelation into a sacramental object, whether it is an object of nature, a human being, an historical event, or a sacred text."[23] He vigorously points out the great loss which Protestantism has undergone in failing to develop, or even to retain sufficiently, this element. Protestantism needs the continuous influx of the sacramental in order to be more than a secular movement, and for this reason it needs the permanent corrective of Catholicism.[24]

The correction could well be reciprocated, he feels, for Catholicism has trouble with some of the forms taken by its expression of participation. He observes a tendency to view the sacramental as more than a manifestation of the divine, to consider particular objects as divine in themselves. This impression made on others by Catholic devotion is the basis of the many accusations of idolatry. Here the purifying, prophetic "Protestant principle" would come forward to reject

21 See *ST*, I, p. 259.
22 Luther, *op. cit.*: "*Igitur peccatum est in spirituali homine relictum; . . . quod qui non sedule studuerit expugnare, sine dubio iam habet, etiamsi nihil amplius peccaverit, unde damnetur. . . . Que non essent sine culpa (sint enim vere peccata et quidem damnabilia), nisi misericordia Dei non imputaret*" (p. 178).
23 *ST*, I, p. 139.
24 See "The Permanent Significance of the Catholic Church for Protestantism," *art. cit.*, 25, 29.

"the temptation of the bearers of the holy to claim absoluteness for themselves."[25] He finds two other difficulties with the Catholic realization of participation. One is the distinction between natural and supernatural, according to which the special participation in the divine is realized outside the center of one's personality. He thinks of this grace as a substance alongside the person.[26] This would be a natural consequence from the more radical difficulty which consists in the conceiving of the divine as an object opposed to us as subjects. When God is reduced to this less than divine status of one being among others, the possibility of participating in him is severely limited.[27] Thus, while participation has a place of honor in Catholicism, its particular realization is considered deficient.

On the other hand, while Protestantism is considered to have much to learn from Catholicism on this point, it is not without its own realization of participation. As noted above, Tillich considers this element to be essential to religion as such. He considers it to be an important factor in the personal experience of Luther which, in the midst of the consciousness of guilt, encountered the divine in an immediate, personal relation of forgiveness. Luther expressed this by the phrases, "he who is unjust is just" and "justification by faith." Tillich would express the same in the modern terminology of despair by "the courage to accept oneself as accepted in spite of being unacceptable."[28] He notes that this is not the courage to be as a part had by the public nature of the sacraments; neither is it the resisting of authority or the transformation of Church or society. Rather, it is a personalism which stands between mysticism and individualism, affirming the individual self in its encounter with the divine person.

This is the very lifeblood of Protestantism as a religion. He finds that it has been threatened with dissolution many times. Hardly had Luther's insight been attained when the

25 *ST*, I, p. 227.
26 See *ibid.*, pp. 258–59.
27 See *TC*, pp. 18–21; cf. *ST*, I, pp. 172–73.
28 *CTB*, pp. 63–64.

attempts to reduce it to a theological system so stressed "the unconditional character of the divine judgment and the free character of God's forgiveness" that the personal situation was replaced by an objective, and then abstract, moral subject.[29] In this way the true existential insight of Protestantism was beclouded. This trend continued as Kant and Hegel developed the notion of the essential man in a supremely rational world. The development of such exaggerated hopes on the part of man's reason made the reaction the more pervading. Schelling's positive philosophy called for an evaluation of things according to the individual's historical situation rather than according to "abstract natures." Marx, Nietzsche, and Bergson found that the modern situation was far from realizing Hegel's reconciliation of man with himself. It was, in fact, reducing the individual to a mere object or thing, an empty space without significance, except inasmuch as something else passed through it. Participation was gone and with it the person. Human existence had fallen into utter meaninglessness.

It is this situation which has to be faced by anything which might be called contemporary Protestantism. As religious it must restore the element of participation in the divine. As Protestant it must keep this from being confused with any mere thing and relate it to the individual as personal forgiveness. At the same time it must be contemporary, facing the problem in the present context of meaninglessness. Religion today must not seek meaning or the participation which is its base beside the totalitarian extension of meaninglessness. It must delve into the meaninglessness itself and there find meaning. Only then can it be a contemporary Protestantism.

Tillich's Philosophy of Protestantism

The varied elements which Paul Tillich intends to integrate in his contemporary Protestant theology are related to the

[29] See *ibid.*, pp. 132–33.

notion of creation. For, "the doctrine of creation is not the story of an event which took place 'once upon a time.' It is the basic description of the relation between God and the world."[30] It includes the complex data concerning God, the production of his finite effects *ex nihilo*, and the response of man from this situation of meaninglessness. Tillich expresses the dynamic interrelationship of these elements in terms of an existential dialectic. He holds this to be the contemporary philosophy because it considers the problems and contradictions of present-day existence at a depth where the ontological principles of essence and existence and the epistemological principles of subject and object can be correlated.

A complete discussion of the relation of essence to existence is identical with the entire theological system. The distinction between essence and existence, which religiously speaking is the distinction between the created and the actual world, is the backbone of the whole body of theological thought. It must be elaborated in every part of the theological system.[31]

Let us see how Tillich's ontological analysis of the present situation reveals a dialectic which might well be termed a contemporary philosophy for Protestantism, since it goes beyond the question of the levels of being to consider their interrelation.

It was observed at the beginning that Tillich insists on the polarity of subject and object as the point of departure for his analysis of reality because both members are presupposed for the ontological question. But if they provide his point of departure, he leaves no doubt that he shares the modern concern to proceed to a point of identity where both subject and object are overcome. This recent concern is the result of the observation that man has been reduced to the status of a thing by allowing himself to be subjected to the objects he produces.[32] The strongest statement of this situation was made by Nietzsche, but the best known is Marx's description

[30] *ST*, I, p. 252.
[31] *Ibid.*, p. 204.
[32] See *TC*, pp. 91–94.

of the reduction of the worker to a commodity. Reality, then, must not be simply identified with objective being, for man must participate in some deeper principle or lose his value and individuality. However, to proceed to identify reality with subjective being or consciousness would be equally insufficient, for subject is determined by its contrast with object. Consequently, what is sought is a level of reality which is beyond this dichotomy of subject and object, identifying the value of both.

The need for a point of identity and its function is better appreciated as one proceeds beyond the subject-object relationship to the investigation of either knowledge or being. "The point of procedure in every analysis of experience and every concept of a system of reality must be the point where subject and object are at one and the same place."[33] Thus, the analysis of experience turns to the logos, the element of form, of meaning, and of structure. In the knowing subject, or self, the logos is called subjective reason and makes self a centered structure. Correspondingly, in the known object, or world, it is called objective reason and makes world a structured whole. There is nothing beyond the logos structure of being.[34] It is, of course, possible to conceive the relation between the rational structures of mind and of reality in a number of ways. Four of these possibilities are represented by realism, idealism, pluralism, and monism. But, according to Tillich, what is of note here is that all philosophers have held an identity, or at least an analogy, to exist between the logos of the mind and the logos of the world.[35] Successful scientific planning and prediction provide a continual pragmatic proof of this identity.

The philosophical mind, however, is not satisfied with the mere affirmation, or even the confirmation, of the fact. There arises the problem of why there should be this correspondence of the logos in the subject with the logos of reality as a whole. This can be solved if the logos is primarily the struc-

33 IH, p. 60.
34 See ST, I, pp. 156, 171–72, 279.
35 See ibid., pp. 23, 75–76.

ture of the divine life and the principle of its self-manifestation. For then it is the medium of creation, mediating "between the silent abyss of being and the fullness of concrete individualized, self-related beings."[36] The identity or analogy of the rational structures of mind and of reality will follow from the fact that both have been mediated through the same identical divine logos.

In this way, "reason in both its objective and subjective structures points to something which appears in these structures but which transcends them in power and meaning."[37] Logos becomes the point of identity between God, self, and world. Of these three, the logos of God is central and is participated in by self and world as they acquire their being. Thus, the logos of reason gives us a first introduction to the concept Tillich has of God overcoming the separation of subject and object to provide a deeper synthesis of the reality of both.

This conclusion of the analysis of experience has definite implications for an analysis of being. For the identity is not merely an external similarity of two things to a third without a basis in the things themselves. The identification of subject and object is the divine and this is within beings. The only nonsymbolic expression of the divine is the term "being-itself,"[38] which, in relation to us, is the ultimate concern. But God is within beings as their power of being, as an analytic dimension in the structure of reality.[39] As such he is the "substance" appearing in every rational structure; the "ground" creative in every rational creation; the "abyss" unable to be exhausted by any creation or totality of creation; the "infinite potentiality of being and meaning" pouring himself into the rational structures of mind and reality to ac-

---

[36] *Ibid.*, p. 158.

[37] *Ibid.*, p. 79.

[38] *Ibid.*, pp. 238–39; cf. "Reply to Interpretation and Criticism," C. Kegley and R. Bretall, editors, *The Theology of Paul Tillich* (New York: Macmillan, 1952), p. 335. To this single nonsymbolic expression of the divine he has added severe limitations.

[39] See *ST*, I, p. 207.

tualize and transform them.[40] God is, then, the ground not only of truth but of being as well. In fact, he can be the ground of truth precisely because he is the ground of being.

These ideas have had a long history in the mind of man. In the distant past the Upanishads viewed the Brahman-ātman both cosmically as the all-inclusive, unconditioned ground of the universe from which the conditioned emanate, and acosmically as the reality of which the universe is but an appearance. The absolute is the "not this, not this" (*neti neti*), "the Real of the real" (*styasya satyam*).[41] This line of thought can be traced through Plato and Augustine to the medieval Franciscans and Nicholas of Cusa. Tillich is fond of relating his thought to these older sources. The proximate determinant of his thought in positing this ontological principle of identity beyond the subject and object is Schelling. At the very first Schelling agreed with Fichte in making the "Absolute Ego" of consciousness the ultimate principle and reality. It is this consciousness which dialectically "becomes" the world of nature. But on further consideration, Schelling failed to see the particular connection between the infinite Ego and the finite object. For this reason he moved the "Absolute Ego" from the conscious side of the dichotomy to a central, neutral position between and prior to both objectivity and subjectivity.[42] Thus, the Absolute is now called not "Ego" but "the unconditional" and "identity." The idealism is no longer subjective, but ontological. This is the insight of the early Schelling which Tillich readily accepts. Thus, he traces the line of his thought in-between, but distinct from, both the subjective idealism of Fichte and the objective realism of Hobbes. Both sides of the polarity must be maintained; the unconditional will be equally the ground of subject and object.[43]

---

[40] See *ibid.*, p. 79.

[41] *Brhadāranyaka-Upanisad*, II, i, 20; IV, ii, 4, cited by T.M.P. Mahadevan, "The Upanisads," Sarvepalli Radhakrishnan, editor, *History of Philosophy, Eastern and Western* (London: George Allen and Unwin, 1952), I, pp. 62–63.

[42] Cf. *TC*, p. 92.

[43] See *ST*, I, p. 171.

Two important specifications must be added to this notion of a divine depth dimension beyond both subject and object. One regards the incapacity of limited beings to exhaust or adequately represent the divine. This indicates the radical individualization of the divine. The other concerns the way God is manifested in the essence of finite beings. This points to the way they participate in him.

The first of these specifications which Tillich is careful to make concerning the point of identity of subject and object is that it is gnostically incomprehensible and ontologically inexhaustible, the former reflecting the latter. "This power of being is the *prius* which precedes all special contents logically and ontologically."[44] It is not even identified with the totality of things. For this reason the divine is termed the "abyss" because it cannot be exhausted in any creation or totality of creations.[45]

Human intuition of the divine always has distinguished between the abyss of the divine (the element of power) and the fullness of its content (the element of meaning), between the divine depth and the divine *logos*. The first principle is the basis of Godhead, that which makes God, God. It is the root of his majesty, the unapproachable intensity of his being, the inexhaustible ground of being in which everything has its origin. It is the power of being infinitely resisting nonbeing, giving the power of being to everything that is.[46]

This position of the divine as the inexhaustible depth dimension of reality is the basis of the distinction and individualization of God in relation to creatures. In the realm of being it implies what Tillich calls the Protestant principle, the protest against any thing being raised to the position of the divine. This extends to any creation of the Church, including the biblical writings which it will not allow to be identified with the divine ground of all.[47] No bearer of the

[44] *TC*, p. 25.

[45] See Paul Tillich, "Symbol and Knowledge: A Response," *Journal of Liberal Religion*, 2 (1941), 203; cf. *ST*, II, p. 6.

[46] *ST*, I, pp. 250–51.

[47] See *ibid.*, pp. 37, 227.

holy may be permitted to claim absolute status for itself.
This reinforces the element of individualization which has
always marked Protestantism as leaving man alone before
God.

In the order of knowledge this implies that, if man is to
proceed beyond finite realities to an awareness of what is truly
divine, he must leave behind the rational categories of technical reason. Such categories limit the infinite. They make
God an object, "a" being among others rather than being-
itself. For this reason God cannot be conceptualized.[48] To
say that God is the depth of reason is to refuse to make him
another field of reason. In fact, he precedes the structures of
reason and gives them their inexhaustible quality simply because he can never be adequately contained in them. Schelling has termed the divine the *Unvordenkliche* because it is
"that before which thinking cannot penetrate."[49] It was the
error of idealism to think that this could ever be completely
reduced to rational forms. Tillich is protected from this error
by his basic ontological observation of the various levels of
reality. "There are levels of reality of great difference, and
. . . these different levels demand different approaches
and different languages."[50] The divine is assigned to the deepest of these levels, and consequently, must be known and
expressed in a manner quite different from that of ordinary
knowledge and discourse. It is this same fact to which Tillich is referring when he introduces the dialectical relationship between these levels and speaks of the divine as the
prius. Here too it will be necessary to proceed beyond con-
ceptualization to an intuitive, personal awareness of the
divine. This will be described below, but one thing is already
clear. Since the categories are the basis for the objective
element in knowledge and the means by which it is made
common, the intuitive awareness will have to be personal
and marked by subjectivity.

[48] See *CTB*, pp. 184–85.
[49] *PE*, p. 76.
[50] "Religious Symbols and Our Knowledge of God," *The Christian Scholar*, 38 (September, 1955), 192.

The other specification made by Tillich concerning the depth dimension concerns its manifestation in the essences of finite beings. The notion of essence is found in some form in practically all philosophers, but classically in Plato and Aristotle. Plato attempted to solve the problem of unity and separation in knowledge by the myth of the original union of the soul with the essences or ideas. Recollection and re-union take place later and in varying degrees. Tillich stresses the point that, in Plato, the unity of soul and ideas is never completely destroyed. Although the particular object is strange as such, it contains essential structures "with which the cognitive subject is essentially united and which it can remember."[51]

In Aristotle there is a retention of the notion of essence as providing the power of being. Essence is the quality and structure in which being participates. But this is still potential; it is the actual which is real. Tillich accepts the Aristotelian position in these general terms and then uses it in order to develop his conception of creation. The divine was described above as the inexhaustible, creative abyss. In order that this divine principle might, in fact, be creative, an element of meaning and structure must be added. This is the second divine principle, the *logos*. It makes the divine distinguishable, definite, and finite. The third principle is the Spirit "in whom God 'goes out from' himself, the Spirit proceeds from the divine ground. He gives actuality to that which is potential in the divine ground. . . . The finite is posited as finite within the process of the divine life, but it is reunited with the infinite within the same process."[52]

In these terms Professor Tillich expresses the positive side of the dialectical relationship of the essences of finite beings to the divine. He attempts to show how these essences can contain, without exhausting, the power of being, while God remains this power. As exclusively positive it might be said to express only the first element of creation. This leaves the essences of finite beings, as it were, in a state of dreaming

[51] See *ST*, I, pp. 94–99.
[52] *Ibid.*, p. 251.

innocence within the divine life, from which they must awaken to actualize and realize themselves.[53] Creation is fulfilled in the self-realization by which the limited beings leave the ground of being to "stand upon" it. Whatever we shall say in the negative section about this moment of separation, the element of essence is never completely lost, for "if it were lost, mind as well as reality would have been destroyed in the very moment of their coming into existence."[54] It is the retention of this positive element of essence which provides the radical foundation for participation by limited beings in the divine and their capacity of pointing to the infinite power of being and depth of reason. As mentioned in the first section, such participation in the divine being and some awareness of it is an absolute prerequisite for any religion.

This concludes our consideration of the first or positive stage in Dr. Tillich's dialectic. By placing the divine as the point of identity beyond both subject and object, he has introduced both elements according to which he evaluated previous religious philosophies. The element of participation so necessary for any religion has appeared, and along with it the element of individualization which seems to be a hallmark of Protestantism. We must now investigate Tillich's attempt to give both of these a context which can be truly called contemporary. The second, or negative, stage of his dialectic provides this for individualization. It will remain for the third phase of the dialectic, the synthesis, to present a contemporary understanding of participation in the divine.

Dr. Tillich turns to the second phase of his dialectic in order to specify the basic infinite-finite structure of the thesis by a contemporary form of individualization. Since a strong statement of this element has always been a distinctive mark of Protestantism, this phase will be of great importance in his construction of a Protestant philosophy. Its contemporary nature lies in its particular relation to nonbeing. Non-

<hr />

[53] See *ibid.*, pp. 238, 255.
[54] *Ibid.*, p. 83; cf. "A Reinterpretation of the Doctrine of Incarnation," *Church Quarterly Review*, 147 (January, 1949), 141.

being is had in God. But it is in him as dialectically driving being out of its seclusion to make him living. It is also in God as dialectically overcome, thus placing being itself beyond the polarity of the finite and the infinite negation of the finite.[55] In beings less than God, the nonbeing is not overcome. The classical statement, *"creatio ex nihilo,"* means that the creature "must take over what might be called 'the heritage of nonbeing.' "[56] It has this along with its participation in being, its heritage of being. "Everything which participates in the power of being is 'mixed' with nonbeing. It is being in the process of coming from and going toward nonbeing."[57] This is finite being.

But if one is to understand this more completely he must integrate what has been theologically stated as the Fall of man. This implies the necessity of avoiding an Hegelian understanding of the dialectical expression of being by nonbeing. Hegel would make existence simply a step in the expression of essence. However, profound observation of the modern world, especially of the cataclysm of the First World War, forced home the point that reality is also the contradiction of essence.[58] This has been expressed by the concept of estrangement taken from Hegel's earlier philosophy and applied to the individual by Kierkegaard, to society by Marx, and to life as such by Schopenhauer and Nietzsche. In fact, since the later period of Schelling it has been commonplace for a whole series of philosophers and artists to describe the world as one of fragments, as a disrupted unity. Its result is that individualization has become excessive and led to a loneliness of man before his fellow men and before God. This, in turn, drives man toward his inner experience so that he becomes still further isolated from his world.[59] The presup-

[55] See *ST*, I, pp. 179–80, 188–91. Böhme's *Ungrund*, and Schelling's "first potency" are examples of dialectical nonbeing in God.

[56] *Ibid.*, p. 253.

[57] *Ibid.*, p. 189.

[58] See *ibid.*, pp. 202–3. Some such distinction of essence and existence is presupposed by any philosophy which considers the ideal as against the real, truth against error, or good against evil.

[59] See *TC*, pp. 104–5.

position of this tragic nature of man is his transcendent Fall.[60]

How is this Fall with its existential estrangement to be understood? First, its possibility is traced to man's finite freedom. As seen above, finite man is excluded from the infinity to which he belongs. In this state freedom gives him the capacity to contradict himself and his essential nature. Furthermore, he is aware of this finitude, of the threat from nonbeing. This adds the note of anxiety to his freedom, producing a drive toward transition into existence. But once this freedom is aroused, man finds a double threat rooted in his finitude and expressed in his anxiety. It is the threat either of not actualizing his potencies and thus not fulfilling himself, or of actualizing them, knowing that he will not choose according to the norms and values in which his essential nature expresses itself.[61] In either case he is bound to lose himself and his freedom.

The finite nature of man's freedom implies an opposite pole, called destiny. This applies even to the freedom of self-contradiction. "It is possible only within the context of the universal transition from essence to existence" and every isolated act is embedded in the universal destiny of existence.[62] This means that the estrangement of man from his essential nature has two characteristics: the one tragic, coming from destiny, the other moral (guilt), coming from freedom. Destiny of itself connotes universality. Since the Fall is the presupposition of existence, there is no existence before or without it.[63] Everything, then, that exists participates in the Fall with its twin character of tragedy and guilt. This applies to every man, every act of man, and every part of nature as well.

[60] See ST, II, pp. 24–25, 45; cf. IH, pp. 60–65.

[61] See Paul Tillich, "The Conception of Man in Existential Philosophy," *Journal of Religion*, 19 (July, 1939), 208; cf. ST, II, pp. 31–35.

[62] See *ibid.*, pp. 32, 38.

[63] See Paul Tillich, "A Reinterpretation of the Doctrine of Incarnation," *art. cit.*, 142.

The conciliation of this absolute universality of the Fall with the freedom which is presupposed is somewhat of a problem. Tillich finds his extension of a part in guilt to nature justified by recent evolutionary theories and depth psychology. But how the inevitability and the freedom of estrangement are to be conciliated remains an enigma. In one recent statement he affirms the necessity of something in finite freedom for which we are responsible and which makes the Fall unavoidable. In another work he considers estrangement to be an original fact with "the character of a leap and not of structural necessity."[64] Despite these difficulties in explaining how man's estrangement is free, Tillich is definite in presenting it as the ontological realization of the Fall of mankind.

This negative phase in the dialectic is mediated to the level of consciousness by the general, and presently acute, phenomenon of anxiety which arises from the nonbeing in finite reality. "The first statement about the nature of anxiety is this: anxiety is the state in which a being is aware of its possible nonbeing."[65] It is, in fact, the expression of finitude from the inside. As such it is not a mere psychological quality but an ontological one, present wherever finitude and its threat of nonbeing are found. Anxiety is then simply inescapable for the finite being. Were it a particular object it might be directly feared, attacked, and overcome. But nothingness is not an "object." There is no way for the finite to overcome nonbeing. Thus, anxiety lies within man at all times. This omnipresent ontological anxiety can be aroused at any time, even without a situation of fear. The emotional element is but an indication of the totality with which finite being is penetrated by the threat of absolute separation from its positive element of infinity, that is, by the threat of annihilating nothingness.[66]

The nonbeing of finitude and estrangement is present on

[64] *ST*, II, p. 44.

[65] *CTB*, p. 35; cf. *ST*, I, pp. 191–92.

[66] See "The Conception of Man in Existential Philosophy," *art. cit.*, 211–14.

each level of being and is there in three ways: ontic, spiritual, and moral. This produces three corresponding types or characteristics of anxiety. Ontic anxiety is the awareness that our basic self-affirmation as beings is threatened proximately by fate, the decided contingency of our position, and ultimately by death. Spiritual anxiety is the awareness of the emptiness of the concrete content of our particular beliefs. It is, even more, the awareness of the loss of a spiritual center of meaning resulting in ultimate meaninglessness in which "not even the meaningfulness of a serious question of meaning is left for him."[67] Moral anxiety is the awareness that, in virtue of that very freedom which makes man man, he continually chooses against the fulfillment of his destiny and the actualization of his essential nature, thus adding the element of guilt.[68]

All three elements of anxiety—death, meaninglessness, and guilt—combine to produce despair, the ultimate or "boundary" situation. One element or another may stand out more clearly for various people or in various situations, but all three are inescapably present. It is guilt that seals Sartre's *No Exit*. For, if there were but the nonbeing of death and meaninglessness, man could affirm both his ontic and his spiritual meaning by his own act of voluntary death. But guilt makes all this impossible. "Guilt and condemnation are qualitatively, not quantitatively, infinite."[69] They point to the dimension of the ultimate and the unconditional from which we have become estranged through our own responsible act. In this way Tillich's contemporary understanding of the situation of loneliness and despair is ultimately specified as Protestant by the pervading element of guilt.

The element of nonbeing is extended beyond this field of being to that of knowledge. After recognizing that existence is both the appearance and the contradiction of essence,

---

[67] *CTB*, p. 48; cf. *ST*, I, p. 189; II, p. 74.
[68] See Paul Tillich, "Freedom in the Period of Transformation," Ruth Nanda Anshen, editor, *Freedom: Its Meaning* (New York: Harcourt, Brace, 1940), pp. 123–24, 131–32.
[69] *CTB*, p. 54.

he adds that "our thinking is a part of our existence and shares the fate that human existence contradicts its true nature."[70] Reason is affected by the nonbeing of finitude and of estrangement. Under the conditions of existence it is torn by internal conflicts and estranged from its depth and ground. Another note of the existential situation of knowledge is its inclusion of actualized freedom. This not only separates thought and being, but holds them apart. There results a special kind of truth, one which is attained, not in an absolute standpoint at the end of history, but in the situation of the knower. Subjectivity becomes the hallmark of truth, which is thereby stamped with the Protestant note of individuality. Furthermore, this subjectivity is of a contemporary nature since it results from separation and despair. "Truth is just that subjectivity which does not disregard its despair, its exclusion from the objective world of essence, but which holds to it passionately."[71] This kind of knowledge is, then, both Protestant and contemporary.

Through this negative stage of the dialectic there remains the original positive element, the bond to the divine. "Man is never cut off from the ground of being, not even in the state of condemnation."[72] However, in this state of existence he does not actualize, but contradicts the essential manifestation of the divine ground. This is more than individualization. It is the tragically guilty estrangement of being and knowing from the divine, and from ourselves as images of the divine. This is the nature of Tillich's systematic analysis of the predicament of modern man. It manifests the true dimensions of the exaggeration of individualization which is experienced as a sense of loneliness and expressed theologically as the Fall of man. It does this in the contemporary context of meaninglessness by questioning not only the supports of previous generations, but the very meaning of support.

The first stage of Tillich's existential dialectic presented

---

[70] *IH*, p. 61.
[71] *Ibid.*, pp. 63–64.
[72] *ST*, II, p. 78.

the essential or potential state of finite reality in union with the divine. The second or negative moment of this dialectic placed individualization in its present context of meaninglessness. This was a powerful and profound expression of the difficulty in actualizing the element of union or participation in the divine which is indispensable to religion. Let us see how the third stage attempts to provide this element in a contemporary fashion, and how well this coincides with the nature of Protestantism.

Since the existential separation and disruption leaves man opaque to the divine, Tillich will not allow the divine to be derived from an analysis of man's experience.[73] If, then, God is to be the answer to the existential question of man, he must come "to human existence from beyond it."[74] The divine depth must break through in particular things and particular circumstances. This is the phenomenon of revelation in which the essential power of natural objects is delivered from the bondage of its existential contradiction. The finite thing or situation can now be said to participate in the power of the ultimate. In this way revelation provides more than a mere representation of the divine. It opens up levels of mind and of reality hidden until now, and produces an experience of the divine, itself the most profound of these levels. The appearance of the divine does vary according to the particular situation. Experienced in correlation with the threat of nonbeing, God would have the form of the "infinite power of being resisting nonbeing," that is, he would be being-itself. In correlation with the question in the form of anxiety, God as the answer would be "the ground of courage."[75] Each would be a form of the particular participation in the divine which takes place in this situation. It is this same participation which bases symbols of the divine. Consequently, their diversification and continuance will depend on the situation.

For a better understanding of the contemporary nature of

[73] This, he says, would be the humanistic-naturalistic or the dualistic approach to God.

[74] ST, I, pp. 64–65.

[75] Ibid., p. 61.

Tillich's religious philosophy it is necessary to investigate further his development of the situation of revelation in the present context of meaninglessness. As cognitive, this encounter includes two elements: one is objective and termed a miracle or sign event; the other is subjective and named ecstasy or inspiration. The objective and the subjective are so strictly correlated that one cannot be had without the other. The truth of revelation is truth only for him who is grasped by the divine presence.[76]

Tillich insists that miracle does not mean a supernatural interference with the natural structure of events. To make this clear he prefers the term *sign-event* as signifying that which produces numinous astonishment, in Otto's sense of that connected with the presence of the divine. Such a sign-event can be realized in the context of meaninglessness because it presupposes the stigma of nonbeing, the disruptive tensions driving towards man's complete annihilation. In particular situations this stigma becomes evident and manifests the negative side of the mystery of God, the abyss. However, such situations also imply the positive side of the mystery of God. For their very reality manifests the divine ground and power of being over which nonbeing is not completely victorious.

The characteristics which Tillich attributes to a miracle will now be sufficiently evident. He speaks of a miracle as "an event which is astonishing, unusual, shaking, without contradicting the rational structure of reality; . . . an event which points to the mystery of being, expressing its relation to us in a definite way; . . . an occurrence which is received as a sign-event in an ecstatic experience."[77] The subjective element pertains to the very nature of a miracle. Thus, even a person who later learns about the sign-event must share in the ecstasy, if he is to have more than a report about the belief of another. An objective miracle would be a contradiction in terms.

[76] *Ibid.*, p. 111; cf. "What is Divine Revelation?" *The Witness*, 26 (April, 1943), 8–9.
[77] *Ibid.*, p. 117.

The subjective element of ecstasy is described as "standing outside one's self" by the term itself. It indicates a state in which the mind transcends its ordinary situation, its subject-object structure. Miracle was seen to be negatively dependent on the stigma of nonbeing. In the mind there corresponds to this stigma the shock of nonbeing, the anxiety of death, meaninglessness, and guilt. These tend to disrupt the normal balance of the mind, to shake it in its structure, and to force it to its boundary line where it openly faces nonbeing. There it is thrown back on itself. But again it is forced to its extreme situation, to the very limit of human possibilities, and there it finds the all pervading "No." It is there, face to face with the meaninglessness and despair which one must recognize if he is serious about anything at all, that one is grasped by mystery. For, in the act of despair, one accepted meaninglessness, and the acceptation itself was a meaningful act. It could be done only on the power of the being it negates.[78] In this way there is manifested within oneself the reality of a transcending power.

This is revelation. The power of being is present in the affirmation of meaninglessness and in the affirmation of ourselves as facing meaninglessness. It comes to one by affirming itself in him in spite of nonbeing.[79] In true ecstasy one receives ultimate power by the presence of the ultimate which breaks through the contradictions of existence where and when it will. It is God who determines the circumstances and the degree in which he will be participated. This rules out the possibility of natural revelation whereby reason grasps God whenever it wills. Natural knowledge of self and world can lead to the question of the ground of being and reason, but in the state of existence it is God who must grasp man.[80]

Tillich calls the cognitive aspect of ecstasy, inspiration. In what concerns the divine he replaces the word knowledge by

---

[78] See *CTB*, p. 176. Despair supposes something positive. "The negative 'lives' by the positive which it negates" (*LPJ*, pp. 38–39).

[79] See Paul Tillich, *Christianity and the Problem of Existence* (Washington: Henderson Services, 1951), pp. 30–31.

[80] See *PE*, pp. 79–80; cf. *ST*, I, pp. 114–20.

awareness. Furthermore, in this area the awareness is not of new objects. This would be to invade reason with a strange body of knowledge which could not be assimilated, and hence would destroy its rational structure. Rather, that which is opened to man is a new dimension of being. It is participated in by all but still retains its transcendence.

It matters little that the contemporary situation of scepticism and meaninglessness has removed all possibility of a content for this act. What is important is that we have been grasped by that which answers the ultimate question of our very being, our unconditional and ultimate concern. This is Tillich's phenomenological description of God. "Only certain is the ultimacy as ultimacy."[81] The ultimate concern provides the place at which the *fides qua creditur* and the *fides quae creditur* are identified, the place where the difference between the subject and the object disappears. The source of our faith is present as both subject and object in a way that is beyond both of them. The absence of this dichotomy is the reason why Tillich refuses to speak of knowledge in this realm and insists instead on awareness. He compares it to the mystic's notion of the knowledge God has of himself, the "truth-itself" of St. Augustine.[82] It is absolutely certain, but the identity of subject and object means that it is also absolutely personal. Consequently, this experience of the ultimate cannot be directly received from others.[83] Revelation is something which we ourselves must live.

In this experience it is necessary to distinguish the point of immediate awareness from the breadth of content. The point of awareness is expressed in what Tillich refers to as the ontological principle. "Man is immediately aware of something unconditional which is the *prius* of the interaction and separation of both subject and object, both theoretically and practically."[84] He has no doubt about the certainty of this

[81] *DF*, p. 17.

[82] See *ibid.*, pp. 8–11.

[83] See "The Problem of Theological Method," *Journal of Religion*, 28 (January, 1947), 22–23.

[84] "The Two Types of Philosophy of Religion," *Union Seminary Quarterly Review*, 1 (May, 1946), 10.

point, although nonsymbolically he can only say that this is being-itself. However, in revelation he has experienced not only its reality but its relation to him.[85] He expresses the combination of these in the metaphorical terms of ground and abyss of being, power of being, ultimate and unconditional concern. Furthermore, generally this point is experienced in a special situation and in a special form. The ultimate concern is made concrete in some one thing. It may, for instance, be the nation, a god, or the God of the Bible. This concrete content of our act of belief differs from ultimacy as ultimacy in that it is not immediately evident. Since it remains within the subject-object dichotomy, its acceptance as ultimate requires an act of courage and venturing faith. The certainty we have about the breadth of concrete content is, then, only conditional.[86] Time may reveal this content to be finite. In that case our faith will still have been an authentic contact with the unconditional itself. It is only the concrete expression which will have been deficient.[87]

This implies two correlated elements in man's act of faith: one is that of certainty concerning one's own being as related to something ultimate and unconditional; the other is that of risk, that of surrendering to a concern which is not really ultimate and may be destructive if taken as if it were. The risk necessarily arises in the state of existence where both reason and objects are not only finite, but separated from their ground. It places an element of doubt in faith which is neither of the methodological variety found in the scientist nor of the transitory type often had by the sceptic. The doubt of faith is, rather, existential, an awareness of the lasting element of insecurity. Nevertheless, this doubt can be accepted and overcome in spite of itself by an act of courage which affirms the reality of God. Faith remains the one state of ultimate concern, but as such it subsumes both certainty concerning the unconditioned and existential doubt.[88]

[85] See *ST*, I, p. 109.
[86] See "The Problem of the Theological Method," *art. cit.*, 22–23.
[87] See *DF*, p. 18.
[88] See *loc. cit.*

Can a system with such an uncertainty concerning concrete realities still be called a realism? Tillich believes that it can, but only if it is specified as a beliefful or self-transcending realism. In this the really real, the ground and power of everything real, is grasped in and through a concrete historical situation. The value of the present moment, which has become transparent for its ground, is, paradoxically, both all and nothing. In itself it is not infinite and "the more it is seen in the light of the ultimate power, the more it appears as questionable and void of lasting significance."[89] The appearance of self-subsistence gradually melts away. But by this very fact the ground and power of the present reality becomes evident. The concrete situation becomes theonomous and the infinite depth and eternal significance of the present is revealed in an ecstatic experience.

Up to this point the positive exposition of Tillich's thought could have been developed without special relation to Christianity. However, he sees in his system the need for a central manifestation of God to serve as a point of over-all unity, and definitively to conquer the contradictions of existence. It is here that Tillich introduces Christ as the final revelation. We shall present this aspect of his system briefly in order to indicate the direction taken by his thought as it enters the properly theological realm.

Since reason remains finite and retains its state of existence even after receiving revelation, new difficulties continue to arise. The corruption was broken in its final power and the conflicts of reason were replaced by reconciliation when man's total structure was grasped by its ultimate concern. Still, because the corruption "is conquered but not removed,"[90] it is able to rise again and attack the elements of revelation. This leads to a mistaking of the bearers of revelation for the ultimate itself, so that faith tends to become idolatrous. Furthermore, the remaining corruption can lead to a loss of the ecstatic, transcending power of reason. In this case, reason forgets that it is but an instrument for aware-

[89] *PE*, p. 78.
[90] *DF*, p. 79.

ness of the ultimate and tends to become an ultimate itself.

Fortunately these distortions of faith and reason can be definitively conquered. The means of this victory is called final revelation. There are various criteria, but all are bound up with the qualities a revelation must have if it is to be the ultimate solution to the conflicts of our finitude in the state of estrangement. The criterion on the part of the miracle is the power which final revelation must have "of negating itself without losing itself."[91] The definitive revelation must overcome the danger of substituting itself for the ultimate by sacrificing itself. This is the Christ on the cross, perfectly united with God, who, in the surrender of all the finite perfection by which he could be a bearer of revelation, becomes completely transparent to the mystery he reveals. He thus becomes a bearer which merely points and can never be raised to ultimacy. This is the perfect fulfillment of the very essence of the sign-event concept. In turn, Christianity receives an unconditional and universal claim from that to which it witnesses, without Christianity as such being either final or universal. On the part of reason another criterion of this special revelation is its capacity to overcome the conflicts in reason between autonomy and heteronomy, absolutism and relativism, emotionalism and formalism. The success of Christ in solving these conflicts provides a continuous pragmatic manifestation of Christ as the final revelation.[92]

The need for a definitive and incorruptible manifestation of the ground of being is cared for by final revelation. As such it is not only the criterion but the fulfillment of other revelations.[93] It becomes the "center, aim, and origin of the revelatory events" which preceded and surrounded it.[94] The preparatory series of revelations mediated through nature, men, and events is called universal revelation, though it occurs only in special and concrete circumstances. It has the function of preparing both the question and the symbols,

[91] *ST*, I, pp. 133–35.
[92] See *ibid.*, pp. 147–54; *DF*, pp. 78–79.
[93] See *ST*, I, pp. 132–33.
[94] See *ibid.*, pp. 138–39.

without which the answer provided by final revelation could neither be received nor understood. But with the advent of final revelation preparatory revelation ceases, and the period of receiving revelation begins. It is now the Church which becomes the bearer of the original fact of Christ and continues the process of reception, interpretation, and actualization. Along with this certainty, it too has the risk of faith. For as final, it believes that it cannot be surpassed by a new original revelation, since its revelation has the power of reformation within itself.[95]

Taking this risk with courage, final revelation is the definitive point where the estrangement of essential and existential being is overcome, where finitude is reunited with infinity, man with God, anxiety with courage, and mortality with eternity. This is the eschatological reunion of essence and existence, foreshadowed and momentarily grasped in universal preparatory revelations. It is definitively established by this final revelation in which Christ becomes the "New Being" and God becomes incarnate.[96] This is "realized eschatology." It has happened only in principle, that is, in power and as a beginning. "Those who participate in him participate in the 'New Being,' though under the condition of man's existential predicament and, therefore, only fragmentarily and by anticipation."[97]

In this context, morality need not remain the empty or arbitrary self-affirmation of a spiritual being. It has an ultimate impulse, a final aim in the expression of a transcendental ground of being. However, its particular contents are received from the culture, and hence remain preliminary and relative. In this way man's actions are to reflect his being as provisional manifestations of the divine depth dimension.

This system, in its expression of the fragmentary nature of reality, includes the objectivity of positivism without its refusal to penetrate into the nature of existence. In its attempt

[95] See *ibid.*, pp. 143–44.

[96] See "A Reinterpretation of the Doctrine of Incarnation," *art. cit.*, 144–45.

[97] *ST*, II, p. 118.

to transcend reality, it also includes the subjectivity of idealism without desiring to remain in the realm of essences.[98]
Both of these insights are synthesized and transcended in a
new mysticism. This is not the classical mysticism which dis-
regarded the cosmos for a direct union with a transcendent
absolute. Instead, it points by faith to the abysmal character of the ground of being and the depth of life as a *prius*
of both subject and object. By restoring the element of participation in the divine it is truly religious. Furthermore, Tillich presents two reasons for considering this mysticism to be
more Protestant than Catholic. One is its refusal to elevate
anything finite to the position of the divine. The other is its
search for the essence of objectivity in the depth of subjectivity, approaching God through the soul.[99] Lastly, since
this approach is made in the context of total meaninglessness, it is also contemporary. Tillich thus concludes to a
philosophy of religion which is both Protestant and contemporary.

Reflections on Tillich's Existential Protestantism

How successful has been this attempt of Paul Tillich to provide a contemporary philosophy for Protestant theology?
There can be little doubt that he has had great success in
presenting the basic notes of Protestantism in a way adapted
to the problems and spirit of much of today's thought. He
has found an ontological structure according to which creatures participate in the divine. This provides a foundation
for the reality of the individual which obliges man to turn
towards the divine in an act of religion. In a dialectical motion, Tillich has specified this act by the contemporary notes
of estrangement, anxiety, and meaninglessness. These express
the Protestant conception of the corruption of human nature and reinforce its subjectivity. The result is a penetrating

[98] See ST, I, p. 236; PE, pp. 66–68, 76–77, 217.
[99] See PE, pp. 69–73; TC, p. 107.

ontological and psychological analysis of the nature of God and man and of the relations between them.

Tillich has been able to do this because his thought has always been marked by exceptional height and breadth and depth. The height stems from the focusing of his attention on the divine. Shortly after he arrived in America some thirty years ago he was able to write: "As a theologian I tried to remain a philosopher, and conversely so."[100] If anything, his years in this country have seen his attention focus even more closely on the divine—the central point of what he would refer to as a "theonomous philosophy." In this his affinity with St. Thomas has been remarked in many quarters. Tillich "shows a concern to relate theology to all knowledge and all culture which reminds one more of St. Thomas than of any contemporary Protestant thinker."[101]

Perhaps Tillich's greatest contribution to the American scene has been his resulting defense of the transcendence of God. Whatever might have to be said about his projection of the divine beyond subject and object, it has provided a defense of God's transcendence. The need for this contribution can be appreciated only when it is observed that the religious atmosphere was dominated by humanistic theism or, at best, neonaturalism. Even should it be remarked that his conception of the divine as a depth dimension of reality is itself too much influenced by humanism and naturalism, his defense of divine transcendence in these terms must still be voted, in the circumstances of the day, the most likely to succeed.

Tillich's thought not only aims at the heights, it also has breadth. Traces of his God are sought in all reality, and thus every field of human inquiry becomes a possible mirror for the revelation of the divine to man and to the present age. It is traces of God that he is seeking in painting, depth psychology, social structure, and all phases of culture. Thus, though wandering far he always seems at home. The reason for this is that here breadth is not allowed to excuse a lack

---

[100] *IH*, pp. 40–41.

[101] Walter M. Horton, "Tillich's Role in Contemporary Theology," Kegley and Bretall, *op. cit.*, p. 27.

of depth. If his patience breaks down at any point, it is with those who would deny the need for an epistemological and ontological foundation. They blind themselves deliberately to the basic principles which determine their thought.[102] Tillich's insistence on an open examination of the philosophical foundations of thought is an explicit rejection of the nineteenth-century neo-Kantians and of our recent positivists. But it is also extended to narrowly biblical theologians, for they must be able to explain the content of their terms and their relation to reality.[103] One cannot but heartily applaud the strenuous objections of orthodox Protestants to Tillich's evisceration of biblical inspiration. But these objections lose much of their force because they are based on such a disrespect for reason that they imply that any statement about God which is not based on revelation is subjective.[104] While much is still to be said about Tillich's epistemology, it is a vigorous and articulate step in the right direction.

It is, moreover, the depth of penetration which permits Tillich to correlate trends in thought as widely divergent as that of Augustine and Wieman. If the interpretation is not infrequently excessively free, the comparison stimulates the reader to deepen his comprehension of the precise position of each. The key to both the depth of penetration and the freedom of interpretation is the use of the dialectical method. This allows him constantly to shift his frame of reference from thesis to synthesis and back to either the positive or the negative aspect of the antithesis. As an existential rather than Hegelian dialectic these shifts are between contradictories rather than contraries. Man, he says, has the freedom to contradict his essential nature, and his fate is to stand under the servitude of this contradiction.[105] The

---

[102] See *ST*, I, pp. 163, 187; "Reply to Interpretation and Criticism," Kegley and Bretall, *op. cit.*, p. 335.

[103] See *ST*, I, pp. 19–21, 163, 187.

[104] See David H. Freeman, "The Philosophical Theology of Paul Tillich," *Philosophia Reformata*, 22 (2nd Quarter, 1957), 54.

[105] See "A Reinterpretation of the Doctrine of Incarnation," *art. cit.*, 140–41.

challenges encountered by the mind in following these steps are not to be underestimated, but neither should they be omitted if they can contribute insights concerning the central issues of a religious philosophy. Paul Tillich's breadth of vision makes it necessary to focus the evaluation on the central issues, first of knowledge, then of being, and finally of participation.

If a realism is to be successful, and Tillich does want to be a realist, the thing itself, as the object, must be the source of the content of knowledge. This can be adequately realized only if the notions and concepts are abstracted from reality in order to give a report on this same reality. But, unless they pertain to being inasmuch as it is, it is not necessary to affirm that they pertain to everything that is. Thus, there are finite and contingent notions which are derived from reality, or at least have a foundation there and tell us about what exists. But, because they do not pertain to existence as such, they need not be predicated of every being. Along with these there are other notions, also derived from reality, which pertain to beings inasmuch as they exist, and hence to all beings. Tillich's system is quite different.

[His categories] are the forms in which the mind grasps and shapes reality. . . . [They] are forms which determine content. They are ontological, and therefore they are present in everything. . . . The categories are forms of finitude; as such they unite an affirmative and a negative element. . . . Both the basic ontological structure and the ontological elements imply finitude. Selfhood, individuality, dynamics, and freedom all include manifoldness, definiteness, differentiation, and limitation.[106]

Two difficulties are of special note here, for each leads to an element of limitation in the divine or excludes any rational knowledge of God. The first of these difficulties is Tillich's position that all ontological elements and categories bespeak limitation. The reason he gives for this affirmation is that selfhood and individuality imply definiteness, which, in turn, implies limitation. "To be something is not to be some-

[106] *ST,* I, pp. 189–90, 192–93.

thing else."[107] Likewise, substance cannot be had without accidents and change. It is evident that his approach is limited to finite beings; and while one must always attend to the limitations consequent upon the human mode of knowledge, these cannot be predicated of that knowledge as intellectual or of its object, being. Accidents do require a substance in which to exist. But there is nothing in the positive notion of existing in oneself which bespeaks the limitation or negation of this perfection of existence. The same applies to the selfhood of such a being. To say that it is not another being does not imply any lack of perfection for this substance, any more than the further multiplication of beings would imply a lessening of the perfection of those which already exist. In fact, the very multiplication of the instances of the perfection of being necessarily implies the existence of a being which simply is this perfection subsistently and without any limitation. This is the classical and necessary sense of that notion of participation of which Tillich makes so much. For when a perfection is had in a limited degree, it cannot be said to be had by that being of its very nature. This implies that the perfection is received from another which does possess it of itself and without limitation.

There is, then, no liberty in constructing the idea of the divine. The implications of the principle of causality impose the recognition that all pure perfections are found in the divine. They must be there formally lest the cause lack some of the perfection of the effect, and they must be there in a subsistent way lest God not be the ultimate cause of all. This remains true through the many purifications by the *via negativa* and the *via eminentiae* which the mode of our finite knowledge must undergo. To deny any pure perfection of God is to deny the divine itself, the simple, infinite, and all-perfect being. God is the most perfect and the most determined being, not the common and indetermined notion of being. "We are not able to know God by understanding him not to be good, just as we cannot know man by under-

---

[107] *Ibid.*, p. 190.

standing him not to be animal: for this removes the substance of God, which is goodness."[108]

It would seem that the closest approach of Tillich to this position is his recognition of a point of contact with the divine and his affirmation that the faith which is generated in this contact does have content. Any affirmation of this today, however, must face the problems of meaninglessness, scepticism, and atheism which constitute the contemporary context. The way in which Tillich describes this problem and his intention of meeting it are important road marks for Christian thought. However, given the limited nature for him of all ontological notions, one might fear that he runs the risk of contracting the disease in attempting its cure, for only the absolute in being and the possibility of some knowledge of it by the intellect can provide immunity against the spreading contagion of meaninglessness.

These fears seem to be borne out when he makes the negation which is meaninglessness the very position of the question of the divine, though that which requires an extrinsic causal principle is rather the positive perfection of limited beings. While the positive element is not eliminated by Tillich in existing being, it is retained only as the essence which the existence contradicts. In this situation the very excellence of the analysis of meaninglessness as a statement of the contemporary situation leads to a disproportionate emphasis of a *via negativa* which cannot then be balanced by a *via affirmativa* in the *via eminentiae*, especially when reduced to ontological terms which are necessarily finite in their intelligible content. As a result, his statement that "the nonbeing of negative theology means 'not being anything special,' "[109] which could be understood simply as a negation of all limitation in God, is not left with any positive counterpart. There is no way of affirming God as the most determined, and under threat of atheism one is left with the choice of affirming God as "being everything" and removing all special con-

[108] St. Thomas Aquinas, *Quaestiones disputatae de potentia*, q. 7, a. 4 ad 8.

[109] *ST*, I, p. 188.

tent from faith.[110] God becomes unavoidable because, as nothing special in this context, he must be either "everything" or nothing at all. Tillich thus becomes quite willing to assert "an element of pantheism," for in the religious realm it has become the only alternative to utter meaninglessness.

The other difficulty which leads Tillich to insert an element of limitation in the divine and to turn from rational knowledge of God would remain even if it were established that some notions did not imply limitation. This problem stems from the origin which he attributes to the categories and to the ontological elements. As the basis for the objectivity of knowledge, Tillich is content to assert that all things have in themselves a structure either identical or at least analogous to the finite categories of the mind. This general correspondence of objective and subjective rational structures is explained by the origin of all from a common logos. Their particular connection in the act of knowing is attributed to factors on the part of the will and emotions. "Emotion is the vehicle of receiving knowledge."[111] He specifies that it is a criticizing *agape* because he wishes to retain critical caution. However, the subjectivity remains an indispensable element, alternating with moments of objectivity which are insufficient in themselves.[112] It is difficult to agree with this analysis of knowledge which has led Tillich to limit rational knowledge to the finite and to project the divine beyond the realm of being. The rejection of abstraction by Kant and the resulting search by the idealists for a source beyond both subject and object is not unfamiliar, but neither are the difficulties thus raised for realistic and objective knowledge. This is demonstrated only too well in Tillich's turn to the emotive in order to connect the separate logical structures of mind and reality. He is sufficiently precise not to say that this gives objective content, and much too keen to be satisfied with mere subjective union. However, his resignation to a situation in which the two alternate is quite unsatisfactory.

---

110 See *CTB*, p. 182.
111 *ST*, I, p. 98.
112 See "Participation and Knowledge," *art. cit.*, 206-9.

True knowledge will be had only when the knower and the known are bound together in a union which is itself objective.

Furthermore, since the categories are not considered to be abstracted from beings, there can be no selective attribution of them to beings. Consequently, all the categories, including those which of their very nature imply limitation, are indiscriminately attributed to all beings. The result of this is the effective elimination of the analogy of being. This is reflected in Tillich's statement that the categories of being are ontological, and therefore in everything.[113] By proceeding in this manner he must conclude that everything which is is finite, for each being must have all the finite categories of the logos structure. "To be something is to be finite."[114] Everything which is, is limited, and subject to the categories of time, space, and cause which express this finitude. The natural implication of such thought is that the divine itself is limited. However, while Tillich is not at all willing to free completely the divine from such elements of limitation, he does not want to say that the divine is simply finite. Consequently, God cannot be said to be something, or a being, or good; although these cannot be simply denied concerning him. God must be placed beyond things, beyond the realm of beings, beyond the subject-object dichotomy of rational knowledge. Our knowledge, then, if it be objective and rational, never will be able to reach the divine or reflect it. For this reason it must be replaced by an awareness of the immediate presence of God as truth itself within the subjectivity of the individual.

In this way the divine is sought in the place and with the instruments with which modern man is most likely to be concerned. Certainly it is most adapted to the more individualistic character of Protestantism. More generally, it is well adapted to the recent more universal appreciation of one's relation to God as the most important and profoundly penetrating dimension of one's life. But if awareness is spoken of, then the intentional order is being distinguished from

[113] See *ST*, I, p. 192.
[114] *Ibid.*, p. 190.

that of being, for one can speak of an awareness of one's being. In regard to this intentional order something must be done to express its particular mode of presence of the divine. To do this Tillich uses "awareness" because he does not feel that "knowledge" sufficiently expresses the personal union. But the act of intentional presence is precisely what is meant by knowledge, and, as will be observed in detail below, it is only the problems of a particular ontological tradition which places an opposition instead of a unity—even an identity—between subject and object. That it be an accident does not separate it from the personal center of the knowing individual, but rather affirms a new way in which that person realizes his existence. In this case it is the greatest of all ways, for it is the realization of God's existence. Finally, since this is really the person knowing, it cannot be isolated or opposed to the person loving God; instead the two must be united.

Ontological problems of the most serious nature could not but accompany these epistemological difficulties of the Protestant philosophy of Paul Tillich. Their background is found in a system of thought earlier than modern idealism and in relation to a difficulty deeper than that of the origin of the concept. Plotinus appreciated that the summit of his pyramid of reality must be occupied by that which is most perfect and, consequently, most one. He felt, however, that knowledge, while it seems to be a perfection, requires a dichotomy between subject and object, *nous* and being. This dichotomy, in turn, implies that each of its elements is finite.[115] Consequently, the supreme One cannot be simply being or knowing. At the same time, the One is not less perfect than these two, since it is the source of both. Therefore, in an improper sense and as a synthesis of both, it is both being and nonbeing, knowing and nonknowing. Nicholas of Cusa expresses these tendencies in his notion of the divine as the coincidence of opposites. Tillich follows in this

---

[115] It is this polar relationship between subject and object which Tillich considers to be the irreducible point of departure for all metaphysical speculation and the norm of all religious thought.

line of thought, but with a more pantheistic and dialectical accent.

As the ground of being, the divine must have the ontological elements. But as transcendent, God is neither potentiality nor actuality, neither becoming nor rest, neither dynamics nor form in the proper sense of these terms. It is just as wrong to speak of God as becoming as it is to speak of him as pure act. In the former case he would be an absolute accident, in the latter he would not be alive. Furthermore, since none of these elements are properly in God, the divine cannot be said to be constructed of a simple combination of each pair. It is possible to affirm each of these elements of God only symbolically, though this implies a true participation in their reality. God unites and balances all of these elements so that there is no tension, or even distinction, between them. Thus, God symbolically has form as intellect and dynamics as will, but they are perfectly balanced in what is properly a higher synthesis. He is the "absolute participant," but only as the "absolute individual," because both are united in the divine life which is "equally 'near' to each of them while transcending them both."[116] As the ground of being he has a negative element. This is overcome as negative in the divine process, but in creatures, where it is not overcome, it remains the basis of their negative element.[117] For this reason simple perfections cannot be properly attributed to the divine, but must be accompanied by a limitation and a negation. The negative is not meant merely to deny that in God these perfections share the limitations of their created state. It is in God as the foundation of the negative element in creatures.

Since these problems arose from the requirement of a subject-object dichotomy and limitation for knowledge, it would seem that the true solution might well be sought in these same areas. The requirement of the dichotomy is true in the case of finite beings precisely because of their potential element. However, of its very nature knowledge is not

[116] *ST*, I, p. 245.
[117] See *ibid.*, pp. 246–47.

a passive reception, but the act of an agent. Consequently, where the reality is pure act and knows itself directly it is by identity both actual intelligence and actual intelligibility. By formal identity God is both subject and object.[118] The act of knowing does not of its nature produce something else. It itself is the perfection intended. This is true of all immanent or vital actions.[119] For this reason it is impossible to accept Tillich's general statements that life must include a separation of potentiality and actuality, or that the nature of life is actualization rather than actuality.[120] The pure act of Scholastic philosophy is unjustly accused of being a static God. He is, in fact, supremely dynamic because the pure act, the supreme being, is the very subsistent act of knowledge, love, and life. In attempting to add an element of dynamics to the divine, modern philosophy corrects its own deficiency, which is based on its interpretation of form in a Platonic and passive fashion. The Thomistic conception does not share this deficiency because of its Aristotelian orientation, according to which form is active.[121]

It will be noted that there is a considerable difference from Plotinus in Tillich's conception of the divine as being itself. It is true, he would affirm, that because of the divine perfection and transcendence the ontological elements and categories can be predicated of God only symbolically. God is neither existing nor nonexisting, neither a person nor not a person. He is beyond cause, substance, and even being. However, and on this Tillich quite insists, this is not to say

[118] See St. Thomas Aquinas, *Summa theologiae*, I, q. 14, a. 2; "His existence is not dissimilar to his intellect" (q. 16, a. 5 ad 2).

[119] In order to retain the true perfection of the divine, motion must be distinguished from operation. The former is always from potency to act and transient; the latter is not transient but only an act and perfection of the agent. As act it does not imply change and consequently is entirely consonant with pure act.

[120] See *ST*, I, p. 246.

[121] See Joseph Owens, C.Ss.R., *The Doctrine of Being in the Aristotelian Metaphysics* (Toronto: Pontifical Institute of Mediaeval Studies, 1957), p. 291.

that he is above beings, for this would make him an idol.[122] The transcendence of God consists in his being the power, the creative ground, the depth within being, without himself being anything special. This would seem to reduce the divine to what is most common because most indetermined and abstract, the common notion of being. However, since Tillich does not want his God to be an abstraction or a supreme genus, he adds to his conception of the divine "an element of pantheism." If what is nothing special is to be anything real, it must in some way be everything. Creation becomes a type of auto-limitation of the absolute, for this absolute has suffered a basic misfortune. It has been confused with a notion of being which is not truly analogous but univocal and, in a sense, pantheistic.

According to Tillich, this pantheism, which considers God to be the substance or essence of all things, is necessary for Christianity. It is the very foundation of that divine presence which becomes actual and manifest in the circumstances of revelation. However, this note of pantheism is mitigated by a dialectic which "tries to unite the structural oneness of everything within the absolute with the undecided and unfinished manifoldness of the real."[123] In this conception the divine is first positively in himself. Then he moves out from himself to the negative state of existence, and returns to himself in the eschatological state. There are expressions in the writings of Tillich which might lead one to conclude that the dialectical movement is sufficiently strong to dissipate the pantheism indicated above. It is remarked that being itself "is not identified with the totality of things,"[124] but infinitely transcends every finite being. This is possible because the abyss is conceived as the inexhaustible ground of being. This notion of the abyss is undoubtedly received from Schel-

---

[122] "Avoid . . . placing the unconditioned meaning beside the conditioned meanings or even beside the totality of meanings. . . . In every 'above' lies a 'beside' and in every 'beside' a 'conditioned' " (*IH*, pp. 222–23).

[123] *ST*, I, pp. 234–35.

[124] *ST*, II, p. 6; I, pp. 237, 250.

ling who held it because of the problem of distinguishing
things entirely from God without placing them outside of
him. This was solved "by things having their basis in that
within God which is not God himself, i.e., in that which is
the basis of his existence."[125] However, in Tillich's philosophy this abyss is the primary essence of God and there is
no "existing" God to be clearly distinguished from it. Furthermore, it is potential and mediated to us by the other element
of God, the logos. The dialectic and its structural determina-
tions fail adequately to expunge pantheism while reinforc-
ing the element of potentiality already evident in his
God.[126]

This question of pantheism being ontological, such a position could not but place a radical deficiency in his ontological
dialectic. The divine is made an analytic depth dimension of
all reality. In these circumstances it becomes necessary to
choose between a denial of individualization, limitation, and
world on the one hand, and the denial of pure act on the
other. Tillich's option for the latter leaves the world without
a sufficient reason, and justly labeled as simply meaningless.
But in this case the lack of meaning merely reflects that of
the pantheism which imposes such a false dilemma.[127]

We may now turn to an evaluation of Tillich's notion of
participation. Since he placed this notion at the heart of religion, it is the particular realization of this which must specify his whole philosophy as Protestant and contemporary. Indeed, it was in order to provide a foundation for participation
without a loss of individualization that Tillich affirmed both
pantheism and elements of limitation of God. What now

[125] Friedrich Wilhelm Joseph Schelling, *Of Human Freedom*,
trans. James Gutmann (Chicago: The Open Court Publishing Co.,
1936), p. 33.

[126] *ST*, I: "If we say God is being-itself, this includes both rest
and becoming, both the static and the dynamic elements" (p. 247).

[127] Tillich's final decision against simple pantheism is based on
the evident fact of man's freedom. While this saves him from the
excesses of some pantheists it does not modify his insistence on "an
element of pantheism" as has been described above (*ibid.*, p. 234).

must be said of his conception of participation as religious, as Protestant, and as contemporary? How successful has it been in providing a speculative synthesis of these factors?

As noted above, Tillich fully insists on the central position of participation in the fact of religion, and in this he is quite correct. To whatever degree we are, we participate in the divine. This is the foundation of our knowledge of God and of our duties toward him. But the question arises whether Tillich's stress on participation is not a turning away from traditional Protestantism and towards the perennial position of the Church. In point of fact, he considers participation, and consequently the substance of religion, to have been best realized and preserved in Catholic doctrine and practice. It is in this light that he has spoken of Catholicism as a permanent corrective for Protestantism.[128]

In this same context it is of special interest that he should choose the Aristotelian ontology when explicitly comparing it with that of Occam.[129] While the *Venerabilis Inceptor* and his school were far from being accepted in their entirety by the reformers, they were considered to be the best of the Scholastics. Their influence on Luther was extensive, especially in opposing analogy and participation in the realms of justification, Church, and the sacraments.[130] The trend Luther most abhorred was the Aristotelian.[131] This contrast

[128] See "The Permanent Signification of the Catholic Church for Protestantism," *art. cit.*, 25–29; *ST*, III, pp. 6, 168–71.

[129] See *ST*, I, pp. 203–4.

[130] See J. Paquier, "Luther," A. Vacant, editor, *Dictionnaire de théologie catholique*, IX–1 (1926), cols. 1187–88, 1251–53; H. Grisar, S.J., *Luther*, trans. E. Lamond (London: B. Herder, 1914), I, pp. 130–65; Robert Fife, *The Revolt of Martin Luther* (New York: Columbia University Press, 1957): "He has put together the framework of a theological structure which is now all but complete. . . . Despite his attack on the Schoolmen its foundations were laid on the doctrine of the powerful, irrational will of God as he had learned it from the Erfurt nominalists" (pp. 225–26).

[131] The strength of this abhorrence may be gauged from Luther's characterizations of Aristotle as "the prince of darkness," and "the damned, arrogant, sarcastic heathen." Such expressions become more

of historical perspective is seen to imply doctrinal opposition
when it is remembered that much of Luther's objection to
Aristotelian thought was directed at its defense of nature and
its powers. On the contrary, Tillich's dissatisfaction with Occam stems from the fact that he has so forgotten essence
and nature that participation is reduced to "an arbitrary commandment imposed by an all-powerful existent on the other
existents."[132] This type of objection to Occam logically extends to the notion of forensic justification, according to
which man's nature remains corrupt and his actions evil, although God no longer imputes this to him. This was held
not only by Luther's followers, but by the reformer himself.[133] For these reasons it would seem that Tillich's development of the importance of participation is, in fact, a
decided step away from classical Protestant thought and toward Catholicism.

These orientations of Tillich's notion of religious participation lend special interest to his attempts to provide it with
a Protestant modality. Positively, these center on a re-
evaluation of the personal character of participation, according to which it effects even the most intimate aspects of
man as an individual subject. There is much in this which
commends it. It brings out the totality of one's dependence
on God and its penetration to the center of one's personality.
In this thought nothing is closer to the Christian, nothing
more real, than the divine. This is what the great mystics
have attempted to express in more poetic language. Unfortunately, it is at this point that Tillich's own stringent and
necessary requirement of pairing participation with individualization places a problem which he cannot solve. He had

---

frequent and violent as Luther progressively separates himself from
many of his earlier philosophical positions.

[132] ST, I, pp. 203-4.

[133] Luther, *op. cit.*: "*Numquid ergo perfecte iustus? Non, sed
simul peccator et iustus; peccator re vera, sed iustus ex reputatione et
permissione Dei certa, quod liberet ab illo, donec perfecte sanet. Ac
per hoc sanus perfecte est in spe, in re autem peccator, sed initium
habens iustitiae, ut amplius querat semper, semper iniustum se sciens*"
(p. 108).

been right in appreciating the necessity of participation, but wrong in attempting to realize it by "an element of pantheism." Now his authentic demand that participation have a personal character bears out the previous error, for when God is a depth dimension of man the individuality of both is lost.

Negatively, Tillich's attempt to provide a Protestant modality for participation led him to twin objections to the Catholic conception of this notion. His first difficulty is with its conception of God as a separate thing. The factors underlying this objection have already been examined. It is sufficient to remark that real participation can be had only in a context of being which is transcendent. This extension of being to the infinite and the supernatural is manifested by the rational proofs for God's existence and by revelation respectively. It is, in fact, the very infinity of the first cause which necessitates its real distinction from its finite effects.

The second difficulty applies the full force of the accusation of externalism and impersonality to the Catholic notion of supernatural participation by grace. It should be recalled, however, that grace is an accident, the nature of which is to modify, not itself, but the subject. The result of such a modification could not be simply an external addition. On the contrary, it makes the subject itself exist in a new manner.[134] The person now exists as participating in the divine in this new way. The personal character of this modification is made even more evident when it is appreciated that all is ordered to charity which, Tillich himself would be the first to insist, is the antithesis of the impersonal. It would appear, then, that one cannot but heartily agree with Tillich's stress on the personal character of participation. Increase in spiritual perfection consists in making this union intimate and more total. But while this is perfectly consequent upon a system of transcendent being, realized by dynamic and static participation in the orders of nature and grace, it is incompatible with the element of pantheism.

---

[134] See St. Thomas Aquinas: "Accidents and nonsubsistent forms are called beings, not as if they themselves had being, but because things are by them" (*Summa theologiae*, I–II, q. 55, a. 4 ad 1).

The last aim of Tillich's Protestant philosophy is to be contemporary by realizing participation in the very midst of meaninglessness. Evidently, this cannot be a participation in nothing, and he strongly objects to placing anything above the world. Thus, he turns to a divine depth dimension of the real which, in the situation of revelation, breaks through to produce such phenomena as justification and symbols. The solution of the contemporary problem of meaninglessness by turning in the equally contemporary direction of subjectivity is an important development of religious thought for today and points up some elements only poorly stressed in the past. It is unfortunate, but not surprising, that this work should include the difficulties mentioned above.

However, this does not negate Tillich's many valuable insights into the nature of the contemporary religious problem. These have been stated above in the positive exposition of his system. It has been the penetrating nature of such analyses of today's crisis of meaning and the ingenuity of the solutions stated in terms of this problem that have made him one of the most influential religious thinkers in the world today. What remains to be done here is to weigh the implications of this contemporary solution drawn from within the emptiness and despair. A discerning light might be shed on this by a consideration of his election of Aristotle over Plato in regard to the foundation of meaning. Tillich's reason for this choice is that Aristotle allows existence to add to essence while keeping it strictly dependent on God.[135] In this way he leaves room for a special participation in the divine which will provide meaning in the midst of today's meaninglessness. One would not question the profound ontological affinity of man for an added participation in the divine beyond that had in the first and second stages of Tillich's dialectic. An analysis of man's spiritual nature would show that, even in the uncorrupted first stage, its ultimate and definitive perfec-

---

[135] See *ST*, I, p. 203. The present author discusses Tillich's assertion that his symbol participates in the reality of that for which it stands and is the same as St. Thomas' analogy; see below, pp. 195–240.

tion could be had only in a direct vision of the divine and the whole order which leads to this. Even if such a vision would be beyond the capacities and potential condition of any creature, the fact that it alone would completely actualize and immobilize man's spiritual capacities points to man's singular affinity for such a participation in the divine beyond that had by his nature. Furthermore, a phenomenological and philosophical analysis of the second, sinful stage more than bears out man's moral inability to observe all of the natural law for a considerable length of time without some special help. This points once again to the moral necessity of an additional participation in the divine.

In this there appear both the validity of Tillich's analysis and the debility of his solution. His contemporary existential analysis unveils the antinomy that is man: a creature torn between the grandeur of his spiritual aspirations and the poverty of his created condition, a capacity which can be filled only by a special participation in the divine. Unfortunately, his solution seeks this participation from within. This places the divine as an interior dimension of all beings, too limited to be pure act and too unlimited to allow for the full individualization of God and creatures. If, then, this participation must rather be sought from without, adding to the essence and existence of the first and second dialectical stages, it cannot be denied the title of supernatural. Despite the considerable distaste which Tillich manifests for this term and the systematic reality it represents, it would seem that it is hardly less called for by his attempt to realize a special participation in the divine in relation to contemporary contradictions, than it is by the notions of deification expressed by the apostles Paul and John. St. Paul speaks of participating as coheirs in the proper heritage of God's divine Son (see Rom. 8:14–17; Gal. 4:1–7), and St. John insists that "we should be called the children of God; and such we are. . . . We shall be like him for we shall see him just as he is. And everyone who has this hope in him makes himself holy, just as he also is holy" (1 Jn. 3:1–3).

V

GEORGE TAVARD

The Protestant Principle and the Theological System of Paul Tillich

Protestantism seen as a whole is hardly a unified phenomenon. The many varieties of it appear so heterogeneous that it is difficult to reduce them to any common principle. Yet, it is significant that Gustave Weigel, S.J., strongly insists on the unity of principle which supports the whole edifice of the Reformation. Father Weigel is one of the more recognized interpreters of Tillich's thought. And what Tillich wants precisely is to bring Protestant thought to an awareness of its profound unity. The critical work of Father Weigel, as that of Paul Tillich, looks for what both of them call the "Protestant principle." For Weigel, Protestantism in all its manifestations is reduced to the fundamental principle of "immediacy in knowing God through a nonconceptual act of awareness."[1] Knowledge of God does not pass through any necessary intermediary. God makes himself known to whom he wills in the way he wills. He has not confided revelation to any priest or prophet, but he is at all times his own priest and prophet.

The Protestant Principle

The Protestant principle, as depicted by Weigel, recaptures, in different terms, what Tillich has himself defined. "Why,"

[1] "A Catholic Looks at Protestantism," Robert McAfee Brown and Gustave Weigel, S.J., *An American Dialogue* (New York: Doubleday, 1960), p. 183.

asks Weigel, "can a Catholic theologian understand Protestantism with the help of Tillich's exposition of it? By reason of the rational coherence that he gives to a phenomenon that seems to be indifferent to all coherence."[2] Tillich places "the divine and human protest against any absolute claim made for a relative reality"[3] at the root of Protestantism. This principle "is the theological expression of the true relation between the unconditioned and the conditioned, religiously speaking, between God and man."[4] The relation must not be understood in the rather Barthian sense of an affirmation of God as totally-other. For Tillich as well, God is the totally-other; this justifies the Protestant principle which refuses to make any created reality a necessary channel for divine communication. But God is totally-other insofar as he is the beyond known through creation. If the totally-other is transcendent, his transcendence is immanent.

The power grasping us in the state of faith is not a being beside others, not even in the highest; it is not an object among objects, not even the greatest; but it is a quality of all beings and objects, the quality of pointing beyond themselves and their finite existence to the infinite, inexhaustible, and unapproachable depth of their being and meaning.[5]

God must be seen as the foundation of being rather than as a being. This implies a condemnation of any attempt to absolutize concrete being in any of its manifestations. According to Tillich, the essence of the Protestant principle is found here. It is a protestation against the divinization of visible forms of being, in favor of the hidden divinity of the ground of being, who justifies and who judges all its manifestations. God is the beyond, toward whom all creation opens a way, without any one road being necessary.

The Protestant principle, therefore, is more negative than it appears in the completely positive formula that Gustave

[2] "Contemporaneous Protestantism and Paul Tillich," *Theological Studies*, 11 (1950), 186.

[3] *PE*, p. 163.

[4] *Loc. cit.*

[5] *Loc. cit.*

Weigel gives to it. But nothing is purely negative for Tillich. In the dialectic of No and Yes each term always includes a form of the other. "The undialectical No is as primitive and unproductive as the undialectical Yes."[6] The more profound negative formulation of the Protestant principle denies the absolute value of the created, whether that created is the Church, the Scriptures, or the sacraments. Every aspect of the Reformation, in its historical form, is included in this negative line. Luther, in denying the absolute authority of the councils, in rejecting the Catholic sacramental order, and in taking liberty with the canon of the Scriptures, was only bringing the Protestant principle to its logical conclusion. By requiring unconditional submission, the Church puts itself up as an adversary to the unconditional, and the pope becomes the Antichrist. But the historical Reformation was itself aware of the positive aspect of its fundamental principle. The Lutheran doctrine of justification by faith without works is only another affirmation of the Protestant principle in its positive aspect; for, if no conditioned being can save, salvation must come from the unconditional. If any human word is not of itself the word of eternal life, then the divine Word, which renders every word at once possible and healing, must give testimony of itself. The "light that enlightens every man who comes into the world" is the light of salvation. We are saved by grace alone, *sola fide, sola gratia.*

Stemming from this is the importance given by historical Protestantism to the affirmation of a divine mono-energism in the work of salvation, as opposed to Catholic synergism. But Luther, Tillich thinks, has not gone far enough in his analysis of the material principle of the Reformation. In the moral order it is not sufficient to teach the *sola gratia* for the forgiveness of sins. This was a critical problem for the reformers of the sixteenth century, insofar as they had to combat what Tillich calls the false supernaturalism of the monastic tradition. Since that time, the dispute between Catholicism

[6] Paul Tillich, "Autobiographical Reflections," C. Kegley and R. Bretall, editors, *The Theology of Paul Tillich* (New York: Macmillan, 1952), p. 13.

and Protestantism, arising at least partially from the very restricted problem of the justification of sinners, has intensified. Recent Catholic tradition, especially in the First Vatican Council and the definitions of Popes Pius IX and Pius XII, decisively indicates that Catholicism is absolute not only in the domain of action, but even in that of thought. Tillich sees here a divinization of the objects of thought as well as of the means of salvation. Thought becomes godlike in the domains of intellect and moral conduct. This would enable Protestantism to understand justification by faith in a manner so profound that it extends to the whole realm of the intellect. Just as no contingent and relative rule can become the ultimate norm of salvation, likewise no doctrine, act of faith, or *credo*, however ancient and universal, can become a necessary means to know the divine. The unconditional never falls under the mastery of human words, not even the words consecrated by the Church.

This is, then, Tillich's idea of the Protestant principle. It is far from being, in fact, the principle of institutional Protestantism. For, if the Protestant principle justifies the Reformation in its protestations against the Catholic tendency to absolutize, it equally condemns the absolutism which has crept into Protestantism. Paul Tillich, therefore, makes himself a prophet of the end of the "Protestant era." His work *The Religious Situation* shows that the religious depth of our times is more apparent in the religiously neutral movements of culture, in science, philosophy, art, and even in politics, than it is in the Churches. In *The Interpretation of History* (1936) and *The Protestant Era* (1948), collections of articles published since 1920, Tillich explains that the socialist movements developing after World War I serve to reveal the religious substance of the twentieth century: in them our age discovers its *kairos*, the providential and eternal direction of modern times. The end of the Protestant era is also the beginning of a new epoch for humanity. Beyond every concrete religious or ecclesiastical form, outside as well as inside the Churches and organized religion, but with no necessary connection with them, this era will neither be heterogeneous, as the modern Catholic would wish, nor autonomous, as the liberal Protestant envisages it. Rather, it will be theonomous, transparent to the ground of being in all of its activities and in all of its institutions. The end of the Protestant era must be the partial disappearance of official Protestantism and its practical identification with bourgeois society, so that the Protestant principle might expand, leading to the eventual appearance of a new theonomous phase in the history of humanity.

Paul Tillich, then, provides a version of the Protestant principle which makes it not only the central element of the Lutheran and Calvinist Reformation, but the very heart of every true religion. A true religious attitude recognizes that all things proceed from the divine initiative. As a consequence, Tillich gives to his contemporaries a universal vision of religious phenomena. Protestantism is no longer a transitory phase in the history of the Western Church; it is the bond of every religion.

There is greatness in such a point of view. It is not, therefore, surprising that Tillich, coming upon the confined environment of American Protestantism, has found an audience. In the years preceding World War II, American Protestantism was divided more than ever between several somewhat contradictory movements. In the South, Protestantism was solidly fundamentalist and pietistic. At the same time, Northern Protestantism held on to a liberalism which was out of style in Europe and which neither Karl Barth nor his American disciples had yet succeeded in counteracting. Many trends were present in American Protestantism of which the "social gospel," inherited from the nineteenth century, remained very active.[7] Yet, not even from such an intelligent author as Reinhold Niebuhr did a universal point of view arise.[8]

---

[7] See Robert Moats Miller, *American Protestantism and Social Issues: 1919–1939* (Chapel Hill: University of North Carolina Press, 1959).

[8] Reinhold Niebuhr's great work *The Nature and Destiny of Man* did not appear until 1941.

Through excessive provincialism, Protestantism ran the risk of finding itself in blind alleys, caught by petty remains of old Puritanism, as happened in regard to prohibition. Practical concerns dominated American Protestant thought, forcing the universal elements of the Gospel to take a second place behind the immediate, short-lived, and often less important questions of the hour.

Paul Tillich was thus the liberator of American Protestantism. He has freed Protestantism in the United States through unification, and he has unified through a principle of judgment which dominates all problems, solutions, and facts. As Walter Leibrecht rightly says: "Tillich's call to theonomy is his greatest challenge to modern thought. His is a vision of culture in which ultimate concern informs the whole web of life and thought and for which the ultimate unity is an ever-present horizon."[9]

Nevertheless, it is necessary to examine Tillich's interpretation of the world and religion, since there are critics who deny any specifically Christian value to Paul Tillich's Protestant principle.

The World and Religion

The Protestant principle, as described by Paul Tillich or Gustave Weigel, does not seem to be the exclusive possession of Christianity. Immediate knowledge of God is affirmed outside of as well as inside the Christian faith. The worship of a God who transcends all contingent forms while sustaining these forms in being is not exclusively linked to the Incarnation of the divine Word. One could even think that its best ground lies in the impersonal oriental religions. The affirmation of a dialectic in which error is a vehicle of truth and through which every intellect is thereby "justified" no

---

[9] "The Life and Mind of Paul Tillich," Walter Leibrecht, editor, *Religion and Culture: Essays in Honor of Paul Tillich* (New York: Harper, 1959), p. 17.

longer requires belief in Jesus Christ. The Protestant principle has, indeed, a universal character, able to be found in all
the great religions.

This, however, does not permit us to deny that Paul Tillich's theology is Christian. For Tillich has given to modern
Protestantism a theological system founded at the same time
on a universal principle, the immanent transcendence of the
divine, and on a historical fact, the Incarnation of the Son
of God.

Paul Tillich constructed his theological system only after
long years of deep study and reflection. Unlike Karl Barth's
Dogmatics, in which the thought evolves from one volume
to the next, Tillich is extremely consistent. The desire for
internal coherence led him to entitle his great work *Systematic
Theology,* endeavoring in it to develop a complete theological system rather than presenting a summary or manual of
theology. "The task of systematic theology is to explain the
content of the Christian faith."[10] This means explaining the
content in itself, as it is presented to the faith by Christian
tradition. A subjective element necessarily intervenes, however, since the explanations are made in light of the principles which support and guide the system. And the choice of
these principles is always governed by the cultural, historical,
and spiritual viewpoint of the theologian. A theological
summa is in some ways timeless, erected to a certain degree
above the successive ages of Christianity. A theological system, on the other hand, is necessarily connected with the
situation prevailing at its birth. When the situation changes,
such a system is in grave danger of degenerating into a cu-
riosity of merely documentary value. Tillich gladly runs this
risk, because it is the vocation of a theologian to make use
of the language of his audience and to take up the problems
of his age in an effort to make men understand the New
Being who is Christ. "The theologian who is not a realist
(and who could never become a realist) . . . uses realism and
becomes a positivist to the positivists, a pragmatist to the

[10] *ST,* I, p. 34.

pragmatists, and a tragic interpreter of life to the tragic interpreters of life."[11]

Tillich's System

Tillich's system uses the method of "correlation." He sees
a necessary correspondence between man's question and God's
answer, between the inquiry of doubt and the affirmation of
faith. The system studies the human dimensions of being,
existence, life, and history. At each stage of analysis it explains the divine response furnished by the Being of the
Father, the Existence of Christ, the Life of the Spirit, and
the History of the Church in strict correlation to the implicit question at hand. Ambiguities of being are resolved in
the Father; ambiguities of existence in the Son Incarnate;
ambiguities of life are resolved in the Spirit; and those of
history in the Church.

This Trinitarian theology is basically Christian. Indeed, if
Tillich's Protestant principle may have a meaning outside of
Christianity and outside of every positive religion, faith in
the Incarnation nevertheless plays a central role in his theological system. There even is, in the dialectic used, an intimate relationship between the Protestant principle and the
Incarnation. The Protestant principle affirms that no contingent being can subsist without the ground of being who is
God. This is why the attribution to being of whatever pertains to its ground is never permissible. All men, therefore,
have a duty of protesting against the idolatry which gives to
being of any sort the singular homage due "this infinite and
inexhaustible depth and ground of all being," who "is God."[12]

Something entirely new in the history of humanity has appeared in Jesus Christ. With him the limits of being, so to
speak, have been broken. The unconditional himself, the
ground, the depth, the abyss of being has appeared in the

[11] *SF*, p. 124.
[12] *Ibid.*, p. 57.

ambiguities of history, subject to the fluctuations of human life and to the uncertainties of existence. "He who is the Christ," according to a favorite expression of Tillich's, is essence manifested on earth under the guise of existence. The essence of which Tillich speaks is that of man at the point where it coincides with the divine ground of being. It is "Essential Godmanhood."[13] "The paradox of the Christian message is that in *one* personal life essential manhood has appeared under the conditions of existence without being conquered by them."[14] The manifestation of essential humanity is, at the same time, the manifestation of the divinity in which humanity has its ground, its limits, and its meaning. "The Christ is God-for-us."[15] In him are resolved the antinomies of existence. Life accepts death and conquers it. Existence, having been separated from God, regains its essential unity with Christ. "Resurrection is not something added to the death of him who is the Christ; but it is implied in his death. . . . No longer is the universe subjected to the law of death out of birth. It is subjected to a higher law, to the law of life out of death by the death of him who represented eternal life."[16]

Jesus Christ, therefore, is a new creature, a new being, whose appearance on earth has changed the meaning of events. "In the face of the Crucified, all the 'more' and all the 'less,' all progress and all approximation, are meaningless. Therefore, we can say of him alone: he is the new reality; he is the end; he is the Messias."[17]

Is Tillich's Christology orthodox? I do not think it is. And I think I have shown in *Paul Tillich and the Christian Message*, that it cannot be so on several points. In particular, his Christology is not true to the teaching of the Council of Chalcedon. Elsewhere I have criticized Tillich's theological

[13] *ST*, II, p. 98.
[14] *Ibid.*, p. 94.
[15] *Ibid.*, p. 100.
[16] *NB*, p. 178.
[17] *SF*, p. 148.

method, which warps many of his conclusions.[18] Father Weigel has written: "Tillichian Christology is Nestorian."[19] And it is interesting to note that Tillich has approved Weigel's article as a whole: "This is the best analysis of my thought I have ever seen."[20]

Tillich's Protestant readers and interpreters are divided on the question of his orthodoxy. Norman Pittenger, an Anglican, professor at the General Theological Seminary in New York, thinks Tillich is orthodox; but Pittenger's own Christology is clearly and knowingly Nestorian, interpreting Chalcedon in a Nestorian sense.[21] Another Anglican, A. T. Mollegen, holds that Tillich's theology is "radically Christocentric" and that his Christology "stands within the classical dogmas."[22]

Some other views are less favorable. According to Jacob Taubes of Columbia University, Tillich's ontological theology corresponds to the naturalist systems and has an affinity with Nietzsche's philosophy. It contains, moreover, certain "Dionysiac" traits, that is, "an ecstatic naturalism, which interprets every supernatural symbol in terms of immanence." Taubes does recognize, however, that these Dionysiac elements are spiritualized in Tillich's thought. Nevertheless, the desire to "reconcile the numinous forces of the abyss and the divine powers of the light" constitute a new chapter in "the history of Dionysiac theology in the Christian frame of reference."[23] In the same vein, but with more severity, Professor William Albright calls Tillich a "modern gnostic," and finds only a

[18] See George Tavard, *Paul Tillich and the Christian Message* (New York: Scribner's, 1962); *idem*, "Christianity and the Philosophies of Existence," *Theological Studies*, 18 (1957), 10–12.

[19] "Contemporaneous Protestantism and Paul Tillich," *art. cit.*, 194.

[20] *Ibid.*, p. 201.

[21] See W. Norman Pittenger, *The Word Incarnate* (New York: Harper, 1959).

[22] "Christology and Biblical Criticism in Tillich," Kegley and Bretall, *op. cit.*, pp. 230–43.

[23] "On the Nature of the Theological Method," *Journal of Religion*, 34 (1954), 22.

superficial resemblance between his system and Christianity.[24]

Nels F. S. Ferré casts some doubt on Tillich's concept of the supernatural. Tillich, in effect, considers the question of knowing whether the eternal essence of man manifested in Christ is natural or supernatural to be a false problem. Writing after the publication of the first volume of *Systematic Theology*, Ferré found that this work shows "no indication of his [Tillich's] accepting the classical Christian presuppositions."[25]

In a more general way, Tillich is condemned for allowing too many nonbiblical elements to enter into his thought, and for not making sufficient use of the scriptural sources of faith. Tillich has tried to justify himself in his book, *Biblical Religion and the Search for Ultimate Reality*. But this small work has not quieted the criticism, and the publication of the further volumes of *Systematic Theology* has only made the critics more uneasy.

Difficulties in Tillichian Theology

The primary difficulty with Paul Tillich's theology, including his Christology, stems from his nonclassical categories and vocabulary. This leads to many misunderstandings. But there are more profound difficulties. Tillich is entirely classical in his insistence on the necessity of expressing Christian mysteries in ontological terms. On this point Catholic readers feel more at ease with him than Protestant readers, in whom Luther's distrust of the theological use of philosophy has left vivid traces. Although it is legitimate to borrow philosophical language, there is, nevertheless, the danger of ontologizing the Christian mysteries and of falling into an on-

[24] Cited in Gustave Weigel, S.J., "Myth, Symbol, and Analogy," *Religion and Culture*, *op. cit.*, p. 125; see below, p. 191.

[25] "Tillich's View of the Church," Kegley and Bretall, *op. cit.*, p. 263.

tologism which would be incompatible with the notion of the supernatural, thereby draining grace of all its substance.

This is exactly what Tillich does. In spite of his existential concern with the concrete and the immediate, so apparent in his writings, the whole of his theological system turns out to be a completely abstract theologico-philosophical construction. It is centered on the postulate that the eternal divine-human essence is manifested in Jesus the Christ and that in him the Protestant principle of immanent transcendence has become flesh, so to speak. Henceforth (and this is the full meaning of Christianity for Tillich), man knows, or is able to know, that his limitations are superficial and that, in the center of his being, there resides an eternal element in which he is rooted and through which he is related to God, the ground of all being. What has been manifested in Jesus the Christ is hidden in us.

For all who understand the Christian message, "the whole man is mortal and immortal at the same time; the whole man is temporal and eternal at the same time; the whole man is judged and saved at the same time, because the Eternal took part in flesh and blood and fear of death."[26] The ground of being is revealed in being; in man, God is revealed; in Jesus, the Christ is unveiled; in every Christian, the New Being resides. This inspires a new ethic, where conscience becomes, beyond moralism and amoralism, "transmoral,"[27] and where the principal virtue of the Christian is, according to the title of a work by Tillich, the "courage to be." "Christianity lives through the faith that within it there is the new which is not just another new thing but rather the principle and representation of all the really new in man and history."[28] But this "really new" is not supernatural in the traditional sense of the word. It is the ontological depth of every experience. Tillich openly denounces "supernaturalism," which, he thinks, makes any mediation between God

[26] *SF*, p. 172.
[27] *PE*, p. 136.
[28] *SF*, p. 186.

and man impossible.[29] Jacob Taubes correctly writes: "[Tillich's] theology of mediation involves the divine in the human dialectic to the point that the divine pole of the correlation loses all supernatural point of reference."[30]

Importance of Tillich's Thought

The actual importance of Paul Tillich's thought comes partly from his influence on the younger generation of American Protestant seminarians. It cannot be said that Tillich has founded a school. But his concern with the existential, his disinterestedness towards the historical Jesus, subordinating him to the Christ of faith, his cult of the great figures of German liberal theology can only prepare a way for the neo-liberalism of Rudolf Bultmann. This is made even easier since American Protestantism still follows the old liberalism, and Karl Barth's influence is at present quite weak in the United States.

But Paul Tillich's theology is worth knowing for better reasons than the short-lived infatuation of seminarians. In the last analysis, Tillich's importance comes from his desire to make the Gospel intelligible to modern man. Even where he seems to abandon the traditional dogmas, his first concern is clearly positive: he wants to interpret the Christian faith in a manner which will be at one and the same time faithful to traditional Protestantism and comprehensible to the contemporary spirit. From this desire comes Tillich's constant preoccupation with those sciences and arts in which modern man expresses what is most profound in him, such as psychoanalysis on the one hand and the plastic arts on the other. Paul Tillich claims to find more religious substance in modern art, even if it is atheistic, than in many formal declarations of the Christian faith. During the German period of his life, Tillich analyzed political movements with this same concern for religious interpretation. This aspect of his activity

[29] See *ST*, I, pp. 64–65.
[30] "On the Nature of the Theological Method," *art. cit.*, 25.

passed to the background in his American period, since the political scene in the United States did not favor his leftist political views. But all artistic, social, and political activities remain a field of reflection for the theologian. The Gospel is a concrete message with an immediate meaning and application in the life of every man. The theologian must seek, in even the most agnostic thought, the preludes and stepping stones to the Christian message. He must then show how the Gospel brings a divine response to bear upon the human questions posed. If this is, according to a current expression in Protestantism, a theology of mediation, then every theology must mediate. Paul Tillich's merit is in seeking a valid mediation between our era and the Christ. The fact that Tillich has not succeeded on all levels and that he has, perhaps, diluted the Christian message to too great an extent is no reason to refuse him our admiration.

VI

KENELM FOSTER, O.P.

Paul Tillich and St. Thomas

The theological writings of Professor Tillich deserve the attention of students of St. Thomas, both for their positive content, which is of the highest interest, and because on fundamental matters they explicitly and sharply join issue with Thomism. They invite the presumption of a certain common ground, certain affinities, and at the same time throw out a challenge which we cannot ignore.

To read these works, especially the great *Systematic Theology*, is to encounter a powerful and original personality, a mind organized to an uncommon degree around a single center. Tillich's peculiar gift is for synthesis; a constructive thinker with a very wide range of interests, he is always striving to correlate and organize these on the basis of a singularly vivid intuition of being in general, the primary *datum* of the mind, which for him—as for St. Thomas—represents the mind's first opening onto reality as a whole, as both containing and transcending human nature. It is this consciously ontological character of Tillich's thinking that seems to distinguish him among contemporary Protestant theologians; as J. H. Randall observes, he "stands in the classic tradition of Western philosophy," in the tradition, derived from the Greeks, of speculative concern with being-itself and wisdom.[1] Let us stress this "concern." "Ultimate concern" is Tillich's

---

[1] See "The Ontology of Paul Tillich," C. Kegley and R. Bretall, editors, *The Theology of Paul Tillich* (New York: Macmillan, 1952), p. 132.

definition of religion, and by "ultimate" he means "that which determines our being or nonbeing."[2] Man for him is the being who "asks the question of being," and since God is "the answer implied in the question of being,"[3] theology is essentially a searching into the same question. Hence, Tillich's emphatic refusal (against the "biblicist" tendencies of a more or less Barthian type) to separate theology from philosophy. For him the difference between the two disciplines consists in this, that while both aim at understanding "the structure of being," the philosopher regards this with "detached objectivity," whereas the theologian is existentially committed to it as to the manifestation of his Lord and God.[4] So the true theologian is also a philosopher, for he too asks the ontological question—that "simplest, most profound, and absolutely inexhaustible question . . . of what it means to say that something *is*"[5]—though from within a concrete commitment to the Christian message.

Yet, despite this philosophical *eros*, this notable drive of his mind toward being, Tillich is a declared and downright anti-Thomist. In this essay I shall state the objection he usually brings against Thomism, and then attempt, briefly, to indicate the ground of this difference in the different ways that he and we reflect on the primary *datum*, being.

Tillich's Clash with Thomism

Explicitly, the clash with St. Thomas occurs over the question of proving the existence of God. With a frequency that betrays a keen personal concern in the matter, Tillich reiterates his opposition to any attempt to demonstrate God's existence. "The arguments for the existence of God," runs a characteristic passage, "neither are arguments nor are they proof of the existence of God. They are expressions of the

2 *ST*, I, p. 24; cf. p. 14.
3 *Ibid.*, p. 181.
4 See *ibid.*, pp. 11–32.
5 *BRSUR*, p. 6.

question of God which is implied in human finitude. This
question is their truth; every answer they give is untrue."[6]
Primarily, it seems, it is not the arguments themselves, as
arguments, that Tillich objects to, but the attitude of mind
that proposes them. This comes out clearly in another typ-
ically strong statement: "It is as atheistic to affirm the existence of God as to deny it. God is being-itself, not *a* being."[7]
The rejection, then, of the proofs for God's existence is evidently part and parcel of a rejection of a certain way—
typified, for Tillich, by St. Thomas particularly—of thinking
about God at all. Though God supremely *is*, he must not
be thought of as *existing*, because this would be to treat him
as one thing along with others, whether one affirmed his
existence or merely put the question. The question should be
"neither asked nor answered."[8] This is not to say that there
is no "question of God"; there is, and it is the theologian's
raison-d'être—but only if and insofar as it is not contaminated
by the question about existence, the question *an sit*.

What then is the authentic, the right, the uncontaminated
"question of God"? It is, first, the ontological question of
"what it means to *be*." To this question God is the implicit
answer, but explicitly its answer is an understanding of the
"structure of being" through certain ultimate principles and
categories—in short, an ontology (this term Tillich prefers to
"metaphysics"). Now the structure of being contains an "unconditional element" which is disclosed to the attentive
mind in terms of certain absolute norms: "*verum ipsum*, the
true-itself," in the theoretical reason, "*bonum ipsum*, the
good-itself," in the practical reason. Rightly to acknowledge
these norms is to acknowledge, to become aware of, God;
for they are "manifestations of *esse-ipsum*, being-itself, the
ground and abyss of everything that is."[9] They are the
presence of God in our mind as the "power of being"; so
that with them arises, beyond the question of mere being,

[6] *ST*, I, p. 228.
[7] *Ibid*., p. 263.
[8] *Loc. cit.*
[9] *Ibid*., pp. 229–30; cf. p. 88; *TC*, pp. 12–16.

the explicit question of God as God. But what sort of question is this; what answer does it expect? If I understand Tillich rightly at this point—and he has not, I think, made himself perfectly clear—he would say, first, that the explicit emergence of the question of God is the expression, in "the depth of reason," of a direct encounter of the finitude of man with the infinite godhead;[10] and secondly, that the "answer" therefore expected is a release from the peril, the "anxiety," of finitude—it is a being given a share in God's eternal being;[11] and thirdly, that the answer that must *not* be expected, that must not even be envisaged, is any assurance of God's existence other than that already given in the awareness of the unconditional element in experience. But it is just here, Tillich insists, that Western theology, between Augustine and Aquinas, went astray. The classic formulation of the unconditional element, in terms of the norm of truth, *veritas*, was given to the West by Augustine, but later distorted into arguments for the existence of God, notably by the Augustinian St. Anselm with his "ontological argument," the value of which lies wholly and solely in the point from which it starts, "the description of the relation of our mind to being as such," as apprehended in the transcendenal notions, *esse, verum, bonum*.[12] The rest of it is utterly invalid—not only as a logical process, as St. Thomas later and Kant saw, but also in what it attempted to prove, namely, God's existence as a *fact*. And this, of course, rules out in advance St. Thomas' quite different proof of the same conclusion.

Tillich, then, denies that one can properly say that God exists: "The Scholastics were right when they asserted that in God there is no difference between essence and existence. But they perverted their insight when they spoke of the existence of God and tried to argue in favor of it."[13] This might be thought a mere question of terms, of the way one

[10] Cf. *ST*, I, p. 88.
[11] See *ibid.*, pp. 181–206, 224; cf. *TC*, pp. 30–39.
[12] See *ibid.*, pp. 227–31; cf. *TC*, pp. 10–29.
[13] *ST*, I, p. 227.

chooses to use the word "existence." For Tillich, certainly, existence always connotes finitude; it is always for him the actualization of some potentiality: "Whatever exists," he writes, "is more than it is in the state of mere potentiality and less than it could be in the power of its essential nature."[14] In this sense of the term, then, plainly God does not exist—for us no more than for Tillich. If this were all the difference between us it could be settled, in theory at least, quite easily. We could reserve "existence" to signify finite actual being and find some other term for the infinite actuality. But the matter is not, it is clear, as simple as that. For one thing, Tillich explicitly and repeatedly rejects any and every argument for establishing the—let us say—"isness" of the infinite being; and for another thing—and here is the more radical disagreement—he appears to reject on principle the judgment *that God is* (as distinct from mere awareness *of* his reality), whether this judgment be made as the conclusion of an inference or simply as a statement of sheer fact.[15] Let us take these two points in turn.

As to the first one, the possibility of arguing to the existence of God, it is not to my purpose here to defend the accepted arguments, or any others, but it is very relevant to understand why Tillich rejects them. He does so broadly for two reasons: because he thinks they are bad arguments and because he thinks that the being whose existence they conclude to falls short of the true, the adequate notion of God. But his main stress falls on this second point. Indeed, so far as I have read him, he offers only one direct, detailed criticism of the argumentative process in question as such. It occurs on pages 217–18 of Volume I of his *Systematic Theology* and deals with the possibility of finding God at the end of a causal series; but as criticism it is quite superficial and so it need not detain us. As I say, his main objection,

[14] *Ibid.*, pp. 225–26; cf. p. 183.

[15] *Ibid.*, p. 227: "God does not exist. He is being-itself beyond essence and existence." This distinction of the true God from the false one, of whom existence is predicated, leads to the statement that "Genuine religion without an element of atheism cannot be imagined" (*TC*, p. 25).

and it springs from the heart of his system, is to the sort of God the arguments are supposed to conclude to. He insists again and again that "to argue that God exists is to deny him"; it is to erect a no-God, an idol, in the place of God.[16] And his three chief reasons for this assertion are, I think, the following: to argue for God's existence is in effect (1) to make God a mere "object" *vis-à-vis* the human subject who reasons about him (whereas in reality he transcends the subject-object division);[17] (2) it is to make God a mere "existent" and therefore, as we have seen, one finite thing among others; and (3) it is to reduce God to a "missing part" of the world from which the argument—in particular the so-called "cosmological argument" of St. Thomas—pretends to derive him; which again is to make God finite.[18]

The point, then, is that a certain way of thinking about God is considered to un-God him. Now what, *au fond*, is this way of thinking? What use of the mind is it that Tillich radically objects to? It is, I suggest, that use of the mind which traditional logic calls *judgment*, and in particular the judgment of fact or existence—"Peter *is*"; "This table *is*." In traditional logic, judgment is, formally speaking, the second operation of the mind. The first is "simple apprehension," whereby one forms a concept, or cluster of concepts, of e.g., the man Peter. Such concepts combine or separate in the mind according to the evidence given by experience or reasoning; and then, in view of this evidence, one *assents* to the combination or the separation: "Peter is a man"; "He is not clever"; "He exists"; "He does not exist." Now it is important here to note two things about the function of the verb "to be" in judgment, as we understand this. First, the verb "to be" is present in every judgment, at least implicitly: to say "Peter writes" is to mean "Peter is writing." And secondly, the verb "to be" has a double function in every judgment, what is called a formal function and a material one. When I say, "Peter is a man," the copula "is" expresses

16 See *ST*, I, p. 227.
17 See *ibid.*, p. 191.
18 See *ibid.*, p. 228.

something about Peter's being, that he has the sort of being we call human; and this is the material function of "is" in the judgment. Its formal function, that which it exercises precisely as completing the act of judging, is to express my *assent* to the fact that Peter is human; it means "Yes, it is so." Moreover, since judgment is, essentially, not mere awareness of some reality, but assent to this awareness, it is not mere knowledge but a knowing that one knows; hence, that function of "is," which is proper precisely to its presence in judgment, is to express a *knowledge that one knows*. And since the mind formally as mind is the power to know, it follows that the mind's conformity to the real, its truthfulness, *veritas*, is only found formally and fully in the judgment[19] —not in our simple awareness of reality, but in the act through which we simultaneously both know and assent to our awareness, in the judgment "*x* is (or is not) *y*"—where "is" expresses both the act of knowledge as such, i.e., the mind as mind's conformity to the real, its immanent truthfulness, and also the objective being of that real to which the mind is now conformed; but the former formally, the latter only materially.

Meeting Tillich's Criticism

With this analysis behind us we are in a position to meet Tillich's criticism of St. Thomas, which is based, I think, on a misunderstanding of the function of the copula in judgment. St. Thomas makes it perfectly clear that the term "being" has two main functions: to signify reality as such, and to signify the mind's conformity to reality. Thus, very early, in the *De ente et essentia*, we read:

The term being (*ens*) is used in two ways: in one way as referring to what is divided into ten categories (i.e., being as real or existing); in another way as signifying the truth of propositions. And the difference is this, that in the second way anything can be called being about which one can form an affirmative proposition, even if nothing is thereby stated

[19] Cf. St. Thomas Aquinas, *Summa theologiae*, I, q. 16, a. 2.

to exist *in re;* and in this sense we speak of privations and negations as "beings," saying that affirmation *is* the opposite of negation, and that blindness *is* in the eye. But in terms of the first way we can speak of being only in referring to something that really exists (or could exist, one may add). And in this sense blindness and so forth are not "beings."

The reference to nonentities like blindness may be confusing, but the point of this quotation for our purpose is simply to bring out the distinction between *ens* as real—i.e., existing or able to exist—and *ens* as expression of the mind's truthfulness. And both senses of *ens* are involved in every judgment, but the second is the one proper to and characteristic of judgment. And in general it is characteristic of the human reason's effort to know reality, if this effort finds its successful issue (in this world at least) only in the formulation of true judgments: "This is so"; "This is not so." Characteristic, therefore, of human rational knowing is a certain indirectness *vis-à-vis* reality-as-in-itself, inasmuch as reason knows most fully by a sort of spontaneous reflection on and assent to its apprehensions, by a sort of *reculer pour mieux sauter,* which expresses reality—through the judgment copula "is"— not simply as reality is in itself, but as it has come to be, conceptually, in the mind. From another point of view we should say that rational knowledge always connotes a certain initial abstraction.

And all this is true of the judgment of fact or existence also, in which the verb "to be" is predicate as well as copula. "The table *is*" means "The table is in being, is an actual existent." And here the copula "is" expresses (1) the table's own existence, which is material of my judgment, and (2) my assent to it, which is form of the judgment. But prior (in nature, not in time) to my assent to it the table's existence must somehow have entered my mind, being "conceived" there in a concept, as we say. I am aware that here I touch on the delicate and difficult problem as to how in fact the concrete singular existence *can* be known through a concept, i.e., not without *some* intellectual abstraction—a problem which Thomists in particular must face, in view of their doctrine that nothing, not even existence, comes within the field

of vision of human intelligence except as a result of a certain
abstraction from sense data. But this further problem must
not detain us; all I wish and need to do here is to point out
that the judgment of existence, being a judgment, also exhibits the double function of the copula explained above.
Precisely as an assent it expresses with its "is"—x is an existent
—primarily the mind's possession of a truth about x—that
it is—and not immediately x's actuality of being as this is, so
to say, in x. And this point is the more evident when x is
not something immediately given in sense-experience or self-
experience, but only mediately known about through inference. St. Thomas held that this is the case with our *scientific*, i.e., rationally established, knowledge of God's existence.
Some infrascientific awareness is indeed allowed for by St.
Thomas at the "intuitive" level of sense- or self-experience;
but the critical reason, he thought, remains unsatisfied until
it has found reason to predicate *esse* of that *divinum aliquid*
which it already, but only obscurely, apprehends. And the
predication is a judgment of existence. It is indeed a very
extraordinary judgment of existence, inasmuch as in this case
and this alone the predicate is the Absolute, subsistent Existence itself, compared with which all other things are as
nothing. It is very mysterious indeed that God can be *judged*
to exist by his creatures. But there are no short cuts past this
mystery. To try to short-cut it from the ontological position
of a Tillich only results in confusion—confusion about human
knowledge and about the nature of God. And to conclude
this inadequate criticism of a man whose greatness I most
readily acknowledge, let me point, more explicitly, to the
former of these confusions.

Confusion about Human Knowledge

It is a confusion about the way we rationally know, and one
passage in *Systematic Theology* is particularly revealing of
Tillich's unawareness of the relevant distinction I have tried
to state, between *ens in se* and *ens* as the mind's expression

of truth. It runs as follows: "In order to maintain the truth that God is beyond essence and existence while simultaneously arguing for the existence of God, Thomas Aquinas is forced to distinguish between two kinds of divine existence: that which is identical with essence and that which is not. But an existence of God . . . not united with its essence is a contradiction in terms."[20] The revealing phrase is "two kinds of divine existence." There is, of course, for St. Thomas only one kind: the *esse Deum* of the judgment "that God exists" is formally and immediately only an expression of the mind's truth, of a truthful state of the human mind. But the answer to Tillich's charge was formulated long ago in the *Contra Gentiles*; it is all too brief but it goes, I think, to the root of the matter. St. Thomas is replying to an objector who would say that if essence and existence are identical in God, and if by reason we cannot know God's existence, it follows that reason cannot demonstrate his existence. The saint's reply may be rendered thus:

It is not a valid objection to point to the identity of essence and existence in God. For this is the existence whereby God subsists in himself, which is as unknown to us as his essence. It is not the existence (*esse*) which denotes an affirmative judgment in the mind. This latter existence, as in the judgment *that God is*, is patient of demonstration inasmuch as, by probative reasons, our mind can be led to form a proposition about God expressing that he is.[21]

Confusion about human knowledge is likely to cause confusion in one's doctrine about God. But I cannot pursue the matter here. Enough to suggest that a certain withdrawal into, or remaining in, one's awareness of the divinity adumbrated in the intuition of being and of its "unconditional elements"—a refusal to analyze, rationally, "Godness" into a clear and distinct concept—that all this is bound to leave our idea of God imperfectly distinguished from our idea of whatever is not God. And this is certainly the case

[20] *ST*, I, p. 262.
[21] *Summa contra gentiles*, I, 12.

PART TWO

Sources and Media of Revelation

What are the sources of systematic theology? What is the medium of their reception? What is the norm determining the use of the sources? The first answer to these questions might be the Bible. The Bible is the original document about the events on which Christianity is based. Although this cannot be denied, the answer is insufficient. In dealing with the question of the sources of systematic theology, we must reject the assertion of neo-orthodox biblicism that the Bible is the *only* source. . . . The Bible, however, is the basic source of systematic theology.

Systematic Theology, I

VII

AVERY R. DULLES, S.J.

Paul Tillich and the Bible

Under the stimulus of recent progress in linguistics and archaeology, biblical studies have flourished remarkably in the present century. Advances on the technical level have been attended by a renewal of interest in the Bible from a theological point of view. Catholic and Protestant theologians alike have been seeking to make use of the new information and to assimilate it harmoniously into their respective systems.

Unlike many other Protestant theologians of our day—the names of Eichrodt, Bultmann, and Cullmann come immediately to mind—Paul Tillich is not outstanding as a biblical scholar. He is primarily a systematic theologian. But his system has, with some justification, been called biblical, on the ground that it is "wholly and finally determined by the revelation of God recorded in the Bible."[1] In his theological writings he has tried to work out a general theory of what the Bible should mean to the contemporary Protestant believer and theologian. Tillich's system holds exceptional interest for the Catholic theologian. His views on the Bible are perhaps especially interesting, since they exhibit some startling approaches toward the Catholic position, and at the same time some fundamental divergences.

The Bible, in Tillich's view, is a uniquely important col-

[1] A. T. Mollegen, "Christology and Biblical Criticism in Tillich," C. Kegley and R. Bretall, editors, *The Theology of Paul Tillich* (New York: Macmillan, 1952), p. 230.

lection of source documents. He sees in it the primary source of God's final revelation to mankind, the original record of man's response to that revelation, and the basic font of Christian theology. We may conveniently consider Tillich's biblical doctrine under each of these three heads, and then conclude our study with a brief critical appraisal.

The Bible and Revelation

In order to understand Tillich's biblical doctrine, one must begin with a clear conception of what he means by "revelation."[2] His theory of revelation is basic to his system and is quite different from that familiar to Catholics. Like most Catholic theologians, he avoids the term "natural revelation" as confusing, if not contradictory. Revelation for him is a special and extraordinary type of knowledge. It is the apprehension of the mysterious—of that which lies beyond the grasp of man's natural powers. In revelation, indeed, God manifests himself; the human intellect is brought face to face with the transcendent God. Now man, in his present existential state—the condition of fallen nature—is estranged from his true self, and consequently from God also. This is indicated by the evident fact that our ordinary knowledge bears on finite beings, which are grasped as "objects" in opposition to ourselves. But God is neither a finite being nor an object. He is the transcendent ground of all being, including our own. Hence, he cannot be reached by ordinary human knowledge. In order to acquire any genuine knowledge of God, therefore, it is necessary for the mind to overleap all finite categories and transcend the ordinary distinctions between subject and object. Extraordinary knowledge of this sort is what Tillich means by revelation.

Revelation has two aspects, objective and subjective. In the objective order, something really happens which manifests the mysterious ground of being. As is evident from the his-

[2] See the chapter on "The Meaning of Revelation" in *ST*, I, pp. 106–31.

tory of religion, revelatory events have always been described as "shaking, transforming, demanding, significant in an ultimate way."[3] Occurrences of this kind are, in Tillich's terminology, called "miracles." The subjective apprehension of revelation, wherein the mind rises above its ordinary limits, is technically called "ecstasy." Revelation, therefore, may be described as the self-manifestation of God through miracle and ecstasy.

The terms "ecstasy" and "miracle" must be understood in the technical sense which Tillich gives them. Ecstasy in his terminology is not emotional overexcitement, nor is it a state of demonic possession destroying the rational structure of the mind. Rather, it is an elevation of the mind whereby it experiences union with the mysterious ground of being. By miracle, on the other hand, he does not mean a supernatural intervention of God in the order of nature. Such an interposition of God in the chain of created cause-effect relationships would, in Tillich's philosophy, be incompatible with the divine transcendence. By a miracle, therefore, he means an unusual event—extraordinary either in its regularity or its irregularity—which somehow points to the ultimate source of reality and of meaning. While Tillich's ontology does not directly concern us in this study, it is important to note at the outset that he denies all supernatural interventions of God in the world.

That which is revealed, as we have said, is strict mystery. It cannot be apprehended by ordinary thought and, for the same reason, it cannot be expressed in ordinary language. Propositions about revelations are not themselves revelatory. This point will be of pivotal importance in Tillich's analysis of the Bible.

On the basis of these observations about Tillich's general view of revelation, we may inquire how he conceives of revelation in the concrete.[4] In the Christian view, he asserts, there is but one final revelation—the manifestation of God in Jesus as the Christ. This revelation was originally made

[3] *Ibid.*, p. 110.
[4] See the chapter on "Actual Revelation," *ibid.*, pp. 132–47.

through Jesus to his disciples. But the final revelation has not ceased. It goes on in the Church, and will go on to the end of time. The original revelation and its reception by the first disciples is the primary source from which all subsequent Christian revelation derives. The latter, therefore, may be called dependent, as contrasted with original, revelation. In opposition to the Evangelicals, who would maintain that the Spirit gives new revelations to individuals reading the Bible, Tillich maintains that the Christian revelation has been given, once for all, in its fullness, and that subsequent revelations within the Christian economy can add nothing substantially new.

Christian revelation, however, is not the only revelation. Tillich differs sharply from Barth who would maintain that the final revelation is cast "like a stone" into the human situation, without any previous conditioning on the part of man. Man cannot receive a revelation which does not answer to a felt need. Hence, the human mind must be disposed for final revelation by revelations of a preparatory character. Preparatory revelation, according to Tillich, may be called universal, not in the sense that everyone receives it, but in the sense that it can occur at any place or time.

The concrete revelations which directly prepared the Jewish people for the final revelation are recorded in the Old Testament. The New Testament contains the basic documents of the final revelation itself. The Bible, therefore, is a record of divine revelation.

But the Bible is not merely a collection of documents about revelation; it is also itself revelatory. The biblical writers were themselves involved in the revelatory events they described; they wrote as witnesses to revelation. It is even true to say that they were inspired writers. In speaking of inspiration, Tillich is careful to exclude any suggestion of supernaturalism. He explicitly rejects the notion that the Bible was divinely "dictated," or that God in any way intervened to shape the thoughts and intentions of the human authors. Inspiration, in Tillich's vocabulary, is the cognitive aspect of ecstasy. "The inspiration of the writers of the New Testament is their acceptance of Jesus as the Christ, and with him, of the

New Being, of which they became witnesses."[5] By literary inspiration Tillich understands simply the vital and creative response of an author to a revelation which he has received.

As a revelatory document, the Bible transmits to us God's self-disclosure in ancient Jewish history, and particularly his final manifestation in Jesus as the Christ. That message, in its revelatory dimension, cannot be set down in ordinary human language. Propositions can express contingent facts, abstract doctrines, or ethical precepts, but they cannot convey revelation. For revelation, in Tillich's view, is not scientific or factual or even practical information. It adds no new content to human knowledge, but gives it a new dimension of ultimate meaning. It manifests the ground of being, that which concerns us ultimately.[6]

While human language, in its ordinary propositional use, cannot serve as a vehicle of revelation, there is a peculiar kind of speech which is appropriate to the task. This is symbolism, which Tillich defines as the use of finite materials in order to create a revelatory situation.[7] Symbolic speech might be described as the miracle of language. Words are so used that their proper meaning is negated, and they point beyond themselves to the ultimate ground of being. The metaphors applied to God in the Old Testament are an excellent example of symbolic writing. Although often described as anthropomorphic, they are not really so; for they are charged with symbolic overtones, and thereby communicate a vivid sense of God's transcendence. Not only metaphors and parables, but also myths and legends, according to Tillich, have value as symbols. The truth of a symbol, obviously, has nothing to do with its literal verification. Symbols have a type of truth peculiar to themselves; they are true to the extent that they adequately reflect the revelatory situation which they are intended to express. In his attitude toward symbolism, Tillich takes great pains to dissociate himself from the mod-

[5] *Ibid.*, p. 35; cf. pp. 114–15.

[6] See *ibid.*, pp. 124–29, 145.

[7] On the question of symbolic assertions about God, cf. *ibid.*, esp. pp. 238–44.

ernists. The latter, he charges, "have interpreted religious language symbolically in order to weaken its seriousness, its power, and its spiritual impact." He is also critical of Bultmann for unjustifiably equating myth with a merely primitive world-view which should be cast aside. For Tillich, on the contrary, myth and symbol are the only way in which revelation can be communicated.[8]

The biblical writers were the recipients of a unique series of revelations leading up to God's final self-manifestation in the person of Jesus. As inspired authors, they used language with singular revelatory power. The Bible, therefore, is a genuine source of revelation. When read by a person with the requisite dispositions, it enables him to enter into the revelatory events described and to share in the ecstatic experience of the biblical writers. As a medium of revelation, the Bible possesses a certain sacramental quality. It is a holy book.

The Bible and History of Religion

Thus far we have considered the Bible as a record and source of revelation. But there is more in the Bible than revelation. Revelation is an act of God which necessarily implies, as its correlative, a reception on the part of man. The human reception of and response to revelation are what Tillich means by the term "religion."[9]

Considered in the abstract, revelation and religion are very different. Revelation moves from God to man; religion moves from man to God. Revelation is divine and absolute; religion is human and contingent. In the concrete, however, revelation is not revelation except insofar as it is actually received; God's self-disclosure is proportioned to the receptive capacities of man. To see how imperfectly men have responded to divine revelation, there is no need to look beyond the Bible.

[8] See Tillich's article, "The Present Theological Situation," *Theology Today*, 6 (1949–50), 306.

[9] See BRSUR, pp. 1–5.

It tells a constantly reiterated story of how men have resisted the word of God, distorted it by superstition, rejected it in favor of idolatry. In order to maintain the purity of revelation, the prophets raised an unceasing protest against these human perversions.

Insofar as it gives an account of Jewish religion, the Bible is a historical work. But the biblical writers, quite evidently, are not historians in the same sense as a Von Ranke or a Trevelyan. Their main interest is to bear witness to divine revelation. They sometimes write about historical facts which, by their miraculous character, have revelatory significance. But they also make use of myths and legends to convey their message. It is theologically unimportant, Tillich maintains, to know exactly where fact ends and fiction begins. The theologian, therefore, can be indifferent to the historical aspects of the Bible. "The truth of religious symbol has nothing to do with the truth of the empirical assertions involved in it, be they physical, psychological, or historical."[10]

Tillich's discussion of creation and the Fall is illustrative of his symbolic method of interpretation. On philosophical grounds he denies that creation and the Fall are two actual past events. They are symbols which aptly express man's existential predicament—the necessarily tragic state of finite freedom. "Finite freedom, when it becomes actual, disrupts the essential, uncontested, innocent unity between finitude and its infinite ground."[11] Through their apprehension of this truth, according to Tillich, philosophers of the stature of Plato and Origen, Kant and Schelling, were driven to invoke the myth of a transcendent, nonhistorical fall. Since the Fall was not a historical event, "it is inadequate to ask questions concerning Adam's actual state before the Fall, for example, whether he was mortal or immortal, or whether he was in a state of righteousness."[12]

[10] *ST*, I, p. 240.
[11] Quoted by Reinhold Niebuhr, in "Biblical Thought and Ontological Speculation in Tillich's Theology," Kegley and Bretall, *op. cit.*, p. 221.
[12] *ST*, I, p. 259.

One of Tillich's colleagues, Reinhold Niebuhr, has power-fully criticized his views on this point, alleging that they falsify "the picture of man as the Bible portrays it, and as we actually experience it."[13] "There is no myth of 'the tran-scendent fall' in the Bible, but only the myth of a histori-cal Fall."[14] Without violence to the clear intent of Scripture we cannot telescope the narratives of the creation and the Fall. "There is significance in the fact that there are two stories, the one symbolizing the beginning of history and the other the corruption of freedom in history. It is impor-tant that the two stories be separated," for that very separa-tion shows that man's act of self-estrangement was a defec-tion from a more ideal possibility. Biblical faith, according to Niebuhr, is distinguished from Platonistic and Oriental speculations by its strong insistence on the significance of history. Tillich, in his biblical exegesis, does not always do justice to the dimension of the historical.[15]

The problem of the relations between revelation and his-tory arises most acutely in the realm of Christology. Does not the Christian faith essentially involve the factual oc-currence in time of certain contingent events such as the Incarnation, the crucifixion, and the resurrection? If so, can Tillich sustain his contention that the truth of revelation has nothing to do with assertions of empirical fact?

The writers of the New Testament, he maintains, are in-terested in transmitting a religiously significant picture of Jesus, not in reporting merely factual data of a sort that could have been picked up by a sound-recording camera. The life of Jesus, as a revelatory event, has been recorded in revela-tory language, that is to say, in symbolic and mythical ex-pressions.[16] It would be erroneous to look to the Bible to give us a photographic picture of Jesus, conceived according to the principles of certain modern schools of historiography. "The original picture, which existed from the beginning, was

13 Niebuhr, *op. cit.*, p. 218.
14 *Ibid.*, p. 220.
15 See *ibid.*, pp. 225–26.
16 See "The Present Theological Situation," *art. cit.*, 307.

of a numinous and interpreted character, and it was this which proved to have the power to conquer existence."[17] From the point of view of religion, there is no need to supplement this picture with one that is merely factual. If scientific history wishes to try to reconstruct a "historical Jesus" according to the principles of its own methodology, it is free to do so, but such a picture will neither add nor subtract anything of theological interest. The scientist can speak with precision about the documents of revelation, but he cannot speak as a witness of revelation and hence cannot add to our revelatory knowledge. Using the techniques of his own science, he can neither confirm nor deny the revealed truth about Jesus; for revealed truth, according to Tillich, "lies within the dimension of revelatory knowledge" alone.[18] A. T. Mollegen, summarizing the views of Tillich, has put the matter well:

This biblical historical Christ is normative for Tillich. The quest of the historical Jesus which Schweitzer so brilliantly described in his book of the same name, and to which he added a revolutionary chapter, can neither replace nor support the biblical portrait inasmuch as faith and theology are concerned. Conservative criticism cannot give us a purely factual Jesus which guarantees the photographic details of the biblical historical Christ's life, nor can theological liberalism, by critical methods, reconstruct a "historical Jesus" who becomes a new canonical scripture supplanting the New Testament portrait, nor can radical criticism destroy the human flesh and blood existence of "the biblical Christ."[19]

Tillich, therefore, is quite unconcerned about the historicity of any particular details in the life of Jesus. But at the same time he is deeply convinced that the Christian revelation has a basis in actual fact. Even as a theologian he can affirm that revelation always occurs in a constellation

---

[17] "A Reinterpretation of the Doctrine of the Incarnation," *Church Quarterly Review*, 147 (1948–49), 145.

[18] *ST*, I, p. 130.

[19] "Christology and Biblical Criticism in Tillich," Kegley and Bretall, *op. cit.*, p. 233.

of ecstasy and miracle. Since we have revelatory writings, we can argue to the occurrence of revelation in and through Jesus. In the objective order, there unquestionably were miraculous events. Indeed, since the revelation given in Jesus as the Christ is the final revelation, the life of Jesus may be called the supreme and ecstatic moment of history. Tillich emphatically repudiates the suggestion that Christianity might have arisen out of some merely subjective experience:

I may express the hope that one false view is excluded by everything I have tried to say: namely, the mistake of supposing that the picture of the New Being in Jesus as the Christ is the creation of existential thought or experience. If this were the case, it would be as distorted, tragic, and sinful as existence is itself, and would not be able to overcome existence. The religious picture of the New Being in Jesus is the result of a new being: it represents the victory over existence which has taken place, and thus created the picture.[20]

The final revelation expressed in the New Testament, then, presupposes as its foundation a human individual, whose life and character were such as to support the biblical picture. Our faith and salvation, in Tillich's view, do not depend merely on the interpreted picture of Jesus, but equally on the events which that picture interprets. The miracle and the ecstasy are strictly correlative. Neither is salvific without the other. "The Christ is not the Christ without the church, and the church is not the church without the Christ."[21] Faith in the Christ is capable of giving us a New Being because, by accepting the revelatory picture, we participate in the reality of the Christ. "The church from its beginning through the present participates in a reality which is different from any other reality and which, therefore, is called the New Being."[22]

Thus, Tillich accepts the reality of Jesus as a human individual. But he does not do so precisely on the authority

[20] "A Reinterpretation of the Doctrine of the Incarnation," *art. cit.*, 145–46.
[21] *ST*, I, pp. 136–37.
[22] "The Present Theological Situation," *art. cit.*, 306–7.

of the biblical writers. He looks to them for the interpretation of the facts, but not for the facts which they interpret.
He recognizes, of course, that the Gospels, like many other
sections of the Bible, purport to relate actual events; they
are not merely symbolic speech. Even though the Bible is
not scientific history, there are factual assertions in the Bible.
As a theologian, however, Tillich passes no judgment on the
value of the Bible as history. When the biblical writers make
historical or scientific affirmations, he would say, their
statements are as reliable as the evidence on which those
statements are based. There can be no such thing as revealed history or revealed science, for history and science,
by their very nature, do not concern us ultimately. They are
not the ground of our being, and hence are not matter for
revelation. The question of factual truth falls within the province of the positive sciences and cannot be prejudged from
a theological point of view. "That which concerns us ultimately is not linked with any special conclusion of historical
and philological research. A theology which is dependent on
predetermined results of the historical approach is bound to
something conditional which claims to be unconditional, that
is, with something demonic."[23]

Many theologians, according to Tillich, have failed to recognize that the Bible was written by human authors who were
fallible as witnesses of historical fact. There has thus arisen
a sort of biblical "monophysitism." The practice of referring
to the Bible as the "word of God" has been one source of this
confusion. It has given support to supernaturalistic theories
of inspiration and the dogma of the infallible book.[24] Great
harm has come to religion from this type of thinking. Theologians, anxiously seeking to suppress elements of truth of
which they were dimly aware, have become fanatical. In their
efforts to reconcile the Bible with science, they have used
"sacred dishonesty." After committing themselves to certain
scientific theories on theological grounds, theologians have
then sought to prevent the diffusion of new theories, only

[23] *ST*, I, p. 36.
[24] See *ibid.*, p. 158.

to capitulate ignominiously when further resistance became impossible. "This ill-conceived resistance of theologians from the time of Galileo to the time of Darwin was one of the causes of the split between religion and secular culture in the past centuries."[25]

Rightly understood, there can be no conflict between science and theology; they move in different dimensions. While scientific investigation cannot dissolve revelation, "it can undercut superstitious and demonic interpretations of revelation, ecstasy, and miracle."[26] Historical criticism, for example, protects us against an idolatrous fundamentalism in our interpretation of the Bible. By calling attention to the mythical elements in Scripture, it removes the false offense of pseudohistory and permits the Gospel to confront men with the true offense of the doctrine of the cross.[27] In such ways as this, the positive sciences are the allies of theology in its struggle against distortions of genuine revelation.

Tillich, therefore, distinguishes sharply between the revelatory value of the Bible and its value as a historical document. Insofar as it is revelatory, it manifests the ultimate ground of being and is not subject to error. Insofar as it deals with historical facts, including religious history, it is neither inspired nor infallible. Even the religion of the biblical writers, Tillich would say, is imperfect. Religion, the reception of revelation, is always inadequate. As a human act, it belongs to the realm of history. Just as the Jews of Old Testament times were not immune from religious error, so too the biblical writers were capable of distorting the revelations which came their way. They were not exempt from the limitations of their own abilities and temperament nor from the unhealthy influence of their secular and religious environment.[28] Thus, the true message of the final revelation, the Christian kerygma, is not the arithmetical sum of the religious ideas which can be found in the Bible. The

---

[25] *Ibid.*, p. 130; cf. pp. 3, 36.
[26] *Ibid.*, p. 117.
[27] See Mollegen, *op. cit.*, p. 237.
[28] See *BRSUR*, pp. 21–22.

sacred writers did not receive the divine message in all its purity.

The Bible, Tillich insists, is not all of a piece. There is a higher level of revelation in the New Testament than in the Old, and even in the New Testament not all parts are of equal value. The high point is the religious picture of Jesus communicated through the interpreted events of the Gospel story and the semimythological reflections of John and Paul. The Gospel, in its main lines, shows us the career of a man completely submissive to the divine demands, surrendering himself even to the death of the cross. St. Paul expresses the significance of these events through the symbolism of a pre-existent spiritual being who takes on the form of a servant.[29] St. John, teaching the lesson of the crucifixion, presents Jesus as saying, "He who believes in me does not believe in *me. . . ."*[30] In this vision of a man totally transparent to the divine we have, in Tillich's opinion, the final and unsurpassable revelation.

But even in the New Testament, Tillich would concede, the gold of revelation is mixed with dross. There is evidence of an idolatrous exaltation of Jesus to a semidivine status. In the miracle narratives of the later New Testament traditions, Tillich detects the incursions of a demonic supernaturalism.[31]

Tillich, therefore, finds it possible to use the Bible insofar as it is revelatory, in order to criticize the Bible as a religious document. In virtue of what he calls the "Protestant principle"—that is, the refusal to exalt anything finite to the level of ultimate concern—he feels entitled to reject certain elements in the Bible itself. "Protestant theology protests in the name of the Protestant principle against the identification of our ulimate concern with any creation of the church, including the biblical writings insofar as their witness to what

[29] See "A Reinterpretation of the Doctrine of the Incarnation," *art. cit.,* 135; cf. Phil. 2:5 ff.

[30] *ST*, I, p. 136; cf. Jn. 12:44.

[31] See *ibid.*, p. 115; cf. p. 15.

is really ultimate concern is also a conditioned expression of their own spirituality."[32]

The Bible and Theology

Theology, in Tillich's synthesis, is clearly distinguished from revelation. It is not revelation, but rather a particular form of man's religious response to revelation. The theologian's task is to construct an ordered body of knowledge concerning revelation.

The Christian message, or kerygma, is, in Tillich's view, identical with the final revelation. Christian theology, therefore, is not the Christian message, but only a reflection on that message. "While the message itself is beyond our grasp and never at our disposal (though it might grasp us and dispose of us), its theological interpretation is an act of the church and of individuals within the church."[33] Religious orthodoxy—of which American fundamentalism is an instance —falls into the error of confusing a particular formulation of the message with the message itself. Such a confusion has "demonic" traits insofar as it ascribes eternal and infinite value to something which is, by its very nature, conditioned, finite, and temporal. Even the "neo-orthodox" theologians —in spite of their principle that "God is in heaven and man on earth"—have committed the mistake of trying to create an unconditioned theology. Barth, while laudably attempting to focus attention on the eternal kerygma, has allowed his work to become tainted with what Tillich might call the heresy of orthodoxy.[34]

Theology, insofar as it is a reflection on revelation, must be based on revelation. The sources of Christian theology are the documents of the final revelation which occurred in Jesus as the Christ. In opposition to the neo-orthodox, Tillich maintains that there are other Christian sources than the

[32] *Ibid.*, p. 37.
[33] *Ibid.*, p. 52.
[34] See *ibid.*, pp. 3, 52.

Bible, such as, for example, ecclesiastical Tradition. But the Bible is the basic source, for it is the original document about the events upon which the Christian Church is founded.[35]

In addition to sources, theology must have a norm, that is, a criterion in terms of which the sources are evaluated and interpreted.[36] The norm, as the formal element in theology, must itself be derived from the sources. If the norm were taken from philosophy or science, one could have a philosophy of religion, but not a genuine theology.

The Bible is not, never has been, and could not itself be the theological norm. For one thing, we cannot learn from the biblical books that they are canonical. The canon of the Bible, therefore, must be determined by something other than the Bible alone. The history of Christianity has shown certain variations of opinion about the limits of the biblical canon. These variations—which Tillich regards as a healthy sign of life and freedom—are due to varying conceptions of the theological norm. Even with respect to books acknowledged as canonical, they have never in practice been treated as all having equal authority. The Old Testament, Tillich observes, has never been directly normative; it has been measured by the New. And even the New Testament has never been equally influential in all its parts.[37]

Tillich is sharply critical of evangelicist biblicism, which attempts to erect the Bible into a self-sufficient norm. Such an attitude, he maintains, is sheer self-deception. The solitary reader of the Bible is more dependent on the Church than he is usually aware. He has received the Bible as preserved by the Church, as presented to him by the Church, and as interpreted by the Church, "even if this interpretation comes to him simply by way of the accepted translation into his own language."[38] It is quite impossible for the contemporary reader of the Bible to leap over two thousand years of Church history and enter into the situation of Matthew or Paul. In

[35] See *ibid.,* pp. 34–35.
[36] See *ibid.,* p. 47.
[37] See *ibid.,* p. 50.
[38] *Ibid.,* p. 48.

point of fact, Tillich observes, the "biblical" theology of the evangelicists is heavily indebted to the dogmatic developments of post-Reformation theology. "Through historical scholarship the difference between the dogmatic teaching of most American evangelistic churches and the original meaning of the biblical texts can easily be shown."[39]

Thus, the norm of theology, although primarily based on the Bible, is not the Bible, nor is it derived from the Bible alone. Historically, the theological norm has always been derived from an encounter between the Bible and the Church. Ecclesiastical Tradition, according to Tillich, plays an indispensable part in the establishment of the theological norm. He does not, however, admit the right of Church authorities to dictate to theologians what their norm should be.[40]

In the concrete, what is the norm of theology? In answer to this question Tillich distinguishes between a negative norm, or critical principle, and a positive norm. We have already mentioned the critical principle in connection with Tillich's evaluation of Scripture: it is the axiom that no finite object should be identified with that which concerns us ultimately. This principle suffices to exclude false theologies, but does not give us the true one. The positive element in the norm is the particular way in which that which concerns us ultimately manifests itself. Since the final revelation is the manifestation of God in Jesus as the Christ, the appearance of Jesus as the Christ is the positive norm for Christian theology.

The total norm, taken in its positive and negative aspects, is the criterion for using all the sources of systematic theology. The norm for the use of Scripture is the final manifestation of what concerns us ultimately in the *biblical* picture of Jesus as the Christ.[41]

Every theologian, even the "biblical" theologian, must take cognizance of the theological norm. Biblical theology should not be treated as though it were a profane discipline. In its

[39] *Ibid.*, p. 37.
[40] See *ibid.*, pp. 50–52.
[41] See *ibid.*, pp. 48–50.

"material" aspect—if it be permissible to introduce a Scholastic term not found in Tillich's exposition—it is a historico-critical discipline, concerned with philological and exegetical problems. But the biblical theologian cannot stop on the scientific level. "Formally" as a theologian he must unite philology with faith and devotion; he must give a genuinely theological appraisal and interpretation of biblical doctrine with reference to the norm of theology. It is exceedingly difficult to strike a proper balance between these two points of view, the critical and the pneumatic. But sound biblical theology is of inestimable importance. "Only such free historical work, united with the attitude of ultimate concern, can open the Bible to the systematic theologian as his basic source."[42]

Just as biblical theology is dependent on philology and history for its contents, so systematic theology derives its material mainly from biblical theology. Systematic theology is the effort to construct a methodical synthesis of Christian doctrine appropriate to the needs of a given age and culture. The precise principles governing the theological synthesis will vary, to some extent, from century to century. For the purposes of his own system, Tillich formulates the theological norm in terms of the "New Being" which became manifest in Jesus as the Christ. This norm is basically biblical, since it is inspired by the Pauline concept of the "new creation." Thus formulated, the norm of systematic theology is adapted to the present state of culture and society. It points to the Christian message as the answer to the anxieties and needs of our age which is haunted by the fear of self-estrangement, dissolution, and conflict.[43]

If it be objected that systematic theology, as he conceives and practices it, is not fully biblical, Tillich defends himself by calling attention to the precedent set by the biblical authors themselves. Textual criticism, he points out, makes it clear that they used and transformed the categories and sym-

[42] *Ibid.*, p. 36.
[43] See *ibid.*, p. 49.

bols current in their own religious and cultural tradition.[44]
The work of adaptation was continued by the primitive
Church—and quite properly so. Tillich repudiates the rigid
biblicism expounded by Ritschl and Harnack, who accused
the early Church of having betrayed biblical religion by relating it positively to the concerns of Graeco-Roman culture.
What Harnack called the Hellenization of the Gospel was a
necessary step, both because the Gospel had to be introduced
into the Hellenistic world and because the discovery of the
ontological question by the Greek mind is universally relevant. "On this point, the early church was right, however
questionable its concrete solutions may have been, and its
nineteenth-century critics were wrong."[45]

This last observation brings us to a final criticism of biblicism with which we may conclude our summary of Tillich's
views on the relations between the Bible and theology. The
biblicists vainly seek to construct a theology which would
avoid the ontological question. Such a theology, according
to Tillich, is impossible. Since theology deals with our ultimate concern, it cannot escape the question of being, any
more than can philosophy. Even the Bible, Tillich points out,
describes the structure of experience in ontological terms.
Not only the sapiential books and the theological meditations
of John and Paul, but even the Synoptic Gospels abound in
terms—such as time, law, life, love, and knowledge—pregnant
with ontological significance.

It is surprising how casually theological biblicists use a term
like "history" when speaking of Christianity as a historical
religion or of God as the "Lord of history." They forget
that the meaning they connect with the word "history" has
been formed by thousands of years of historiography and
philosophy of history. They forget that historical being is one
kind of being in addition to others and that, in order to
distinguish it from the word "nature," for instance, a general
vision of the structure of being is presupposed. They forget
that the problem of history is tied up with the problems of

---

[44] See Mollegen, *op. cit.*, p. 237.
[45] *BRSUR*, p. 60.

time, freedom, accident, purpose, etc. . . . The theologian must take seriously the meaning of the terms he uses. . . . Therefore, the systematic theologian must be a philosopher in critical understanding even if not in creative power.[46]

Thus, Tillich, while relying on the Bible as the basic source of the final revelation, directly opposes the narrow biblicism which has tended to stunt the growth of Protestant theology in the past. Against Pascal and many Protestant fideists he loudly proclaims that the God of Abraham, Isaac, and Jacob is the same as the God of the philosophers.[47] Tillich has been bold enough to undertake a statement of the Christian message in fully ontological terms. However one may appraise the results of his efforts, he has unquestionably made a great contribution to the revival of metaphysical thinking within Protestant circles in our day.

Evaluation

For the Catholic reader the most disconcerting element in Tillich's treatment of the Bible, as in other areas of his thought, is his total rejection of the supernatural. His position in this regard radically affects his entire understanding of the Christian revelation. The Bible, for him, is not a supernaturally inspired book, nor does it contain revealed precepts, doctrines, or history. The biblical account of man's creation and Fall is valid as symbolism, but tells us nothing about the prehistoric past. Even the Incarnation and the redemption, which for classical Christianity constitute the central message of the Bible, are not, in Tillich's view, events which actually occurred. While admitting that these terms have mythical value in symbolizing the union of human existence with its creative ground, he refuses to accept them as properly descriptive of what objectively transpired. The notion of a unique ontological union between God and creature, such as underlies the traditional doctrines of the Incarnation,

[46] *ST*, I, p. 21.
[47] See *BRSUR*, p. 85.

the Mystical Body, and sanctifying grace, in Tillich's eyes is idolatrous. His so-called Protestant principle is but one expression of his conviction that there can be no *communicatio idiomatum* between God and created natures.

Although Tillich continues to speak of the Christian revelation as "final," his conception of Christianity has little in common with what is usually understood by that term. In the words of one Protestant critic:

> If Tillich is right, the objective faith of the apostles and of the great company of Christian witnesses throughout the ages was wrong, and he plainly tells us so. . . . There is, for Tillich, no personal God who *objectively is*, who rules the nations and our lives, and who has judged us and saved us in Christ Jesus by his own coming into the world, being crucified, and being raised from the grave. Nor is there, for him, any life after death for us all, and thus no eventual solution to the tragedies and evils of our existence.[48]

To go into Tillich's reasons for excluding the supernatural would take us beyond the limits of the present study. In part they are philosophical. Since he does not admit the analogy of being as understood by Scholastic philosophers, he does not conceive of God as the Absolute Being, subsisting in himself, fully distinct from creatures. Rather, God is for him the immanent-transcendent ground of finite being. For Tillich, therefore, it seems repugnant that God should act on creatures externally, as an efficient cause, or that he should preferentially unite himself to some rather than others. To assert any such intervention, he maintains, is to degrade God to the status of a particular, finite being—one which acts upon, or unites with, others existing alongside of itself.

To many of his critics it has seemed that, in his rejection of the supernatural, Tillich inevitably falls into a sort of naturalism. This criticism has been made from the Catholic side by Gustave Weigel, S.J., and from the Protestant side by Nels Ferré. It has also been made from a nontheistic point of view by J. H. Randall, who shrewdly observes that "revela-

---

[48] Nels F. S. Ferré, review of *BRSUR*, in *Christian Century*, 72 (1955), 1273.

tion" for Tillich "would seem to be a symbol for the power of reason to do what revelation notoriously does."[49] Sometimes Tillich himself refers to his system as "self-transcending or ecstatic naturalism,"[50] a term which suggests that he is basically a naturalist, though not of the reductionist stamp. But if Tillich is a naturalist, it is not because he wants to be. His constant endeavor has been to find a middle path between naturalism and supernaturalism. He has affirmed: "My thinking is not naturalistic. Naturalism and supernaturalism provoke each other and should be removed together."[51]

While Tillich's blanket rejection of the supernatural order is clearly unacceptable to the Catholic, it should be remarked that his critique of "supernaturalism" contains elements of great worth. It is true, for example, that naturalism tends to generate, by way of reaction, an unwholesome supernaturalism. Efforts to demonstrate the reality of the supernatural with quasi-mathematical exactitude from alleged violations of physical laws have all too often been based on an uncritical acceptance of rationalistic presuppositions. As Tillich puts it: "A kind of rationalist irrationalism develops in which the degree of absurdity in a miracle story becomes the measure of its religious value. The more impossible, the more revelatory!"[52] Tillich renders a valuable service in stressing that antinaturalism of this sort does small honor to God, and that the prodigy-aspect of miracles should not be allowed to overshadow their function as religious signs. Thus far he is in line with biblical thinking. The notion of miracle, as found for example in Exodus, is hardly equivalent to the violation of a physical law. As G. E. Wright has said: "In the Bible a miracle is something quite different. It is any spectacular happening or 'wonder' which is a 'sign' of God's working."[53]

---

[49] "The Ontology of Paul Tillich," Kegley and Bretall, *op. cit.*, p. 149.

[50] *Ibid.*, p. 341.

[51] From a letter to G. Weigel, S.J.; see above, p. 23.

[52] *ST*, I, p. 115.

[53] "The Faith of Israel," *The Interpreter's Bible* (Nashville: Abingdon, 1952), I, p. 366.

Beginning with the time of Newman, many Catholic authors have pointed out the inadequacy of defining miracles as though they were simply contraventions of the laws of nature, and the urgency of restoring the traditional emphasis on the religious and revelatory dimension.[54] Miracles, according to this conception, are astonishing events in which contingent causes are raised to a higher pitch of efficacy, producing effects which betoken the kingdom of God. Normally, at least, these wonders admit of a twofold interpretation—like the heavenly voice which the Jews explained as thunder (Jn. 12:29). But the whole context of a miracle is such that the religious-minded inquirer is able to recognize the direct activity of God. Such a view of miracles embodies a supernaturalism which is the reverse of antinaturalistic. It affirms that nature, instead of being a completely self-enclosed system, is open to the intervention of a higher Liberty, and that God can make use of created agencies to bestow gifts that are divine.

A similar critique may be made of Tillich's comments on inspiration. He rightly rejects the "supernaturalistic" view which would depict God as dictating the Bible or as substituting his own activity for the natural processes of the human mind. Inspiration is indeed—to use Tillich's own term—essentially ecstatic. That is to say, it implies that the rational structure of the mind is preserved and elevated, although transcended. It is quite true that some theologians, wishing to stress the divine authorship of the Bible, have pictured scriptural inspiration as a "demonic" possession of the mind by God. But no such charge can be made against official Catholic teaching or against the doctrine of St. Thomas. Aquinas ceaselessly emphasized the fact that God respects the freedom and rationality of the human author. Strictly scriptural inspiration, in the Thomistic view, does not involve any infusion of new information. It does not dispense the author

---

[54] This point of view is well expressed by André Liégé, O.P., "Réflexions théologiques sur le miracle," *Pensée scientifique et foi chrétienne* (Paris: Fayard, 1953), pp. 206–18. See also the accompanying bibliography, p. 223.

from gathering his facts and forming his conceptions by natural methods, nor does it prevent him from expressing himself according to the thought-patterns and idioms of his own age and culture. For this reason, St. Thomas explains, the hagiographers "more commonly spoke about matters which could be known by human reason, and not, as it were, in the name of God, but in their own name (*ex persona propria*), although with the assistance of the divine light."[55]

Thus, Tillich's attack on supernaturalism is directed less against the perennial Catholic doctrine than against the rationalistic distortions which tended to infect Christian apologetics in the era of Newtonian scientism. The same may be said of Tillich's biblical theology in general. He is mainly concerned with refuting errors and exaggerations which have arisen in the past few centuries, especially that radical biblicism which is distinctively Protestant. Catholics, who have never looked on the Bible as a self-sufficient source of revelation, can concur in many of Tillich's strictures on biblicism.

As regards the authorship of Scripture, the comments on inspiration in the preceding paragraphs indicate both the justice and the exaggeration in Tillich's views. He is on solid ground when he protests against a "monophysitism" which would ignore the role of the human author. He is right in insisting that the Bible did not drop down from heaven without any relation to the human situation, but that it reflects the patient pedagogy by which God gradually prepared mankind for the fullness of revelation in Christ. But Tillich goes to the opposite extreme and falls into a sort of inverse monophysitism. He tends to overlook the divine element in Holy Scripture, and in effect denies that it is the word of God. Thus, he needlessly repudiates an article of faith as

---

[55] St. Thomas Aquinas, *Summa theologiae*, I–II, q. 174, a. 2 ad 3. The Thomistic doctrine of scriptural inspiration is admirably expounded by P. Synave, O.P., and P. Benoit, O.P., *Prophecy and Inspiration*, trans. A. Dulles, S.J., and T. L. Sheridan, S.J. (New York: Desclée, 1961).

ancient and sacred as Christianity itself, and leaves the Christian believer without authoritative guidance.

Tillich does well, once again, in refusing to interpret the Bible with a literalism that would be sheerly verbalistic. The Catholic tradition has always recognized that Holy Scripture, in its literal meaning (*sensus litteralis*), is rich in imaginative, poetic, and figurative features. In recent years, moreover, the typical and secondary senses of Scripture have been made the object of intense theological study. As regards the historical sections of the Bible, every Catholic exegete would agree with Tillich's assertion that they are not "pure history" as conceived in the secular tradition of post-Renaissance times. In order to ascertain the precise qualities of biblical history, one would have to make a more detailed analysis of the individual books than Tillich has done. As for the Gospels, there is no doubt that the evangelists wrote as witnesses to their faith, eager to convey the religious significance of the events they related. But it should also be noted that they attach great importance to the reality of some of these events. St. Paul, likewise, goes to great pains to establish that the resurrection was an objective occurrence, attested by competent witnesses. He even states that, if Jesus had not truly risen from the dead, the Christian's faith would be a miserable deception (1 Cor. 15:1–19).

Tillich unduly minimizes the historical elements in the Bible. He even proclaims that "theology does not imply factual assertions," since particular occurrences do not concern us ultimately.[56] Yet, he solemnly affirms, as we have seen, that there was a Jesus who lived on earth and spoke with his disciples. In making this assertion, is he not in fact relying somewhat on the results of modern biblical criticism, which generally affirms that there is a historical "core" to the Gospel story? Dorothy Emmet, who puts this question, remarks that Tillich seems to want "to have it both ways."[57] More fundamentally: Does the question whether Jesus was a historical

[56] See *ST*, I, p. 130; cf. above, p. 164.
[57] "Epistemology and the Idea of Revelation," Kegley and Bretall, *op. cit.*, p. 213.

character fall within the province of theology? If so, Tillich must admit that theology and history can overlap, and that theologians and historians, operating within their own proper fields, might contradict each other. If not, he has no right to maintain as a theologian that Jesus was a real person. Logically, he is bound to admit that the Christian revelation could be a product of merely subjective experience. It does not seem that Tillich has succeeded in erecting a theology which is fully insulated from empirical fact. The relations between Christianity and history are better indicated by Cullmann's suggestive formula, "revealed prophecy concerning history."

When he turns to the relations between the Bible and theology, Tillich makes many observations with which Catholics will agree. He clearly demonstrates that the Bible is not the sole source of Christian theology, and that ecclesiastical Tradition is a legitimate theological quarry. His assertion that "dependent revelation" continues to be given in the Church through the power of the Spirit inevitably reminds the Catholic of his own belief that there is a legitimate development of dogma.[58]

Catholics will agree also with Tillich's insistence that the Bible is not itself the theological norm. Neither the canon of Scripture nor a coherent interpretation of its contents can be arrived at without consulting ecclesiastical Tradition.[59] Tillich even goes so far as to maintain that Church decisions have a certain normative force, although he does not grant that they are binding on theologians. The Catholic, of course, accepts the Church's claim to teach with divine authority.

[58] Cf. G. Tavard, "The Unconditional Concern," *Thought*, 28 (1953), 244.

[59] In this connection it is interesting to observe how frequently the councils, in their authoritative interpretations of sacred texts, invoke the witness of Catholic tradition. The expression, "*quemadmodum Ecclesia catholica ubique diffusa semper intellexit*," or its equivalent, recurs frequently. For examples, see Denzinger-Schönmetzer, nn. 223, 1514, 1740, 3054.

Tillich does well to emphasize that Christian doctrine cannot be a static thing. The radical biblicist, in his unwillingness to depart from the letter of the Bible, is unfaithful to its spirit. As Tillich points out, the Gospel cannot have its due impact unless it is presented in ways suitable to the needs and capacities of each successive generation. Although Tillich's conception of the kerygma does not quite coincide with the Catholic notion of the "data of revelation," his efforts to distinguish between the kerygma and theology will prove stimulating to many Catholic theologians. His emphasis on the "answering" function of systematic theology is in full accord with Catholic teaching on doctrinal development and adaptation. As Father Weigel has written: "The Tillichian principle of correlation is not a new discovery but only an urgent exhortation to use efficiently the principle always functioning in the theological enterprise, though it often functions with less than desirable energy."[60]

Finally, Tillich gives a very sound exposition of the relations of biblical theology to scientific criticism, on the one hand, and to systematic theology on the other. Biblical theology, as he rightly holds, is an intermediate discipline, essentially ordered toward systematic theology. Catholics, accustomed to the dogmatic syntheses of the Scholastic doctors, generally recognize that theology cannot confine itself to merely biblical categories. The Christian message should be set forth, as far as possible, in genuinely metaphysical terms, answering to the ontological hunger of the human mind.

But speculative theology is a delicate enterprise, never entirely free from the risk of denaturing the Gospel. One must be on guard against trying to squeeze divine revelation into any man-made framework of metaphysical speculation. The great Scholastic theologians recognized this. While making use of Platonic and Aristotelian conceptual schemes, they allowed the data of revelation to correct, enlarge, and inwardly transform their philosophical categories.[61] They saw, likewise, that

---

[60] See above, p. 49.

[61] The transfiguration of Platonic and Aristotelian philosophy under the impact of Christian dogma has been brilliantly sketched by

every metaphysical transposition of Christian teaching must, of its very nature, fall short of the divine message, grasped in faith. They were, therefore, content that their theological systems should echo, faintly but not unfaithfully, the truths of revelation.

It is here, more than anywhere else, that Tillich goes astray. Like the Scholastic doctors, he sets out to achieve a Christian wisdom. He brings an impressive array of philosophical tools to the task. Familiar with nearly the whole range of Western philosophy, he makes particularly fruitful use of modern German speculation. The idealism of Schelling, the subjectivism of Schleiermacher, the phenomenalism of Otto, and the existentialism of Heidegger all provide him with valuable insights. But he does not sufficiently purify his philosophical categories in the light of the revealed message. Instead, he lets the exigencies of his philosophical system determine in advance what God's revelation can and cannot be. The biblical message is reduced to the dimensions of an all-too-human philosophy.

Because of this initial error in method, Tillich's efforts to translate the "primitive personalism" of biblical religion into a sophisticated theological scheme are vitiated at the source. Inevitably, the living God of Abraham and Isaac loses his distinctive traits and becomes merged into an amorphous, "transpersonal" ground of being—the product of philosophical speculation. In the name of his private metaphysical theories, Tillich denies that God has really performed those deeds of love which have always been regarded as the very substance of the biblical teaching.

E. Gilson in *The Spirit of Mediaeval Philosophy* (New York: Scribner's, 1936), especially the last two chapters.

VIII

RAYMOND SMITH, O.P.

Faith without Belief

Broadly speaking, two elements can be distinguished in Dr. Paul Tillich's concept of faith. One line of thought seems to be saying, in existential terminology for the most part, what the Catholic Church herself teaches. Another aspect of this notion of faith seems to be contradicting, even denying outright, what is regarded as sound Catholic doctrine. Since the writings of Professor Tillich have had a definite appeal to our age, one would be unrealistic not to examine his insights into the problem of faith and the modern man.[1]

Dr. Tillich has given us a clear enough definition of the term from his point of view: "Faith is the state of being ultimately concerned; the dynamics of faith are the dynamics of man's ultimate concern." Whatever it is that claims man, if it is truly ultimate "it demands the total surrender of him who accepts this claim, and it promises total fulfillment, even if all other claims have to be subjected to it or rejected in its name." When man places his faith in what is truly ultimate, he has true faith; if in anything less, for example, the nation, it is idolatrous faith.[2]

---

[1] See C. Kegley and R. Bretall, editors, *The Theology of Paul Tillich* (New York: Macmillan, 1952). Pages 3–21 contain extremely valuable autobiographical reflections of Dr. Tillich. At one point he remarks: "Nevertheless, I was and am a theologian, because the existential question of our ultimate concern and the existential answer of the Christian message are and always have been predominant in my spiritual life" (p. 10).

[2] See *DF*, pp. 1, 12. In fairness to Dr. Tillich and his critics on

Moving quickly to the center of Tillich's position on true faith, we can discover it from his definition of an act of faith which he says is "an act of a finite being who is grasped by and turned to the infinite."[3] The finite being is man. The infinite, in religious terms, is God. Faith is an existential encounter with the power of being-itself. Such an understanding of faith has that Protestant emphasis which insists on the truth that faith unites man to God or gives man the experience of Christ within his very being.

Tillich, however, is careful to avoid some extremes into which certain sects of Protestantism fell. Faith is not an emotion; nor is it something that destroys reason or is in conflict with reason; rather, faith "is a total and centered act of the personal self, the act of unconditional, infinite, and ultimate concern." In other words, faith is a function of the whole person, not some part of man, be it intellect, will, or emotion.[4]

All of this is in harmony with Catholic teaching, although the faithful sometimes miss the points made by Dr. Tillich. Were an average Catholic asked to define faith, no doubt the answer would be the standard catechism one: A virtue by which we believe the truths which God has revealed. Although the answer is correct, it can be misleading. Faith thus defined seems merely some function of the mind assenting to a list of truths revealed by God and proposed as such by the Church. Yet, Protestantism can rightly point to the New Testament and show that such a meaning of faith is not central to the Gospels or the writings of St. Paul.[5]

---

the issue of faith, two observations of his are worth noting. At the end of *Dynamics of Faith* he writes: "Almost every word by which faith has been described . . . is open to new misinterpretations. This cannot be otherwise" (p. 126). In his treatment of "The Spiritual Presence," he warns: "These statements presuppose a full discussion of faith and love in order to be understandable. Such discussion could fill a large volume. I myself have dealt with faith and love, each in a small book" (*ST*, III, p. 129).

[3] *DF*, p. 16; cf. *ST*, I, p. 156; *CTB*, p. 172.

[4] See *DF*, pp. 8, 40.

[5] See A. Henry, editor, *The Virtues and States of Life* (Chicago: Fides, 1957), p. 48.

Christ simply asks for faith in himself. There is an encounter with Christ. The person is grasped by the personality and power of our Lord. Faith results. No question of a short course in dogma arises. In Tillich we see this idea stressed constantly. Something of that truth seems lost to many Catholics who too often receive only the benefits of theological conclusions without having studied the Bible.

Also, we can discern a great similarity and perhaps even agreement with Paul Tillich in his double notions of faith as being "ultimate concern" and the act of faith involving the whole man. In place of ultimate concern a Catholic would say that every man is seeking happiness, as indeed many pagan philosophers have said without the help of revelation. Happiness is man's ultimate concern, and obviously he can place it in many objects—even the apparently good and ultimate, as Tillich does in his understanding of faith. St. Thomas Aquinas tells us clearly how man rightly reaches his genuine ultimate concern: "The theological virtues direct man to supernatural happiness."[6]

In this citation we also note that St. Thomas says these virtues direct man; not merely man's intellect or will or emotions, but the whole man is directed by them to God. Thus, we are on common ground again with Dr. Tillich. Likewise, the personal encounter with God through faith is the constant doctrine of the Church and her theologians. St. Thomas has expressed this truth many times, for instance: "Christ works in two ways. First, inwardly, by himself, and thus he prepares man's will so that it wills good and hates evil";[7] "Grace causes faith. . . . God is always working man's justification, even as the sun is always lighting up the air."[8]

[6] *Summa theologiae*, I–II, q. 62, a. 3.
[7] *Ibid.*, III, q. 68, a. 4 ad 2.
[8] *Ibid.*, I–II, q. 4, a. 4 ad 3.

The Protestant Principle and Faith

Other affinities, as well as some divergences, can perhaps be better appreciated if Dr. Tillich's theory of "the Protestant principle" is explained. This principle must not be identified with any religious form at all, including Protestantism. Were that the case, then Protestantism would be complete with its treasury of eternal truths. Such cannot be the case. For one thing, the human situation is constantly changing, and man is assailed by doubts which he must face and be free to answer. In this sense, "Protestantism as a principle is eternal and a permanent criterion of everything temporal."[9]

On Tillich's terms, faith is not a gift from God which frees man from further investigation into the meaning of life; much less is it the royal road to a life hereafter, permitting one to ignore the responsibilities of his present earthly existence.[10] In order to appreciate the full implications inherent in the Protestant principle, as understood by Dr. Tillich, one must consider how he arrived at his interpretation of Protestantism and, consequently, at this aspect of his idea of faith.

A constant theme in Dr. Tillich's thought is his distinction between being and nonbeing, the finite and the infinite, the conditional and the unconditional.[11] Being-itself, the infinite, the unconditional, are most adequately described by the expression, "the ground of being." Since the ground of being is in and through everything and working out its own existence, history becomes of paramount importance in Tillich's notion of faith. He writes: "History became the central problem of my theology and philosophy."[12] History, however, is not to be merely a record of past events, but it is viewed and

[9] *PE*, p. xii.
[10] See *CTB*, pp. 171–78.
[11] E.g., *PE*, pp. 32–51; *ST*, I, pp. 186–204; *ST*, II, pp. 10–12; *ST*, III, p. 284; *TC*, pp. 22–26.
[12] *PE*, p. xvii.

pondered from the point of view of *kairos,* the right time. "*Kairos* in its *unique* and universal sense is, for Christian faith, the appearing of Jesus as the Christ."[13]

Each moment in history has its own decision to make and this requires a new theonomy, that is, a new directing of an age to the divine.[14] From a description of theonomy one can see why faith becomes, for Tillich, a kind of tension. "Theonomy asserts that the superior law is, at the same time, the innermost law of man himself, rooted in the divine ground which is man's own ground: the law of life transcends man, although it is, at the same time, his own."[15] Only when man attains the really real, the ground of being, will he have faith in the Tillichian connotation.

> Faith is an ecstatic transcending of reality in the power of that which cannot be derived from the whole of reality and cannot be approached by ways which belong to the whole of reality. . . . Hence, we are led to the result that faith and realism, just because of their radical tension, belong together. For faith implies an absolute tension and cannot be united with any attitude in which the tension is weakened; . . . self-transcending realism accepts the tension.[16]

For Professor Tillich everything we do and have done in history is ambiguous in character, and all is subject to what he calls "the law of historical tragedy."[17] He finds it much more realistic to announce "the tragic destiny of all human truth and goodness" than to pretend that man has some body of eternal truths.[18] Just how tense faith can make us, if we fully realize the actual state of affairs, is vividly stated:

> Protestantism must proclaim the judgment that brings assurance by depriving us of all security; the judgment that declares us whole in the disintegration and cleavage of soul and community; the judgment that affirms our having truth

---

[13] *Ibid.,* p. 46; the emphasis is Tillich's.
[14] See *PE,* p. 44.
[15] *Ibid.,* pp. 56–57.
[16] *Ibid.,* pp. 67–68.
[17] *Ibid.,* p. 190.
[18] See *loc. cit.*

in the very absence of truth (even of religious truth); the judgment that reveals the meaning of our life in the situation in which all the meaning of life has disappeared.[19]

The Protestant principle for Tillich is never idle. Its work is never finished. No one has all the answers to the meaning of life, not only because the concept of life is so broad and sweeping, but also since life itself is ever changing. The Protestant principle has always existed in the minds of thinkers daring enough to challenge the complacency of an age. Moreover, Tillich does not hesitate to see the Protestant principle outliving Protestantism itself.[20]

From these brief observations on the Protestant principle, the following three considerations can be made: Dr. Tillich rejects the idea of faith as belief; his doctrine on the Christ will be bound up with the concept of the finite, the ground of being, and history; faith will include elements of uncertainty and doubt.

Faith vs. Belief

Dr. Tillich seems fairly convinced that faith "is continually being confused with belief in something for which there is no evidence."[21] He has put his general concern very vividly in these questions: "Do I really believe? Is not my belief a transitory suppression of doubt and of cognitive honesty? And, if I do not really believe, is my salvation lost? The terrible inner struggles between the will to be honest and the will to be saved show the failure of doctrinal self-salvation."[22]

In this sense it is perfectly natural for Professor Tillich to say that the Christian "should not even have faith in the Bible."[23] Such being the case, then one wonders what is his understanding of revelation. Some of Tillich's statements on

[19] *Ibid.*, p. 204.
[20] See *ibid.*, p. 163.
[21] *ST*, III, p. 130; cf. *TC*, p. 47; *DF*, p. 31.
[22] *ST*, II, p. 85.
[23] *DF*, p. 32.

revelation seem close enough to the teaching of the Church. One such definition is: "A revelation is a special and extraordinary manifestation which removes the veil from something which is hidden in a special and extraordinary way." Nor would a Catholic theologian probably quarrel with his explanation: "Whatever is essentially mysterious cannot lose its mysteriousness even when it is revealed. . . . God has revealed himself and . . . God is an infinite mystery."[24]

Gradually Tillich returns to a familiar theme: "Revelation is the manifestation of what concerns us ultimately," and two very important observations: "Revelation, as revelation of the mystery which is our ultimate concern, is invariably revelation for someone in a concrete situation of concern"; "There are no revealed doctrines, but there are revelatory events and situations which can be described in doctrinal terms."[25]

What seems to be at issue basically is that tremendous problem of biblical inspiration. Dr. Tillich has no separate treatise on this difficult subject, although one might compose an interesting volume by checking his many writings on this one point. He does say this: "The Bible does not contain words of God . . . but it can and in a unique way has become the 'Word of God.' "[26] Catholic Scripture scholars certainly do not hold that any version of the Bible is the very word of God or even that such a mode of speech could accurately describe the question of God's role in the composition of the Bible. Also, Catholic theologians do not claim that the Bible has a neat package of dogmas which one simply learns and has faith by belief in them. Thus, Tillich and the Catholic position may not be so far apart as at first seems.

What would seem to make the positions even closer is the fact that Tillich's notion of faith is really an insistence that God, and not a list of doctrines, is the object of faith. However, the Catholic position cannot possibly eliminate belief. The distinction made by St. Thomas includes Tillich's asser-

[24] *ST*, I, pp. 108, 109.
[25] *Ibid.*, pp. 110, 111, 125.
[26] *ST*, III, p. 124.

tion, but then goes a step beyond. Aquinas points out that God is the formal or immediate, direct object of faith. All else relative to God falls under the material object of faith. To make his claim clear, St. Thomas refers to God in this context as First Truth. Then he takes up the question of propositions, that is, putting the truths about God into sentences. He says this must be done, not because of God, but because of man, since "the mode proper to the human intellect is to know the truth by synthesis and analysis."[27]

With a degree of reluctance, Dr. Tillich does employ the word unbelief. This is one of the factors in man's estrangement from God. Such estrangement will be overcome by accepting Christ as the "New Being." Jesus as the Christ is the New Being because there are no traces of estrangement between Christ and God. Never does Christ remove himself from the center of the divine being. Always God is the subject of his ultimate concern. Thus, Christ escapes the estrangement of unbelief. Further, Christ conquers the many temptations to self-elevation and concupiscence.[28] Man's task is to realize the example of Christ in himself. "To say that Jesus as the Christ is the concrete place where the Logos becomes visible is an assertion of faith and can be made only by him who is grasped by the Christ as the manifestation of his ultimate concern."[29]

Since it would exceed the limits of this article to examine in detail what Dr. Tillich understands the nature of Christ to be, as well as the significance of his death and resurrection, we need only remark that surely Christ is most intimately involved in the Christian's faith. Beyond that statement the area of agreement with Dr. Tillich's doctrine on Christ is rather limited.

[27] *Summa theologiae*, I–II, q. 1, a. 2; see also a. 1.
[28] See *ST*, II, pp. 47–55.
[29] *BRSUR*, p. 76.

Uncertainty and Doubt

The third point noted above was the inclusion of uncertainty and doubt in the act of faith by Tillich.

> Faith is certain insofar as it is an experience of the holy. But faith is uncertain insofar as the infinite to which it is related is received by a finite being. This element of uncertainty in faith cannot be removed, it must be accepted.[30]

> Faith includes both an immediate awareness of something unconditional and the courage to take the risk of uncertainty upon itself. Faith says "Yes" in spite of the anxiety of "No." It does not remove the "No" of doubt and the anxiety of doubt; it does not build a castle of doubt-free security—only a neurotically distorted faith does that—but it takes the "No" of doubt and the anxiety of insecurity into itself.[31]

The same point is made in this way:

> God, in the divine-human encounter, transcends man unconditionally. Faith bridges this infinite gap by accepting the fact that, in spite of it, the power of being is present, that he who is separated is accepted. Faith accepts "in spite of"; and out of the "in spite of" of faith the "in spite of" of courage is born.[32]

Doubt is implicit in every act of faith, according to Dr. Tillich. However, it is not a methodological doubt or that of a skeptic; rather, he calls it an existential doubt. Obviously, the point at issue is the very act of faith viewed mainly in its psychological aspects. Isolated in this way we can discover some grounds of agreement between Tillich and Aquinas. For instance, St. Thomas points out: "It is clear that imperfect knowledge belongs to the very nature of faith."[33] Then he cites the definition of St. Paul: "Now faith is the

[30] DF, p. 16.
[31] BRSUR, p. 61.
[32] CB, p. 172; cf. DF, p. 20.
[33] Summa theologiae, I–II, q. 67, a. 3; I–II, q. 2, a. 1.

substance of things to be hoped for, the evidence of things that are not seen" (Heb. 11:1). Later in the *Summa*, St. Thomas takes up the problem along psychological lines, expounding the definition of St. Augustine, namely, "To believe is to think with assent." St. Thomas points out that, when the mind of man lacks a clear sight of the truth, he deliberates, as happens in doubt, opinion, and suspicion. Since the object of faith is not clearly seen, man does experience a certain cogitation of the mind. Like the eye, the intellect wants to see its object clearly, but as a wayfarer man must say with St. Paul: "We see now through a mirror in an obscure manner. . . . Now I know in part" (1 Cor. 13:12).

Nevertheless, the believer does not have any lack of firmness to believe on the part of God revealing. True, even saints were assailed by doubts; but that is quite different, it seems, from Dr. Tillich's understanding of the act of faith. To make an act of faith "in spite of" the possibility of being wrong and in so grave a matter seems foolishness rather than prudence. Further, it would indicate that the person was suspecting the genuineness of his being grasped by the ground of being and would lead him no further towards a solution to the meaning of life than before the "revelatory experience." For the Catholic, the act of faith is not a hypothetical act, but a genuine conviction made possible by the grace of Christ.

The crucial point with Dr. Tillich's concept of faith is not with his penetrating analysis of the act of faith, but with other aspects which might be called peripheral but, nevertheless, which carry serious consequences for the Catholic. An important factor in Professor Tillich's thinking on faith is his desire to preserve human autonomy. He offers a definition with which a Catholic thinker would readily concur: "Autonomy means the obedience of the individual to the law of reason, which he finds in himself as a rational being."[34]

Dr. Tillich apparently finds submission to any type of authority unreasonable, because he fears it will destroy man's autonomous responsibility. As a result he must, of necessity,

[34] *ST*, I, p. 84.

reject the Catholic concept of papal infallibility.[35] Without attempting here to untie that knotty problem, one need only reply that, for the Catholic, such obedience is not unreasonable and one's freedom is not forfeited by accepting the doctrine that God teaches man through his Church.

Besides Dr. Tillich's concern over man's freedom, relative to accepting doctrines imposed by some authority, he has a fear which is well expressed in this sentence: "Faith as a set of passionately accepted and defended doctrines does not produce acts of love."[36] No doubt he has in mind not only religious persecutions, but also the sad plight of his native Germany under Hitler. Yet, one must ask Dr. Tillich to distinguish. Surely, if the doctrines are those of racism and hate, no love will result. If one means, on the other hand, the teachings of Christ, then only love should follow, for Christianity teaches that God is love.[37] Faith as including a list of beliefs need not be condemned outright simply because, on the natural level, some political system, such as Communism, proposes class hatred, or, on the supernatural plane, some individuals use religion as an excuse to suppress others.[38]

In spite of rejecting the idea of doctrines as relevant to faith, Dr. Tillich himself does use what he calls the biblical norm and finds this "unambiguously" stated in Deuteronomy 6:5: "You shall love the Lord your God with all your heart, and with all your soul, and with all your might." This expresses the character of genuine faith because it demands "total surrender to the subject of ultimate concern."[39]

This observation of Dr. Tillich's is of the greatest importance, for it is, in the final analysis, the command of love

[35] See *ST*, I, pp. 49, 84–85; *PE*, p. xvi; Kegley and Bretall, *op. cit.*, where he writes: "What I have called the 'Protestant principle' is, as I believe, the main weapon against every system of heteronomy" (p. 8); also see *ST*, III, pp. 166–67.

[36] *DF*, p. 113.

[37] See Mt. 5–7; 1 Jn. 4:8.

[38] Cf. *CEWR* where Dr. Tillich speaks of religions and quasi-religions.

[39] *DF*, p. 3.

repeated by Christ and achieved by his life. If this one doctrine is accepted, cannot the Catholic theologian say that the other doctrines are flowing from and related to this central norm? If the teachings of the Church are correctly understood, her dogmas are not meant to take man away from God, but to lead man to God, forever grateful for the teachings of the Bible which do provide us with much information on God and his providence over mankind.

No doubt Dr. Tillich's complaint that literalists distort the message of the Bible has validity. Few, if any, Catholic theologians would dispute with his demand that God be spoken of in analogical terms. However, one might question his meaning of symbols which leaves us with an extremely tenuous knowledge of God.

Although between Tillichian theology and the teachings of the Catholic Church often a giant gap does exist, one must not overlook the points of contact, or fail to profit from the insights of Paul Tillich, or least of all fail to capture the spirit of his ultimate concern for making the Christian message meaningful for our times.

It is commonplace to hear and to read that our age is one of crisis. Indeed, the inner struggles of so many men throughout the world recall that personal struggle of St. Augustine, preserved for us in his *Confessions*. Paul Tillich seems to paraphrase the most frequently quoted sentence from this book: "Thou madest us for thyself, and our heart is restless, until it repose in thee," when he writes: "The human heart seeks the infinite because that is where the finite wants to rest."[40] That rest is possible to the human heart even while it is on earth, not perfectly of course, but the effects of divine love in the heart produce peace and joy.

[40] *Ibid.*, p. 13.

PART THREE

The Knowledge of Revelation

The question, it seems to me, is not the distortion
of revelatory truth by speculative truth, but the
question is the conflict between revelatory experiences of a preparatory character, symbolized in
myths and conceptualized in metaphysics, and the
revelatory event, on which Christianity is based.
The existentialist approach implied in the metaphor encounter must be applied to all of them.
This leads to the problem of religious language
generally, the problem of symbol and myth.

Some Questions on Brunner's Epistemology

IX

GEORGE F. McLEAN, O.M.I.

Symbol and Analogy:
Tillich and Thomas

In order to appreciate the importance of Paul Tillich's thought it is necessary to note that his arrival in America came at a most opportune moment. By 1933 the great economic depression had sufficiently disenchanted men of the excessive optimism which had beguiled them into humanistic theism. The time was ripe for the return to a theocentric philosophy of religion. Unfortunately, the voices which announced this return were those of the neonaturalists speaking only of a God who was a process wholly immanent in the universe.[1] It was at this point that Tillich arrived upon the scene with the prophetic cry of Barthian neo-orthodoxy's "totally other" ringing in his ears. He set about re-echoing it in America, but only as translated into the terms of a philosophy grounded especially in Schelling and existentialism. This defense of a transcendent God has perhaps been his great contribution to the philosophy of religion in America. It has not replaced the older naturalistic conception, nor has it dissipated the antimetaphysical prejudices. But it has effectively eliminated the logical positivists in this field and orientated most minds toward an interest in some form of transcendence.

There is a danger for the prophet lest he overstate his truth. It would have been natural enough for Tillich's in-

---

[1] Cf. Henry Nelson Wieman, "Faith and Knowledge," *Christendom*, 1 (1936), 777–78; *American Philosophies of Religion* (Chicago: Willett, Clark, 1936), pp. 295 ff.

sistence on God's transcendence to be reflected in a radical agnosticism, for his "totally other" to be totally unknown and totally unknowable. But Tillich's is a much more balanced mind than this. He has seen the errors of most and, within the limits of his epistemology and ontology, attempts to overcome them. In the question of man's knowledge of the divine he does this by his notion of the symbol, or of the analogy of being to which he equates it.[2] "If the knowledge of revelation is called 'analogous,' this certainly refers to the classical doctrine of the *analogia entis* between the finite and the infinite. Without such an analogy nothing could be said about God."[3] For this reason Tillich has, of recent years, done considerable work on the notion of the symbol. He has attempted to restore to it as much reality as is possible, and in doing this has perhaps made a distinctive step toward the Thomistic position.

The importance of any such step becomes apparent if one considers many of the main differences between Catholic and Protestant theology to be reducible to their varying answers to the one basic philosophical question of whether the created can participate in the divine. The Church answers in the affirmative and proceeds to interpret ecclesiastical authority, the internal life of grace, and the sacraments as forms of this participation. Protestantism has answered in the negative and proceeds to reject each of these doctrines. It is of great interest, then, when a non-Catholic philosopher and theologian sets out to make the religious symbol something which "participates in the power of the divine to which it points."[4] The first step will be to investigate and evaluate the exact meaning Dr. Tillich has given to the symbol. It will then be possible to weigh the particular value of his conception of the religious symbol and to appreciate its im-

---

[2] Paul Tillich, Letter to G. Weigel, S.J., cited in *Theological Studies*, 11 (1950), 201: "I speak of symbolic knowledge and mean with it exactly what St. Thomas means with *analogia entis*. The reason I used symbol more than analogy is a methodological difference between St. Thomas and myself."

[3] *ST*, I, p. 131.

[4] *Ibid.*, p. 239.

plications as he employs it in the task for which he invented it, man's knowledge of God.

The Nature of Symbol in Tillich's Philosophy

Dr. Tillich approaches the symbol as something which has been lost to his contemporaries. It is not that they do not speak of it, but rather that they have made it simply equivalent to the sign. In order to restore the symbol, it is necessary to revive its distinctive notes. This has been his central task. There is, of course, a generic identity of sign and symbol, for both have the function of pointing beyond themselves to something else. But here the similarity ends. Signs, as such, "point to something different in which they do not participate at all."[5] In themselves they are quite empty, since all their reality and, consequently, all their meaning resides solely in the thing signified. It is true that they designate one particular reality, but they do this only because they are chosen for this purpose. What is more, this choice is entirely arbitrary, for signs have of themselves no essential or necessary relation whatsoever to that to which they point. Tillich exemplifies this by referring to the use of the letters of the alphabet in words and to the function of traffic signals. Their relation to the signified is completely extrinsic and arbitrary. For this reason they can be exchanged at will, with expediency as the only norm.[6]

Unfortunately, in recent times the expression "only a symbol" has come into vogue. The phrase is an example of semantic confusion, because what it really means is "only a sign." This is indicative of the general confusion by which all reality has been removed from the symbol. "Only a symbol" continues the error, and for this reason is strongly rejected by Dr. Tillich.[7] How is it that the symbol has been

[5] Paul Tillich, Letter to G. Weigel, S.J., see above, p. 55.

[6] See *PE*, p. 98.

[7] Paul Tillich, "Reply to Interpretation and Criticism," C. Kegley and R. Bretall, editors, *The Theology of Paul Tillich* (New York: Macmillan, 1952), pp. 334-35.

so reduced? Our author indicates three causes. First, there is the reduction of reality to empirical reality by many of the modern philosophies. Secondly, there is the simple confusion of terms just mentioned. Lastly, there has been the symbolic interpretation of religious language by modernism and Protestant Hegelianism, with the intention of dissolving its meaning.[8] These factors have steadily and effectively reduced the symbol to the position of the sign.

Tillich's symbol is intended to be truly different. It participates in the reality, the power, and the meaning of that to which it points and for which it stands.[9] In this way it goes beyond the object itself which is used, and even beyond the use of this object as a sign. By its newly acquired inherent power, it is placed nearer to the reality it expresses. This might be exemplified by the privileged position of a flag over a letter of the alphabet, and by the difference between the uses of words in liturgy and poetry and the use given them by the logical positivists.

It is evident, then, that an understanding of the nature of this restoration of the symbol lies in a determination of the new power it attributes to the symbol. The background of this idea lies in a conception of nature, a "new realism," which Tillich received from Rilke, Goethe, and especially Schelling. This seeks the power and meaning of nature within and through its objective, physical structures rather than separating the two. It seeks this power and meaning on a level which is prior to the cleavage of our world into subjectivity and objectivity, and "deeper" than the Cartesian dichotomy. But it is here that the great difficulty arises. For how is one "to penetrate into something 'nonsubjective' with categories of a subjective mind and into something 'nonobjective' with categories of objective reality"?[10]

With this question in mind Tillich viewed other modern work on the symbol and the myth. He was dissatisfied with

8 See ST, I, p. 241.

9 See Paul Tillich, "Religious Symbols and Our Knowledge of God," The Christian Scholar, 38 (1955), 189–90.

10 Loc. cit.

what he calls the negative theories or those attributing merely a subjective character to the symbol. Marx had a sociological conception of this type and derived the total reality of symbols from the will to power. Freud and Jung had similar psychological conceptions, which considered the symbol as a sublimation rising out of the unconscious. What Tillich disagreed with here was not the subjective element itself, but the recognition of this aspect alone.[11] For this reason he was also interested in what he called the positive theories of symbols. One of these is the cultural-morphological interpretation of symbols proposed by Oswald Spengler. It retained the subjective element, limited now to the selection of the symbol. But it went beyond mere subjectivism by considering this subjective factor in essential relation to the objective reference of symbols. This was part of a total philosophy according to which all cultural creations were symbols for a psychic and formative vital principle, but with a symbolism which was "broken" by their objective and empirical character.[12] The neo-Kantians proceeded further to produce the critical idealist theory of symbols, typified by Ernst Cassirer. He went so far as to identify the symbolic and the objective character of the symbol in such a way that cultural reality was symbolic reality and existed only in that form.[13]

Tillich would seem to have been searching for a tenable and consistent position between the negative and the positive theories, or rather, one which combined elements of both. He considered that the subjective aspect contributed to more than the mere choice of a symbol, but was not, of itself, sufficient. The objective aspect, on the other hand, was neither the total reality nor, of itself, symbolic. It could not be symbolic because reality in existence is fallen reality, which not only expresses but contradicts the true essence or nature of things. For this reason it is only in very special conditions that existing beings are symbolic. Until recently Tillich's

[11] See Paul Tillich, "The Religious Symbol," *Journal of Liberal Religion*, 2 (1940), 15–19.

[12] See *ibid.*, pp. 19–21.

[13] See *ibid.*, pp. 21–23.

work has been more concerned with this general context of
the symbol and with the German thought on the broken
and unbroken myth. However, in a number of later articles
he has centered his attention immediately on what is in fact
the central problem of analogy, namely, in what way is its
participation in the reality of the symbolized to be understood?[14] In point of time, this participation arises when the
natural reality of the symbol and the symbolic meaning and
power become bound together in a special way. In virtue of
this union the natural power of the symbol becomes the
necessary and, for the time, inseparable bearer of the power
of meaning of the symbolized.[15] The reality of this union
is then the reality of the symbol as such, and it consists in
both an objective and a subjective element. This has led
Tillich to a more complete study of these two elements of
the symbol.

On the objective level the symbol can be a word, idea, or
physical object; it can be anything at all. It is necessary, however, that its immediate and nonsymbolic nature have some
original affinity to the symbolic content which it is to contain. There must, then, be some objective predisposition.
Two of Tillich's examples may be of some help toward a
preliminary notion of the extent of this objective element.
One is that of water which is used in the purifying ceremony
of baptism becuse of its original cleansing power as a natural
element. A more interesting example is, as we shall see, his
use of the word "God," with what he considers to be its false
overtones of a highest being, in order to symbolize the divine,
conceived as the unconditional ground and abyss of all
being.[16] In actual use as a symbol, this objective reality is
both affirmed and denied. It must be affirmed, for it is the
basis for pointing beyond itself. But it must also be denied
in its proper meaning by that to which it points.[17] Since

---

[14] See Letter to G. Weigel, S.J., see above, pp. 53–55.

[15] See *PE*, p. 98.

[16] See Paul Tillich, "Symbol and Knowledge: A Response," *Journal of Liberal Religion*, 2 (1941), 294.

[17] See *ST*, I, p. 239.

there is this objective basis for the symbol, it cannot be considered to be merely subjective.

Nevertheless, the union of the special power to this object, in order to make it a symbol, also has a subjective basis, and it is a very considerable one indeed. Tillich considers it but natural that there should be one, since the purpose of symbols is to mediate between those who use them and the objects symbolized. In what does this subjective element consist? It consists in what he would term a creative encounter with reality.[18] This will be investigated further in a moment. But here it is necessary to observe two characteristics of this subjective element: it is both collective and unconscious. It is collective, since a symbol, to be of value, must be accepted by the group. It must be socially rooted and supported. For this reason, though a sign may be invented by an individual, it cannot become a symbol until it is accepted by the community.[19] The second characteristic of the subjective element is that it be subconscious. Since, as we shall see, the function of the symbol is not merely to represent something but to "open up" levels of reality and levels of the mind otherwise hidden,[20] the symbol must be born out of a creative encounter with reality, which takes place in the group or collective unconscious. The symbol is, then, born out of a group which acknowledges in this thing its own being.

The Origin and End of Symbol

What has just been said leads to one of the most prominent characteristics of the symbol as distinct from the sign. A symbol is not the result of mere subjective desire. It can neither be invented at will nor be freely exchanged for an-

[18] See Paul Tillich, "Theology and Symbolism," F. Ernest Johnson, editor, *Religious Symbolism* (New York: Harper and Brothers, 1955), p. 109.

[19] See Tillich, "The Religious Symbol," *art. cit.*, 13–14.

[20] See Tillich, "Religious Symbols and Our Knowledge of God," *art. cit.*, 190–91.

other symbol more or less adequate.[21] It cannot even be consciously removed. All these things are possible with signs, but not with symbols. The symbol is not made but "born."[22] It is the result of a creative encounter with reality such as that had in all true art. In this encounter the symbol receives its power by a sort of necessity or creation and is thus established as such.[23] While this correlation between what is symbolized and the persons who receive the symbol lasts it retains its power and lives.

But once the encounter ceases and the correlation is broken the symbol loses its power, its life's blood, for it no longer participates in the meaning of that which it represents. Thus, it "dies" along with the situation of the encounter in which it was born. It is reduced to a mere sign without an ontological foundation. This might be exemplified by the death of the polytheistic gods along with their situations. However, since one of the elements of the symbol is subjective, we can never be sure that the correlation has ceased to exist for a certain group. This is known only from the inside, from the point of view of the group, for only there is it evident when a symbol ceases to "say" something.[24]

One interesting application Tillich makes of this regards the Catholic devotion to the Blessed Virgin Mary. It may well be, according to him, that Mary is still a powerful symbol for Catholics. If so, then, provided the usual precautions are taken to keep separate the symbolic and the natural values of the symbol, the figure of the Blessed Virgin can be of great service to Catholics. For Protestants the situation of correlation with the divine has changed, and for this reason the symbol of Mary has lost its value for them. For example, the importance they attribute to immediate relationship to God

[21] See CTB, p. 25.

[22] See Tillich, "Religious Symbols and Our Knowledge of God," art. cit., 191–92.

[23] See Tillich, "The Religious Symbol," art. cit., 13–14.

[24] See Tillich, "Religious Symbols and Our Knowledge of God," art. cit., 191–92.

removes for them the value of the symbol of Mary as mediatrix. Furthermore, being themselves outside the particular Catholic encounter, they have no capacity to judge concerning the value of this symbol for those who are within. Tillich does not see the question of historical fact as being of any importance here.[25] It is a question of subjective symbolic value for a particular group. If this is had, then it is good to retain the symbol. Nevertheless, complete subjectivism is avoided by positing the necessity of an "innersymbolic" critique. If the symbol itself were to contradict some other truth, as he conceives the Virgin Birth as contradicting the humanity of Christ, then the symbol must be rejected. But again, this is not solved on historical grounds, but on an evaluation of the inner coherency of the symbol with the total religious truth.[26]

The Function of Symbols

In a recent work on symbols Tillich clearly distinguishes between two fundamental functions of symbols—the basic and the main function. The former is particularly clear from what has been said about the difference between sign and symbol. This basic function is to represent something which it is not itself, but for which it stands and in the power of which it participates.[27] Thus, symbols point beyond themselves in the power of that to which they point. This is their figurative quality, their special power of representing something which they are not. Because of this quality, in considering symbols it is more important to keep in view what is symbolized than to attend to the symbols.[28] Only in this way can a full consideration of their truth and their meaning be had.

[25] He does not admit that Mary's mediatory powers or the Virgin Birth have any foundation in objective historical fact.

[26] See Tillich, "Religious Symbols and Our Knowledge of God," *art. cit.*, 196–97.

[27] See *ibid.*, pp. 191–92.

[28] See Tillich, "The Religious Symbol," *art. cit.*, 13–14.

The main function of symbols is somewhat different. Here the symbol is seen not only as pointing to something already known, but as becoming an instrument for new knowledge. It opens up levels of reality otherwise hidden and beyond our grasp.[29] The conception of levels of being or of dimensions of being is of the greatest importance in Tillich's thought. It is this which provides the key by which his otherwise disparate ontology and epistemology are reconciled. For, in speaking of various areas of reality and of our capacity to know them, he does not have in mind new beings beside, above, or beyond other beings. Rather, he conceives of levels within the one being progressively less transparent to our faculties of knowing as we descend through them to the very interior nucleus of reality. The levels of being which are opened up by the symbol are in some way intrinsically transcendent, invisible, or ideal. The symbol makes these levels of being perceptible. Furthermore, it exposes to our view special levels in the mind or soul corresponding to these levels of reality and of which we would not otherwise be aware.[30] For there is a structure of the mind which corresponds to that of reality, and this too is progressively less open to our consciousness as we penetrate its deeper levels. The symbol also has the function of opening these levels of our mind to us.

This is the function of all symbols. It is immediately seen in the field of visual arts, where a painting, even a completely naturalistic one, reveals a level of reality to which only the artistic creation, following upon the artist's creative encounter, has an approach. It reveals something which otherwise we would never have seen.[31] This function of symbols is also found in ontological concepts. They use some realm of experience to point to characteristics of being itself which cannot be expressed literally since being itself lies above

[29] See Tillich, "Religious Symbols and Our Knowledge of God," art. cit., 191–92.

[30] See Tillich, "The Religious Symbol," art. cit., 13–14.

[31] See Tillich, "Theology and Symbolism," op. cit., p. 109.

the split between subjectivity and objectivity.[32] We shall see much more about this in considering Tillich's use of the religious symbol. What must be kept in mind is that, of themselves, symbols do not provide us with objective knowledge. They point to reality, which is then seized according to its proper mode.[33]

The Analogy of St. Thomas

Recalling the circumstances and method of Tillich's approach to the problem of the symbol and of analogy, it is especially noteworthy that his work on this subject has been done with a very concrete object in mind: the salvation of man's capacity to speak of a God who is the absolute, the infinite, the unconditional. It has also been done within the framework of the rehabilitation of the term "symbol" which had lost all meaning by its reduction to the state of an arbitrary and external sign. Tillich's task has been the re-establishment of the internal content of the symbol, in order that it might be of some use in the particular function of speaking about God and his relations with man. Other considerations are merely incidental and illustrative. One will not fail to recall that St. Thomas also struggled for an ever more precise expression of analogy, in attempting to clarify the value of our words about God.[34] But, if it was generally when treating of God that St. Thomas most extensively considered analogy, he used the occasion to provide a general division of terms according to their similarity and dissimilarity. Indeed, follow-

---

[32] See CTB, p. 25.

[33] See Tillich, "The Religious Symbol," *art. cit.*, 13–14.

[34] See Hampus Lyttkens, *The Analogy between God and the World, An Investigation of Its Background and Interpretation of Its Use by Thomas of Aquino* (Uppsala: Almqvist & Wiksells Boktryckeri AB, 1952), p. 199. Examples of treatments of analogy by St. Thomas in this context are: *In I Sent.*, q. 5, a. 2 ad 1; *Summa contra gentiles*, I, 34; *Summa theologiae*, I, q. 4, a. 3 and q. 13; *De verit.*, q. 2, aa. 3, 11; *De pot.*, q. 7, a. 7.

ing Aristotle, he does this even without reference to the divine at all.[35] His approach to the question is thus able to be at the same time more systematic and less restricted.

Two elements of this Thomistic analogy are of particular immediate interest in comparison with the concept of the symbol in Paul Tillich. The first regards the relative proximity of analogy to univocity and to equivocity. Is analogy so close to the former that its use in theodicy is but a subtle and devious form of anthropomorphism? Or does it approach equivocity sufficiently to preserve the transcendence of God while still avoiding agnosticism? The second question concerns the extent to which the element of similarity is real and intrinsic to the analogates. This will provide the Thomistic term of comparison to the element of participation which Tillich has attempted to clarify.

Approximation to Equivocity

According to relative proportions of similarity and dissimilarity, St. Thomas classifies all reality as univocal, equivocal, or analogous. The first is characterized by identity, the second by diversity. Both of these are somehow included in the third which is partly the same and partly different. This is the way things are and this is the way we grasp them.[36] An analogous term might be defined as one which is predicated of many things following upon an aspect which is simply different, though somewhat the same because of a bearing toward some one thing. (*"Quod dicitur de pluribus secundum rationem simpliciter diversam sed secundum quid eandem propter habitudinem ad aliquid unum."*)[37] Both Aristotle

[35] See *In XI Metaph.*, lect. 3, nn. 2195–97.

[36] See *ibid.*: "*In univocis enim nomen unum praedicatur de diversis secundum rationem totaliter eandem. . . . In aequivocis vero . . . secundum rationem totaliter diversam. . . . In his vero quae praedicto modo dicuntur, idem nomen de diversis praedicatur secundum rationem partim eamdem, partim diversam*" (n. 2197).

[37] Paulus Dezza, S.J., *Metaphysica generalis* (Rome: Universitas Gregoriana, 1952), p. 43. Cf. John of St. Thomas, *Logica*, II, q. 12, a. 2 (B. Reiser, O.S.B., editor [Turin: Marietti, 1930], pp. 481–82).

and St. Thomas seem to attach analogy more closely to equivocity than to univocity, making it rather a subdivision of the former.[38] Thus, Aquinas calls equivocal what is clearly analogical. This special proximity to equivocity is of particular importance in avoiding anthropomorphism in man's knowledge of God. It would seem to be inevitable for the following reasons.

If analogy were to be equally and necessarily related to univocity and equivocity, then contraries would enter into the very definition and be mutually exclusive.[39] If, on the other hand, the relation were equal, but only by accident, then, without being more clear than the case just mentioned, there would be the added difficulty of defining things by that which is had only by accident. The relation of analogy to the two extremes can then only be unequal. But this inequality cannot be in favor of univocity, making the definition: simply the same and in a way different. If this were to be so, then analogy would be identified to such a degree with what we consider to be univocity that the very concept of analogy would be redundant. The only escape from this would be a system of pantheistic monism where all individuation would be suppressed. A special proximity of analogy to equivocity remains, then, the only alternative.[40] This same conclusion might be reached from the fact that any substantial addition or subtraction changes the species of a being, and thus its definition. Beings, then, which are not simply univocal are necessarily of different species. No matter to what degree this difference might be moderated, they are "things which have one name in common, but different definitions."

[38] See Aristotle, *Nicomachean Ethics*, I, 4, 1096 b, 23–29; St. Thomas Aquinas, *Summa theologiae*, I, q. 13, a. 5, corp. and ad 1.

[39] This is the opinion of J. Le Rohellec, C.S.Sp., "De fundamento metaphysico analogiae," *Divus Thomas* (Piac.), 3–3 (1926), 88–91. He would define the analogous as that whose name is common but whose character signified by the name is simply the same and simply different.

[40] See J. Ramirez, O.P., "De analogia secundum doctrinam Aristotelico-thomisticam," *Ciencia tomista*, 24 (1921), 34–38.

This is Aristotle's definition of equivocals.[41] This question
of approximation is, of course, not to be conceived as one
of mechanically mixing diverse elements. But it is important
to clarify the leaning of analogy toward equivocity for those
who, like Tillich, are antipathetic toward analogy precisely because of a possible anthropomorphism to which it might lead.
God's transcendence is in no way questioned by something
which is simply diverse.

Intrinsic Similarity

This, then, is the general nature of analogy, and St. Thomas
goes about subdividing and analyzing it. If the fact that
analogous realities are "simply different" will protect God's
transcendence, the fact that they are "somewhat the same"
will make it possible to know him. By subdividing the possibilities for sameness, St. Thomas clarifies the notion of
analogy and lays the foundation for knowledge of God. Let
us now see what these divisions are and to what degree Tillich's claim to have Aquinas' "*analogia entis*" is justified.

Having determined the element of equivocity, one further
classification of analogy can be made according to the various
realizations of the univocal or "something the same" element. This sameness can be had either according to being
or according to intention or according to both.[42] The first
way refers to what is generically common and identically
participated in by many. This is widely used in the fields of
the first two degrees of abstraction, but since it is basically
univocity it is not pertinent to the comparison we wish to
make.[43] The second type of analogy is that according to intention and not according to being. This is similar to the
pros en relations of Aristotle. It is generally called analogy

---

[41] See Aristotle, *Categories*, 1, 1 a 1; cf. Joseph Owens, C.Ss.R.,
The Doctrine of Being in the Aristotelian Metaphysics (Toronto:
Pont. Inst. Med. Stud., 1951), p. 51.

[42] See St. Thomas Aquinas, *In I Sent.*, d. 19, q. 5, a. 2 ad 1.

[43] See James Anderson, *The Bond of Being, an Essay on Analogy
and Existence* (St. Louis: Herder, 1949), pp. 26–38, 90.

of attribution or of proportion because in this case the analogous reality is realized intrinsically and formally only in the prime analogate, while the others are related to this one.[44]

The question of intrinsic realization of the element of similarity is of special interest because of its possible relation to Tillich's main consideration in his present work on symbols; their participation in the power of that which they symbolize. It is necessary, then, to determine to what degree the similarity is intrinsic in St. Thomas' analogy of attribution. What is to be admitted here is the presence of an intrinsic relation in the secondary analogates considered formally as such.[45] Their title to the common name is based on this relation which consists in their suspension from a common term by what is ultimately a varying bond of external causality.[46] The relation is commonly based on something intrinsic in the secondary analogate. But this, in turn, together with the relation based on it, must be distinguished from the analogous reality which is formally and intrinsically realized only in the primary analogate.[47] There-

[44] See Aristotle, *Metaphysics*, IV 1003 a, 18–2, 1003 b, 5. He gives the example of health being predicated of the nonliving things which are either the source or the sign of health. St. Thomas notes that, *"intentio sanitatis refertur . . . non tamen secundum diversum esse, quia esse sanitatis non est nisi in animali"* (In I Sent., d. 19, q. 5, a. 2 ad 1).

[45] See St. Thomas Aquinas, *Summa theologiae: "Quamvis sanitas non sit in medicina, nec urina, tamen in utraque est aliquod per quod hoc quidem facit, illud autem significat sanitatem"* (I, q. 16, a. 6). John of St. Thomas explains this further in his *Logica* (B. Reiser, editor): *"Herba habet intrinsece relationem ad sanitatem propter virtutem sanandi et ideo intrinsece dicitur respiciens sanitatem, sed non intrinsece denominatur sana. Et sic sanitas in animali habet rationem formae, respectu herbae rationem termini extrinsece denominantis"* (II, q. 13, a. 4, p. 490).

[46] See M. T.-L. Penido, *Le rôle de l'analogie en théologie dogmatique* (Paris: Vrin, 1931), pp. 37–40, 53–57; cf. St. Thomas Aquinas, *Summa theologiae*, I, q. 16, a. 6.

[47] See Marianus Deandrea, O.P., *Praelectiones metaphysicae* (Rome: Offic. Libri Catholici, 1951), p. 172.

fore, from this intrinsic relation it is necessary to distinguish
intrinsic denomination. While the point is a disputed one,
it would seem that the latter, which would imply intrinsic
attribution, is to be rejected. Such a concept would destroy
the very existence of the analogy of attribution both from
within and from without. Attribution would be internally
excluded, since once the secondary analogates formally contained the analogous form itself, there would be no more
need for further specification from without. It would also be
excluded externally, since such a form would have to be
either different or identically or proportionately the same in
relation to the other analogates. Thus, it would come under
equivocity, univocity, or analogy of proportionality.[48] For this
reason intrinsic attribution is to be excluded and the likeness
is to be considered more as existing between the analogates
than in them.[49] In insisting on the limitation of attribution
to extrinsic attribution, one is, of course, speaking merely
formally, i.e., of attribution as such. It does in fact happen
that there are cases of a material coincidence of intrinsic and
extrinsic denomination, thus producing mixed analogies. But
to speak of intrinsic attribution is to speak materially.[50]

Nevertheless, it is possible to carry the similarity to the
very interior of the being. This is what happens in the third
type of analogy, that according to both intention and being
or the analogy of proper proportionality. Aristotle was conscious of the rather recent discovery that the middle terms
in a mathematical proportion were interchangeable because
they were two proportions of the same mutual relation. To
this he added an appreciation of the fact that philosophical
analogy expressed the likeness of the relations only proportionately, and not univocally.[51] St. Thomas made full use

[48] See John of St. Thomas, *Logica*, II, q. 13, a. 4 and q. 14,
a. 3 (*op. cit.*, pp. 488, 513).

[49] See C. Ryan, O.P., "God and Analogy," *Blackfriars*, 25
(1944), 139.

[50] See Penido, *op. cit.*, p. 37; R. Garrigou-Lagrange, O.P., *God,
His Existence and His Nature* (London: Herder, 1954), II, p. 207.

[51] See Lyttkens, *op. cit.*, pp. 43–46.

of these discoveries.[52] This analogy, then, will consist in a proportion of proportions. While its external form can be had when using metaphors, we are interested in its analogical reality which implies that the analogue be formally realized in each of the analogates.[53]

The analogy of proper proportionality is based on a reality, for example, life, goodness, or being, which realizes itself in various beings according to diverse modes. What is important to note is that these modes are immanent in this reality and expressed confusedly by it. Thus, one passes from one of the analogates to another, not by the addition of specific differences, but by making more explicit the diverse modalities already included in it. The foundation is thus the very essence of the thing itself.[54] The analogy of proper proportionality is based on a perfection existing objectively and fulfilling three conditions: first, that it be realized intrinsically in each analogate; secondly, that the realization take place according to essentially diverse and graduated modes; and thirdly, that the realization be such that nothing in these modes is extrinsic to the analogical perfection in which they are united.[55]

The Symbol of Paul Tillich

Having thus briefly reviewed the nature of analogy according to St. Thomas, especially as regards its priximity to equivocity and its degree of internal reality, we may now proceed

---

[52] Note the similarity between Aristotle, *Nicomachean Ethics*, V, 3, 1131 a 30–1131 b 4 and Aquinas, *De verit.*, q. 2, a. 3. It extends even to the indication of its mathematical origin.

[53] See Aristotle, *Metaphysics*, XIV, 6, 1093 b 18–24.

[54] "*In analogia consideratur non diversae realitates, sed diversi modi essendi eiusdem realitatis*" (St. Thomas Aquinas, *De pot.*, q. 9, a. 2 ad 6); "*Ens contrahitur per decem genera quorum unum quodque addit aliquid supra ens, non aliquod accidens vel aliquam differentiam quae sit extra essentiam entis, sed determinatum modum essendi qui fundatur in ipsa essentia rei*" (*De verit.*, q. 21, a. 1).

[55] See Penido, *op. cit.*, p. 56.

more directly to the evaluation of the symbol of Dr. Tillich.
What kind of analogy is he able to establish and justify in
his philosophical system? To what degree will his symbol
have internal reality, so that it can become an instrument of
knowing and speaking meaningfully of God and of the nature
of his existence?

According to Tillich, the nature of symbols is specified by
their participation in the power of that which they
signify.[56] On the determination of the exact value of this
statement depends the value of Tillich's symbol and its
approach to St. Thomas' analogy of being. Unfortunately, it
is not a conception which our author has found easy to clarify
and determine. It would seem that he sees the necessity of
making this power something real, but that being enmeshed
in his general philosophical background he is unable to ac-
complish this task. Thus, while at times he seems to identify completely symbol and analogy,[57] elsewhere he would
appear to make a special connection between analogy and
his conception of God as the ground of all, and to consider
analogy as the basis for the symbol.[58] Generally, however,
he merely stresses that the symbol participates in the power
of the thing symbolized. Rather than approach the question
of the value of this power directly, when Tillich himself has
had little success in solving it, let us first consider the symbol
from the point of view of its origin and function. Immediately it appears that his concept of analogy is still quite distant from St. Thomas' analogy of proper proportionality.

The symbol arises from a creative encounter by men with
the reality for which it stands.[59] It is only in such an encounter that the symbol receives its power, and this power
remains only as long as the correlation between the symbol-

[56] See Tillich, "Religious Symbols and Our Knowledge of God,"
art. cit., 189–90.

[57] ST, I: "The knowledge of revelation . . . is analogous or symbolic" (p. 131).

[58] See *ibid.*, pp. 239–40.

[59] See Tillich, "Religious Symbols and Our Knowledge of God,"
art. cit., 191–92; "The Religious Symbol," *art. cit.*, 13–14.

ized and the person. Thus, far from being a reality capable of contributing to the original encounter between the subject and that for which the symbol stands, the symbol is a result of such an encounter. This is the basic difference between Tillich and Thomas regarding the reality of analogy and symbol. The extent of this difference becomes even more striking when it is observed that this encounter is subjective because it is an act which is ultimately dependent on the person's emotions, and that it is relative because essentially determined by the moment of time in which it takes place. These two elements pervade the whole philosophy of Paul Tillich and quite naturally determine the nature of his symbol.

Subjectivism

In order to evaluate the subjective influence so common in modern philosophy since Kant, it must be noted that, according to the conception of Tillich, both mind and reality are rationally structured. Both have originated through the mediation of the divine *logos*. This common mediation guarantees that the two structures will be either identical or at least analogous, as all philosophers have supposed.[60] Working with the structures of the mind, technical reason as the power of reasoning can provide a scientific knowledge which is safe but not ultimately significant.[61] When it comes to direct and ultimately significant knowledge of beings and situations, something more is required, since the structures of the mind are "a priori in the strictest sense of the word."[62] For this reason receiving knowledge is added to provide the element of union or participation in reality. Unfortunately, the vehicle for this type of knowledge is emotion,[63] though he attempts to retain the rational by referring

---

[60] See *ST*, I, pp. 23, 75–76.

[61] See *ibid.*, p. 166.

[62] See *ibid.*, pp. 72–73, 105.

[63] See *ibid.*, p. 98.

to it as "a criticizing and accepting *agape* which is detached and involved at the same time."[64] Without wishing to give in to complete subjectivism, he would seem to hold that objective rationality by itself is incapable of grasping the real with its basic self-world content. This implies the necessity of a subjective element of participation by emotion, which alternates with the moments of objectivity which are insufficient in themselves.[65] There is thus introduced an element of subjectivity into every meaningful encounter with reality, and it is placed at the focal point of union or participation.

It is from this encounter with its inherently subjective note that the symbol arises. It depends on this encounter for its own essential note of participation in the reality of that for which it stands. In this way, subjectivity is introduced into the very essence of the symbol and it becomes evident why this symbol is incapable of providing objective knowledge. Furthermore, there is required a second and perhaps unconscious act on the part of the community in order to constitute a symbol. This is the act of acceptance and it is indispensable.[66] The result is that symbols are "born" and "die" as the subjective situations of encounter and assent arise and disappear.[67]

This birth and death of symbols, together with particular external situations and their dependence on subjective acts of the community, demonstrate clearly that they differ from the analogy of St. Thomas. As we have seen above, his analogy is based on either a relation of dependence of the thing itself on that to which it is analogous (analogy of attribution) or on the internal realization of the same note according to diverse modes (analogy of proper proportionality). These two adequate foundations are realities which exist independently

[64] Paul Tillich, "Participation and Knowledge, Problems of an Ontology of Cognition," in *Sociologica*, Vol. I of *Frankfurter Beiträge zur Soziologie*, Theodore W. Adorno and Walter Dirks, editors (Stuttgart: Europaische Verlagsanstalt, 1955), p. 206.

[65] See *ibid.*, p. 209.

[66] See Tillich, "The Religious Symbol," *art. cit.*, 13–14.

[67] See Tillich, "Theology and Symbolism," *op. cit.*, p. 109.

of the knowing subject and the community; they are realities which pertain to the analogous material, either by its nature or by the fact of its concrete existence. Thus, for St. Thomas, it is reality itself as it objectively exists which is analogous. For Tillich, on the other hand, reality is neither analogous nor symbolic, but can be used by man as the material for symbols.

Nevertheless, Dr. Tillich also postulates an objective basis for the symbol. The immediate nonsymbolic nature of the material used as a symbol must have an original affinity with the thing symbolized. In this regard it is necessary to observe two things. First, this objective basis is not sufficient for the establishment of a symbol. To it must be added the subjective situation of encounter and the oftentimes subconscious acceptation by the community which follows this encounter. Secondly, it would seem that this objective basis can have any degree of reality whatsoever. Tillich cites the example of water, whose nature is to cleanse physically, being used to symbolize the spiritual purification which takes place in baptism. But he also uses as an example the word "God" in what he considers to be its false connotation of a supreme being who is transcendent by being above the world. This becomes a symbol of the true divine which is transcendent without being either a being or above the universe.[68] Of itself the word "God" is a denial of transcendence, though it does bring the notion of transcendence to the mind. It would seem, then, that the function of this objective basis is not, as it is in St. Thomas, to give real content to the symbol. For Tillich, the symbol is denied in its proper meaning.[69] Rather, the function of this objective basis would seem to be that of favoring the subjective act by which this reality is joined to the object it is to symbolize. Again it is the subjective element which comes to the fore. The scant importance which is given to the relation of the objective basis to the thing symbolized would seem to indicate that Tillich's

[68] See Tillich, "Symbol and Knowledge: A Response," *art. cit.*, 204.

[69] See *ST*, I, p. 239.

symbol does not, of itself, get beyond St. Thomas' conception of the analogy of metaphorical proportionality. There the nature of the material chosen does not have the importance it has in the other analogies, since it is intended to fix the attention not on what is literally asserted, but on what is in some way similar to it. It is, then, the external appearance which is of importance here.[70] However, even in this type of Thomistic analogy, one arrives at the metaphorical sense only by the medium of the proper sense of the term.[71]

What, then, has happened to the power in which the symbol participates? It has clearly been separated from the internal participation which St. Thomas has in his analogy of proper proportionality. Such an idea would not interest Tillich, since his interest is primarily with symbols for God, and his conception of the nature of the absolute excludes any such participation by creatures. The power participated in is not entitative but significative power. It is not being but meaning. However, for Tillich, meaning has a particularly real signification. This is the result of the line of thought which came to him through Rilke and Schelling. He has spoken of his philosophy of meaning as the basis for his whole system,[72] and explained "meaning" as "a correspondence [which] exists between the human spirit and reality."[73] This would seem to confirm the predominant subjective element which has been appearing constantly. He does not philosophize directly about being, but about reality as subjectively grasped. The power which he places in his symbol depends essentially, though not exclusively, on this subjective element.

It would seem that his desire to overcome the negative conceptions of the symbol, which excluded all objective content, has not been as effective as he would desire. Neverthe-

[70] See Luigi Ciappi, O.P., "Valore del Simbolo nella Conoscenza di Dio," *Sapienza*, 1 (1948), 52–53; cf. St. Tomas Aquinas, *In I Sent.*, d. 16, q. 1, a. 3 ad 3.

[71] See St. Thomas Aquinas, *Summa theologiae*, I, q. 13, a. 6; Penido, *op. cit.*, p. 44.

[72] See *IH*, p. 38.

[73] *Ibid.*, p. 61.

less, his intention of making room for the objective aspect must not be forgotten, since it is in itself a contribution toward the correction of prevalent errors. It is the general context of his ontology, to the degree that it depends on Schelling and incorporates elements of his developmental dialectic, that gives some realization to this desire of restoring the objective element in symbols. But when it comes to the more particular questions of the construction of individual symbols, subjectivism seems to enter at every turn. This is not merely an isolated or arbitrary instance within his philosophy, but a natural consequence of the step his ontology has taken beyond Schelling by incorporating the "Fall" and the epistemology which corresponds to it. Subjectivism is firmly rooted in his philosophy and its presence in his theory of the symbol is inevitable and intentional.

From this there follow two corollaries regarding the part of symbols in knowledge. First, it is understandable that symbols cannot give objective knowledge or be the basis for objective reasoning toward the construction of a rational structure. Without the existence of a situation of correlation and the consequent constitution of this material as a symbol by the acceptation of the community, it would neither point to anything nor tell us about anything. Therefore, since this subjective element is essentially and inseparably contained in the symbol, knowledge and reasoning, which depend on the symbol simply, are not entirely objective.

Secondly, since the subjective act which constitutes the symbol as such can only be the result of an existing situation of encounter and of correlation of object and subject, the symbol cannot be the means of first coming to a grasp of what is symbolized. The object must first have been grasped at least by one person, and generally by a representative portion of the group, in order that the group acceptation of this symbol be able to take place. Once accepted it can serve as a symbol for the enlightenment of the whole society. Tillich has here a difficult dialectical relation between the grasp of the object necessary for the constitution of a symbol for it and the contribution of this symbol to the knowledge of the object. There is possibility of avoiding contradiction here, provided a distinction is made either between the subconscious and conscious levels of the mind with their many shadings, or between the various members of the community which uses the symbol. Both these distinctions will allow for a progression in knowledge to which the symbol can contribute. Thus, the relation mentioned above can be truly dialectical and not simply contradictory. In fact, it is a consideration which makes excellent use of the social and unconscious aspects of human knowledge and will be well worth further development by Dr. Tillich. However, it is clear that, since the symbol thus conceived requires some explicit knowledge of the object from the beginning, it cannot by itself contribute to completely new knowledge.

Relativism

There is another element in Tillich's philosophy which has a special bearing on his notion of the truth of the symbol: it is the element of relativism. This arises from two sources: one is a fear lest his philosophy be static; the other is his desire to protect the transcendence of God. Together they prepare him to accept the concept of a changing God, including both nonbeing and potency, whose very nature is subject to his freedom.[74] Since the truth of things depends on their relation to God, this produces a relativism.[75] This is reinforced on the finite level by his situation of the norm of truth in the *kairos*, that is, "qualitatively fulfilled time . . . the moment of time approaching us as fate and decision."[76] This *kairos* is of supreme importance to one who has conceived of essence and idea as irreducibly dialectic. Having rejected any absolute standpoint from which to view

[74] See *ST*, I, pp. 246–48; II, pp. 22–23.
[75] See St. Thomas Aquinas, *Summa theologiae*, I, q. 16, a. 1; cf. the commentary on this by A.-D. Sertillanges, O.P., *Dieu*, I, Questions 12–17, *Somme théologique* (Paris: Desclée, 1926), p. 363, n. 152.
[76] *IH*, p. 129.

this dialectic as a total process, the norm of truth becomes complex. It is essence, but essence as of this moment. "Dialectics is the attempt to comprehend the fate of ideas from our *kairos*, from the fate of our period."[77] As a result he comes to the relativism of the statement, "not everything is true at every time."[78] Truth is continually changing along with its norm, the *kairos*. It is the "problem of actual reason . . . to make the dynamics of reason effective in every act of subjective reason and in every moment of objective reason."[79]

Turning now to the symbol and its truth, a double consequence of this relativism appears. First of all, the community aspect of the symbol is reinforced; for, since the *kairos* is a norm for all members of the group at this time, the situation of encounter and the symbols which follow upon it can have a true meaning for the entire community. This eliminates the danger of a completely individualistic subjectivism which would result in a set of symbols for each person and exclude them as a means for transmitting and increasing awareness. Since the symbol is valid now for the community or one of its subgroupings, it can be a means of communicating and of "opening up" levels of reality.[80] However, if the danger is overcome in the dimension of space, it remains in the dimension of time. True symbols become false and then their use is deadly. It is the fruit of relativism and the result of a philosophy which puts actualization above actuality.[81]

Tillich's symbol remains, then, an inspiration and a disappointment. As an attempt to rise above the sign and to regain a participation in the reality it represents, it is a significant step toward the notion of analogy which was developed in

[77] *Ibid.*, pp. 167–69. In rejecting the absolute standpoint he wishes to separate himself from Hegel.

[78] *PE*, p. 33; cf. *ST*, I: "There are no right decisions" (p. 152).

[79] *Ibid.*, p. 78. Thus, both objective and subjective reason changes: "Human nature changes in history" (p. 167).

[80] See Tillich, "Religious Symbols and Our Knowledge of God," *art. cit.*, 191–92.

[81] See *ST*, I, p. 246.

the peripatetic and Scholastic schools of philosophy. It represents an awareness of the philosophical bankruptcy which must follow on an exclusive positivism, and a realization of the need to construct a means for penetrating to the notion of being and for ascending to being-itself. It is unfortunate that the subjectivism and relativism of Tillich's system should have entered to determine the origin, structure, and truth of this symbol. But since existing being is not analogical, a subjective act must be had in order to constitute a symbol; and the truth of this act is relative to the group which makes it and the moment of time in which it is made. In this way the symbol ceases to be a means for objective knowledge. While the accent of present-day philosophy remains on subjectivity, it is hardly likely that this defect will be overcome. But it is not unreasonable to hope that Paul Tillich's notion of the symbol and its importance will contribute to a revival of interest in this central concept.

Tillich and Religious Symbol

A more complete understanding of the symbol in the system of Paul Tillich cannot be had without a thorough investigation of his religious symbol. It was noted above that his interests are centered on the divine and that his great contribution is the eloquent defense he has made of God's transcendence. But lest this transcendence exclude man from any religious considerations, there must be something which carries one's attention toward the divine and supports it in this quest. This is the religious symbol, and of recent years Tillich has come to understand that his investigation of it must be proportionate to the work done on the divine transcendence. Since it is in this religious context that much of his work on the symbol in general has been done, it is now necessary to examine his religious symbol and his use of it with regard to man's awareness of God.

The nature and necessity of the religious symbol in the philosophy of Paul Tillich depend directly on the phenomenological and ontological conception which he has of the divine. Phenomenologically he conceives God as man's ultimate concern. This is the common element in all classical approaches to the divine as "being-itself," "universal substance," "progressive integration," or "absolute spirit."[82] It is also the element common to the religious symbols actually used by men.[83] By "ultimate" Tillich wishes to make God the unconditional, free from all peculiarities of character or circumstance, and to assert his total and infinite penetration of all places and times. By "concern" Tillich wishes to introduce the existential aspect of the divine as a matter of infinite passion and interest for the individual.[84] He concludes that "whatever concerns man ultimately becomes god for him, and, conversely . . . a man can be concerned ultimately only about that which is god for him."[85]

From this phenomenological consideration, Tillich easily changes to the ontological perspective in which he conceives the divine as being-itself. Only that can be of ultimate concern which has the power of determining, threatening, and saving our being and meaning. Here being does not mean existence in time and space. Its import is "the whole of human reality, the structure, the meaning, and the aim of existence."[86] This statement that God is being-itself is the only statement about the divine which means directly and properly what it says. All others are symbolic.[87] Such symbolic statements of the divine express God as "the power of being" overcoming nonbeing in all its forms, "the substance" or the "logos" appearing in every rational structure, the "abyss" as inexhaustible by any creation or totality of crea-

[82] *Ibid.*, pp. 9–11. These are respectively the approaches of the Scholastics, Spinoza, Wieman, and Hegel. Ultimate concern is also found in the supreme scriptural commandment to love God with one's whole heart, soul, mind, and strength.

[83] See *PE*, p. 32, n. 1.

[84] See *ST*, I, pp. 11–12; "Existential Philosophy," *Journal of the History of Ideas*, 5 (1944), 51–54.

[85] *ST*, I, p. 211.

[86] *Ibid.*, p. 14; cf. p. 230.

[87] See Tillich, "Reply to Interpretation and Criticism," Kegley and Bretall, *op. cit.*, p. 335.

tions, "the ground" as creative in every rational creation, and "infinite potentiality of being and meaning" as pouring himself into the rational structures of mind and reality to actualize and transform them.[88] These expressions bring out the structure of Tillich's ontological thought. For him, being is made up of levels or dimensions of which God is the depth dimension or ground—"an analytic depth dimension in the structure of reality."[89]

Turning now to the religious symbol, it is possible to gain a preliminary appreciation of its nature and necessity. The nature of the religious symbol is specified by the fact that the object it represents, the divine, transcends everything in the empirical order. This type of symbol must point to the ultimate level of things, to the depth dimension of reality and of reason. This is the level of being-itself and of the ultimate power of being. It is not another thing but the ground of every other depth and of every other dimension.[90] In pointing to the divine, the religious symbol points to what is of ultimate concern for us, to the "infinitely meaningful and the unconditionally valid."[91] It is with this that religious experience is concerned and the content of this experience is expressed by religious symbols.

A further preliminary insight into the nature of the religious symbol is to be had from a consideration of the necessity of such symbolism. If phenomenologically God is man's ultimate concern, the object of such concern cannot be considered with detached objectivity. Indeed, it cannot be considered as a separated object, a highest "thing."[92] Neither can this object as ultimate be derived from mere subjectivity,

[88] Tillich, "Symbol and Knowledge: A Response," art. cit., 203; "The Two Types of Philosophy of Religion," Union Seminary Quarterly Review, 1 (1946), 11; ST, I, pp. 79, 236.

[89] Ibid., p. 207.

[90] See Tillich, "Religious Symbols and Our Knowledge of God," art. cit., 192–93.

[91] Tillich, "Theology and Symbolism," op. cit., p. 110.

[92] For this reason Tillich has begun to use "ultimate concern" and "unconditional concern" rather than "the ultimate" and "the unconditional"; see ST, I, p. 12.

for in demanding our total surrender it also demands the surrender of our subjectivity.[93] In this way the subject-object schema disappears in ultimate concern; and that about which one is concerned is present as both subject and object and as beyond subject and object.

Ontologically, "the unsymbolic statement which implies the necessity of religious symbolism is that God is being-itself, and as such beyond the subject-object structure of everything that is."[94] On the contrary, man's reason, being finite, is bound to the subject-object schema and must use categories which would turn the "Source" (Jasper's *Ursprung*) into an object dominated by human reason as subject.[95] It is evident that, if its categories of thinking are not false, they are not used literally. This also appears from the fact that revelation is the self-manifestation of the ground of the onto-logical structure of being. If this be so, then no word or con-cept or thing which bears the revelation could be identical with the mystery revealed, without being its own ground.[96] Therefore, the relation cannot be one of complete identity. Neither can it be one of absolute difference, for then the expressions would be without any value whatever. The true position is in-between these two. It includes a Yes and a No, both of which together point beyond to something hidden. This is the symbol; and such a religious symbol is indis-pensable in all thought concerning the divine.

It must be noted that the religious symbol is not a means for discovering something new about God; it is, rather, the form in which all knowledge of revelation must be ex-pressed.[97] Its purpose is to allow us to make concrete state-ments about God in order to give content to the cognitive function in revelation.[98] We shall see later what the truth

---

[93] See *ibid.*, pp. 12, 214.

[94] Tillich, "Reply to Interpretation and Criticism," Kegley and Bretall, *op. cit.*, p. 334.

[95] See Tillich, "Existential Philosophy," *art. cit.*, 55–57.

[96] See Paul Tillich, "Authority and Revelation," *Harvard Divinity School Bulletin*, 49 (1952), 31–32.

[97] See *ST*, I, p. 131.

[98] See *ibid.*, p. 239.

content of such statements is, but first let us determine in
what these symbols consist.

The Elements of the Religious Symbol

If an assertion is to be concrete, it must use a segment of
finite experience. Furthermore, since the divine is the depth
dimension of all reality and the power of all being, the religious symbol is able to take its material from all the realms
of finite reality which we experience in our daily life. Natural,
personal, and historical reality can all be used. In fact, Tillich
goes so far as to say that everything in time and space has
naturally been at some time, in the history of religion, a
symbol for the holy,[99] and to suggest that we must now
find the germs of religious symbolism not only in cult and
doctrine but in the whole of today's practical life.[100]

In themselves these finite things are not ultimate. "They
all are of preliminary import. They have limited meaning,
they have a conditioned validity."[101] Being-itself, on the
other hand, is absolutely transcendent. It is as far removed
from any material taken from natural or personal reality as
the infinite is from the finite. This ultimate, then, is beyond
the finite material with its framework of time and space.
Furthermore, the very multiplicity of the materials used
divides the ultimate into several figures (necessarily as we
shall see), and thus tends to undermine its ultimacy.[102] For
this reason the proper meaning of the concrete reality used
must be negated even while it is being affirmed as a symbol.

Tillich stresses nothing more than the fact that God must
in no way be reduced to the level of objects and of beings.
Therefore, if he admits and even finds it necessary to affirm
that objective symbols are an indispensable basis for speak-

[99] See "The Religious Symbol," art. cit., 192–93.

[100] See "The Permanent Significance of the Catholic Church for
Protestantism," Protestant Digest, 3 (1941), 29.

[101] Tillich, "Theology and Symbolism," op. cit., p. 110.

[102] See DF, p. 49.

ing in any way about God, he is always the first to stress that "a symbolic expression is one whose proper meaning is negated."[103] Tillich is much concerned about what he considers to be the idolatrous character of traditional theology and of popular beliefs about God. He observes in them a tendency to make God one thing among others, to raise the materials used in symbolism to the level of God himself, and to consider them as divine. Such symbols become demonic and their use is idolatrous the moment they try to replace *the* Holy to which they point.[104] The first step in the deterioration of religion is the identification of symbols with the world of finite relations which furnishes the material for symbols. It is Tillich's concentration on combating this error which makes his understanding of analogy, in his own words, "more negative-protesting than positive-affirming."[105] An example of the vigor with which he stresses this negation of the literal meaning of the finite material is to be found in the following conclusion to one of his articles: "That which is signified lies beyond the symbolic material. This is the first and last thing we must say about religious symbolism."[106]

However, the symbol is not all negative. "Every religious symbol negates itself in its literal meaning, but it affirms itself in its self-transcending meaning."[107] This affirmative aspect provides the symbol with a basis for fulfilling its task of pointing beyond itself. This is what keeps it from being overcome by nonbeing. But, in participating in this ground of being, things participate in its power of being. Thus, there is a basic possibility for the material used as a religious symbol to fulfill in a most excellent way that specific characteristic of a symbol—that it participates in the power of that which it represents. It is not "only a symbol" just as it is not a mere sign. On the ground of this participation, the section of finite reality used as a religious symbol is not entirely strange to

[103] *ST*, I, pp. 239–40.
[104] See Tillich, "The Religious Symbol," *art. cit.*, 192–93.
[105] Letter to G. Weigel, S.J., see above, p. 55.
[106] "Theology and Symbolism," *op. cit.*, p. 116.
[107] *ST*, II, p. 9.

that which it represents, nor is it arbitrary.[108] It is really a two-edged sword, expressing at the same time what is symbolized and that through which it is symbolized. It forces the infinite down to the finite, but only inasmuch as the finite element used is lifted up to the infinite by being consecrated and made theonomous.[109]

This idea of the necessity of lifting finite reality and making it theonomous introduces the necessity of a proximate foundation for the religious symbol—a necessity which can be understood only in the context of the dialectic which is the dynamics of Tillich's thought. Any being which is to be used as a religious symbol must be lifted up because of the transcendental fall of all reality. The Fall stands as the antithesis between the essential state where all was united with God and the eschatological state where this unity will be re-established in a new synthesis. It was an idea of the later Schelling, developed by Kierkegaard, that the state of existence is not only the actuation and expression of essence but its contradiction as well.[110] In this contradiction, or fall, the polar unity of the ontological elements in finite reality is disrupted. Thus, whereas in principle all reality would be sacramental or transparent to the divine—a condition Tillich terms theonomous—in our state of existence it is not so.[111] Existing beings, though existing on the divine power of being and including a potential participation in God's perfect unity, now are separated from it. They are opaque to the divine. The potential participation is merely enough to allow us to speak of God in terms of a quest for him.[112] Existing man can only ask the question of the divine and, in fact, man's existence in its disruption is the question. The answer must be received; the holy must break

[108] See Paul Tillich, "Religion and Secular Culture," *Journal of Religion*, 26 (1946), 84.

[109] See *ST*, I, pp. 240–41; *PE*, p. 61.

[110] See *IH*, pp. 61–64.

[111] See *PE*, pp. 110–11.

[112] See *ST*, II, p. 9.

through in particular things and particular circumstances. This is the phenomenon of revelation.

The term revelation is used by Tillich more despite its supernaturalistic implications than because of them, for the divine does not speak to man. But because it transcends the situation of an object whose structures are presented to a subject for his knowledge, a cognitive encounter with the divine does imply the manifestation of something hidden, and may be termed a revelation. The manifestation in turn involves both an objective element, called a sign-event, and a subjective element, called ecstasy. A sign-event is a situation which astonishes by allowing the stigma of nonbeing in reality to appear more clearly and in relation to us as death, meaninglessness, and guilt. In this way the negative or "abyss" aspect of the divine appears. The positive aspect, or God as the ground and power of being, is manifested at the same time by the very fact that nonbeing is not completely victorious.[113] The mental state which accompanies a sign-event is termed ecstasy. This is had in one's anxiety before the clear appearance of nonbeing. There, in the extreme situation at the very limit of one's possibilities, one must at least affirm meaninglessness. This itself is a meaningful act, for it can be done only on the power of the being it negates.[114] The power of being is thus present in the affirmation of ourselves as facing meaninglessness. In this way it grasps one by affirming itself in him in spite of nonbeing.[115]

This encounter of revelation, in which the divine as the depth dimension of mind and of reality is opened to our awareness, establishes a theonomous situation and thus gives birth to symbols. For, when particular realities become connected with the correlation of revelation and take on its meaning and openness to the divine, they become "theonomous," and for the time being escape the contradictions of

[113] See *ibid.*, I, pp. 108–10, 119.

[114] See *CTB*, p. 176.

[115] See Paul Tillich, *Christianity and the Problem of Existence*, three lectures delivered at Howard University, Washington, D.C., April, 1951 (Washington: Henderson Services, 1951), pp. 30–31.

the state of existence in which their natural transparency to
the ground of their being became opaque. When this happens, these realities begin actually to participate in the power
of the Holy which begins to show through. Thus, the remote
foundation becomes proximate, and these finite beings become, for faith, bearers of sacramental power—symbols. They
represent and open up the depth dimensions of mind and
of reality hidden until now, and participate in the power of
the ultimate to which they point. Because of this participation
in the Holy itself, religious symbols are holy. In turn, this
participation places a limit to the meaning, power, and holiness of symbols. It means that they themselves can never
be the Holy, the matter of ultimate concern, without becoming idols.[116]

The element of participation would seem to be connected
to the concept of analogy in a particular way by Tillich, although this is not always the case. Sometimes he seems to
use symbol and analogy as absolutely synonymous.[117] At
other times he seems to make a particular connection between analogy and God as the ground and the power of
all being, making this analogy the basis for the symbol.[118]
If this distinction is really contained in his thought, it is a
distinction to which he does not always adhere. He seems
more interested in noting that the symbol participates in
the reality to which it points than in stressing its pointing
character, and more interested in analogy as giving us the
possibility of speaking about God than as based on God as
being-itself.

Tillich observes that, by symbol, he means exactly what
St. Thomas meant by "*analogia entis*," but that he uses the
term symbol because of a methodological difference between
him and Aquinas.[119] This may be an indication of his particular connection of analogy with participation, which, of
course, would be the prime consideration of St. Thomas in his

---

[116] See Tillich, "Theology and Symbolism," *op. cit.*, p. 110.
[117] See *ST*, I, p. 131.
[118] See *ibid.*, pp. 239–40.
[119] See Letter to G. Weigel, S.J., see above, p. 196, fn. 2.

metaphysical approach. Tillich, being more influenced by epistemological questions, would naturally be particularly concerned with the representative or more specifically symbolic aspect. His stress on the transcendence of the divine, and hence on the negative element in the symbol rather than on the more positive aspect of analogy, might also have had a considerable influence on this decision.

The Perfection of Religious Symbols

The combined positive and negative elements in the religious symbol lead to the possibility and necessity of a multiplicity of symbols. Since the unconditional transcends reality and multiplicity, it can be represented and partially expressed by any number of types of reality without ever being exhausted by them. At the same time, because of this transcendence, any one symbol would be hopelessly inadequate in helping the human mind to grasp the unconditional. Thus, a multiplicity of symbols, in fact all the basic qualities of reality, are called for.[120]

While all reality can and should be used for the symbolic expression of God, it is not a matter of indifference which aspect of finite reality is used in a particular symbol. Tillich sees a profound difference between the proportion stone—infinite—and the proportion man—infinite.[121] Beneath man the elements themselves are not had as completely as in man, and "this difference is the basis of the possibility whereby God is manifest according to his innermost nature in man, but not in a stone."[122] The difference is also based on the degree of unity of the ontological elements in finite

---

[120] See *IH*, pp. 267–70.

[121] See Letter to G. Weigel, S.J., see above, p. 55.

[122] *Loc. cit.*; cf. *ST*, I, pp. 241–44; John Rodman Williams, *The Doctrine of the Imago Dei in Contemporary Theology: A Study in Karl Barth, Emil Brunner, Reinhold Niebuhr and Paul Tillich* (unpublished Ph.D. dissertation, Dept. of Philosophy, Columbia University, 1954), pp. 150–53.

reality, since each approach to a perfect unity is an approach
to the perfect identity of these elements in the identity of
God. Thus, man is the image of God because, in man, dynamics and form, freedom and destiny, individuality and
participation are particularly united, even while retaining
their polar relationship. This unity is far greater in the essential and eschatological states than in the disrupted state
of existence where the polar relation becomes one of tension
and even disruption. Thus, in order to have religious symbols, the correlation which is the encounter of revelation is
indispensable because it re-establishes the unity.

Since they are the expression of this encounter in which
man is grasped, rather than grasps, religious symbols cannot
be produced—not even by the "collective unconscious, the
great symbol-creating source."[123] Neither can they be
changed[124] or destroyed.[125] Having been born with the encounter of revelation, they change and die with the encounter,
and rational criticism can cause none of these events. Does
this limit the perfection of the religious symbol and make
it irrational? Tillich rejects this opinion. Provided that reason
is taken in the sense not of the power of reasoning, but of
the logos structure of mind and reality, the religious symbol
is rational. It agrees with this structure and thus is adequate
to the situation of ultimate concern which it expresses. It
constitutes a whole of meaning and shows the ultimacy which
gives it its character as an object of faith. Since it is not
irrational, reason can investigate its meaning, elaborate it,
and correlate it with that of other symbols. On the other
hand, it is not conceptual and cannot be established or
changed by reason. Rather, it is the given and depends entirely on the encounter in which the symbol arises.

[123] ST, I, p. 241.
[124] See Paul Tillich, "Religion and Its Intellectual Critics," Motive (1955), 30–31.
[125] See Tillich, "Theology and Symbolism," op. cit., p. 111.

Types of Religious Symbols

Tillich distinguishes various types or levels of religious symbols. According to his division, symbols fall into one of two main groups: the transcendent and the immanent. Immanent symbols are found within the encounter with reality on the level of the appearances of the divine in time and space. The immediate function of these symbols is to point beyond themselves. For this reason he once called them "self-transcending" religious symbols. But what many of them point to directly is not being-itself but another, a deeper, level of symbols by which they are supported: the transcendent religious symbols. These symbols are beyond the empirical level. He calls them "objective religious symbols," since they form the level in which religious objectivity is established.[126]

Transcendent religious symbols form, then, the basic level, which includes representations of the unconditional transcendent and of our relations to this unconditional.[127] In particular, Tillich distinguishes three levels of transcendent symbols. The basic level here is God himself. Even "God," "Supreme Being," and the world of divine beings are symbols. They have a symbolic element and a nonsymbolic element, a Yes and a No. We shall attempt to determine just what these are in another section.

The second level of transcendent religious symbols is composed of symbols which concern the nature of God, his qualities and attributes. These are taken from qualities which we have experienced in ourselves and applied symbolically to God. The third level concerns acts of God, for example, creation of the world. These last two levels propose God as an object and apply our categories of time, space, cause, and substance to him. Therefore, unless these statements are to be absurd, they must be considered to be figurative. This

[126] See "Religious Symbols and Our Knowledge of God," *art. cit.,* 193–96; "The Religious Symbol," *art. cit.,* 26–28.
[127] See Tillich, "The Religious Symbol," *art. cit.,* 14–15.

has been traditionally expressed in the awareness that all our knowledge of God has a symbolic character.[128]

Immanent religious symbols comprise natural and historical objects which have been drawn into the sphere of religious objects to become religious symbols. Empirical existence can be both affirmed and denied of them. In order to be of use to men as pointers, they must have historical existence. But as symbols they do not have a place in the objective world. It is evident, then, that historical existence cannot be understood apart from the symbolic intuition, and as symbolic it must have a Yes and a No.[129] In this class of immanent symbols are a very large number of signs and actions containing reference to the "Supreme Being." The basic level here is the incarnation of the divine beings in men, animals, and things. These have become more necessary whenever the transcendence of God has been stressed. A second level includes all the sacramental objects—sections of reality which have become bearers of the Holy in special ways or special circumstances. Finally, there is a last level, which Tillich calls "sign-symbols." This level is composed of signs which, as such, are able to be replaced, but which have been consecrated by tradition. The cross might be an example of this.[130]

All these immanent religious symbols which have come down to us in history were once holy and bore great sacramental power. This power has not entirely disappeared, for then they would no longer symbolize. However, due to the natural tendency to objectify their reality and to make them into unconditioned transcendents, this power is almost gone.[131] This is the danger of every religious symbol. The fight against it is the task of every religious person.

But there is more to do than fight against aberrations.

---

[128] See *ibid.*, pp. 28–31; "Religious Symbols and Our Knowledge of God," *art. cit.*, 193–96.

[129] See Tillich, "The Religious Symbol," *art. cit.*, 28–31.

[130] See Tillich, "Religious Symbols and Our Knowledge of God," *art. cit.*, 193–96.

[131] See Tillich, "The Religious Symbol," *art. cit.*, 28–31.

There is also the task of seeking God in symbols and, Tillich proposes hesitantly, even beyond symbols. The highest aim of theology, he says, might be to find the point where the contrast between reality and symbol is abolished and reality speaks unsymbolically of both self and the unconditional. This would mean speaking properly of the depth in which things are rooted. The presupposition of this would be a point where reality stands in God who has become all in all. It would be a completely theonomous point. Tillich notes that we are now in a distant state from God; but the interesting thing is that he does not, for this reason, absolutely rule out all possibility of such a point. Instead, he merely concludes that it must be at least rare.[132] Is he referring here only to revelation? Unfortunately this section must end on that question mark.

A Critique of This Religious Symbol

It is time now to evaluate this religious symbol which Paul Tillich has constructed within the framework of his philosophy. Two questions would seem to be of particular importance. First, to what extent has Tillich been successful in his attempt to give real content to his religious symbol to make it more than a mere sign? Secondly, in what way does this content compare with the analogy which has existed in the Scholastic tradition? A point of departure for this evaluation is provided by the note of relativism which was treated previously, since its implications for the notion of reality and of truth are many and far-reaching.

The relativism which was found to be a basic element in Tillich's philosophy diminishes the reality of things in man's immediate experience by conceiving their nature as dependent on a changing God and a changing *kairos*. The result is a mutable, intrinsic truth-value for all the common realities which might be used as symbols. In order for such changing

[132] See *ibid.*, pp. 31–33.

realities to acquire the power of pointing, which is essential
to a symbol, a subjective act must be added. Only then is
the direction of this pointing determined and the participation in the power of the object of the pointing completed.
This subjective act takes on special importance in a system
such as Tillich's where "meaning," or being in relation to us,
is given almost the importance which is attributed to the
simple concept of being in Scholastic philosophy.

When it comes to the knowledge of God, this weakness
makes it necessary to look through the external realities to
their "depth dimension," in order to find sufficient reality and
sufficient similarity to make up the symbol of the divine.
This implies that, what gives Tillich the possibility of having a symbol of the divine at all, is his dialectical system by
which God goes out from himself into the state of existence,
where his essence is realized and participated in existentially
by the multitude of beings, especially man. Beings can, of
themselves, be symbols of the divine precisely because of this
divine depth dimension within them. Their Yes element is
the divine itself. It appears from this that the basic possibility
of divine symbols depends on this element of pantheism in
the system of Paul Tillich and advances only as this element
is stressed.

This is not to say that Tillich is a pantheist. It is, rather,
one of the orientations in his philosophy which he wishes to
balance by its dialectical contrary. He states that "the pantheistic element in the classical doctrine that God is *ipsum
esse*, being-itself, is as necessary for a Christian doctrine of
God as the mystical element of the divine presence."[133]
But he adds that it must be overcome by a metaphysical and
dialectical realism which unites "the structural oneness of
everything within the absolute with the undecided and unfinished manifoldness of the real."[134] Nevertheless, while
ontologically the divine remains an analytic depth dimension

---

[133] ST, I, p. 234. Tillich defines this pantheism as the doctrine
"that God is the substance or essence of all things, not the meaningless assertion that God is the totality of things."

[134] *Ibid.*, p. 235.

of reality, the "pantheistic element" on which he insists is balanced only by his dialectic, and not eliminated.[135]

It is, in fact, only the Fall which impedes this pantheistic element from making all beings symbols of the divine. Creation could have taken place in such a way that existence would only express and not contradict essence. However, as a simple matter of fact, the Fall accompanied the transition into existence in such a way that existence not only expresses but contradicts essence. It is obtuse to God. This situation can be overcome only in the situation of revelation. It is in this encounter with the divine as showing through the contradictions of concrete existence that various realities regain their power of actually pointing to the divine. This is where the religious symbol is born, and it lasts as long as there remains the correlation of God and man which takes place in revelation.

Note the implications of this as regards both method and content. The method makes the symbol not the means, but the result of religious knowledge. The correlation of revelation as an already existing fact is a necessary element in the production of the symbol. As a result, the symbol cannot contribute completely new knowledge of the divine. Furthermore, as was mentioned above, for Tillich, religious knowledge essentially implies a subjective act of the will and emotions at its focal point of union. The result is that this knowledge "is not a theoretical, it is an existential truth, that is, a truth to which I cannot have the spectator-attitude, to which I must surrender in order to experience it. In this sense the 'symbols provide no objective knowledge.'"[136] The subjective element thus infects religious symbols, and the death blow is dealt to any contribution symbols might have made to an objective knowledge of God's nature.

The implications of making religious symbols a product of

---

[135] Tillich's final decision against pantheism is motivated by his desire to protect man's freedom, but it fits so well with his dominant religious interest in the transcendence of the divine that he cannot be accused of simple pantheism.

[136] Tillich, "Symbol and Knowledge: A Response," *art. cit.*, 204.

revelation are equally disappointing regarding the content of symbols. What is contained in the religious symbol, as such, is not information about the nature of God or even the roots of such information. It is simply the experience of the reality of the depth of being and of our relation to this reality.[137] A variation of symbols does not give us a new note concerning God, an additional "belief that," but only represents a new correlation to God, an additional "belief in." What is varied is only our relation to God in the encounter and not the knowledge we have of God himself. Again it is the subjective and relative aspect which begins to show through and to weaken the nature of the symbol. The true value of the religious symbol becomes its power of pointing to God. The variation of the conceptual content follows and implies a variation of meaning only on our side of our special correlation to the divine.

A Thomistic Evaluation of Tillich's Religious Symbol

Just as it was natural for Tillich's reduced conception of analogy and the symbol to leave him in a weak position concerning knowledge of the nature of God, so it is natural for the internal reality which St. Thomas places in his analogy to make a definite contribution regarding this knowledge. When treating before of St. Thomas' analogy, we considered its equivocal element and its various types. Now let us take a look at the univocal element contained there, for if the analogous are "simply different," they are still "in a way similar" (secundum quid unum). It is by studying this bond of union, however tenuous it may be in the various types of analogy, that we shall come to a comprehension of how our intellect is able to proceed to a knowledge of God's nature.[138]

---

[137] See ST, I, p. 109.

[138] "L'analogie se meut dans le 'simpliciter diversum,' mais c'est pour y retrouver le 'secundum quid unum'; elle veut ordonner la diversité; dans la multiplicité du réel elle recherche l'unité relative, dans le dissemblable, la similitude proportionnelle. Et par là, elle s'af-

St. Thomas, in arriving at the answer to the question of existence (the *an sit*), affirms the existence of a supreme cause on which all other beings depend. In doing this he posits the prime analogate needed to automatically turn the relations of dependence in the orders of efficiency, finality, and exemplarity, which had first been observed in reality, into analogies of attribution. All that was needed to constitute the reality of those analogies was the reality of the term to which they were related and by which they are designated.[139] This is true to the degree that if, *per impossible*, being did not belong intrinsically to God, it could still be attributed to him inasmuch as he is the cause of the being of creatures and known to exist as such by the five ways. This is the basis for the objection of Maimonides which we shall consider in just a moment. At this stage, then, what is known of God is known by analogy of attribution. We see that, behind the facts of experience, there must be a cause-of-them, not-them. This other is known only in relation to the created realities and in its distinction from them.[140] Note that here the analogy of attribution is only virtual.[141]

This is not enough, however, for the analogy of attribution tells us only about the relations to this cause and nothing about the nature of the cause. In fact, it leaves room for the

---

firme encore comme doctrine de juste milieu" (Penido, *op. cit.*, p. 62).

[139] *"Creator et creatura reducuntur in unum, non communitate univocationis, sed analogiae; . . . ex eo quod unum Esse et Rationem ab altere recipit, et talis est analogia creaturae ad creatorem; creatura . . . nec nominatur ens nisi in quantum Primum Ens imitatur"* (St. Thomas Aquinas, *In I Sent.*, Prolog., q. 1, a. 2 ad 2).

[140] See Ryan, "God and Analogy," *art. cit.*, 140–41.

[141] See John of St. Thomas, *Logica*, II, q. 14, a. 3. For a consideration of the implications of the necessity of an intrinsic foundation for the relations of dependence, cf. Deandrea, *op. cit.*, pp. 170–75. This concludes in rejection of the incompatibility of formal realizations of the two types of analogy and a reinforcement of the intrinsic element of the analogy of attribution. The more commonly accepted opinion expressed above is that of John of St. Thomas and might be considered a maximum approximation to Tillich's position by Scholasticism.

objection of Maimonides that the effect need be in the cause but virtually, with the result that one is able to conclude only that God exists and not that he has being or any perfection in himself. The conclusion might be valid except that we are now working with pure perfections. A mixed perfection, such as corporeity, considered as a perfection, could be indifferent to its mode of realization with or without its imperfection. But a pure perfection cannot be in its cause in a different way without the cause lacking some of the perfection of its effect. This would lead to the contradiction of an effect being more perfect than its cause—or something coming from nothing. Thus, we must place the analogous reality formally in God.[142] Lest, however, the order of reasoning and that of reality be confused, it is necessary to bear in mind that the perfection itself comes from God to creatures who participate in it, and not vice versa.

It will be noted that this is, of necessity, quite contrary to the position of Paul Tillich. Without a vigorous conception of the intrinsic reality of the analogy of proper proportionality and of the radically analogous character of being itself, the ideas expressed above would, as Tillich affirms, be quite idolatrous. The interest in the analogy of proper proportionality arises when one asks what is meant by the statement that the perfections we know are in God. This cannot be known by the analogy of attribution, for this deals only in extrinsic relations—those of other beings to God. It does not tell anything about the relation of the nature of this cause to the nature of the effects. For this reason, St. Thomas calls on the analogy of proportionality to establish a proportion within God which will in some way indicate how the pure perfections of creation are in the Creator. Is there a reality on which this type of analogy can be based? The answer is affirmative, for, if the five ways lead to an uncaused cause, they also lead to a nonparticipated being to whom being belongs essentially. Since this can be but one, and all causality is a giving of being, all things participate in this being. There is, then, the imperfectly one reality which

---

[142] See St. Thomas Aquinas, *Summa contra gentiles*, I, 28–29.

realizes itself according to diverse modes in God and in
finite beings. With this as a basis, it is possible to institute
a relation of proportions. The proportions will be those of the
terms with their own acts of being, for example:

Creature : its being : : God : his being.

With this proportion of proportions established, one can
know something about God. One can know the proportion
between the two created terms on the left and know that
this proportion is somehow realized between the uncreated
terms on the right. Thus, within the unknowness of God
there is something positively known, namely, the formal realization of this perfection and its verification of this proportion. However, in what way the proportion is realized in God
is not known, because it depends on the central relation—
that between the two proportions.[143]

To all of this Tillich makes a number of objections, most
of which are based on his notion of the symbol and of the
nature of God. These were treated above. However, there
remains one central difficulty stemming from the infinity of
God. Tillich's conception of the divine, not as another being but as the depth dimension of being, while not preclud-
ing any consideration of him, is such that any word about
God as he is in himself is unfounded. A proportion of proportions concerning God would then contain the famous two
unknowns. Tillich might be able to admit Thomas' reasoning were it about creatures alone, because both proportions
together with the proportion between them would be known
from experience. But in the case of a proportionality between God and creatures, man does not know what it is for
being to be in God. From this there follows the objection
that, rather than one unknown there are two—both terms
which concern God. The result is a form of agnosticism in

---

[143] "If we happen to know one of the terms of the remote proportion independently of the central proposition, this to some extent determines the actual proportion, and correspondingly determines our knowledge of both the remote proportion and its remaining
unknown term" (Ryan, "God and Analogy," *art. cit.*, 140–41).

which man can point to the divine but never know about him.

It would seem that the reason why this objection is not valid is that the fourth term, the existence of God, is, in fact, already known to us by another analogy—that of attribution—as seen above.

In these equations there are two terms directly known, one uncreated term which is indirectly known by appealing to the principle of causality, and we infer the fourth term, which is indirectly known in a *positive* way, from what it has analogically in common with creatures, in a *negative* and *relative* way as regards its proper divine mode.[144]

Man has, then, a knowledge of the nature of God which is drawn from an analogy of proportionality. That much is basic and must be admitted. But logically prior to this, one has an analogy of attribution expressing the existence of God. This analogy of attribution does two things: first, it supplies the needed term so that the analogy of proportionality can become operative and tell us something about God; secondly, it binds the two sides of the analogy of proportionality together. It refuses to allow the two essence-existence relations to remain separate, but joins them in a union fruitful to our knowledge of God. Without proportionality we could but virtually predicate things of God. Without attribution we could not avoid agnosticism. The two, remaining distinct but united in a tightly interlocked union which might be called a mixed analogy, are necessary for true knowledge of God.[145] Thus, the Thomistic system uses its realistic conception of a radical analogy of being in all its amplitude in order to make success possible in man's highest task, knowledge of God.

[144] Garrigou-Lagrange, *op. cit.*, II, p. 220.
[145] See Eric Mascall, *Existence and Analogy* (London: Longman's, Green, 1949), p. 113.

X

GUSTAVE WEIGEL, S.J.

Myth, Symbol, and Analogy

One of the characteristic traits of the Gospel of St. John is the device often used by the author whereby an obviously figurative statement of Christ is interpreted by his hearers with gross literalism.[1] This is, of course, a stylistic artifice, but it points up clearly the nature of the Christian kerygma. It is clear from the four Gospels, and most of all from the Gospel of John, that the verbal formulas are not always to be understood in their *prima facie* vulgar sense.

Little satisfaction is achieved by attempting to construct historiographically the events of the life of Christ, as the bewildered quest of "the historical Jesus" showed. Today the majority of theologians are of the mind that not too much can be accomplished by the rigid application of the rules of the modern historian's sober craft to the New Testament documents. Nor is this a new persuasion, for the Alexandrine expositors, in the tradition of Clement and Origen, looked on principle for a meaning of the words far below the surface. We call their approach pneumatic, spiritual, mystical, allegorical, typical, symbolic. This kind of interpretation was dear to the Christians for many centuries. The medieval distich—

> *Littera gesta docet, quid credas allegoria,*
> *Moralis quid agas, quo tendas anagogia—*

gives it high importance, for the *credenda* of Scripture were

[1] See 2:19–20; 3:3–4; 4:10–11; 4:32–33; 6:51–52; 7:33–35; 8:18–19; 8:56–57; 11:11–12; 12:32–34; 13:8–9; 13:36–38; 14:3–5; 14:7–8; 18:33–37; 21:22–23.

assigned to the allegorical sense. What is more, for many medieval doctors, such as St. Thomas, the anagogic and moral senses were, in their way, symbolic.[2]

Hermeneutical Orientations

However, the tendency to seek first the symbolic sense of the scriptural dicta always had an opposition. The Antiochians, in the spirit of Theodore of Mopsuestia, were uncomfortable with symbolic hermeneutics. They preferred to stick to the letter. It was not so much that they advocated a puerile literalism, but rather they wished to transpose the kerygma and *didache* into simply intelligible propositions in the light of common logic and the philosophic assumptions of their times.

These two rival hermeneutical orientations simultaneously march down the centuries of the Christian era. The Fathers and the earlier Scholastics had a keen eye for the symbolic content of revelation, while the Age of the Reform was strongly inclined to remain with the more obvious burden of the words. This inclination, with time, helped to produce the historicism of the nineteenth century with its chimeric search for the "historical Jesus." Today, a reaction against rationalistic historicism has brought us back again to the possibilities of allegory and symbol.

Thomas Aquinas wished to mediate between the two tendencies, and his views prevailed in the Catholic Church. He gladly admitted the validity of allegorical interpretation, but gave the primacy to the text as it stood; it was the "historical" or "literal" sense (the literary sense, as we would say today) which must first engage the attention of the interpreter. In its light there could be a transition to the allegorical dimensions of the message. The "historical" sense was basic, and only under its guidance could an appeal be made to the "spiritual" meaning.

The multiplicity of scriptural senses does not make the

---

[2] See *Quaestio quodlibitalis* VII, q. 6, a. 15.

Scriptures equivocal or in any way multiple in meaning. As was said above, there are many senses in the Scripture without implying that the same word has many meanings. The multiplicity of senses derives from the fact that the objective things signified by the words can, in turn, have a symbolic function with reference to other things. Consequently, there is no confusion in Scripture, for all the senses are founded on one alone, namely, the literal sense. Moreover, when arguing from Scripture, evidence must be drawn exclusively from the literal meaning. Allegorical interpretation is no argument, as St. Augustine saw.[3] This involves no loss of scriptural content, because there is nothing necessary for faith to be grasped from the symbolism which is not clearly expressed elsewhere by the literal sense.[4]

St. Thomas had solved the problem of hermeneutics, at least to his satisfaction. He was both Antiochian and Alexandrine; he could go along with both without any negation of the valid insights achieved by either camp. Thomas' philological method would hardly come up to the standards set today, but the textual critic and philological investigator on the Thomistic principle must be considered as formally, even though subsidiarily, engaged in the theological enterprise.

Perhaps the weightiest objection to fundamentalist literalism, or even to the moderate historicist position of Aquinas, was clearly put by Reinhold Niebuhr: "I do not know how it is possible to believe in anything pertaining to God and eternity 'literally.' "[5]

The support for this objection is found in the finitude of human conception and the inevitable bondage of human language to the finite God is the Infinite, the Trans-human, the

---

[3] *Epistula contra Vincentium Donatistam:* "Is it not the height of impudence to interpret an allegorical locus to one's own advantage, unless the obscurity of the allegory is removed in the light of testimonies whose meaning is clear?" (Ep. 93, c. 8, n. 24, *PL* 33:384.)

[4] See St. Thomas Aquinas, *Summa theologiae*, I, q. 1, a. 10 ad 1.

[5] "Reply to Interpretation and Criticism," C. Kegley and R. Bretall, editors, *Reinhold Niebuhr, His Religious, Social, and Political Thought* (New York: Macmillan, 1956), p. 446.

"wholly Other." Hence, human language and human thought cannot express him as he is. At most they can only point to the ultimate reality, Tillich's ground of being, in terms of existentialist concern.

In the place cited, Niebuhr makes it clear that he cannot subscribe totally to Rudolf Bultmann's call for "demythologization." This does not mean that Niebuhr and Bultmann are in disagreement as to the nature of the biblical message. For both of them it is a stimulus to existentialist reflection, and in the reflection "revelation" is achieved. The difference between the men, and Tillich would go along with Niebuhr, is that Bultmann thinks there is too much myth in the Scriptures, while Niebuhr, admitting the presence of myth, would consider that much of the so-called myth is really valid symbol. We have here two concepts in play: myth and symbol.

Myth and Symbol

So much has been written about these two terms that one is afraid to say any more about them.[6] Yet, something more must be said, for there is much confusion on this score. For Bultmann, the Scriptures must be demythologized, not because myth can ever be eliminated from the formulation of the biblical message, but because the mythology employed by the Bible stands in the way of modern man's achievement of the biblical truth. By biblical mythology Bultmann means the ancients' accepted image of the universe in terms of their physics, cosmology, psychology, and sociology. That image is so thoroughly in conflict with the image functioning in our day that the former inevitably alienates our age, which does not believe in miracles, angels, demonic possession, an-

[6] Two newer studies are well worth mentioning: E. C. Blackman, "The Task of Exegesis," W. D. Davies and D. Daube, editors, *The Background of the New Testament and Its Eschatology, In Honour of Charles Harold Dodd* (Cambridge: University Press, 1956), pp. 3–26; and in the same volume, H. Riesenfeld, "The Mythical Background of the New Testament Christology," pp. 81–95.

thropomorphic divinity, autocracy, slavery, and other constituents of the classical world vision. The biblical message must, therefore, be couched in harmony with the image accepted by current man in order to be effective in our day. Just how this is to be done is not so clear. Although Bultmann wishes to reform the expression of the kerygma, he does not want to rewrite the Scriptures nor does he want to edit out large or small sections of the books.

There is one fundamental assumption in the demythologizing plea which has not been criticized sufficiently. Is it true that myth is a barrier to the correct understanding of substance? The Greeks had various terms for "word." Three of them are relevant to our purpose: *rhema, mythos,* and *logos. Rhema* was neutral; it referred to the material vocal (or written) sign, much as does the Latin *vox* or *sermo. Mythos* implied the image-evoking value of the word. *Logos* referred to the intellectual content of the term, rendered in Latin as *ratio.* Every word is simultaneously *rhema, mythos,* and *logos.* Any word can be considered from all of these three viewpoints. Thoroughgoing demythologization, in consequence, can only be achieved in completely wordless communication. That is something humanly difficult, if at all possible. The myth dimension of human communication is no obstacle to correct understanding. Ronald Knox somewhere points out that the scriptural phrase "the bowels of his mercy" is not English, for we would rather speak of a man's kind heart. The observation is true enough, but the initial distraction of the image does not rob it of its power to communicate accurate meaning. With time and familiarity we may even ignore a term's image so that we can say that the sun rises and the sun sets, though the astronomical assumptions of today's prevailing myth reject any notion of the sun's movement around the earth.

The mythological component of language is no defect of language; only a sign of man's dependence on image for thought. Effective works of literary communication fuse the functions of imagery and thought evocation, with the consequence that it would kill the precise message of the writer if we were to change his imagery. The reader will not grasp such images exactly as the writer formed them in his own fantasy, but the *ratio* is still carried genuinely by the kindred image produced.[7] To demythologize the Scriptures means to substitute a different message from the one contained there.

One cannot help but suspect that the champions of demythologization unconsciously want to change it. They seem to manifest a loss of nerve because of which they cannot retain the biblical burden as they find it. Of course they recognize so many good things in it. Hence, they hope that a radical reconstruction will give us something better to take its place. This is an understandable endeavor, but why call its result Christianity?

Barth, Tillich, and Niebuhr seem to see the flaws in the project of demythologization. But, with Bultmann, they feel that there is a *scandalum pusillorum* involved in biblical rhetoric. They do not, however, bridle at the presence of myth in the Scriptures, because they readily appreciate that only children, young or old, identify *logos* with *mythos*. They recognize that an adult easily and effectively distinguishes between the two. The difficulty vexing the existentialist theologians concerns not the *mythos* but the *logos* of the Bible. This difficulty is eminently and properly theological because it stems from the theological principle that the *logos* of Scripture cannot be taken literally, since no human *logos* is equipped for the task of revealing the transcendent God.

What, then, is the solution of existentialist theology? Neither demythologization nor fundamentalist or historicist literalism, but in their stead symbolism. Perhaps the most stimulating definition of theological symbolism was given by Tillich when he said:

One of the things I aways forbid my students to say is "only a symbol." This bad phrase is rooted in the confusion of sign and symbol. Signs point to something different in which they do not participate at all. Symbols participate in the power of what they symbolize.[8]

[7] This point is well illustrated in an article by Heinrich Schlier, "The New Testament and Myth," *The Relevance of the New Testament* (New York: Herder and Herder, 1967), 76–93.

[8] Letter to G. Weigel, S.J.; see above, p. 55.

If we may examine this statement somewhat, it seems true to say that a symbol is a sign but not simply a sign. It is more than a sign because it shares in the reality which it signifies. The green light at the street crossing is a simple sign of an open street, because its being is totally alien to the being of the street. Open street and green light are only mythically conjoined. In the phenomenon of fire, however, smoke is a constituent element of the integral phenomenon, and thus smoke is a symbol of fire. It is not all of it; it is not even its essence, but it shares existentially in the essential being of fire.

In this sense the Scriptures must be understood as symbolic statements. Hence, when they speak of God as Lord, as Creator, as Father, as King, we are in the realm of symbolism. It is not stated that God is literally any one of these things, but rather that lordship, contingent reality, paternity, and dominion have their roots in God, the ground of being, and in their way point to him in telling fashion. When Jesus as the Christ is called God, we are not told that Jesus of Nazareth was God, but rather that in the encounter with the phenomenon of Jesus, God was revealed to man definitively under the guidance of man's ultimate concern.

Similarly, Niebuhr can take the third chapter of Genesis and see in it not merely a myth of primal innocence and its loss, but rather the symbolic affirmation of man's estrangement from God through the fact of sin. The myth in its literal dimensions is not the object of concern. What concerns us is the symbolic affirmation that man, any man, from his origin estranges himself from transcendental righteousness through the selfishness operative in all his works. Niebuhr, in this position, considers himself as reading the symbol differently from Tillich. As Niebuhr sees it, Tillich has man estranged from God by the mere fact of creation, while the Bible shows man estranged not by creation but by sin. However, the difference seems not to be too great, for Niebuhr's man will inevitably sin as soon as he is created.

Seeing symbol where Bultmann sees only myth gives the symbolists a great advantage. They have no need of demythologizing. On the contrary, they see the definitive value of the Bible precisely in its effective symbolism. In Scripture we are faced not with "prescientific myths" but "permanently valid symbols."[9] In consequence, they can wholeheartedly agree with the current cry that theology should take its categories from the Scriptures, where the history of revelation is most genuinely given.

However, the symbolist pays a price for his advantages. The historical concreteness of the biblical accounts, patent to any reader, is swallowed up into a transhistorical awareness of existence. Christ is risen indeed, but this does not state that Jesus of Nazareth physically rose from the dead. We are only told symbolically that the man of perfect faith rises above death, which then loses its existentially constrictive menace. The man of faith lives "eternally," in dimensions beyond time.

In such a hermeneutic it is postulated that the Bible as a record of revelation does not teach history, for history is not a matter of ultimate concern. Tillich has been reported as being quite explicit on this point.[10] As a record of revelation, the Scriptures make no historiographic statements, and to look for such betrays a misunderstanding of their nature. If a historian uses the Bible as something less than a record of revelation, he is using a document of dubious trustworthiness, because any historiographic value in the books is completely irrelevant to the real significance of the reports. The Bible is a record of revelation and not the historiographic presentation of secular events. The symbolists make much of the meaning of history, but as theologians they ignore on principle any historiographic validity of the Bible.

The eminent Orientalist William F. Albright grows somewhat uneasy with this hermeneutical method. He has called Tillich a "modern gnostic."[11] "Tillich has grafted C. G.

---

[9] Loc. cit.

[10] See Avery Dulles, S.J., "Paul Tillich and the Bible," in this volume.

[11] A pertinent study of gnosticism and the New Testament is given by R. P. Casey, "Gnosis, Gnosticism, and the New Testament," pp. 52–80, in the memorial volume to C. H. Dodd mentioned above in fn. 6.

Jung on Schelling's pantheism . . . and produced a theological system which resembles traditional Christianity only in superficial aspects."[12]

Tillich and the symbolists deny such an accusation vehemently. They see themselves as very genuine Christians, following a middle way already previsioned dimly in the reformers. Unlike fundamentalists, who consider every proposition of the Bible or of dogmatic intent as a statement of secular event or secular fact, they reject literalism. The symbolist insists that he does not take the affirmations literally; but he equally insists that he takes them seriously. In his position he avoids the unseriousness of absurd literalism and the equally unserious treason of those who will not take the scriptural affirmations as statements of truth. The truth, of course, is existential, the answers to man's ultimate concern. Biblical propositions indeed speak of history, but not historiographically.

This is brilliant. But it nonetheless gives the impression that history is no longer a concrete flux, but rather a nonfluid comprehensive abstraction, dialectically opposed to the nonhistorical. In this opposition, history becomes so dehistorized that it can stand in homogeneous polar relationship with metahistory. *Contraria sunt eiusdem speciei.* Can thoroughgoing transhistorical symbolism do justice to the historical preoccupations of the Christian message? It is understandable that so able a historian as William F. Albright should become irked when history, which he knows through lifelong work, suddenly means something which for him is not history at all.

It is all very well for Niebuhr to say that his symbolic approach to the record of revelation must not be identified with Bultmann's ideas on demythologization. Proximately they are not the same, obviously. Ultimately, however, there is a high degree of coincidence. Bultmann is still concerned with the mythical level of revelational language, but the symbolists, on principle, ignore it from the outset. They concentrate on

[12] "Toynbee's Book on Religion Reviewed," *Evening Sun*, Baltimore, Sept. 11, 1956, p. 20, col. 7.

the transhistorical meaning of mythical expression and thus render it a symbol. Bultmann makes a plea for demythologization. He is too late; the symbolists have effectively anticipated his need.

Bultmann's call appears to show that there are unresolved problems in symbolist hermeneutics. Undoubtedly, the main obstacle confronting the symbolists is the refusal of the human community to share their assumption that religious truth can be equated with the answers to man's ultimate concern, which latter is irrevocably a subjective experience. Professor Ben F. Kimpel of Drew University put it very well:

> No religious individual believes that his experience constitutes the source of his security. The source of the security is the reality in which he believes, and to which he orients his life in complete trust. Hence, he wants to know the nature of this reality. . . .
> A belief about the nature of the divine reality is, therefore, not the criterion by which a religious individual proposes to select from among the competing claims to knowledge those beliefs which are true. An earnest religious individual wants to know the divine reality, and yet, his earnestness is not a sufficient condition for selecting true beliefs from other beliefs which may be held with equal earnestness. Earnestness is a condition for learning, but it is not a criterion by which the character of belief can be ascertained.
> According to religious faith, the criterion for the truth-character of interpretations of the divine reality is a knowledge of the divine reality.[13]

The symbolists use the word "serious" very often. On last reduction does their seriousness coalesce with Kimpel's earnestness?

In the light of the dissatisfactions aroused by both symbolic and demythologized hermeneutics, a rapid glance at the generic solution of Aquinas may be helpful. Passing over the positive core in demythologization, let us face the strong point in the symbolist position. The symbolists cannot see how any

[13] *Religious Faith, Language, and Knowledge: A Philosophical Preface to Theology* (New York: Philosophical Library, 1952), p. 72.

human word can be applied literally to God. Therefore, they must look for a nonliteral meaning in the affirmation.

Perhaps we are being misled by the word "literal." Is it simply true that we cannot use any word "literally" of God? It is universally recognized that we refer to God with words. The symbolists do it no less than others, and Tillich has said that God "is not the 'ineffable' simply and unconditionally; but on the basis of his ineffability much can and must be said about him."[14]

As Tillich has seen, symbolism is similar to Thomistic analogy. Now, Thomas cannot be logically compelled to choose one or the other of the members in the disjunction: literal or symbolic. On his principles of predication the disjunction is a false one, for he can logically add a *tertium* with ease. He did so when he insisted that the biblical content was simultaneously literal and symbolic, though the literal enjoyed a normative primacy in theological dialogue.

Analogy

The ambiguous word in our current hermeneutical discussions is "literal." Aristotle distinguished literal predications by establishing the dichotomy between univocal and equivocal.[15] With something less than profound insight, he placed analogy, an inferential process known to Plato and the mathematicians before him, under equivocation. Mathematics and philosophy continuously reworked the concept up to the time of Thomas. Aquinas then produced his own theory without, however, explaining its totality explicitly. Yet, the general lines of his doctrine can easily be detected in his writings.[16]

---

[14] Letter to G. Weigel, S.J.; see above, p. 55.

[15] See Joseph Owens, C.Ss.R., *The Doctrine of Being in the Aristotelian Metaphysics* (Toronto: Pont. Inst. Med. Stud., 1951), pp. 49 ff.

[16] Cf. Hampus Lyttkens, *The Analogy between God and the World, An Investigation of Its Background and Interpretation of Its*

According to Thomistic thought, a word in its literal sense can be predicated univocally, simply equivocally, or analogously. In all three instances we are dealing with the word literally. The symbolic power in the term need not be touched at all. When I say "rook," the word may mean a crow or a chess piece. This ambiguity occurs by reason of the literal power of the word. A simple equivocation faces us, and in fact we do not encounter the same word in two cases. It is not *una vox*, except as *rhema*. Actually two different words are offered us, though the sign structure is equal—*aequa vox*.

But when I speak of the leg of a man and the leg of a table there is neither univocity nor simple equivocation. In both cases the word is used literally. It is absurd to say that the leg of the table is a symbol of a human leg, for it is neither the symbol nor the sign of it. Of course it is true that the leg of a table is analogous to the leg of a man. The proposition, "This is the leg of the table," immediately affirms something literal of the table, and on ultimate reduction also affirms that there is a proportion between a human leg and a table leg. This proportion is literally true. The partial function of a human leg with respect to a man is equivalent (not equal!) to the partial function of a table leg with respect to the table. We rightly use the term "leg" in both instances literally, but with analogy. And let it be remembered that analogy must not be reduced to metaphor, though any truth content of a metaphor is derived from the prior principle of analogy.

Analogy or proportionality is not the conquest of a mystical perception nor the object of an experience so baffling as that suggested in some of the descriptions of the symbolists when they try to explain the existential perception of the ground of being. Any child recognizes the similarity which really exists between two relations. What is more, analogy can be employed in reasoning, for the mathematics of proportion is a purely logical achievement.

Use by Thomas of Aquino (Uppsala: Almqvist & Wiksells Boktrycheri AB, 1952). The older work of the Brazilian, Maurilio Texeira-Leite Penido, *Le rôle de l'analogie en théologie dogmatique* (Paris: Vrin, 1931), is highly esteemed in Catholic circles, though Lyttkens has found shortcomings in it.

The recognition of the role of analogy seems to explode the difficulty against the literal predication of human terms to God. Could it be that that eloquent symbolist, Karl Barth, glimpsed this when he declared, probably in irritation, that *analogia entis* was the invention of Antichrist? Whoever invented it certainly drove a powerful wedge between the horns of the supposed dilemma: univocal literalism or unliteral symbolism. The concept of analogy tells us that there is the a priori possibility of analogous literalism. Nor need we assign the discovery of analogy to Antichrist. The demon is the *simia Dei* (ape of God). He can only misleadingly imitate God. Now, which is the real thing and which the fraudulent copy: analogy or gnosticizing symbolism? We must discern the spirits, and in the relatively long history of Christianity the analogous understanding of the scriptural statements concerning God has a record of piety, whereas cavalier impatience with the letter has always been suspect.

Nor need the symbolist fear that the "utter otherness" of God is denied by an analogous understanding of the formulas which speak to us of God. In a proportion we do not say that the half of an orange is in any way equal to the half of a melon. We only say that in ratio of whole and half they are equivalent. When the Scriptures call God our King, they are not saying that God is our Nero. It is only affirmed that Nero's proper power in his limited field of direction is relatively equivalent on his side of the equation to the absolute dominion of God over us on the other side. There is no univocity; no equality. We all know that we cannot conceive God's dominion absolutely. We only conceive it relatively to what we know of human dominion, for proportionality is a reality of the order of relation. Nor does this give us only formal knowledge. When I am told that the boy before me looks like his father, I know something about the father I have never seen.

Analogy does not immediately answer the problem which Bultmann tries to solve by demythologization, though indirectly it can offer us a different solution. The historiographical aspects of the Scriptures can be safeguarded, nor need they be cast into the discard. Analogy pervades all language.[17] It is vexing to a foursquare rationalist that this is so, for he wants only univocal terms, so that all valid inference can be restricted to an Aristotelian syllogism.

But reality itself stubbornly resists the rationalist's prejudice. The realism so characteristic of the English language accepts analogy without a qualm, so that the same word can be a substantive, verb, and adjective—all with different levels of meaning. The genuine root-meaning is not precisely the same in all instances, but an analogical perception makes diverse uses easily intelligible without confusion. Now, "history" is a chameleon word in English. It can mean the flux dimension of empirical reality. It can mean historiography. It can mean a philosophy of history. And it can mean a theological interpretation of history.

The formulas of Christian revelation, scriptural or nonscriptural, are in large part theological interpretations of history. For this function, the methodological precision and detailed accuracy in the presentation of historical data are not called for. Historical data can be referred to in many ways. Folklore does it. So does epopoeia. Theological interpretation rightly telescopes the data or even poetizes them, but the genuine data are referred to, even if the reference is not to ultimate sources nor given with rigid definition.

It is true enough that the methodologically exact historian uses the scriptural monuments at his own risk, but it is equally true, as experience has proved, that historiography can successfully and profitably use the Scriptures in its work. The rhetorical exaggerations and fanciful reconstructions inevitable in a small people's chauvinism are not imprecisions. They are merely evidence that, in the selected literary genre, precision in the offering of data was not contemplated.

In the light of this rapid sketch we can glimpse values and defects in symbolism and demythologization. With the symbolists we can consider as unserious and rather puerile the

---

[17] This is admirably brought out by J. V. Langmead Casserly in "Event-Symbols and Myth-Symbols," *Anglican Theological Review*, 38 (1956), 127–37, 242–48.

assumption that the biblical writers were writing history with the purpose a modern historian pursues in his work. This is fundamentalism, which always runs the risk of becoming ridiculous. On the other hand, to refuse to see any kind of historiography in the Scriptures seems willful and unfaithful to the books before our eyes. Scriptural historiography is analogous to ours. It must be understood, not by the canons of Bernheim, but by the modes and styles of the past, and according to the theological purposes of the authors. To ignore, overlook, or discard the analogously historiographical dimensions of the Bible is to change a record of flux into static Platonic didacticism. Seriousness, earnestness, plain unvarnished candor prevent such a procedure.

XI

ERICH PRZYWARA, S.J.

Christian Root-Terms: Kerygma, Mysterium, Kairos, Oikonomia

The thought of Paul Tillich, in its innermost intention, is directed to the examination of Christian root-terms. This focus emerges early, in his interpretation of Schelling who himself had sought for a "philosophy of revelation," not for the purpose of taking up revelation into a final philosophical concept (as did Hegel), but rather to understand revelation in terms of its own immanent concepts. As Schelling was dependent upon Boehme and Franz von Baader who developed such an immanent philosophy of revelation, so Tillich, in his turn, interpreted this tradition in his first works,[1] attempting to draw from it the final consequences for the development of a possible "Christian grammar." Such a grammar, for Tillich, culminates in the *kairos*, around which his whole thought moves.[2]

[1] See *Die religionsgeschichtliche Konstruktion in Schelling's positiver Philosophie* (Breslau: H. Fleischmann, 1910), and *Mystik und Schuldbewusstsein in Schelling's philosophischer Entwicklung* (Gütersloh: C. Bertelsmann, 1912).

[2] See *Kairos: Zur Geisteslage und Geisteswendung* (Darmstadt: Otto Reichl, 1926), and *Protestantismus als Kritik und Gestaltung* (Darmstadt: Otto Reichl, 1929); see also the author's analysis of Tillich's philosophy of religion in *Humanitas* (Nürnberg, 1952).

Material Christian Root-Terms

Christian root-terms can be understood materially or formally. Taken *materially*, root-terms refer to the content of Christian revelation and point to the fulfillment of its particular revelation. This centrality of a *particular* revelation appears in the history of thought from Irenaeus to Augustine, in terms of the *admirabile commercium* or the *commutatio:* the "spiritual barter" between God and man fulfilled in Christ as the "Mediator" who functions as a dynamic "medium."

The special material root-term of the Christianity of the Middle Ages, particularly in Thomas Aquinas, was the *ordo universi* in a *perfectio universi:* that is, "sacral ordering of all," understood as the ground of revelation in the Prologue of John the Evangelist and in the Epistles to the Ephesians and Colossians. (Christ "before the foundation of the world" to "the new heavens and the new earth" as *archē, anakephalaiēsis,* and *synhestēken* of the "whole creation," of the "whole cosmos," of "everything in heaven and earth.") This material root-term, having the same intention of meaning as the original Christian "spiritual barter," is now expressed in terms of a "Christian ordering of all" in Christ as *Logos* and the Holy Spirit as *Paraclete*.[3]

Out of this interpretation in the Middle Ages arose the special root-term of the Reformation: "justification by faith alone." In it there is a return to the situation of the Epistle to the Romans and the Epistle to the Galatians. As Paul counters the "sacramental justice" of Judaism with a "divine justification" by the justice of God, so the Reformation counters the static institutional justice of the Middle Ages with a dynamic "justification," in which the pure receptive potentiality of man becomes the divine expression of justice in the dialectical claim of justice and grace. The Reformation

[3] Cf. the author's *Christentum gemäss Johannes* (Nürnberg, 1943), pp. 229 ff.

doctrine of "justification" as the article by which the Church
stands or falls (*articulus stantis et cadentia ecclesiae*) excludes all juristic thinking in its appeal to the primordial
mysterium of *Deus irae et gratiae* which (according to
Romans 11) is the "abyss of the deep and the high (*bathos*),"
expressed in Luther's "volcanic" experience, made a cardinal
principle in the cosmic theosophy of Jacob Boehme, and
today again emphasized in Paul Tillich's philosophy of religion.[4]

But this material root-term of "justification through faith
alone" has met in our day a counter root-term in the rediscovery of the cult emphasis in the Epistle to the Hebrews:
the *High Priesthood of Christ in the Holy Temple*, whom
"God ordains and not man"; a High Priest not only in heaven
but "announced from the *Agora*," in the markets of the
world. Christian salvation is thus seen not as a simple ontic
"barter," nor merely as an aspect of a divine dialectic, but
rather has its determinate center in the "Here He is"—as in
the conclusion of the prophecy in which Ezekiel names the
"new temple." It is this new root-term which occasioned the
rise of the so-called "liturgical movement" in Catholicism following the First World War. In a similar manner, a liturgical-sacramental Protestantism grew following the Second
World War.[5] Eastern Orthodox Christianity has seen in
these Catholic and Protestant movements a renewal of spirit,
since from the very beginning the Epistle to the Hebrews,
with its teaching on the High Priesthood of Christ, has been
the determining charter of Eastern Orthodoxy.

Formal Christian Root-Terms

One must clearly distinguish the material Christian root-
terms from the *formal* Christian root-terms. The latter do not

[4] Cf. "Religionsphilosophie," Max Dessoir, editor, *Lehrbuch der
Philosophie* (Berlin: Ullstein, 1925), and *Das Daemonische*
(Tübingen: J. C. B. Mohr, 1926).

[5] Compare with the program of the "Evangelishen Michaels-
brudershaft," *Credo Ecclesiam* (Kassel, 1954).

refer to the content of the Christian revelation insofar as this
has its determinate center in the fact of revelation itself, but
rather refer to the form in which the totality of revelation
appears concretely: in the annunciation, or *kerygma*; in the
sacramental *mysterium*; in the historical *kairos*; or in the
transhistorical *oikonomia*, the "order of salvation."

The formal root-term, for ancient prophetism as for the
new evangelism, is the *kerygma*. *Kerygma*, derived from
kēryssein and *kēryx* and rooted in *geryo*, means basically "to
sound" (as also animals "make sounds"). "Sound" is here understood as the "sounding" of a state, military, or sacred authority which, through a "crier," calls together the people,
the militia, or the believers for a public gathering, for train-
ing, or for a sacrifice. Insofar as the authority "sounds out"
through a "crier," the crier becomes the representative of the
authority, the "messenger," or "he who is sent." As representing messenger he is a "herald" in the original meaning of the
term. *Kerygma* means, therefore, official messenger announc-
ing the official message, and is thus internally bound up with
a "kingdom": a kingdom in a free public gathering, a kingdom over which the warriors engage in battle, or a kingdom
before God in the act of sacrifice. *Kerygma* also appears in
the story of the apostles and in Paul as the central form of
the Messianic message (see Is. 16:1); as the message of the
Messias as announced by John the Baptist (see Mt. 3:1);
as the message of the Messias in his own words (see Mt.
4:17); as the message of the Messias through his apostles
as "messenger in the whole world" (Mt. 10:7; Mk. 16:15); as
"narrator of the message of Christ the Crucified" (1 Cor.
1:21, 23). So also *kerygma* is inextricably bound up with the
basileia as the "Kingdom of God" or the "Kingdom of
Heaven": that is, as "messenger of the kingdom." In this sense
kerygma is simply *evangelion* in the historical meaning of
the word—not in the sense of a fortuitous "happy message,"
but as a message from the Roman Caesar to the whole of
the Roman Empire, whose message is in itself "holy" (following from the divine character of Caesar), quite independently of whether it comprises a message of punishment or
clemency. Therefore, *evangelion*, in its historical form, means
"message of the kingdom," just as *kerygma* means "official

message," thereby presupposing a kingdom. In this similarity of *kerygma* and *evangelion* there is finally the *Pater immensae Majestatis*, as expressed in the *Te Deum:* the divine Majesty which proclaims itself through its messengers, the *kerygma* and the *evangelion.*

Kerygma and *evangelion* are, therefore, necessarily rooted in the "Word of God" as expressed by the Gospel of John, leading back to the *Logos* as the "Word of God." As this Word of God is the one *Logos*, the one "Word" of the *kerygma* and *evangelion*, so the root of all Christian *kerygma* and *evangelion* is the one "I am with you" in the *Logos*. This central form of the *kerygma* provides the formal criterion in the theology of Origen, since for him all revelation-words of the old and new covenants, in his method of *analogia fidei*, become a *kerygma* of the "Logos of God," so that all faith and all life in faith is a "participation in the Logos," thus leading to a *Logos* Christianity.

During the late Middle Ages this centrality of the *kerygma* of the *Logos* became the foundation of the medieval Dominican teaching on the *ordo praedicatorum*, which was a reaction against the centrality of liturgy among the Benedictines. In extreme Calvinism or Zwinglianism, the absolute form of this central *kerygma* arises in preacher-centered worship, wherein all sacraments and liturgy are only pictorial remembrances and commemorations, and the sermon itself becomes the determining principle. Karl Barth's theology provides the interior metaphysics for this centrality of the *kerygma*; for him the *kerygma* is ultimately rooted in the mystery of the Trinity itself.

The second formal Christian root-term, *mysterium*, is so basic to Pauline thought that today both the Catholic "*Mysterien* theology" and the Protestant liturgical-sacramental movement take the word *mysterium* as a designation of a new Pauline emphasis, in contradistinction to a "Pauline *kerygmatic*." In its etymological meaning, *mysterium* means "concealed truth" (*terein*). It has at one and the same time a tellurian and a psychic-spiritual meaning. This separation into a tellurian and a psychic-spiritual dimension opens the view into the inner duality of the historical *Mysterien*. The telluric side is expressed particularly in the *mysterium* of the *hieros gamos,* holy marriage, which stands in the center of the Babylonian Mysteries. The psychic-spiritual side is expressed in the specific ancient Greek Mysteries which affirm a metaphysical-religious "resurrection in death."[6] This telluric-spiritual dualism posits a "terrifying abyss" as the essence of the *mysterium.* In the words of the learned philologist Walter Otto, *mysterium* is the "repetition of a divine event" in the cult whereby "man is ethereally lifted to the divine and works together with the divine."[7]

With the concepts of a spiritual marriage and a resurrection in death, we are already in the center of the Christian *mysterium.* Mystery in the Christian sense signifies, in the Gospel of Matthew, "the mystery of the Kingdom of God" (13:11), and in Paul, in whom the "Gentiles are fellow heirs, members of the same body, and partakers of the promise" (Eph. 3:6), as well as the "cosmic *mysterium*" of the "all in all in Christ." This Christian mystery finds its constant renewal in the self-fulfillment of the Church as the body and the consummation of the one Christ (see 1 Cor. 12:12 ff.; Eph. 5:25 ff.), and therefore, as the new living celebration of marriage in its members (as *epi-chor-hegume-non* and *synbibazomenon*), and as a marriage feast in which there is the objective *memoria et praesentia* in the bread and the cup of the "body and blood of the Lord."

This is the Magna Charta of the Christian *mysterium* and forms the basis of the *Mystagogical Catechism* of Cyril of Jerusalem, as well as of Augustine's sermons (*Tractatus in Johannem* and *Enarrationes in Psalmos*), wherein Christianity is acknowledged as the new, living cult which, under the sign of the one bread and the one cup, celebrates the true mystery—wherein the crucified and resurrected One, in his resurrection is now married to the many members in one body (see 1 Cor. 12:12).

---

[6] See W. Otto, *Die Gestalt und das Sein* (Düsseldorf, 1955).
[7] *Ibid.,* pp. 80, 86.

Kairos and Tillich's Philosophy of Religion

Both *kerygmatic* Christianity and Christianity as *mysterium*, taken alone, are susceptible to an overemphasis of a trans-historical Christianity. In the version of Origen, *kerygmatic* Christianity tends to become an intelligible structure understood as a "System in the Logos," and a Christian-Platonic *topos noētos*. The danger of a pure transhistorical *mysterium* Christianity can be seen in Eastern Orthodoxy in which the Platonic *topos noētos*, the ideal world of the icon, and the ideal world of a transhistorical liturgy converge. But Christianity essentially implies the incarnation of the divine in the human, in which the eternal God fully becomes historical man and continues to live in the historical Church, in humanity, and in the world as the Christ who is the same yesterday and today and forever (see Heb. 13:9). It is at this juncture that *kairos*, the third formal Christian root-term, makes its appearance. This is the root-term which has particular significance for Paul Tillich's philosophy of religion.

Christianity inextricably means eternity in time: absolute, divine Eternity in relative human time, and thus within the duration of yesterday, today, and tomorrow. The full implication of this notion can only be grasped by exploring three words used by the New Testament Greek to express the mystery of historical time: *chronos, kairos, aiōn*. *Chronos* denotes simply the duration of time in a temporal succession. *Aiōn* has reference to the content of a temporal or a world age, in the sense of an "early age," "middle age," and "modern age." As *chronos* focuses primarily upon the *successive* character of time—"chronology" is thus made possible by virtue of which one becomes conscious of the transitoriness of time—so *aiōn* crystallizes the "relative eternity" of this transitoriness into an "absolute eternity," as expressed in the liturgical form: *per omnia saecula saeculorum*. In contrast to the emphasis on transitoriness in *chronos* and the emphasis on eternity in *aiōn*, *kairos* emphasizes the situational Appositeness, "right time," in the manner of the Latin word *opportunitas*—the "opportune moment." The right time as opportune is rooted in a "pre-established Plan," but becomes concretely opportune in specific historical circumstances. It is opportune by virtue of an ideal "determination from above" and by virtue of a "real situation below." *Kairos* is "time in the right measure," which is at one and the same time a trans-temporal "measure of real circumstances."

It is in this sense that the Lord, in his parting words to his apostles when they asked concerning the "time" of the coming kingdom, distinguished the *chroni* as *kairoi*, "which the Father has fixed by his own authority" (Acts 1:7). That is to say, the Father, as "originator without origin" (*principium sine principio*), enters the temporal succession *chronoi* by an interruption at the opportune moment's *kairoi*. As this entering into time is essentially Messianic, the word *kairos* is particularly applicable to the Christ; for the Lord himself, in the Gospel of John, speaks of "my *kairos*" (7:6). However, insofar as the Messianic *kairos*, in its essential content, is set over against Satan as the "ruler of this world" (Jn. 14:30; 2 Cor. 4:4) and the "Antichrist," the word *kairos* indicates also the time for this opposition, as is expressed in Luke: "And when the devil had ended every temptation, he departed until an opportune time" (4:13). Thus, the *kairos Christi* is essentially the "*kairos* of salvation" as this salvation occurs in the conflict between God and Satan, between Christ and the Antichrist.

It is this duality in the *kairos* which Paul Tillich, in the tradition of Jacob Boehme, Franz von Baader, and Schelling, as well as of the Russians, Tschaadajev, Frank, Chestov, and Berdyaev, has expressed in his concept of the divine as "ground and abyss." In his criticism of Rudolf Otto, Tillich argues that the Holy must be understood as an intrusion through the realm of meaning which is its abyss and its ground.[8] In his *Religionsphilosophie* he argues that theism and atheism are rooted in this divine "ground and abyss":

---

[8] See *Rechtfertigung und Zweifel* (Giessen: Alfred Töpelmann, 1924), p. 28.

"In every theism . . . an abyss of atheism is present."[9] In
the same writing he speaks of a "differentiation of the Holy
into the Divine and the Demonic," wherein the demonic is
"the Holy which contradicts the Divine."[10] *It is here that we
see the tradition of Origen becoming transparent in the
thought of Tillich,* wherein "the Kingdom of Satan as the
Ruler of this Age" is understood as the last antithesis to
God, which itself is taken up in the final "divine synthesis"
of the "complete restoration" in which "God is all in all"
(1 Cor. 15:28).

The Final Christian Root-Term

But the fourth formal Christian root-term gives the answer to
such dubious undertakings in Tillich's thought. Beyond all
the contraries of the "Kingdom of God" and the "Kingdom
of Satan" in the history of salvation stands the *oikonomia
tu pleromatos ton kairon;* rooted in "the mystery of his will
according to his purposes" (Eph. 1:8), in which are "united
all things, things in heaven and things on earth" (Eph. 1:10).
All *kairoi,* in their inner history of salvation within the duality of the "Kingdom of God and his Christ" and the "Kingdom of Satan and his Antichrist," are grounded, live, and
move in an *oikonomia tu pleromatos ton kairon,* wherein resides the inscrutable and unsearchable abyss of God's Being;
God's "abyss in depth and height" (Rom. 11:33), which
alone the *Pneuma,* the Spirit of God, can comprehend (see 1
Cor. 2:11). Although the Epistle to the Romans comes close
to affirming a final dialectic between God and Satan, it
moves exclusively in the "depths of the riches and wisdom
and knowledge of God," from whom and through whom and
to whom are all things (see Rom. 11:33–36).

The history of salvation is thus finally and exclusively
grounded in the appearance within history of the "inscrutable
justice and unsearchable ways" of the one *bathos,* the one

---

[9] Dessoir, *op. cit.,* p. 804.
[10] *Ibid.,* p. 808.

oikodespotes, the one *oikonomia,* as the sovereign ordering of the incomprehensible and unsearchable "height and depth of the divine abyss." For this reason, *Catholicism has this Christian root-term* oikonomia, *as its most fundamental term.* If the divine *oikodespotes* and *oikonomia,* ruling and ordering, belong together, and if the Divine became human entering the world and history, then he is present in this world as human ruler and as One who orders through law. Catholicism sees the dialectical character and double significance of the *kairoi* as rooted in the final Christian root-term, *oikonomia,* and represented in the ordering of the Church through ecclesiastical lords. Hence, Majesty and Glory are the final "sound" and "breath" of this divine-human *oikonomia.*[11]

[11] See the author's *Alter und Neuer Bund* (Vienna, 1956), and *Gespräch Zwischen den Kirchen* (Nürnburg, 1957).

PART FOUR

Final Revelation

We want only to communicate to you an experience we have had that here and there in the world
and now and then in ourselves is a New Creation,
usually hidden, but sometimes manifest, and certainly manifest in Jesus who is called the Christ.
. . . And we should not be too worried about the
Christian religion, about the state of the churches,
about membership and doctrines, about institutions
and ministers, about sermons and sacraments. This
is circumcision; and the lack of it, the secularization
which today is spreading all over the world is un-
circumcision. Both are nothing, of no importance,
if the ultimate question is asked, the question of
a New Reality. . . . The New Creation—this is our
ultimate concern; this should be our infinite passion—the infinite passion of every human being.
This matters; this alone matters ultimately. In comparison with it everything else, even religion or non-
religion, even Christianity or non-Christianity, matters very little and ultimately nothing.

The New Being

XII

GEORGE TAVARD

Christology as Symbol

An outline of the Christology of Paul Tillich must, in the first place, take account of the levels of existence that Tillich distinguishes. Since Christology is the answer of the Christian Church to man's universal quest for the Unconditional, such an answer will be adapted to the several planes of human existence. From the point of view of theology there are several such levels, each providing a vantage point from which one may look at the Christian answer. Each, in its sphere, is valid; and this validity is delimited by the scope of that sphere. This is to say that the Christian tradition has seen the rise of several Christologies or that Christology has developed several aspects and several formulas. These may, or may not, be contradictory. The important point is not to determine their absolute truth in the abstract, but their meaning in the concrete. One must perceive their relevance to the existence of man in its several depths.

The deepest level at which Christology may be studied is called by Tillich the "ontological awareness of the Unconditional." As "the concern about our existence in its ultimate whence and whither,"[1] it precedes every formula of a solution and every formula of a search. "The faith which conquers sin by receiving reconciliation and a new being, must precede the search for ultimate reality."[2] If Christianity's claim to

---

[1] BRSUR, p. 61.
[2] Ibid., pp. 55–56.

universality is valid, a Christian answer must be found at this level. Christology must be ontological. It must provide an answer at the very depth where the quest for the Unconditioned is ontologically preformulated. This ontological requirement corresponds to what Tillich calls "the ontological principle in the philosophy of religion," and which he thus expresses: "Man is immediately aware of something unconditional which is the prius of separation and interaction of subject and object, theoretically as well as practically."[3] But we have to pass a hurdle here. At this level of existence, the implication cannot be directly formulated, it can only be pointed at. The Christian answer, like the answer of any religion, philosophy, or revelation, will be *symbolic* and will be true only insofar as the symbol is grasped.

A second level of truth corresponds to the next plane of existence, that of history. Our experience is conditioned by historical circumstances. History has developed a culture which has profoundly influenced both our conscious thinking and our subconscious psyche. The Christian answer has precisely been couched in historical terms. Christ is presented as a historical person. This will therefore provide a second point of view: Christology as *historical*.

A third level of truth corresponds to the largely artificial distinction, in man, between his intellectual activity and other elements of his personality. In terms of beliefs, Christianity has been embodied in dogmas. These have an intellectual appeal and must be grasped rationally. We shall, therefore, study Christology as *dogmatic*.

Finally, another analysis of human behavior sees man as an ethical being, whose convictions, principles, and assumptions prompt him to adopt definite standards of conduct. Morality is not severed from assent. On the contrary, it expresses faith in the realm of ethical behavior by cloaking the Christian answer in the garments of moral principles. A study of Christology should thus devote some time to Christology as *ethical*.

[3] TC, p. 22.

Theology as Symbolic

That Christian theology is symbolic follows upon the fact that it claims to be a formulation of faith. Faith, as man's attempt to assert the Unconditional, cannot be expressed in conditioned language. But all language is conditioned. It is limited by the very concepts that it seeks to express and by the linguistic tools at its disposal, which themselves result from long historical evolutions. To speak of formulating man's search for the Unconditional would, therefore, be to march towards a mirage, if there were no such thing as an indirect, symbolic use of language. And not only words are involved in this problem. Words correspond to concepts, which themselves depend on a previous or simultaneous experience of knowledge. Tillich's analysis of faith thus posits a fundamental critical problem concerning the structure of theological knowledge. As he has noted, "the center of my theological doctrine of knowledge is the concept of symbol."[4]

The Unconditioned makes itself known through symbolic situations. In other words, it reaches us through symbols. The symbol belongs to the world of appearances. It may be a word, an image, a concept, a fact, a gesture, a person. It may be, literally, anything. For anything which has been involved in a concrete experience of the Unconditional may retain, for the mind which has known it in the fire of communion with being-itself, a flavor of remembrance. It has kept the power of reminding us of that experience. It has been endowed with a sort of secondary revelatory power; and whenever we meet this symbol, we shall be thrown back into the revelatory constellation that was once connected with this particular symbol. This is the main Tillichian use of the word symbol: it denotes the elements that have been associated with a revelation and that have retained some of the revelatory power then manifested. A second use of the term

[4] C. Kegley and R. Bretall, editors, *The Theology of Paul Tillich* (New York: Macmillan, 1952), p. 333.

follows. We cannot speak of the Unconditional directly. Even to say "Unconditional" is to see it as contrasted with the conditional, and this conditions the content of the word "Unconditional." There is no way of expressing the ultimate ground of being unless we use symbolic terms. The terms are understood as pointers to, not as copies of, reality. God does not mean a God, but points to a reality that no language can circumscribe. Were the word "God" nonsymbolic, it would be identical with "a God." But God is not a God. As Unconditional, he is beyond the realm where "a" is meaningful, beyond singular and plural; as Unconditional, he is neither subject of the verb "to be" nor object of the verb "to know," but he is beyond object and subject. "It is highly symbolic language which must be used at this point. But its symbolic character does not diminish its truth; on the contrary, it is a condition of its truth. To speak unsymbolically about being-itself falsifies the real situation."[5]

A symbol is, therefore, not a mere sign. Paul Tillich strongly insists on the difference between signs and symbols. A sign points to a meaning with which it has no intrinsic connection. It is an agreed, conventional way of saying something. Highway codes are made of signs, not of symbols. A symbol, on the contrary, has characteristics that distinguish it from a sign. In *Dynamics of Faith*, Tillich lists four such marks. *First*, a symbol "participates in that to which it points."[6] This is a consequence of the fact that it became a symbol in the midst of a revelatory situation. Its association with revelation has lingered, and this makes it still participate in the power of that which was revealed. The "beyond itself" to which it points is no other than the revelation that was then perceived. A *second* characteristic logically follows: "It opens up levels of reality which otherwise are closed for us,"[7] namely, those levels to which we were raised in the original revelatory experience. *Thirdly*, it "not only opens up dimensions and elements of reality which otherwise remain unap-

---

[5] *TB*, p. 180.
[6] *ST*, II, p. 42.
[7] *Loc. cit.*

proachable, but also unlocks dimensions and elements of our soul which correspond to the dimensions and elements of reality."[8] A revelation would be unperceived unless we had the capacity to perceive it. And only in the revelatory experience itself do we gauge the depths of our soul. What Tillich has called "ecstasy" corresponds to "miracle." The miracle is the correlation of elements having revelatory power. The ecstasy is the opening of the soul's depths to the depths of the situation.

Fourthly, "symbols cannot be produced intentionally."[9] In Tillich's theology, this is a principle of tremendous importance. That a symbol cannot be invented is evident, once it has been defined by its participation in a revelatory constellation. One does not create revelation, and only revelation creates symbols of itself. This is important for defining the function of theology. "Theology as such has neither the duty nor the power to confirm or to negate religious symbols. Its task is to interpret them according to theological principles and methods."[10] The theologian cannot discard traditional Christian symbols; that they are symbols and, as such, endowed with divine power, is enough for him. This cuts the ground from under much of liberal Protestantism and its rejection of Catholic symbols. Yet, the theologian should criticize symbols: he "may discover contradictions between symbols."[11] He may also, by his prophetic insight, contribute to the surge of a new revelatory situation out of which new symbols will grow. This, for Tillich, condemns the "static" character which he attributes to Catholic sacramentalism and Catholic theology.

Fifthly, symbols, "like living beings, grow and die."[12] "They grow when the situation is ripe for them, and they die when the situation changes."[13] This seems a difficult point

[8] *Loc. cit.*
[9] *Ibid.*, p. 43.
[10] *ST*, I, p. 240.
[11] *Loc. cit.*
[12] *DF*, p. 43.
[13] *Loc. cit.*

to accept. It creates no problem with respect to artistic or social symbols. With religious symbols, however, a question arises. If these develop from revelatory situations, the revelation that gave them birth will always be a revelation. One may conceive that, after years have passed, it may have lost some power, that people will no longer fully perceive in what way this particular situation was revelatory. But the fact will always remain that, through these concrete symbols, the Ultimate was once perceived. Tillich admits it: symbols that have become "latent" may be revived in favorable circumstances. Yet, he maintains that religious symbols can undergo a "disintegration,"[14] losing their symbolic power.[15] This is a serious matter, for how can a symbol disintegrate if it truly partakes of the power of being-itself which it expresses? How can it fail to be revelatory, unless the reality of which it partakes also disintegrates?

Tillich rightly insists that "it is not theoretical criticism that kills religious symbols."[16] Theoretical refutation is powerless before the existential pregnancy of the symbol. But when he adds that symbols are killed by "a change in the actual encounter,"[17] one may ask how ultimate was the Ultimate that was perceived in that situation, if it can disappear? If the Unconditional is unconditional, it should be beyond the reach of the situation in which it was perceived. The situation was a necessary, symbolic mediation for it to be perceived; but a person that has intuited the Unconditional knows it once for all, even after the various elements of the revelatory correlation have separated and lost their power. This leads to a basic criticism. If Tillich is right in connecting religious symbols and the Ultimate, he cannot be right in thinking that religious symbols die; for the Ultimate does not die. A symbol which is no longer made powerful by the existential context in which it became symbolic of Ultimate reality, remains symbolic of it by the very power of

14 PE, p. 62.
15 See ibid., p. 63.
16 RS, p. 111.
17 Loc. cit.

Ultimate reality already perceived. A symbol which has been truly symbolic of God is always symbolic of God. When it no longer leads to God, God comes to man through it. This would seem to be the conclusion logically to be drawn from Tillich's doctrine: "A symbol *has* truth: it is adequate to the revelation it expresses. A symbol *is* true: it is the expression of a true revelation."[18] Tillich fails to be consistent when he does not add: A symbol remains true as long as what it reveals is the truth. Since ultimate truth does not disintegrate, neither do its symbols. It is true that Tillich offers an explanation for the disintegration of religious symbols: "Religious symbols are double-edged. They are directed towards the infinite which they symbolize *and* towards the finite through which they symbolize it."[19] One can easily understand that "the symbol and, along with it, the reality from which it was taken" may disintegrate "in mutual interdependence."[20] Yet, one cannot see why the Infinite lacks the power to maintain the symbolic relation even when the situation is no longer revelatory.

A last point concerning Tillich's conception of religious symbols should now be mentioned: A constellation of religious symbols forms what he calls a religious "myth."

"Myths are symbols of faith combined in stories about divine-human encounters."[21] One finds such myths in pagan religions, and they are present in the Old Testament and even in the New. In Tillich's usage, the word "myth" is not derogatory. Myths are as necessary as symbols. The correlation of several symbols even manifests an element of man's perception of the Unconditional which a symbol, by itself, would not convey, namely, the historical and the cosmic relevance of the Unconditional. It "puts the stories of the gods into the framework of time and space."[22] In Tillich's view, this is legitimate if it expresses the transcendence of

18 ST, I, p. 240.
19 *Loc. cit.*
20 PE, p. 63.
21 DF, p. 49.
22 *Loc. cit.*

God above space and time. But it is radically ambiguous. Myths can contribute to unseat the Unconditional and to make man conceive of it as subject to time and space. This is why so many myths imply polytheism: myth "divides the divine into several figures, removing ultimacy from each of them without removing their claim to ultimacy."[23] Like symbols, therefore, myths must be criticized, and all great religions have done so. In modern times, and in the Christian context of the New Testament, this criticism has been given the name of demythologization, a matter which will claim our attention later. At this point it is enough to note that, for Tillich, myth and demythologization belong together, just like symbol and symbol-criticism. A myth which is not understood as symbolical but as literally true is a "pure myth." Its religious value is distorted by literalism. It is taken as a transcendent history of the life of God and of God's intervention in the life of man. Such myths must be broken. Only a "broken myth"[24] has undoubted religious value, precisely because its value has resisted the radical criticism of demythologization. But the criticism of myth should bear on the real, not on the imagined shortcomings of the mythical story. Pagan mythology has often been criticized for its supposed immorality, yet, as Tillich rightly points out, "these attacks are only partially justified. The relations of the mythological gods are transmoral; they are ontological; they refer to structures of being and to conflicts of values."[25]

The only ultimately valid criticism of a myth must take account of the religious dimension of the myth. It must be seen as an attempt to perceive and express the concept that God is living and the experience of man faced with the fascinating mystery of the holiness of God's life. Because it is made of symbols that are themselves the products of a series of revelatory situations, a myth may be successfully criticized only from within its own revelatory context. This is what Tillich calls the "theological circle." Only the Unconditional

[23] *Loc. cit.*
[24] *Ibid.*, p. 50.
[25] *ST*, I, p. 224.

which the myth wants to express can judge the myth. Only in its light can the myth be considered inadequate, misleading, or, perhaps, fallacious. In the light of the Ultimate, however, all myths are ambiguous; for if they combine symbols, that is, revelatory situations, the system into which these are united is not itself a revelatory situation. It is, precisely, a myth, arising out of religious imagination. Because of this bipolarity—combining genuine revelatory situations into imaginative patterns—myths must be neither destroyed, negated, nor accepted in their literalism. They must be "broken," understood on the level of the ultimate dimension of existence, which they depict in ambiguous traits and colors.

Tillich's Christology

"Christianity was born, not with the birth of the man who is called Jesus, but in the moment in which one of his followers was driven to say to him, 'Thou art the Christ.' "[26] The cornerstone of Tillich's Christology is that the revelation carried by Jesus must have been known in a revelatory situation. This implies the convergence of a "miraculous," power-revealing situation and of someone grasping the meaning of this situation in an ecstasy of faith. The most striking such moment, as recorded in the New Testament, is the confession of Peter professing his faith that "Thou art the Christ." We will concentrate on the meaning of the confession "Thou art the Christ," for the term "Christ" is evidently the central symbol of Christology. It is in the light of it that every other symbol is meaningful and that every Christian assertion about Jesus must be criticized. In the light of it, too, Christians will judge the attempts of other religions to identify the Christ differently from what Christianity asserts. With the symbol of the Christ we are at the cosmic crossroads of all religions.

The term Christ, in Christianity, gives a name to the Unconditional, the eternal ground of all that is. But it is more

[26] *ST*, II, p. 97.

than a name; it is an identification with an event of history. There has been a man in whom "Essential Godmanhood has appeared within existence and subjected itself to the conditions of existence without being conquered by them."[27] By Essential Godmanhood Tillich means the eternal ground of man. The analysis of man's existential estrangement, which classical theology calls original sin, shows that, by the very fact of his existence, man has fallen from his essential being to an existential situation. The essential being of man corresponds exactly to his point of contact with the Absolute. It is not only manhood as experienced in existence, but it is also manhood as created in God, ontologically before the fall into existence. This Tillich calls Godmanhood. Essential Godmanhood is thus the being of man prior to existence. It is man in God. "To essential man belongs the unity of his finiteness with his infinity, and it is precisely this unity which I call Godmanhood, because it is an expression of the dialectical interdependence of finiteness and infinity."[28]

Christianity claims that this Essential Godmanhood has, in a concrete event and a concrete man, appeared within the conditions of existence, inside the weft of history, without falling from essence and without being distorted by the ebb and flow of existence. In Christ "Eternal Godmanhood"[29] has been seen. When it was seen Jesus was known as the Christ, the expectation of mankind finally fulfilled, the One who brings in the new eon, the New Being. Because he was thus perceived, Tillich may say: "Jesus is the Christ for us."[30] And because the Christ means Essential Godmanhood, he may add: "The Christ is God-for-us."[31] Jesus would not have been the Christ, and, as the Christ, he would not have been the manifestation of Eternal Godmanhood, if manhood had

[27] Ibid., p. 98.
[28] "A Reinterpretation of the Doctrine of the Incarnation," Church Quarterly Review, 294 (January–March, 1949), 143.
[29] ST, II, p. 100.
[30] Ibid., p. 101.
[31] Ibid., p. 100.

not acknowledged him. For there is no revelatory situation without the ecstasy of recognition in which one discovers a manifestation of being-itself.

The symbol of the Christ, therefore, which is borrowed from the Jewish conception of the Messias, or King, or Anointed, can easily be distorted. Jesus as the Christ must not "be seen as a God walking on earth,"[32] as "a divine-human automaton without serious temptation, real struggle, or tragic involvement in the ambiguities of life."[33] This would be a misunderstood myth. It could not be the manifestation of a reality in which one partakes. It would not be the revelation of the ground of being. Caught in existential estrangement, man could not grasp the meaning of a divine-human avatar. A human being named Jesus who would not be subject to the involvements of existence could not be revelatory, since man could not step into the nonexistential theological circle where he would make sense. On the contrary, the Christ has been known, "touched with our hands, seen with our eyes." And he has been known, not only as a man named Jesus, but as "Jesus who is called the Christ."[34] This means that, in Jesus, we have "the picture of a personal life which is subjected to all the consequences of existential estrangement, but wherein existential estrangement is conquered in himself and a permanent unity is kept with God."[35] The ground of being, which we only perceive in hope, to which we are unconditionally committed without the evidence that we are in contact with it, dominated the ambiguities of existence in the Christ. Under its power, the Christ did not undergo "original sin"; his existence did not imply a fall: it maintained in its integrality the dominion of Essential Godmanhood over the tragedies of life.

The universal quest of mankind has been for this return to unity, for this recovery of the ground of being which supports us and from which we are estranged. To perceive it in

[32] *Ibid.*, p. 133.
[33] *Ibid.*, p. 135.
[34] *Ibid.*, p. 98.
[35] *Ibid.*, p. 135.

the Christ is to hear the good news that "the Christ is the one who brings in the new eon," to expect "the coming of a new state of things through him,"[36] the state of things in which we ourselves have recovered Essential Godmanhood and have risen from the state of estrangement to that of re-union with being-itself. Tillich uses the symbol "New Being" to point to this. Man's quest has been for a New Being that would conquer the dichotomy between subject and object. "New Being is essential being under the conditions of existence, conquering the gap between essence and existence."[37] This symbol itself can be misread. The Being which is manifested in the Christ is new indeed, but not in the sense that it has done away with the circumstances of estrangement that mark existential being. Tragedy is still there, but henceforth it has been conquered. It is there, but no longer as victorious. "The New Being is new insofar as it is the undistorted manifestation of essential being within and under the conditions of existence. It is new in two respects: it is new in contrast to the merely potential character of essential being; and it is new over against the estranged character of existential being."[38] In the Christ alone, man's relation to the ground of being is fully actual and fully undistorted. In ourselves, subject as we are to existential estrangement, Godmanhood is only potential; it is a state of dreaming innocence in which we never were and from which, speaking symbolically, we fell when we came into being. Our actual being is divorced from it, and the constant dream of man has been for a return to the beginning, a restoration of that which has been lost because we never had it, innocence, essence, Godmanhood. This is the New Being we long for. In Christ it has been manifested. Essential being has come to existence without distortion. Innocence has become experience without losing its pristine virginity. Estrangement has been conquered. "The New Being has appeared in a personal life."[39] Tillich's

36 *Ibid.*, p. 118.
37 *Ibid.*, p. 119.
38 *Loc. cit.*
39 *Ibid.*, p. 120.

formula for the Christian message is this: "We want to communicate to you an experience we have had that here and there in the world and now and then in ourselves is a New Creation, usually hidden, but sometimes manifest, and certainly manifest in Jesus who is called the Christ."[40] Out of their participation in the revelatory situation in which Jesus is perceived to be the Christ, Christians witness to the vision they have had of the New Reality, which is "reconciliation, reunion, resurrection . . . the New Creation, the New Being, the New state of things."[41]

Tillich insists that "Jesus as the Christ is the bearer of the New Being in the totality of his being, not in any special expressions of it."[42] Various Christologies have concentrated on his words, his deeds, or his suffering. These are enlightening if not cut off from the being of Christ. But rationalism separated his words, pietism his deeds, and orthodoxy his suffering from his being; these systems forgot "that the being of Christ is his work and that his work is his being, namely, the New Being which is his being."[43] When theologians overlook the being of Christ, they cannot place the New Being at the center of their thought. Concentrating on his acts, they unavoidably distort their meaning and relevance. They then no longer relate the Christ to the universal quest for a conquest of estrangement. This makes the Christ himself a stranger in mankind.

On the contrary, we should remember that the traditional symbols of "salvation," "redemption," "grace," "atonement," "mediation," as applied to the function of the Christ, emphasize the universality of his role. The New Being in the Christ has universal significance. It is universally expected. On account of this, "Jesus as the Christ is the Savior through the universal significance of his being as the New Being."[44] What is this significance? Simply that the revelatory correla-

[40] *NB*, p. 18.
[41] *Ibid.*, p. 24.
[42] *ST*, II, p. 121.
[43] *Ibid.*, p. 168.
[44] *Ibid.*, p. 169.

tion in which Peter acknowledged his Messiasship remains revelatory for every man. The main point here is that this revelatory constellation has universal scope. In this sense it is "final," not that no more revelations may take place, but that all other revelations will be subordinated to it.

The revelatory event is Jesus as the Christ. He is the miracle of the final revelation, and his reception is the ecstasy of the final revelation. His appearance is the decisive constellation of historical (and by participation, natural) forces. It is the ecstatic moment of human history and, therefore, its center, giving meaning to all possible and actual history. . . . But it is only for those who received him as the final revelation, namely, as the Messias, the Christ, the Man-from-above, the Son of God, the Spirit, the Logos-who-became-flesh, the New Being.[45]

Implications of Tillich's Symbols

One should examine the implications of the symbols of Christ and of New Being as far as the formulation of faith is concerned. Certainly traditional Christology has not expressed the meaning of Christ as Tillich does. His basic point, that Christ is the historical manifestation of Eternal Godmanhood, is filled with implications. All Christian dogmas, both in their Catholic form and in the form that was classical in Orthodox Protestantism, must be radically reinterpreted in the light of Tillich's interpretation of the basic Christian symbols. This all-important question may be shelved, however, until Tillich has given us more insights into his thought. The problems raised by his explanation of symbolic Christology are twofold. In the first place, we should ascertain to what extent history backs up his interpretation, and, in the second, confront his world view with the traditional Christian dogmas. What is the status of history in symbolic Christology? And what is the dogmatic meaning of the same Christology?

[45] ST, I, p. 136.

In particular, can Essential Godmanhood, as manifested in the Christ, be identified with God? The classical dogma has called the Christ God. Does Tillich's Christology permit such an identification? This will be the center of the dogmatic problem as we shall have to examine it. Before being able to answer these questions, we should unfold some of Tillich's interpretations of other Christian symbols. Christ and the New Being are no doubt fundamental, yet they are not alone. Other aspects have to be pointed to by means of other symbols. One of these brings us to the brink of the dogmatic question of the divinity of Christ. It is the symbol of Christ as the Logos or Word of God. "Jesus as the Christ is the Logos."[46] Such a statement, in Tillich's language, is "paradoxical." That is, it "contradicts the *doxa,* the opinion derived from man's existential predicament and all expectations imaginable on the basis of this predicament."[47] This opinion formulates the universal fact of estrangement. The paradox is that a human being, living under the conditions of estrangement, nevertheless conquered and dominated them. One should not examine this from the standpoint of logic, but from that of experience: "The paradox is a new reality and not a logical riddle."[48] Statements concerning the Christ are not, therefore, to be justified on the level of philosophical logic. They stand or fall on the strength of the revelatory situation which imposes them, which is all the more remarkable since "Logos" and "Word" are of philosophical origin and have philosophical connotations.

At this point, the symbol of the Word interlocks with Trinitarian thinking. The Word is the Word of God, the self-manifestation of the divine life, not an added achievement of it, but the divine life as such. That God may be called not only God, but also Word, is one of the bases of Trinitarian theology.

[46] *ST*, II, p. 57.
[47] *Ibid.,* p. 92.
[48] *Loc. cit.*

The New Being

The symbols that point to the New Being as manifested in the personal life of Jesus may be misunderstood. They actually have been, whenever man's hunger for spiritual security has led him to distort the nature of the New Being. It is especially the Catholic temptation to picture the New Creation as the introduction into the world of a new institution. Shelter-like, the Church offers protection against the disintegrating forces of the world. She staves off false philosophies and leads the good fight for the law and the rights of God. She has assembled a whole arsenal of protective devices with powerful psychological impact. This, as seen by Paul Tillich, is her tragedy. The "mechanizing of her hierarchial apparatus"[49] was to be expected, for she overlooked an important aspect of Christology, which it would be the vocation of Protestantism to restore. It has been traditional in Lutheranism to present Luther's theology as a *theologia crucis*, as distinguished from the *theologia gloriae* of Catholicism. Christianity is a theology of the cross. The Christ did indeed appear in glory; but nowhere was his glory seen more directly than on the cross. In Tillich's categories, the proclamation of the cross forms the essence of the Protestant principle. "Protestantism must proclaim the judgment that brings assurance by de-priving us of all security; the judgment that declares us whole in the disintegration and cleavage of soul and community; the judgment that affirms our having truth in the very ab-sence of truth (even of religious truth); the judgment that reveals the meaning of our life in the situation in which all the meaning of life has disappeared."[50]

The New Being that is perceived in Jesus as the Christ and of which we catch an obscure glimpse whenever, in the ecstasy of a revelatory situation, we are infinitely concerned, is new because it is old. It is as old as being-itself, transcending

---

[49] *PE*, p. 195.
[50] *Ibid.*, p. 204.

time and space, having been before anything concrete was. It is the second principle of the Trinitarian life of God. But it is known nowhere by man except in the estranged situation which is the stuff of existence; it is perceived only "in the radical experience of the boundary-situation."[51] In the story of Christ, this insight is expressed in the symbol of the cross; the Christ, who dominates existence, yet slaves under its harsh conditions. "The first relation of the Christ to existence is his subjection to it. . . . The subjection to existence is expressed in the symbol of the cross of the Christ."[52] It is not complete and final, being correlated to the conquest of existence and its symbol, the resurrection. It is, nevertheless, central. A Christology which would not see that the manifestation of the New Being takes place nowhere but in a boundary-situation would miss the main point of Christianity. The interdependence of the cross and the resurrection, of defeat and victory, gives universal relevance to an otherwise sad story. "The cross of the Christ is the cross of the one who has conquered the death of existential estrangement. Otherwise it would only be one more tragic event (which it *also* is) in the long history of the tragedy of man."[53] It also constitutes the unique contribution of Christianity to a philosophy of religion. In general, religions have worshipped God as "Lord and Father"; they have adored him as Creator and Judge. Hence, they have organized priestly castes for mediation, and hence they have provoked prophetic protests: "The Lord who is only Lord" and "the Father who is only Father"[54] "cannot be man's ultimate concern."[55] For besides reverence and sentimental love, such religions also inspire revolt and contempt. Christianity alone has conceived of "the manifestation of the Lord and Father as Son and Brother under the conditions of existence."[56] The conditions of existence mean

---

[51] *Ibid.*, p. 203.
[52] *ST*, II, pp. 152–53.
[53] *Ibid.*, p. 153.
[54] *ST*, I, p. 288.
[55] *Loc. cit.*
[56] *Ibid.*, p. 289.

tragedy. They make failure inseparable from effort, stumbling necessary in the search for an ideal. He who is the Christ was doomed. He had to meet his fate on the cross.

Christianity centers on the cross, with its "universal symbolic significance." The story of the cross "is the myth of the bearer of the new eon who suffers the death of a convict and slave under the powers of that old eon which he is to conquer."[57] The faith of Christianity expresses the meaning of this symbol: "the surrender of him who is called the Christ to the ultimate consequence of existence, namely, death under the conditions of estrangement."[58] The symbolic meaning of the cross has many aspects.

In terms of life, the cross points to the insight that the new life cannot be superadded to the old. "The new life would not really be new life if it did not come from the complete end of the old life. Otherwise it would have to be buried again. But if the new life has come out of the grave, then the Messias himself has appeared."[59] In Tillich's view, Christian theology is not a "supranaturalism" whereby something is added to nature as a result of an heteronomous decision. Rather, it is "self-transcending"[60] through self-sacrifice. It teaches the redemption of nature through the negation of nature. In this way the cross becomes the pattern for faith and theology. In the symbol of the cross the Christ "stands the double test of finality: uninterrupted unity with the ground of his being and the continuous sacrifice of himself as Jesus to himself as the Christ."[61]

In terms of Godmanhood, the cross is a symbol "of the divine paradox of the appearance of the eternal God-man unity within existential estrangement."[62] Nowhere else should we look for the power and the glory, not in the birth of Jesus, not in the transfiguration, not in the miracles, not in the

[57] ST, II, pp. 153–54.
[58] Ibid., p. 155.
[59] SF, p. 168.
[60] ST, II, pp. 6 ff.
[61] ST, I, p. 170.
[62] ST, II, p. 159.

preaching of the beatitudes, not in the resurrection—unless all these are seen as leading to, or flowing from, the "paradox of the cross, that God is present in an actual human body and that it is just in suffering that his majesty is revealed."[63] The cross is by no means the only symbol of the manifestation of the ground of being. Yet, "it is the central one, the criterion of all other manifestations of God's participation in the suffering of the world."[64]

In terms of Protestantism, the cross is the ultimate symbol of the Protestant principle: what takes place at the cross is the same as what happens, according to Tillich, wherever true Protestantism is to be found: "In the power of the New Being, the boundary-situation is preached, its No and Yes are proclaimed."[65] This is the acted event of justification by faith. The Christ dying is also resurrecting, thus revealing his unity with the New Being. "No longer is the universe subjected to the law of life out of birth. It is subjected to a higher law, to the law of life out of death by the death of him who represented eternal life."[66] The Protestant principle of the justification of him who is unjust is a Yes and a No: No to oneself and Yes to oneself. No alone would entail despair, and Yes alone would breed arrogance. In Christians both Yes and No are true, because when they say, "Amen through Christ," they express their ultimate certitude: "There is no ultimate certitude except the life which has conquered its death and the truth which has conquered its error, the Yes which is beyond Yes and No."[67] The message of the cross is that Jesus as the Christ is the only reality "where there is not Yes and No, but only Yes."[68]

Tillich's analysis of the main Christian symbols corresponds exactly to his analysis of faith. Faith is simply a more or less confused awareness of being-itself, beneath all the

[63] *RS*, p. 170.
[64] *ST*, II, p. 175.
[65] *PE*, p. 205.
[66] *NB*, p. 178.
[67] *Ibid.*, p. 103.
[68] *Loc. cit.*

concrete experiences of man's existence. The Christ represents this ground of being when it is known in an intense
intuition and feeling of regeneration. The Christ is thus the
New Being, the New Creation. He is also the Word of God;
for the New Being is identical with being-itself, the Ultimate,
for which the word "God" provides a traditional symbol. He
is the Word because he represents the ground of being in its
second aspect, its life-containing capacity. He is crucified because the cross is an adequate symbol of self-transcendence
through self-sacrifice, of the subservience of conscious being
to being-itself. The Christ is, therefore, not merely the God
of Christianity; he is the universal God for whom all have
been seeking and whom all have obscurely perceived even in
their ignorance and doubt.

How close Tillich's position is to Protestantism we may
gather from John Calvin's protest: There are those who
"claim that truth may be held in error, light in blindness, and
knowledge in ignorance." Of Tillich's faith in the ground of
being of the philosophers above the concrete being of the
Christian God we may say with Calvin: "But it is mockery
to attribute the name of faith to pure ignorance."[69] Calvin was objecting to the concept of implicit faith found in
Roman Catholic theology. How much more to the point his
protest is as we face the even more remotely implicit faith
of Paul Tillich, with its ontological transcendence of concrete symbols!

[69] *Institutes*, Bk. III, chap. 2, n. 3.

XIII

GEORGE TAVARD

Christ as the Answer to Existential Anguish

The human situation is a situation of estrangement. In these words we sum up Paul Tillich's description of the conditions of man's life on earth. Most of his writings constitute an analysis of this situation of estrangement. The first work that made him known to Americans, *The Religious Situation*, studies how forces of union are today counteracting forces of estrangement in the various fields of science, art, politics, ethics, and institutional religion. In the terms of this book, what makes a situation "religious" is precisely the appearance, within conditions of estrangement, of an inner core of union, or reunion, eventually capable of overcoming estrangement. This analysis rests on the assumption, which is basic to Tillich's thought, that no situation is totally, irremediably estranged. There is indeed tragedy in life. The essence of tragedy is the appearance of an element of fatality even within liberty; it is the encounter of a demonic dimension under what appeared superficially to be a smooth, perhaps angelic, surface. Existence is ambiguous. When we have been betrayed by a person we considered our friend, when we have found that the men we have admired had secret flaws that have finally burst open leaving a bad sore naked, when we are drawn to ask the question: "Is there any way to trust anybody? Is life always a lie?", then we encounter tragedy: we fall under the impression of a dominant fate dooming our best constructions and ultimately giving all our dreams the frightening colors of nightmares. We do not live with a companion, a mate, or a friend, sharing our concerns and loves, but with a werewolf, coming in and out of a mystery that we can never reach. And we ourselves suspect, if we do not know, that we also are, to him, a werewolf.

Expressed in literary terms, this is tragedy, which was described with profound insights by the Greeks, which constitutes the substance of oriental religions, which appeared in Western literature with the "classics"—Shakespeare in England, Racine in France, Cervantes in Spain—which gained acceptance in modern philosophy under the differing impacts of Schopenhauer, Kierkegaard, and Nietzsche, and which has acquired academic status with the existentialism of Heidegger and Sartre, with the unavoidable result that the tragic that can be lectured about in a classroom or a lecture hall loses its tragic character.

Human Estrangement

Paul Tillich stands in the line of those who, in our time, have emphasized the tragic nature of life.

> There is a separation among individual lives, separation of a man from himself, and separation of all men from the ground of being. This threefold separation constitutes the state of everything that exists; it is a universal fate; it is the fate of every life. And it is our human fate in a very special sense. For we as men know that we are separated. We not only suffer with all other creatures because of the self-destructive consequences of our separation, but also know why we suffer.[1]

Tillich is not satisfied with mere description. His theological analysis does, as it must, go further. His main contribution to the investigation of human estrangement is the concept of the demonic.

Where does the tragic aspect of life come from? Philosophers can suggest answers, some of which may indeed open

[1] SF, p. 155.

new insights into the human situation. Tillich appreciates the existential philosophies which, in his terms, have described "man's existential situation or present estate as finitude," this finitude being "connected with the contrast between man's present estate and what he is essentially and therefore ought to be."[2] To the ontological explanation that abyss separates essence and existence, Tillich adds a theological explanation: creation is "demonic," not in the Greek sense of *daimon*, the inspiring spirit, but in the biblical sense. The demons in the Old Testament, and still in many passages of the New, are ambiguous beings, ethically neither good nor bad, with capacities for good and bad, innocent, if innocence means unawareness of good and evil, and by the same token instruments of both good and evil. Thus, in the Book of Job, Satan obtains permission from God to tempt Job, in order to see how good he may be. Jesus, in the New Testament, drives out demons.

Tillich does not take these instances literally, yet he considers them important elements of biblical faith and of the Christian message. He does not believe that there is a fallen angelic being called demon. Yet, all things and all beings for him are demonic. The demon is a symbol for a dimension of life and a category of being: he represents the ambiguous aspect of the creaturely state, the polyvalence of existence, the bifocal ellipse or the multifocal figure in relation to which every man may be located. What is demonic is meaningless, insofar as it holds the possibility of a double meaning. The demonic is that which has not yet chosen between good and evil, between life and death, between order and chaos. That Jesus drove demons away means that he gave meaning to existence, that the person who has been freed from demonic possession has now found himself and his truth, that he is no longer estranged from self, that he has made his choice. That the demons are being chased off is a sign of the kingdom and its coming, because the Messianic kingdom is the ideal state of mankind beyond hesitancy between good and evil, beyond the multiplicity of possible ethical options, and

2 *TC*, p. 102.

beyond the threat of estrangement between man and man. Thus, the demonic is a religious category. It is not simply a mythical description of the situation of estrangement, but a "structure of being." If the demons are symbols of the ambiguity of life, they are also occasions for transcending this ambiguity. The aspect of ambiguity, which is inseparable from life as we experience it, implies a counteraspect: the desire to rise above ambiguity, to choose and by one's choice to drive away the power of the demons. Demons were, for Jesus, not simply enemies to be defeated and overcome, but occasions for the manifestation of his divine power and mission. That he himself saw them in this light is patent: "If it is by the Power of God that I drive away demons, then the Kingdom of God has come for you" (Mt. 12:28).

In other words, the dimension of the tragic, which is also the religious dimension of the demonic, is a gap in the structure of our universe, through which the divine ground and meaning of existence and life may be perceived. Without this failure of the world to make sense at first sight, we might be satisfied with a sort of "animal faith," to borrow the words of Santayana, looking at the world and accepting it without even suspecting its tragic depth. Existential anguish, the subjective response to the demonic elements of nature, is the wedge which forces our self-satisfied, complacent universe to break and make room for the one solution to the conundrum of existence, the remedy to the disease of the universe, the one who heals the discrepancy between being and being—Jesus the Christ.

Applying his analysis of estrangement and demonic potentialities to our generations, the generations of the two World Wars, Paul Tillich paints the most dismal picture ever seen:

We have become a generation of the End. . . . The End is nothing external. It is not exhausted by the loss of that which we can never regain: our childhood homes, the people with whom we grew up, the country, the things, the language which formed us, the goods, both spiritual and material, which we inherited or earned, the friends who were torn away from us by sudden death. The End is more than all this; it is in us, it has become our very being. We are a generation of the End and we should know that we are.[3]

Such is the time chosen for the Christ to manifest himself. The true epiphany was not when a baby was recognized by wise men amid all the trimmings of a poor but happy childhood. It was when a man dying on a cross between two thieves exclaimed: *Eloi, eloi, lamma sabacthani:* "My God, my God, why hast thou forsaken me?" This is the token that God has selected to reach a generation of the End. And every human generation, ultimately, is a generation of the End.

The Divine Answer

Paul Tillich's basic approach to the Christ, as implicit in all his works and developed in Volume Two of his *Systematic Theology,* presents him as the divine answer to mankind's anguish when the estrangement of existence bursts into our consciousness. Then we are not only aware of self, but also of self-estrangement, not only aware of being human, but of being humans separated from humans. Can no bridge be thrown from man to man? Are we doomed to loneliness and isolation, next to other human beings equally doomed to equally unbearable loneliness and isolation? Unlike the philosophers of existentialism, Tillich affirms that we are not so doomed. Eager as he is to integrate philosophical insights and Christian faith, he believes that the situation of estrangement, which is part and parcel of the human condition and is especially acute between individuals and societies, in our century, is a springboard for what Kierkegaard called a "leap of faith," for the faith that, in the historical appearance of Jesus the Messias, one man at least overcame the dilemma of the separation between essence and existence in himself, of the abyss between subject and object, of the estrangement between himself and other men and between himself and na-

[3] *NB,* p. 172.

ture. The concept of the Messias is that "of essential man appearing in a personal life under the conditions of existential
estrangement."[4] "The paradox of the Christian message is
that in *one* personal life essential manhood has appeared under the conditions of existence without being conquered by
them."[5]

What this means concerning the man Jesus is that he also
suffered, like all of us, under the experience of estrangement;
he also experienced separation from those he loved and who
loved him; he also fought with the demonic dimension of
nature, which assailed him in the desert and tried to lure
him away from his divine peace; he struggled with misunderstanding and misrepresentation among the leaders of his
people; he eventually fell victim to estrangement, when he
was condemned under trumped up charges. The paradox of
Jesus the Christ is that, for him, none of these experiences
was ultimate; each one of them was transformed in the
furnace of his "Courage to Be" into a positive power of reunion; each of these spiritual and physical deaths found its
meaning in a resurrection. In him "the New Being has conquered the old being."[6] The old being is that which we experience in estrangement from ourselves and from each other;
the New Being is that which appeared on earth, for the first
time, in Jesus the Christ, a Being of reconciliation and peace,
which replaces estrangement with reunion, misunderstanding
with forgiveness, hatred or indifference with love. "Existence is separation,"[7] and this man existed. But his existence
paradoxically manifested grace. "Grace is the *reunion* of life
with life, the reconciliation of the self with itself. Grace is
the acceptance of that which is rejected. Grace transforms
fate into meaningful destiny; it changes guilt into confidence
and courage."[8] It is the privilege of Christians to recognize
this in the picture of Jesus; where others see human failure

[4] ST, II, p. 95.
[5] Ibid., p. 94.
[6] Ibid., p. 114.
[7] SF, p. 155.
[8] Loc. cit.

at its worst, the failure of a great and good man, to see divine victory. "When the apostles say that Jesus is the Christ they mean that in him the new eon which cannot become old is present."[9] Faith in him is the ecstatic conviction, the revelatory intuition that, at the supreme moment of his unsuccess, in his death, he resurrected; and this paradoxical success has dominated human history ever since. Tillich writes in a moving page:

Even the greatest in power and wisdom could not more fully reveal the heart of God and the heart of man than the Crucified has done already. Those things have been revealed once for all. "It is finished." In the face of the Crucified all the "more" and all the "less," all progress and all approximation, are meaningless. Therefore, we can say of him alone: He is the new reality; he is the end; he is the Messias. To the Crucified alone we can say: Thou art the Christ.[10]

A question keeps arising at this point in the Catholic mind: Does Tillich believe that this man is also God, the second Person of the Blessed Trinity, the Word made flesh, the Lord Incarnate? The question is, of course, legitimate. But it should, perhaps, be asked in terms that are more adequate to Tillich's approach. An existential approach to the mystery of Christ must be consistent. And if we interrupt its course to ask the dogmatic question: "Is Jesus God?" we introduce a nonexistential concern into the argument. Tillich's problem is not to establish the norms of Christological orthodoxy; it is to show the relevance of the Christian message to the estranged man of today, torn with anguish, sick with loneliness, and bristling with revolt. It is certainly the Church's duty to judge all Christological attempts according to its unvarying doctrinal norms, but the attempt to correlate the Christian message and the existential quest for life is valid independently of the more or less inadequate doctrinal standards of Paul Tillich's own faith. Here I am concerned mainly with his attempt at correlation, having dealt elsewhere with his orthodoxy. One may say, however, that the question

9 *Ibid.*, p. 186.
10 *Ibid.*, p. 148.

would be more meaningful for Tillich were it couched in different categories. The categories of God, man, and material creation, which characterize a several layer universe, are mythical categories: they form a myth, necessary to most of us, of a God "above" this world and lording over it. But God is neither above nor beneath; he is not a being that can be connumerated with others. The transcendence of God cannot allow us to think of him in those terms. We should think of him as the Absolute, the One and Only, the *Ipsum esse* of the Schoolmen, the One "than whom nothing greater can be conceived" of St. Anselm. We should think of him in the untranslatable terms of Dom Claude Martin, the son of the Venerable Mary of the Incarnation, the Ursuline of Quebec: "*L'Être de Dieu est un Être de Grandeur.*" Yet, this very God, perceived in the darkness of faith, negatively as St. Thomas insists we know him in this life, has made himself immanent in one human being, in the personal life of Jesus the Christ. The same act of faith reaches God as the almighty Creator of heaven and of earth, as the One who spoke by the prophets and as the One who reveals himself in Jesus the Christ. In this perspective, I think Paul Tillich would have no hesitancy in saying that Jesus the Christ is God revealing himself: "He represents the original image of God embodied in man, Essential Godmanhood."[11] "The Christ is God-for-us."[12]

The appearance of the divine in a personal human life must make sense for man, for all men. This is its purpose. God has no other reason to send the Logos into the flesh than to make it possible for all men to be related to himself. The Word made flesh comes as divine grace, that is, as communication with God, as mediation, as redemption. The correlation between existential estrangement and the epiphany of divine reconciliation is not made as long as what is manifested in Jesus the Christ, once for all in a unique historical setting, cannot be shared, to some extent, by all men in whatever conditions of time and space. Jesus is not the Christ by

[11] *ST*, II, p. 94.
[12] *Ibid.*, p. 100.

himself. Tillich insists that Jesus is manifested to be the Christ in the answer given to him by his disciples. That is to say, a Church, a community of believers, is essential to the meaning of salvation. Without the Church to acknowledge him as the Christ, the bearer of the glad tidings, the New Being, Jesus would simply be known as Jesus of Nazareth, a carpenter and itinerant revivalist. The Church, in this context, is the gathering of those who have, with gladness, received the news of the appearance of the New Being in Jesus. Access to it is a matter of faith. Faith is the basic way of overcoming estrangement in ourselves and of sharing the manifestation of the New Being in the Christ.

I need not elaborate on Tillich's concept of faith. It will be enough to note that, true to his Protestant heritage, Tillich understands faith more as confidence, *fiducia*, than as belief. He calls it "unconditional concern," and he sees it essentially as the awareness of a divine depth within human consciousness and activity. His recent lectures, *Christianity and the Encounter of the World Religions*, have repeated that such an unconditional concern, and therefore genuine faith, is found in all religions. This does not imply the equivalence of the concrete religious formulations accepted in the various religions. On the one hand, Tillich admits that "none of the various elements which constitute the meaning of the holy are ever completely lacking in any genuine experience of the holy, and, therefore, in any religion." On the other hand, "this does not mean that a fusion of the Christian and the Buddhist idea of God is possible, nor does it mean that one can produce a common denominator by depriving the conflicting symbols of their concreteness."[13] Under irreducible concrete formulations and systems, however, the experience of the holy unites all in an unconditional concern which is saving faith. This faith opens man to the realm of the New Being.

How does man incorporate in his own life and experience the manifestation of the divine in Jesus the Christ? By faith indeed, and by faith understood in the most radically Protes-

[13] CEWR, p. 67.

tant way possible. Not only the faith which justifies the impious—this is, after all, a Catholic concept, developed at length in the sixth session of the Council of Trent—but, furthermore, the faith which Tillich expresses as "the Protestant principle": "The power grasping us in the state of faith is not a being besides others, not even the highest; it is not an object among objects, not even the greatest; but it is the quality of pointing beyond themselves and their finite existence to the infinite, inexhaustible, and unapproachable depth of their being and meaning. The Protestant principle is the expression of this relationship."[14]

The Experience of Love

It seems to me, however, that Tillich provides a second answer to our question, and that in so doing he comes nearer to a Catholic pattern of thought. The application to our personal life of the Christian solution to the dilemma of existence is expressed, in Catholicism, both in terms of faith and in terms of sacramental life. Faith is, for us, the starting point of a sacramental participation in the mystery of Christ. Tillich, who shows great understanding for the sacramental principle, fears that the Catholic way of sacramental participation in Christ makes the relative absolute by giving more importance to the symbols of the sacraments than to their transcendent significance. Yet, his ethical concepts endow at least one human experience with sacramental value comparable to that of the Catholic sacraments. This is the experience of love, which dominates his ethics, and provides a starting point for a life of participation in Christ within our situation of estrangement.

Love, as Tillich understands it, is a power of reunion in spite of estrangement. "Love alone," he writes, "can transform itself according to the concrete demands of every individual and social situation without losing its eternity and dignity

[14] PE, p. 163.

and unconditional validity."[15] That is to say, love is the only human experience in which estrangement is overcome, in which the depth of the beings who are uniting themselves in love is unconditionally affirmed. If estrangement is the doom of every human being and every human situation, and if salvation consists in the gratuitous gift, manifested in Jesus the Christ, of life unified and reunited, then love is itself radically Christ-like, and it is already, even in our unredeemed state, a participation in ultimate reunion.

The structure of love, as Paul Tillich understands it, has been described in *Love, Power, and Justice* (1956). It is, for him, the universal phenomenon of beings in quest of each other. It is not only human, but is found in all realms of creation. "Life is being in actuality and love is the moving power of life"; it is "the drive toward the unity of the separated."[16] Love is a particularly human experience, because it "cannot be described as the union of the strange but as the reunion of the estranged."[17] That is to say, love implies an original oneness, from which precisely we have been estranged; and it is the intrinsic power of life to desire a recovery of this oneness. Love is inseparable from estrangement insofar as we experience our estrangement in our wish to overcome it. Love manifests our estrangement, since it is in our discovery of the other person whom we love that we find ourself insuperably impeded in our wish for unity with him. We cannot become he and he cannot become we. We remain separated by an abyss from the banks of which we call to each other. Love thus makes estrangement painful. It replaces innocence by experience, the innocence of selfish complacency by the experience of separated selfhood. But because it implies this appeal for reunion, love also makes it evident that we are somehow united. It shows that, under the surface of our separations, there is a continuity between us and that, at a deeper depth, we are one. "Without an

[15] *Ibid.*, p. 155.
[16] *LPJ*, p. 25.
[17] *Loc. cit.*

ultimate belongingness no union of one thing with another can be conceived."[18]

The supreme manifestation of love took place in Jesus the Christ: "The love of Jesus as the Christ, which is the manifestation of the divine love—and only this—embraces everything concrete in self and world."[19] That God, in the words of St. John, is love, implies that he is at the same time Absolute and Related. This is expressed dogmatically in the doctrine of the Blessed Trinity: the Absolute nature of God being self-related in the threefold way of the Personal Relations, Father, Son, and Spirit. To say that God is love is also to say that he relates himself to creation and especially to the spiritual creature, man, in a bond of unity. The Absolute makes itself neighbor to the contingent, the Eternal to the temporal, the Permanent to the temporary. In this mystery of love, which is the fundamental mystery of creation, we find the ultimate origin of the mystery of redemption, of God's determination, in spite of all, to reach unity with his creatures, the children of his love. This was supremely expressed on the cross, when the Word of God manifested love for all by overcoming the hostility of all creatures through his acceptance of failure. In the cross, in the renunciation of success and the acceptance of defeat, in the final humiliation of the Servant of God, "bruised for our sins," God's love affirmed its ultimate power to reconcile all things in heaven and on earth. "The Christ had to suffer and die, because whenever the Divine appears in all its depth, it cannot be endured by men."[20] This is one aspect of the crucifixion; the other aspect comes next: "Yet, when the Divine is rejected, it takes the rejection upon itself. It accepts our crucifixion, our pushing away, the defense of ourselves against it. It accepts our refusal to accept and thus conquers us. That is the center of the mystery of Christ."[21] The hour of the crucifixion was the hour of truth. Face to

[18] *Loc. cit.*
[19] *ST*, I, p. 152.
[20] *SF*, p. 147.
[21] *Loc. cit.*

face with God, dying through our fault, we discovered that he was actually dying for our salvation. This was the revelation of love, the good news that divine love is able to bring order out of chaos, union out of estrangement, acceptance out of revolt, good out of evil, redemption out of the murder of Jesus the Christ. At that hour a New Being appeared: the being of the one who suffered death at the hands of those he loved, and who, resurrecting, made them able to love him whom they had murdered. The New Being, "born in the grave,"[22] will now spread fire on the earth.

In all experience of love, therefore, we share to some extent, however faintly, the function of the Christ; for, we share his experience of accepting estrangement, thereby making reunion possible. Love joins two aspects, absolute, by which it always gives itself, and dependent, by which it shapes its gift on the concrete nature and situation of the one who is loved. "The absoluteness of love is its power to go into the concrete situation, to discover what is demanded by the predicament of the concrete to which it turns."[23] At each minute all men can say with Tillich: "The other one and I and we together in this moment in this place are a unique, unrepeatable occasion, calling for a unique, unrepeatable act of uniting love."[24] When we recognize this occasion for uniting love, for reunion of those who are estranged from each other, and from themselves, and from nature, and from God, we participate in the Christ, following the example of him who achieved God's reconciliation of the supreme estrangement of sin, being transformed into him, being made images and likenesses of the very love of God. When we fail to recognize these occasions, we deepen the estrangement into which we were born and which hangs over mankind, dooming all men to separation. The permanent dilemma of man is that he has to choose—and he cannot avoid choosing—between love and indifference, between reunion and estrangement. Estrangement is overcome by an attitude which respects the

22 *Ibid.*, p. 164.
23 *ST*, I, p. 152.
24 *NB*, p. 32.

distance between being and being: it is not identity and
fusion between two beings, who would thereby lose their
absoluteness, but the joining together of those who find a
ground for unity in their very distinctiveness. When this takes
place, then the Christ has done his work; faith is fulfilled; the
unjust is accepted through grace, in spite of his injustice;
the other becomes mine while remaining other, and I become his without becoming he. Then the human situation
is no longer one of estrangement; it is one of reconciliation.
"Love," Paul Tillich writes, "is the source of grace. Love accepts that which is unacceptable and love renews the old
being so that it becomes a new being."[25]

Conclusion

In the preceding pages I have let Paul Tillich speak, although I have interspersed my own comments with his analysis. For I feel that the main point of this essay, that Christ
is the answer to existential anguish, is a fundamental insight
which Catholics have tended to neglect in a smug unconcern
for those who have brought this anguish to the fore of modern thought. We should be grateful that we can learn something about Christ, that at least some aspects of Christology
can be emphasized with the help of modern thinkers, be they
Protestant like Tillich or agnostic like many philosophers of
existentialism.

The second main point, that the experience of love, if it
is genuine love, implies a Christ-like attitude, seems to me
to have always been an essential point of Catholic ethics and
spirituality, even though it has often remained implicit. This
suggests, I believe, that Catholic theology ought to develop
a theology of love. It is better equipped for this than Protestantism, which remains impeded by an excessive stress on
faith as the one virtue of Christian life. The liberal Protestantism of the nineteenth century, which became a philan-
thropy rather than a dogmatic teaching, shifted the center of

25 TC, p. 145.

Protestant virtue from faith to love. Paul Tillich attempts to strengthen the often vague altruism of liberal Protestantism through a better grasp of fundamental theological categories. He thus helps to restate the importance of faith while keeping love at the center of Christian life. Catholic theology should be in a still better position to investigate the relationships between our acts of love, in which we are reunited to those from whom we are estranged, and the supreme act of divine love, which brought reconciliation between God and creation.

I do not know if it is necessary at the end of this essay to raise once more the question which seems to be predominant among the reviewers and interpreters of Paul Tillich who belong to strong doctrinal traditions, especially Catholic, orthodox conservative Lutherans, and those who, in all traditions, have felt the impact of Karl Barth: Is Tillich's thought, as distinguished from his intention, Christian? To ask the question in these terms is to make a meaningful answer impossible, for Tillich's thought cannot be divorced from his intention. His intention is to establish an existential correlation between the human condition today and the Christian message. His thought stresses, understresses, or overstresses the aspects of Christianity that need to be stressed, understressed, or overstressed in order to make such a correlation meaningful. The resulting "system," as he calls it, cannot be integrated as such and without changes into an established type of Christianity; it is not Catholic or Orthodox; nor is it, for that matter, Protestant, as Luther and Calvin were Protestant. Yet, whatever label we give it, and how much we may wish to rewrite his thought for the sake of orthodoxy, we should heed Paul Tillich's eagerness to interpret Christianity for the man of today, for the estranged, the puzzled, the frightened man of today.

XIV

MAURICE B. SCHEPERS, O.P.

Paul Tillich on the Church

A common observation concerning the ecumenical movement is that its development on the Continent of Europe, especially in Germany, owes its vitality primarily to the situation which Christians faced in common during the days of the Nazi rule and persecution. Out of this observation we may distill a more general remark, namely, that the political milieu in which the Christian community is immersed influences the forms the Church uses to express her inner life. It is not necessary to cast our glance across the Atlantic to perceive the truth of this remark; for American Christianity, whether Catholic or Protestant, has certainly been modified by contact with the American way of life.

The case is somewhat the same on the individual level. In fact, we can scarcely begin to penetrate into the core of any man's thought unless we are aware of the politics of his origins. By "politics of his origins" is simply meant the principle movements which characterize the society in which he was formed and in which he abides.

The following remarks are not presented as a sort of colossal machine whereby a given story is entirely unraveled without a shred of inexplicable material remaining. It is inevitable, however, that a person who becomes acquainted with the thought of such a great contemporary theologian as Dr. Paul Tillich asks questions something like the following: "Why does Tillich see paradox *everywhere?* How is it that he cannot envisage or admit the possibility of our being *in the truth* in such a way that doubt ceases to be the defining category of our lives?"

This is not the place even to attempt a definitive answer to such questions; nevertheless, the observation must be made that, for Tillich, the society in which he presently abides is not "his" society, i.e., the society of his formation. "This is too obvious to be significant," someone may say. Perhaps, but I would submit that Paul Tillich is essentially a *European* theologian, who happens to be living and writing in the United States. It is certainly significant that, among all the theologians who do live and write within the borders of our country, Dr. Tillich stands out as the one who is the most preoccupied with the ambiguity of everything which is not of ultimate concern and, therefore, with doubt as the dominant factor in religion.

I do not intend by this to slight Dr. Tillich; for, as a matter of fact, it is altogether possible that our native theologians are somewhat blinded to the ambiguities which do pervade the world in which we live and do tend to underestimate the moment of doubt as a religious category. If this is true, the reason might be traced to the "American success," in which we are all, to a greater or less degree, immersed. So be it! The voice of Tillich, however, must actually sound somewhat foreign, because it is the expression of another experience. If we can adjust, by understanding somewhat the experience from which this expression flows, we may have a better chance of profiting from what he has to say, and also of making a fair criticism of the system which he proposes as the representation of his experience.

As far as the system itself is concerned, this essay limits itself to that portion of Volume Three of Dr. Tillich's *Systematic Theology* which deals ostensibly with the mystery of the Church. Direct reference to the entire Tillichian system seems unnecessary for two reasons: (1) universal claims have not been made either for its authenticity or for its universality; (2) the following pages are meant only to elucidate a specimen in the thought patterns of Dr. Tillich as he theologizes concerning what he sees in the life of the Christian churches.

The immediate context of the doctrine concerning the Church is that part of the *Systematic Theology* entitled "Life and the Spirit." The beginning of this section consists in an analysis of the ambiguities which may be discovered in life itself, together with certain indications concerning the symbols of "unambiguous life." There follows a section on the "Spiritual Presence," where we are introduced to notions leading to a direct confrontation with the mystery of the Church. Such, for example, is the idea that Jesus is not *the Christ* when separated from those who receive him in faith and love, which leads to mutual service. A final entree to the matter we wish to analyze is Tillich's discussion of the term "Spiritual Community," a reality which, he affirms, can and does appear in both latent and manifest forms, so that "the qualities invisible and visible must be applied to the church both in its latency and in its manifestations."*

The method employed in the following pages is simply that of reconstructing, with as great accuracy as possible, the line of thought established by Tillich concerning the Church, along with a few indications of what seems to be crucial matter for a valid understanding and criticism. This will be followed by a brief critique, in order to make as clear as possible what position Dr. Tillich takes in the matter of the Church's self-reflection and self-justification.

The Meaning of Spiritual Community

The first task Paul Tillich undertakes in investigating the meaning of the Church is to define precisely "Spiritual Community." The term is used here designedly without the definite article, because of Tillich's insistence that Spiritual Community is "not a group existing beside other groups, but rather a power and a structure inherent and effective in such groups" (p. 162). By the same token, however, Spiritual Community is not to be conceived of as standing for an ideal being that

* ST, III, p. 153. Further references to ST, III, will be placed in parentheses after quotations from the work.

can be contrasted with the reality of the churches (Tillich prefers always to use this term in the plural and without capitalization). Finally, it would be a mistake to interpret Spiritual Community as an "assembly of so-called Spiritual Beings . . . the saved from all periods and countries represented on earth by . . . hierarchies and sacraments" (p. 164).

Not ideal but real, not a concrete thing yet susceptible of discernment, neither a visible Church beside other churches nor an invisible Church embracing all the just of every age, Spiritual Community is the one absolute in the ecclesiology of Paul Tillich. It is the "quality in the churches which makes them churches" (p. 164). This statement is based, of course, on everything that has been said previously in the *Systematic Theology* concerning Spiritual Presence, through which the ambiguities of religion are overcome. A parallel is at least suggested: just as Spiritual Presence is operative for the resolution of ambiguities present in religion on the individual level, so also Spiritual Community effects the resolution of all the paradoxes which characterize the churches. Implied, therefore, is a reference to the unambiguous life of God. Thus, the vertical relationship is definitive for the churches.

Dynamic Essence of the Churches

All else is paradox; and this is verified first of all in the dynamic essence of the churches. Woven into the very fabric of the sociological phenomenon called "church" there is discernible a theological aspect, which points to the presence of unambiguous Spiritual Community. This presence is, however, symbolic, in the sense that it cannot be isolated and distilled out of those concrete things which we call "the churches." The churches' holiness, for example, is paradoxically present in institutions, doctrines, ritual, devotional activities, and ethical principles, which point to the presence of the New Being. And to be "paradoxically present" means to be hidden beneath that which appears as unholy. Likewise with the attribute of unity, Tillich sees the ambiguity of unity and division in the churches' historical existence as not susceptible of resolution by means of a force such as the ecumenical movement. The reason for this is simply that ecumenism and similar movements are operative principally on a horizontal plane, whereas the unity of the churches consists in a relation that is vertical, the terms of which are the sociological phenomenon of the churches and the Spirit.

Even as unity is paradoxically present in the divided churches and holiness in the ambiguous institutions through which they propagate themselves, so universality (catholicity) is present, both intensively and extensively, in the churches' particularity. Intensive universality is defined, then, as the "power and desire to participate as church in everything created under all dimensions of life" (p. 170); while universality's extensive armature is conceived of as the "validity of the church's foundation for all nations, social groups, races, tribes, and cultures" (p. 171).

To take a given factor in the sociological structure of the Church, therefore, we would have to say that it offers simultaneous opportunities for holiness and unholiness, unity and division, isolated particularism and universality. And this would have to be said of *any* given factor, without regard for the apparent source of its being constitutive of the churches.

These ambiguities are carried over into every aspect of the life of the churches, even into the wholly interior realms of faith and love. Thus, for example, the churches are distinguished from other religious groups in that they are communities "of those who affirm Jesus is the Christ" (p. 174). This affirmation—one of faith—is the foundation of the churches. (It is, by the way, one of the bases for a given church's membership in the World Council of Churches.) This being true, it follows necessarily that any denial of this principle results in exclusion from the Church; and the denial itself would ordinarily be given the name "heresy." Tillich perceives an ambiguity even here and prefers to state the case as follows: The rejection of the foundation of the churches is not, in itself, heresy, but rather "separation from the community in which the problem of heresy exists" (p. 176). Concretely this would mean, of course, that the Church itself, as a sociological phenomenon, does not have the right to label such a rejection heretical, nor to stigmatize as a heretic the person who makes the rejection his own.

So too, when the churches are viewed as communities of love (this is the complementary factor of the churches' interior life, according to Tillich), certain judgments are called for. At the very limit, of course, this judgment or crisis has to do with whether or not a person is disposed to live "in communion" with the Church; and the indisposition would ordinarily be termed "schismatic." In the present state of affairs, moreover, the crisis occurs both within a given church and in the relation of the separate churches with other religious groups and with one another. Tillich's position here is analogous to that which he holds regarding the community of faith. Because of the ambiguity of even the interior life of the churches, all final judgment must be suspended. Although the problem of schism does exist and plague the churches, it is not possible to render a decision concerning the rupture. Perhaps it might be said that an absolute criterion does exist, but that the churches themselves are not allowed to apply it absolutely to an altogether ambiguous situation.

Here we may note that Tillich's views concerning the Church as community of faith and love seems to be the very core of his ecclesiology. It is the point at which direct dependence on the Christ is established, although the manner in which this dependence is conceived is certainly worthy of further discussion. We will return to this point in the critical part of the present study.

External Functions of the Church

According to Tillich the external functions of the Church, which flow, as it were, from the interior life of faith and love, belong to four genera of functions: the constitutive, expanding, constructing, and relating functions, respectively. Each of them is characterized by a sort of tension which he calls paradoxical or ambiguous. The following ideas are a summary of his notions concerning these functions.

"The constitutive function of a church is that of receiving"

(p. 189). This statement introduces us into Tillich's explanation of how the churches are held in existence. Essentially it is through some sort of mediation, a condition wherein one person ministers to another person. The Church exists in virtue of the preaching of the Word and the administration of the sacraments; in these actions there is always a giving and a receiving. Tillich is at pains to point out, however, that "he who preaches preaches to himself as a listener, and he who listens is a potential preacher" (p. 189). Thus, he obviates the necessity of according the churches a structure in which some members would be definitely hierarchical (mediators), while others would be laymen (receivers). In this connection he notes too that, in worship, which includes adoration, prayer, and contemplation, the churches respond to the ultimate ground of their being.

In the complex act of the constitution of the Church, therefore, Spiritual Community is established through one or another mediating principle; and the churches thus enlivened express themselves in forms of worship which seem appropriate. The paradox or ambiguity found here consists in a certain tension between "tradition" and "reformation." Tillich's idea is indicated by the following observations: "The identity of reception and mediation excludes the possibility of the establishment of a hierarchical group which mediates while all the others merely receive" (*loc cit.*). In other words, the structures through which Spiritual Presence or the New Being is mediated are, although given according to a certain "tradition," always susceptible of "reformation," and this to the degree that altogether new structures come into being.

The expanding functions of the churches include the missions, education, and evangelism. Tillich describes the first of these as the "actualization of the Spiritual Community within concrete churches all over the world" (p. 193), putting the emphasis thereby on the geographical aspect of the churches' expansion. Evangelism or revivalism comprises, in contrast, those activities "directed toward people who have belonged or still belong to the realm of Christian civilization, but who have ceased to be active members of the Church or who have become indifferent or hostile toward it" (p. 195).

The paradox inherent in these functions is between verity and adaptation, i.e., between adherence to the true sources of the mission of the churches and the shifting of emphasis dictated by the circumstances of those to whom the mission is directed.

Through a process of mediation, then, the churches are constituted, and they expand especially through mission activity. These two genera of functions refer immediately to the community of faith and love, which Tillich designates as the dynamic essence of the churches. The functions yet to be described appear to be related less intimately to the interior core of the churches, but they are still integral parts of Tillich's view.

Constructing functions are those "in which [the Church] builds its life by using and transcending the functions of man's life under the dimension of the spirit" (p. 196). The latter phrase—"man's-life-under-the-dimension-of-the-spirit"— is a sort of technical name for activities authentically human on account of their coming under the dominion of the Spiritual Presence. At this point, of course, the discerning reader is already asking himself which is cause and which is effect, i.e., whether the constructing functions "of the Church" are constitutive of it, so that the Church becomes an aggregate of men whose lives are led under the dimension of the spirit, or whether these functions flow, as it were, from the very being of the Church in circumstances where assimilation is called for. Tillich does not come to grips with the problem at this point, however; hence, it will be introduced more explicitly as his own ideas unfold.

Two species may be distinguished within the genus of constructing functions: functions which go by the name, "theoretical," and those which are called "practical." The former species, moreover, includes the aesthetic and cognitive functions; the latter is further distinguished into the communal and the personal. The ambiguity which pervades this entire genus is an opposition between "form-transcendence" and "form-affirmation"—"form" here designating the modes of human activity which become common through an experience of their relative worth.

Hence, in the area of the aesthetical, two principles control the authenticity of religious art in the service of the Church: the principle of consecration, "an application of the larger principle of form-transcendence"; and the principle of honesty, "an application of the general principle of form-affirmation." On the one hand, it appears that the whole of creation is susceptible of being *consecrated* and thereby put to the use of the artist, whatever his peculiar talents may be. The artist must, however, have reverence for the form of the material which he uses, a form which is "affirmed" by nature itself. On these bases Tillich ventures the opinion that religious art will be in the authentic service of the Church, i.e., really a constructing function, to the extent that it exhibits expressionist elements.

By the same token he sees two factors in the cognitive function which we call theology: meditation and discourse. "The meditative act penetrates the substance of the religious symbols [thus transcending their form]; the discursive act analyzes and describes the form in which the substance can be grasped" (p. 202). Tillich does not conclude, however, that theological discourse is bound to any particular set of symbols. On the contrary, it is "infinitely open in all directions" (*loc. cit.*). Tillich's own "system," wherein the terms and concepts canonized by long use are at least scrutinized, if not set aside, bears witness to his convictions in this regard. Nevertheless, he is very candid in affirming that, with regard to the philosophical vehicle for theological discourse, the existential approach seems the most apt, because herein the "question of human existence in time and space and of man's predicament in unity with the predicament of everything existing is asked and answered in symbols of their conceptual transformation" (p. 203).

In the realm of praxis the churches are concerned with the "interdependent growth of community and personality" (p. 204). And it would appear that the churches are the locus wherein the ambiguities of communal life ought to be striven against, if not completely overcome. This is, in fact, verified, according to Tillich, in four different areas. First of all, communal life in the Church is characterized by *inclusive-*

ness, "insofar as the Church claims to be all-inclusive beyond any social, racial, or national limitations" (p. 205). Again, *equality* is a property of the practical life of the churches, insofar as they acknowledge "the equality of all men under sin (which they confess) and . . . of all men under forgiveness (which they confess)" (p. 206). A third quality of the churches' life is *leadership*. Within the ecclesial community certain members actually exercise a governing role; and the genuine growth of the community demands, on the part of all, the recognition of the simultaneous presence of the holy and the demonic in this religious leadership. The existence of *legal form* in the churches is a final quality to be met with in this sphere. As in all the other cases, here too is an ambiguity; for the churches must recognize that such forms, though not of ultimate concern, are necessary to the life of the churches.

The churches' inclusiveness is in danger of becoming monolithic. Equality in a corrupted state is egalitarianism. Leadership can, even within a religious community, decline and tend to become tyrannical. Legal forms can become empty formalities. All these dangers are inherent in the churches' life; yet, they are susceptible of being overcome, at least in a sort of fragmentary way. Such a systematic presentation of the difficulties which beset the churches in their effort to *do* the will of Christ touches very closely the notions of the catholicity and the unity of the Church as well as the principles from which they might be derived. Therefore, we shall have to return to this point.

The other armature of Church praxis has to do directly with personal functions: these include the ambiguity of self-determination and the ambiguity of the determination of others. The former is expressed concretely in the apparent opposition between asceticism ("self-denial") and humanity ("self-assertion"). All men experience the inner conflict to which these terms refer, and Tillich affirms that the asceticism which resolves the conflict consists in "the conquest of a subjective self-affirmation which prevents participation in the object" (p. 211). Obviously, the emphasis is placed upon the interior factor; but the expression, "participation in the object," harks back to Tillich's notion concerning the existential estrangement of man, i.e., his separation from others through his very existence, which is overcome through the New Being. With regard to the determination of others, Tillich makes the following incisive statement:

> In the actual processes of education and guidance . . . he who is nearer to the *telos* of humanity is continuously aware of the fact that he is still infinitely removed from it, and that therefore the attitude of superiority and the will to control the other one (for his good) is replaced by the acknowledgement that the educator or the guide is in the same predicament as the one he tries to help (p. 212).

"Relating functions" is the name Tillich gives to the actions which result from the churches' encounters with other sociological groups. Here he makes use of a classic schema; the attribution to the churches of the priestly, prophetic, and royal functions derived from the Christ. It is remarkable, however, that in each case Tillich observes a mutual interaction between the churches and other groups. For example, there is a *silent-interpretation* of "priestly-substance" between the churches and other groups. Both the churches and other groups in society also exercise *critical judgment* (the prophetic function) on one another, and this "in the name of the Spiritual Presence" (p. 214). *Political establishment* is the name Tillich gives to the mutually exercised royal function; and here he notes that there is "also a justified political impact on the churches from the side of society" (p. 215).

Spiritual Presence

Paul Tillich's final systematic consideration of the churches is entitled, "The Individual in the Church and the Spiritual Presence." It is concerned with the experience of entering into the Church and of being in it. The rubrics of this section are very simple; and the points Tillich makes are consistent with the principles he has laid down heretofore. Sev-

eral rather significant points are made, however, and it may
be helpful to put them in their proper context.

To enter into the Church is to experience conversion. This
statement, may, however, be taken in two senses: and there
actually exist two radically different interpretations. The question concerns, of course, which has the ontological precedence,
the Church or the individual. Those who emphasize the predominance of the Church over the individual and conceive of
the Church as "objective," maintain that conversion consists
in a person's being introduced into a community which is
already in existence, in the being and perfection of which the
individual may share. On the other hand, those who emphasize the predominance of the individual over the Church
look upon the experience of conversion as the assuming of
a covenant relationship. The Church thus comes into being
through the conversion experience.

Once within the Church, the individual is free to experience the New Being. This experience takes place on three
levels. In regeneration, i.e., through faith, New Being is experienced as "creation." Here again the radical character of
Tillich's thought becomes evident; for, in this context he states
that to be thus under the impact of the Spiritual Presence
is to believe oneself to be acceptable (to God) even though
unacceptable. This is one aspect of the ecclesial experience,
a necessary factor in the living of the life of the community
of faith and love. We may be prone simply to interpret a
statement such as this in a Lutheran sense, i.e., to make it
mean that man sees himself as *simul justus et peccator*. Tillich leaves us with the impression, however, that he has followed Luther all the way—and even further than Luther would
himself have wanted to go. For Tillich, existential estrangement means radical separation from God and self through
existence itself.

The second armature of the individual person's ecclesial
experience (justification) is felt as "paradox." In discussing
this aspect of the question Tillich shows that in every age
this paradox is expressed in a different way. The constant and
"central element in the courage of faith is the courage to
surrender one's own goodness to God" (p. 226). For St. Paul,

however, courage was concretized in his titanic effort to be free from the law; whereas, Luther asked how he might find a merciful God. In our times, says Tillich, the question is, rather, how it is possible to find meaning in a meaningless world. One possible answer, of course, is simply to *accept* the meaninglessness of the world. Then, however, another question arises, namely, whether or not this surrender is really made to God or to the idol of our own despair.

Sanctification of the individual in the Church is experienced as "process." This is a complexus of spiritual realities. It includes increasing "awareness," i.e., attention to the paradoxical presence of the Spirit in the world. Tillich observes that such growth in awareness comprises attention to "the demonic as well as to the divine" (p. 231). Sanctification means also increasing freedom, i.e., "mature freedom from the law" (p. 233); increasing relatedness; and a certain measure of self-transcendence. As is abundantly evident from all the writings of Tillich, this latter term stands for an "attitude of devotion toward that which is ultimate" (p. 236). At this point precisely the uninitiated are prone to ask: "And what *is* the ultimate?"

To be reborn, justified, and sanctified are experiences that lead to a certain perfection; and Tillich's final point concerning the mystery of the Church is in the form of a question: Is "the transcending of the split of subject and object . . . a possibility in man's existential situation?" (p. 242). In other words, do such experiences as these, which we should recognize as the opening out of the human person, have as their term something which is unambiguous? It would appear that Tillich is of the opinion that it is not the churches' business to give categorical answers to questions such as these.

Final Critique

Before launching a critique of Tillich's thought, one or two observations, which seem to fall within the category of method, must be made. First of all, we must keep in mind that Tillich's theology is a "systematic theology." Therefore, it is of some moment to understand the rationale of the "system," i.e., to locate the point of view of the author. Obviously, this cannot be done all at once; this is the reason we have attempted to *follow* Tillich in his comparatively brief study of the Church. Ordinarily, such a method is valid, since, sooner or later, an author will reveal the location in which he feels most at home. In this same vein we must acknowledge the breadth of Tillich's view of the Church, which takes in its dynamic essence, ambiguities of all sorts, both in the interior life and the external functions, and the complex relationships of the individual to and within the Church.

One of the questions to be asked of any theologian who stands in the tradition of the Reformation is, "*Where* does he stand in that tradition?" In this connection it would be somewhat helpful to see the relation between the ecclesiologies of Luther and Calvin and Tillich's doctrine concerning the Church. This can be done most conveniently within the context of his description of Spiritual Community, where he takes his stand in relation to the reformers, though perhaps in not so many words.

The following is one interpretation of his delimitations of the meaning of Spiritual Community. His ruling out Spiritual Community's being a group beside other groups would seem to be a sort of reaction against the "orthodox" Lutheran notion of an *ecclesiuncula,* i.e., a little remnant of a Church composed of all those who effectively hear the Gospel when it is preached and who profit from the evangelical sacraments when they are rightly administered. Here too Tillich rejects a notion recognizably Calvinist, namely, that the Church is composed of all the predestined of every age and place.

Are we to conclude from this that Tillich does not stand *at all* in the ecclesiological tradition of the Reformation? This is not necessary, especially if we reflect that the common factor in this tradition is the emphasis which is placed upon the vertical relationship between God, the ultimate, and the community which makes up the sociological phenomenon we call the Church.

To say this, of course, is, at least implicitly, also to ask how Tillich's thought concerning the Church is related to the tradition we call Catholic. To answer this question, we must observe, first of all, that this tradition recognizes both vertical and horizontal factors in the constitution of the Church. This means simply that the Church is viewed as a mystery which consists in a complexus or network of relations, the *principal* one of which is the relation of Christ to the Church as his body, a relation which founds, however, a real communion of persons within the Church. We say then—and this in at least verbal agreement with Paul Tillich—that the Church is a community of faith, and love is an absolute dependence on Christ, whom Tillich would designate as the source of New Being.

The difficulty that underlies this verbal agreement, however, would seem to be in the understanding of what is consequent upon "dependence on Christ." When persons "depend on Christ" what follows as far as their relation one to the other is concerned? Notwithstanding the all too obvious ambiguities—to which we will refer again in a moment—can it be said that the horizontal relations within the Church, insofar as they are *established* by Christ, are necessarily involved in a definition of the Church? Catholic tradition would, of course, answer this question in the affirmative, because the Church is conceived of as a real communion (in faith and love) among persons, based upon the communion with God established through the Son of God's having taken our flesh. The Church exists, first of all, in the glorified body of the Lord, no longer limited in its power by the "ambiguities" of time and space. The Church also really exists, however, in the persons who are incorporated into that body of his through the sacraments; and this we should designate as the essentially horizontal existence of the Church, even though the structure of the Church conceived in this way includes factors which we call "hierarchical."

In saying these things we may seem to be really out of tune with Paul Tillich; nevertheless, it is necessary to state the antinomy in order that the similarities and agreements which do exist may not be misunderstood. It is possible to feel great sympathy for many of the observations Tillich makes concerning the life of the Church, and even to wish that Catholic theologians would be as realistic in their appraisal of the life of the Church as he is, but still have serious reservations, based ultimately in the conviction that Tillich misunderstands some of the central dogmas of Christian tradition.

The elements of Tillich's theory concerning the life of the Church which are most telling are the thoughts he expresses in connection with the process of sanctification. It is true that in the Church—in the Catholic Church and in the other Churches of divided Christendom—certain claims are made for *inclusiveness*, i.e., for a realized catholicity. Other claims are set forth regarding an *equality* of recognition that could not possibly be matched in any society which had its origins in either the natural propensity to share goods or in a covenant of men to enter into communion one with another with a view toward some common goal. *Leadership* in the Church is also vaunted as having its source in the "episcopacy" of Christ himself, and therefore having his seal upon it. Finally, we claim that the *legal forms* in which the Church is garbed have a certain divine guarantee.

The *aggiornamento* initiated by Pope John XXIII in the Catholic Church consists in an honest critique of these claims. How is catholicity to be realized today? Perhaps Paul Tillich has something to say to us in this regard. To what extent is equality in the Church of God realized? Speaking from the Protestant tradition Tillich certainly has valid remarks to make concerning this question. So too with the questions of leadership and legal forms, in fact one of the principal factors in Catholics coming to know how better to discern the essential from the accidental is dialogue with those Christians who have been living according to their own traditions for several centuries.

The basic weakness of Paul Tillich's ecclesiology is the tendency, which he shares with all the theologians who live and think within the tradition of the Reformation, to "maximize" the rupture between God and man to the extent that men themselves are not reconciled one with another in the Church. Still, this tendency is modified in Tillich's thought by his preoccupation with the ambiguities he sees in the *modern* world. We cannot say that his experience of these ambiguities is not genuine; by the same token, however, they ought not to be universalized. On the American scene they do put us into direct contact with the thought of the Old World. And this is good for us!

XV

CHRISTOPHER KIESLING, O.P.

The Life of the New Being

Volume Three of Paul Tillich's *Systematic Theology*, which appeared in the autumn of 1963, is part of a comprehensive, tightly knit system of theology, approaching the Christian message with the brand new conceptual equipment of the twentieth century. Tillich's theology of the Christian life, found in Volume Three, can be summarized without loss of its logic. But how can it be summarized without loss of its insights and its attractiveness to the modern mind? Since the approach is so new, the terminology so unfamiliar, how can this theology of the Christian life be presented to an unprepared audience in a favorable light in the limited space of an essay, where it would be stripped of its context and severed from the analysis of the concepts fundamental to the whole system?

The best approach seems to be to examine the goal of the Christian life as Tillich sees it. Concentration on this one point brings in its wake consideration of other aspects of the Christian life. But limited space requires this essay to be further restricted to a consideration of the goal of the Christian life for the individual person in this life, abstracting from the goal of the Church and Christian society in general and from the goal of the Christian life beyond time and space.

The chief value of Tillich's theology may be its unique, masterful, systematic use of mankind's most modern thoughts about reality in order to render the Christian message intelligible to the modern mind—not the mind flooded with faith, but the mind without faith or with weak faith, the mind searching for a final answer to life's puzzles in the twentieth century. This essay approaches Tillich's theology positively, with the intention of welcoming those elements compatible with Catholic thought, rather than with the intention of criticizing its divergencies from Catholic doctrine. The aim of this essay, as a consequence, is simply to present Tillich's idea of the Christian life in its conceptual newness. To achieve this goal, Tillich's own existential terminology and categories of thought have been used and then related to more familiar terms and patterns of thought. Tillich's ideas are not controverted here, but where he differs from Catholic thought is pointed out.

The first step is to formulate a definition of the goal of the Christian life in Tillich's own terminology. Then, the meaning of the various phrases making up this definition will be studied in detail.

The Goal of the Christian Life

In Tillich's theology, several different expressions (he calls them symbols) can be used to designate the goal of the Christian life. In terms of his whole theological system, the most proper expression for the goal of the Christian life is the New Being in Jesus as the Christ.[1] The New Being in Jesus as the Christ is the organizational center of Tillich's theology; it is to Tillich's theology what God is to St. Thomas' theology. Tillich has chosen the New Being in Jesus as the Christ for the organizational center of his theological system because his is an "answering" theology, as he calls it; his theology is essentially an apologetic.[2]

Such a theology must meet the needs of men. Men of the twentieth century have been disillusioned with regard to the rationalistic and progressive ideologies of the previous century; they have been thrown into uncertainty, first by two unprece-

[1] See *ST*, I, pp. 24, 49–50.
[2] See *ibid.*, pp. 6–8.

dented World Wars and then by the specter of atomic annihilation; they have been caught up in the chaos of technological and social change consequent upon rapidly advancing
scientific knowledge and economic progress. Men today need
purpose, certainty, stability. But this is an age also of existential philosophy, so the need must be expressed in terms of
being, existence: men today need New Being. And since Tillich is committed to the Christian message, he offers to men
of today, in answer to the questions inherent in the human
predicament, the New Being in Jesus as the Christ.

While the New Being in Jesus as the Christ is the goal of
the Christian life in terms of Tillich's entire theological system, in terms of the fourth and fifth parts of that system
in the third volume of his *Systematic Theology*, the goal
is designated by other symbols, namely, Unambiguous Life,
the Spiritual Presence, the Kingdom of God, and Eternal
Life.[3]

In these last parts of his system, Tillich considers the New
Being precisely as Unambiguous Life conquering the ambiguities of human life. This Unambiguous Life can be seen
from different points of view and denominated by correspondingly different biblical symbols. It has for its immediate
subject the human spirit (although indirectly it conquers the
ambiguities in all the realms of life); moreover, it is known
by analogy with the life processes of the human spirit. Hence,
the Unambiguous Life of the New Being is expressed by
the symbol of the Spirit of God dwelling in the human
spirit or, in a phrase, the Spiritual Presence. Unambiguous
Life also has an historical dimension, as does man and the
human spirit; the historical dimension has social and eschatological aspects over and above the aspect of spirit. In this
more comprehensive sense, it is designated by the symbol of
the Kingdom of God. Since the Unambiguous Life does in fact
transcend history, from this point of view it is signified by the
symbol of Eternal Life.

We have, therefore, several terms for the goal of the Christian life in Paul Tillich's theology. Here, we shall concentrate

[3] See *ST*, III, pp. 107–10.

on the goal of the Christian life as it is designated by the symbols of the New Being in Jesus as the Christ, Unambiguous Life, and the Spiritual Presence.

When we speak of the New Being or Unambiguous Life or the Spiritual Presence as the goal of the Christian life, we refer to these in their purity and perfection. Tillich speaks of them also as men participate in them fragmentarily and by anticipation.[4] As participated, they are the power of being and meaning behind the Christian life, the efficient and formal causes of the Christian life, as we would say. The New Being, Unambiguous Life, the Spiritual Presence is even now in men as they struggle with the ambiguities of life; it drives them forward toward the perfect manifestation of the New Being, Unambiguous Life, and the Spiritual Presence. In a similar vein, we say that charity or the divine life is the goal of the Christian life, meaning these in their perfection; but we say, too, that even now charity vivifies men and the divine life animates them as efficient and formal causes whereby men tend to the plenitude of these gifts.

In the fourth part of his theological system, Tillich considers the Spiritual Presence especially as it is the power of being and meaning in the Christian life rather than as the goal.[5] In the light of this fact and of what has been said above, we can state the goal of the Christian life in Tillich's terminology in these words: *the New Being in Jesus as the Christ conquering the ambiguities of life by Unambiguous Life under the impact of the Spiritual Presence*. We will now probe into the meaning of the several phrases which make up this statement.

[4] See *ibid.*, pp. 138–40.
[5] See *ibid.*, pp. 111–20: Tillich does not say this explicitly, but he writes of the divine Spirit "breaking into" the human spirit, "driving" the human spirit beyond itself, the human spirit "under the impact" of the divine Spirit, etc.

The New Being in Jesus as the Christ

A Catholic could accept the statement that the goal of the Christian life is the New Being in Jesus as the Christ, but he would attach a much different meaning to these words from the meaning Tillich gives to them. A Catholic would understand the New Being in Jesus as the Christ to be the supernatural, divine-like life acquired by incorporation into Christ and derived from the glorious Jesus, Head of the Mystical Body, from whom energy and life descend from the Father to quicken the members with new life, so that each member can say very literally, "It is now no longer I that live, but Christ lives in me" (Gal. 2.20).

For Tillich, the New Being in Jesus as the Christ signifies what kind of thing the goal of the Christian life is—New Being —and where the supreme exemplar and criterion of this kind of thing is to be found—in Jesus, certainly not the mere man Jesus of Nazareth, but neither an incarnate God named Jesus of Nazareth, rather Jesus as the Christ, that is, the man "sent" by God as the manifestation of the New Being and recognized as such by his disciples in a revelatory experience.[6] Let us explain this more fully.

The New Being, according to Tillich, is man in whom existential estrangement is overcome. Existential man, man deciding his being from minute to minute each day, becomes estranged from his essential being, from what he could and should be, for every choice closes off forever other choices, and some choices are positively detrimental to self or others. Since man must choose, he has no alternative except to exist, to go forth from his essential being, to become estranged, to be "fallen" man. The New Being is man in whom existential estrangement is overcome, in whom existence—choosing one's being—does not lead away from what man can and should

[6] For the ideas in the remainder of this section on the New Being in Jesus as the Christ, see especially *ST*, III, pp. 141–52 and, for more details, *ST*, II, pp. 119–65.

be. Since man's essential being is from God, to remain true to his essential being is to remain true to God; it is to be united to God, the ground and abyss of being.

Such New Being is found in Jesus as the Christ. Here is one man who, though he lived under the conditions of existential estrangement, never "fell" from his essential being, never sinned, never lost contact with the ground of his being, God. Such New Being is found in other men, but not with the perfection that it has in Jesus as the Christ, nor as the central manifestation of New Being in history under the continuing creativity of divine Providence, nor as the criterion whereby New Being is recognized and judged wherever and whenever it appears. The New Being is said to be in Jesus "as the Christ"; for only insofar as the man Jesus is recognized as the bearer of New Being, as the Messias, the Christ, is he, in fact, the central manifestation and criterion of New Being. "The New Being in Jesus as the Christ" designates for Tillich, then, the kind of being which is the goal of the Christian life and where the supreme exemplar and criterion of that goal is to be found.

In more familiar ascetical or pastoral terminology, Tillich is saying that the goal of the Christian life consists in the imitation of Jesus as the bearer of the New Being. This brings up the practical question of precisely in what respect Jesus is the bearer of New Being.

Jesus is the bearer of New Being insofar as he remained always in contact with the ground of his being and transparent to the infinite and ultimate, never usurping the claims of infinite power, being, and meaning. Jesus of Nazareth could have been king of the Jews very literally; he could have demanded and obtained the allegiance of men to him alone; he could have gathered for himself the treasures of worldly wealth that go with kingship; he could, in a word, have set himself up as an idol in place of God. In fact, however, Jesus resisted, by the power of the New Being in him, all these tendencies of estranged humanity; he insisted always that the word he preached was not his but the Father's, that he had come to do not his own will but the Father's. Rather than usurp the place of God in men's lives, he went to an ignominious death, obedient to the Father unto the end. Thus, he was never estranged from his essential being, from what God intended him to be, even though he lived under the conditions of existential estrangement. In the more familiar terminology of Christian thought, Jesus is the bearer of New Being precisely in his loving obedience to the Father and his humility unto death. Or, more true to Tillich's thought, these characteristics of Jesus are the chief signs that he is the bearer of the New Being; his entire life was a manifestation of New Being, but the ultimate proof of the authenticity of New Being in him was his humble, obedient death.

Imitation of Jesus as the Christ, as the manifestation of the New Being, does not involve any ontological or moral union with a risen, living, glorious Jesus, any mystical union with Jesus reigning at the right hand of the Father, any becoming a member of a mystical body with Jesus as head. The resurrection, ascension, and glorious reign of Christ are symbols for the truth that Jesus is the Christ, is the one who has conquered existential estrangement, is the bearer of the New Being *par excellence* and is recognized as such by his disciples. There was no empty tomb; there is no transmuted body of Jesus in some place called "heaven."

These mysteries or myths of Jesus as the Christ are not unfounded fictions of the mind: they do point to an historical reality, Jesus as the bearer of the New Being recognized as such by his disciples, all of which is a divine revelation. But these mysteries or myths do not signify a Jesus in heaven, head over a real but mystical body. Jesus is head and the Church is his body insofar as he is the prime exemplar and criterion of the New Being; and all those who look to him as such constitute, as it were, members of a community or "body" dependent upon him who is, so to speak, the "head." This, obviously, is the Church, or in Tillich's terminology, the Spiritual Community.

The New Being in Jesus as the Christ, then, as the goal of the Christian life, means something far different for Tillich from what it means for the Catholic, although there is a sliver of common ground.

The Ambiguities of Life

According to the definition of the goal of the Christian life in Tillich's terminology, the New Being conquers the ambiguities of life by Unambiguous Life. We must now investigate the meaning of "the ambiguities of life" and "Unambiguous Life."

Tillich's theology is, as we have noted, an "answering" theology. The method of procedure in such a theology requires, first of all, an analysis of the human predicament in order to bring to light the questions implicit in this predicament, in order, finally, to give the answer of the Christian message.[7] Examining human life, Tillich discovers that it is ambiguous and that man, experiencing such life, yearns for its opposite, which is to be found in the New Being, the creation of the Spiritual Presence.[8]

This ambiguity of life consists in the double value, the goodness and badness, that attaches to the results of every function of the life process, especially those of the spirit. In more familiar terminology, we would speak of the imperfection of everything we attempt to do or of the evil by-products that follow upon even the best of our accomplishments. This ambivalence of life is manifest, and particularly important theologically, in the realm of the human spirit, the realm of the properly human functions of life—morality, culture, and religion.

Morality is the function of self-integration in the life process whereby man strives to form his personality. Man is, at the outset, a person, a centered-self; but he must grow, must experience reality and other persons and assimilate this experience into his own personality, thus growing as a person. But in this process of assimilating experience, man must neither destroy the delicately balanced centeredness of the self, which

---

[7] See *ST*, I, p. 62.

[8] Tillich carries out this analysis in *ST*, III, pp. 30–110; the high points of this analysis will be summarized in the rest of this section.

he already has (by intemperate use of alcohol and, perhaps, consequent alcoholism, for example), nor destroy what he experiences (by "using" other persons for his own gratification, for example). The moral law lays down the norms for this function of self-integration; the moral law confronts man with the structure of his essential being, what he can and should be.

But, in his state of existential estrangement, man finds it impossible to develop his personality as he should. It is not always clear to man what the moral law is, so that man is without a guide in the function of self-integration. If the law is clear, its application is often obscure. If, for fear of making a mistake because of the ambiguity of the law, man refuses to act at all, then his personality is stunted, he does not grow morally. On the other hand, if he acts, he may very well actualize potentialities of his being which will lead to evil, or which will violate other persons, or which, though good in themselves and their consequences, will prevent the actualization of other, perhaps better, potentialities. Existential man is at an impasse: he must act, but to act is to achieve at best an ambiguous result. Man does do good; in this Tillich is a remarkably optimistic Protestant theologian. But man's good, his best, is never perfect, and the evil present, physical or moral, is much too great to be ignored, so that morality for existential man, "fallen" man, is ambiguous.

Culture, like morality, is a specifically human function of the life process. Culture is the function of self-creativity whereby man tends to make a meaningful and purposeful world for himself. This involves his reacting to the experienced world by knowledge (sciences, history, etc.) and aesthetic expression (the fine arts), both of which are directed to finding meaning in the experienced world. Culture involves also man's acting upon the world through technology and social institutions; these functions also ought to lead to a meaningful, purposeful, world. Through all of this cultural activity man ought to grow personally or morally, finding his true, essential being and the ground of his being, God. In other terms, man's cultural activity ought to make a world that speaks on every side of God and leads to sanctity.

But here again man, in existential estrangement, is trapped in the ambiguities of life. Language, which is fundamental to cultural activity of any sort, obscures, hides, and omits meaning as much as it reveals and conveys it. Words make possible not only communication but also misunderstanding. One social group, for the good of many, excludes others, and perhaps even threatens the good of others. Technology, as we know so well, raises living standards; but it also creates moral problems—the dulled personality of the assembly line—and cultural problems—overpopulation in certain areas, a civilization of gadgets, shallow thinking, bureaucracy. Instead of leading to sanctity and being transparent to God, culture is forever obscuring or concealing humanity (Tillich's term for the classical "virtue"), justice (human relatedness of every sort), and the ground of being (God). Culture, in existential estrangement, is ambiguous.

The third function of the human spirit is self-transcendence. Man seeks not only to shape his personality and to fashion a meaningful world by morality and culture, he also seeks to go beyond himself towards the infinite. The more common name for this function of life is "religion." Religion is man's effort to transcend his finitude in the direction of the infinite. Man is aware that his being and all his achievements are finite and conditioned; this readily leads to an awareness of the infinite and unconditioned ground and abyss of being, the sacred, the divine, God. With this awareness is born an *eros*, a yearning for the infinite ground of being. Man seeks to lay hold of the infinite, but, of course, he cannot, for everything he does and all the means at his disposal are finite, conditioned.

What man can and in fact does do in this effort to transcend his finitude is to symbolize the infinite for himself with materials drawn from his morality and culture. He fashions a religion with a particular moral code, with "saints" exemplifying this morality, with myths or doctrines expressive of the nature of the infinite ground of being, with social groups called "temples" or "synagogues" or "churches" or "societies." All of these finite, conditioned entities point to the infinite and transcendent ground of being, to God, and through them man expresses the self-transcending function of life.

But, if ambiguity plagues morality and culture, it plagues religion even more. Since religion uses the material of morality and culture in its effort at self-transcendence, all the ambiguities of morality and culture are found in religion. The moral code of a particular religion is unclear in its prescriptions; or if clear, its application to particular instances is obscure. It is difficult to distinguish truly saintly action, truly self-transcending action in the direction of the infinite, from neurotic oddity, which is a further falling away from man's essential being, a disintegration of personality. Myth or doctrine becomes not only a language binding men together in their ultimate concern for the infinite ground of being, but a source of misinterpretation, misunderstanding, dispute, division, even religious war. Social organization not only joins men together in their effort to transcend their finitude, but tends to exclude other men and thus to destroy rather than to promote the brotherhood of men.

But religion suffers ambiguities proper to it, distinct from the ambiguities it suffers because of the moral and cultural elements it uses. Religion is self-transcendence toward the infinite by means of finite symbols. In religion there is always the danger, and even the fact, of the finite symbols usurping the place of the infinite: the symbols become an idol worshiped in place of the living God. Whenever absolute claims are made for any facet of religion, whether it be for a particular code of morals, a particular set of doctrines, or a particular social organization, then religion has become demonic and turned to idolatry. The religious morals, myths, doctrines, and social organization have ceased to be transparent to the divine ground of being, to facilitate transcendence beyond the finite to the infinite.

For Tillich, this demonization of religion is not merely a danger which occasionally becomes a fact. The danger is so great and the fact so widespread that religion, in the state of existential estrangement, is, simply speaking, universally ambiguous. Every world religion claims to be the true religion: hence, every world religion is demonic, setting itself up

as an idol. Catholicism, according to Tillich, is demonic in
its claim of infallibility for the pope. Fundamentalist Protestantism is demonic in its claim of infallibility for the Bible
literally interpreted. These examples can be multiplied by
running through the claims of the world religions and all their
sects. Religion, man's noblest function of self-transcendence,
that which seeks to give ultimate meaning and purpose to all
of life's functions, is not a total failure, but neither is it a
total success; it is ambiguous.

Tillich's systematic analysis of the negative side of the goal
of the Christian life is, in the opinion of this author, brilliant. The scanty sketch of the previous paragraphs by no
means does it justice. It is not, however, without its faults.
While the association of morality and personality is extremely
valuable, the schematic separation of morality from religion
is a disadvantage. The dovetailing of culture with morality
and religion is a distinct contribution to theology. The approach to religion provides a broad basis for theology to account for the multiplicity of world religions and Christian
denominations in a way that respects the good and true in
them and does not merely criticize them. But the danger of
religious relativism haunts this approach which, as it stands,
lessens the unique meaning of the Christian revelation. This
is not to say, however, that the approach could not be modified to overcome its shortcomings, and this to some extent
on the basis of Tillich's own principles.

Unambiguous Life

The goal of the Christian life is the conquest of the ambiguities of life by Unambiguous Life. The Christian life
tends towards, is in fact the fragmentary anticipation of, Unambiguous Life. What does this mean?

Unambiguous Life, properly, is the life of God.[9] Only in
the ground and abyss of being is there life without ambiguity.
The ambiguities of life are rooted ultimately in the tensions

[9] See *ST*, I, pp. 241–52.

and threats to dissolution which are inherent in the polar structural elements of finite being—essence and existence, potentiality and actuality, self and world, subject and object, individualization and participation in the universal, dynamics (motion) and form, freedom and destiny. Precisely because of the composite ontological character of finite being, finite life is marked by tensions and forever threatened with dissolution: the functions of such life are necessarily ambiguous. But God is being-itself. In him essence and existence are identical. All the structural elements of finite being have their analogous counterpart in God as the ground and abyss of being; but, in God, their opposition, tensions, threats of dissolution are transcended. In being-itself there can be only Unambiguous Life.

If we compare by analogy the life processes of God with those of man, we can get some faint glimpse of what this unambiguous divine life is like. What corresponds to self-integration, personality development, and morality, in man, is found in God without tensions and without ambiguity, precisely because God's existence is his essence: he is what he can and should be. No moral law stands over against his existence in judgment. He is the norm of his own being.

What corresponds to self-creativity or culture in man is found in God without ambiguity, for the Father generates the Logos without disrupting the unity of the divine being, without a split between the subject and object in uttering the divine Word, without a gap between the depth of the divine being and its meaning. When man creates language, science, art, crafts, social institutions, the polar structure of composite finitude leads inevitably to a gap between reality as it is or should be in itself, and as man knows it and shapes it. In God, the power of being and meaning are one.

What corresponds to self-transcendence or religion in man is found in God without ambiguity, for, though God cannot transcend himself, there is in him a profound unity of infinite power and meaning in life at its maximum perfection. (The Spirit in God is the symbol of this living unity of infinite power and meaning in God.) What man seeks for in self-transcendence—infinite unity of being and meaning—God is.

The New Being, under the impact of the Spirit, participates in the Unambiguous Life of God. This participation is fragmentary and anticipatory here and now, to be perfect beyond time and space under the symbol of Eternal Life. If we wish to characterize this participated Unambiguous Life, the best way is to describe it as an ever-increasing unity of the functions of the human spirit and ultimately also of the polar structural elements of finite being.[10] This increasing unity must be explained.

As St. Thomas' interpretation of the Christian life in the second part of the *Summa theologiae* is grounded in his metaphysical and anthropological interpretation of the Christian revelation in the first part of the *Summa,* so Tillich's interpretation of the Christian life is grounded in his metaphysics and anthropology. We have seen some of the elements of this metaphysics and anthropology necessary to appreciate, to some extent, Tillich's view of the Christian life as participated Unambiguous Life. We noted above the composite nature of finite being and the polar elements which make it up; and we have already described the three functions of life under the dimension of the spirit—morality, culture, and religion. Just now we have seen that in God there is a transcendent union of all these elements and functions, for God is being-itself. In man, on the contrary, there is tension between all these elements and not only the threat but the tendency to dissolution.

Now, under the impact of the Spirit grasping man through faith and love (*agape*), that dissolution is resisted, gradually overcome, and will be ultimately conquered completely in Eternal Life. The Christian life under the impact of the Spirit is a movement toward human integrity, a restoring of shattered unity, a healing of creation, which is good as it comes essentially from God, but corrupt as it exists.

This note of unity as characteristic of participated Unambiguous Life becomes evident in the principles according to which the Christian life develops, as Tillich sees it. He offers

---

[10] See *ST*, III, pp. 129-30, 138-40, 157-61, 401-3.

four principles which determine the New Being as process,[11] thus offering modern man a fresh set of norms for what is known traditionally as sanctification.

The first of these principles is that of *increasing awareness*. In the process of sanctification, man becomes increasingly aware of his actual situation, the evils that beset him, his needs. He is increasingly aware of the predicament of others. He becomes aware and sensitive to authentic being in himself and others. All of this awareness is more than human, more than an aristocracy of nature; it takes place under the impact of the Spirit. In Catholic theology we would speak of growing in knowledge and correct evaluation of self, neighbor, and the world in the light of God, especially through the gifts of the Holy Spirit.

The second principle of sanctification is that of *increasing freedom from the law and the contents of the law*. This does not mean abandonment of law in favor of willfulness; willfulness is, in reality, a symptom of estrangement, of "fallen" nature, a slavery to conditions and compulsions. Freedom from the law means an interiorization of law. Law has the connotation of an exterior norm confronting, compelling, judging, condemning. But the law represents man's essential nature, what he can and should be. Under the impact of the Spirit, man more and more is what he should be; less and less is the law something outside of him, judging him. As he acts more and more spontaneously according to his essential nature, he grows in freedom from the law as confronting him from without. In Catholic theology this idea is expressed in the idea of loving obedience to God. St. Thomas Aquinas,[12] following St. Paul,[13] speaks of the New Law as being different from the Old Law in that the New Law is inscribed in the heart of man, is the grace of the Spirit within; it is the law of liberty, as St. James says.[14]

---

[11] See *ibid.*, pp. 231–37.

[12] See *Summa theologiae*, I–II, q. 106, a. 1.

[13] See Rom. 3:27, 8:2; Heb. 8:8–10.

[14] See Js. 1:25; cf. St. Thomas Aquinas, *Summa theologiae*, I–II, q. 108, a. 1.

Freedom from the content of the law means a facility in applying the law to concrete situations. We noted previously that, even when the moral law is clear to man, its application is often ambiguous. But under the impact of the Spirit, through what Catholic theology would call infused prudence and the gift of counsel, man learns how to live by the spirit of the law rather than being enslaved by the letter. Catholic theology, however, would insist that, in reality, one never acts without the guidance of some law; it may appear that one is acting against the law, but if the action is truly good, one is, in the final analysis, bypassing a lesser law for some higher law. Tillich's interpretation would be much the same, it seems, but his manner of expressing it (freedom from the contents of the law) and his examples of it leave the impression that at times one bypasses law altogether.

The third principle determining the process of the Christian life is *increasing relatedness*; the New Being as process drives towards a mature relatedness. Under the impact of the Spirit through *agape*, man overcomes self-seclusion with its accompanying loneliness and hostility. No other human relatedness or love can conquer these conditions. At the same time, this conquest of self-seclusion does not exclude solitude, for in solitude (which is not the same as loneliness) the mature Christian turns from self towards, not other men, but God. This mature relatedness is not only towards others but also towards self: the self as subject and the self as object are reconciled, so that man neither exalts himself nor despises himself, but accepts himself. This self-relatedness is the term of that "search for identity" so much spoken of in psychiatry and sociology. In all of this we see what is more familiarly expressed as the Christian life's being a growth in love of neighbor and God (relatedness to others) and in true love of self (self-relatedness).

The fourth principle determining the process of the Christian life is the principle of *self-transcendence*. Awareness, freedom, relatedness cannot be attained without continuous transcendence of the self in the direction of the ultimate and infinite ground of being, the holy, God. This self-transcending towards the ultimate is what is meant by the word "devotion." Devotion does express itself in particular "devotional" practices, such as prayers, church services, etc., but, precisely as self-transcendence towards the ultimate it can and does express itself in other ways. In fact, it may express itself outside the framework of religion altogether; it may even express itself in criticism of religion, in the narrow sense of the word, that is, as institutionalized symbols of ultimate concern. Self-transcendence towards the ultimate may express itself in dedication to, let us say, better education or civil government, seeking to fashion these in such a way that they become transparent to the ground of being; it may express itself, according to Tillich, in establishing a new church, a new religion in the narrow sense of the word.

Tillich comprehends under the idea of devotion something akin to what St. Thomas envisages. For Thomas, devotion is the primary act of religion, the ready will to serve and honor God.[15] This devotion expresses itself in prayer, sacrifice, and the like; it expresses itself also in the nursing nun's care for the sick, the lay catechist's instruction of children, the Christian mother's solicitude for her family, the apostolic businessman's and worker's social concern: all these people are devoted to God in working for the welfare of their neighbor. And through such devotedness, they grow in awareness of themselves and others and the human situation, they interiorize the moral law, and they grow in love.

In the light of these four principles which guide the development of participated Unambiguous Life in the New Being, we can see more clearly the note of increasing unity characteristic of Unambiguous Life with regard to the functions of the spirit—morality, culture, and religion—and to some extent with regard to the ontological elements.[16] As

[15] See *Summa theologiae*, I–II, q. 82, aa. 1–2.

[16] The principal section of Part IV of Tillich's system is devoted to showing how the ambiguities of life are overcome by Unambiguous Life under the influence of the Spirit. This and the following paragraphs summarize the theme of *ST*, III, pp. 162–274. This increasing unity must not be interpreted as the obliteration of the polar elements and the functions of life or their confusion into some

man grows aware of himself, others, and God in the human situation; as he more spontaneously and from within fulfills the law; as he grows in relatedness within himself and with others and God; as he transcends himself in more and more of life's activities by concern for the ultimate in them, he obviously grows in self-integration, the function of morality; and the disunity between the structural elements of essence and existence tends to be overcome. In this condition of increased self-integration, man can make a world of meaning, a culture, which is true, beautiful, purposeful, humane, and just, in which the disruption between subject and object is overcome.

A culture transparent to the infinite ground of being fashioned by self-integrated man reciprocates by providing man with suitable materials for further self-integration in the moral life. Self-integration requires assimilation of the experienced world; this self-integration will be moral, conformed to God's intention, a union of essence and existence, if this experienced world is transparent on all sides to God.

The more man attains to self-integration through a culture transparent to the holy, the more religion or self-transcendence ceases to be a special function of the spirit, a department of life, and is found in every phase of life. Everything man engages in becomes an expression of self-transcendence in the direction of the ultimate; man's whole life becomes religious. The people of the Middle Ages expressed their self-transcendence in their morality and culture: their moral ideal was the saint devoted to God; in their culture, time was measured by the hours of worship; the arts and crafts were employed in the erection of cathedrals; kings and armies went on crusades to regain the Holy Places. The Middle Ages were not perfect by any means, but we do see there a shadow of that tendency toward unity characteristic of human participation in the transcendent union of Unambiguous Life.

---

general amalgam; rather, this increasing unity is the establishment of balance between the polar elements and the achievement of integration among the functions of life, a state which will be attained only in Eternal Life (see ST, III, pp. 401-3).

Spiritual Presence

The New Being conquers the ambiguities of life by Unambiguous Life under the impact of the Spiritual Presence. We must finally consider the impact of the Spiritual Presence as a factor in the goal of the Christian life.

New Being participating in Unambiguous Life is the creation of God.[17] Man cannot of himself achieve New Being and Unambiguous Life. Only if he is grasped by the divine, driven beyond himself into ecstasy in faith and love (*agape*), can he become New Being and participate in Unambiguous Life.

The experience of God present and active in the human spirit, driving it beyond itself, is expressed in the symbol of the Presence of God or the Presence of the Spirit of God or, the phrase Tillich prefers, the Spiritual Presence. Spiritual Presence, therefore, signifies God or the Spirit of God grasping the human spirit and driving it towards the goal of the Christian life.

The first effect of the Spiritual Presence is faith and love (*agape*).[18] Faith and love are, in a sense, the totality of the

[17] See *ST*, III, pp. 111–12.

[18] See *ibid.*, pp. 129–38. Tillich has developed his own concept of faith. To judge it fairly, we must keep in mind the following points: (1) faith in Tillich's sense means something akin to the choice of, and adherence to, a concrete ultimate end in Catholic theology; (2) if this concrete ultimate end is the infinite ground of being, or God manifested in Jesus as the Christ, then we can speak of Christian faith in Tillich's sense of the word and ours (we would speak of "living faith," "faith with charity," for such faith implies definitive choice of, and adherence to, God as our ultimate goal); (3) if this concrete ultimate end is God, but known through symbols other than Jesus as the Christ, we can go along with Tillich and speak of true but implicit faith, provided, of course, that the person involved is truly open to God, is seeking for God, doing the best he can in view of his circumstances and the interior grace of God; (4) if this concrete ultimate end is some finite being, then faith in Tillich's sense

Christian life, as they are the totality of any authentic religious life. Through faith man is in a state of ultimate concern; he is aware of, and concerned about, the infinite ground of being and meaning; his spirit breaks through preliminary concerns (means to ends and intermediate ends) to the ultimate concern (the true final end); he resists the temptation to attribute ultimacy to preliminary affairs and thereby rejects self-sufficiency, which feeds on preliminary goals within the reach of man.

Through love, which is another side of the state of ultimate concern, man participates in the transcendent unity of Unambiguous Life, albeit fragmentarily and in proportion to the intensity of his faith and love. Love is, after all, unifying; it is relatedness. In the state of ultimate concern man is related to the ground of his being, God. To be related to the ground of his being is to recover his essential self, which is from God; this is to be self-related. One's essential self can be had only in community with others, for man is by definition a social being; this means the essential self can be had only by recognizing the individuality of other centered-selves and establishing relatedness with others. As we saw above, this threefold relatedness is another way of speaking of love of God, self, and neighbor.

Growth in awareness, freedom, relatedness, and self-transcendence, which we saw above to be the principles determining the progress of the Christian life, we can now see as simply aspects of the growth in faith and love of the New Being, the fundamental effects of the Spiritual Presence.

The Catholic reader has probably asked himself more than once in the course of reading this essay if the New Being

and in our sense is corrupted into idolatry; (5) according to St. Thomas, the terminating object of faith is not the propositions of faith but the reality we know through propositions which can never adequately grasp the mystery of the divine Being (see *Summa theologiae*, I–II, q. 1, a. 2; q. 8, a. 7); (6) St. Thomas shows that there is something akin to the restlessness of doubt in the act of faith when he comments on the suitability of St. Augustine's definition of the act of faith as *cum assensione cogitare*—"to consider (or ponder) while assenting."

and Unambiguous Life are supernatural realities for Dr. Tillich. If the question were put to him, probably he would say "No." But if he did, perhaps he would be answering, not the question put to him by a Catholic, but his own question with his own understanding of it. In his *Systematic Theology*, Tillich fortunately uses the term "supra*natural*" rather than the term "supernatural." As he describes supra*natural*istic interpretations of faith,[19] the Catholic can only agree with Tillich in rejecting such explanations of the relationship of God to creatures. But Catholic theology does not intend by supernatural what Tillich describes as supra*natural*.

The supernatural is not one more being alongside other beings, different only because it is immensely bigger and more powerful than the other beings. The supernatural does not break into the natural order as a foreign element strange to the natural and contradicting it. The supernatural transcends the natural order, perfects it, leads it to depths of being it could not attain of itself. God is, as Tillich so wonderfully describes him, the ground and abyss of being. God is intimately present in all things, more present to them than they are to themselves; things are "in" God, not in a pantheistic sense, but as effects sustained in being by the unique cause of being.[20] The divine invasion of the order of nature is not an invasion at all in the final analysis, for God already is there, and nature is his creature with which he can do what he wills in accord with his wisdom. Nature is in obediential potency (to use Thomistic terminology) to being driven by God beyond its intrinsic limits without its structure being violated.

We said above that man can attain New Being only if the Spiritual Presence grasps the human spirit and drives it beyond itself into the ecstasy of faith and love. There is a supernatural character about this, in the Catholic sense of supernatural. Tillich consistently maintains that man cannot have New Being and conquer the ambiguities of life unless God's active creativity works in man. In existential estrangement, man can do nothing other than continue in estrange-

---

[19] See *ST*, II, pp. 5–10.
[20] Cf. St. Thomas Aquinas, *Summa theologiae*, I, q. 8, a. 1 ad 2.

ment while struggling to overcome it. Only God can save
man. If existential estrangement is natural to man (not essential but natural, proper to man in his native existence),
then it can be said that conquest of estrangement and ambiguity of life is supernatural, beyond the native capacity
of man to effect or attain, for only God can bring it about.
Thus, the New Being, the goal of the Christian life, is supernatural in its cause and manner of being reached.

When the Spiritual Presence grasps the human spirit, it
drives it into ecstasy.[21] Faith and love are ecstatic states.
Tillich does not mean by "ecstasy" a state of trance or some
extraordinary psychic reaction or even simple enthusiasm. He
uses the term in its root significance of "standing out of oneself." The Spiritual Presence produces in man a state of
being in which man is beyond what he could be as existentially estranged, beyond what he could be in his natural existential condition. But this ecstatic state does not destroy or
violate the structure of being, man's essential nature; rather,
it tends to close the gap between the essential and existential.
Thus, faith and love, as ecstatic states, are beyond any knowledge and love that estranged man as such could have, but
they do not contradict reason in its depth nor love in its
manifold forms. The whole idea of ecstasy—what it is, its
relation to essential being and the existential situation, and
its origin from the Spiritual Presence—corresponds to the
Catholic idea of supernatural.

But in what sense is the New Being supernatural—in its
essential content (*quoad substantiam* in Thomistic terminology) or only in its manner of being (*quoad modum*)?
The goal of the Christian life, as characterized above, is the
restoration to unity of the divergent functions of the spirit
and of the split ontological elements of finite man. The Spiritual Presence driving man to ecstatic self-transcendence drives
man, not beyond his essential nature, but beyond his existential estrangement to the restored unity of essential nature.
The New Being is not supernatural in its content, but in the
manner in which it comes to be. To put it another way, and

[21] See *ST*, III, pp. 112, 114–20; *ST*, I, 111–15.

in traditional terminology, for Tillich grace is not elevating but only healing.

While there is, then, a supernatural element in Tillich's theology, this supernatural is not the essentially supernatural to which Catholic theology assigns first place. However, it would not be difficult to find a place in Tillich's theology for the essentially supernatural. If God is all that Tillich claims for him in the first volume of his *Systematic Theology*, if the divine creativity is the source of man's essential being and capable of overcoming existential estrangement, and if man's essential nature includes what Tillich calls "ontological reason" and the "depth of reason,"[22] there seems to be no obstacle to speaking of a substantially supernatural destiny for man. Tillich's system is not closed to the Catholic notion of obediential potency. Tillich describes Eternal Life as "essentialization."[23] If man's essence is what man could and should be, could not "essentialization" under the impact of the Spirit include not only conquest of existential estrangement but also transcendence of native essential being in the direction of a profounder participation in the abyss of being? Could grace be not only healing but also elevating?

Conclusion

This essay has attempted to present Tillich's idea of the Christian life viewed in terms of its goal—the New Being in Jesus as the Christ conquering the ambiguities of life by Unambiguous Life under the impact of the Spiritual Presence.

In judging Tillich's idea of the Christian life as well as the rest of his theology, we must keep in mind that his theology is essentially an apologetic for the Christian message based on the intrinsic motives of credibility—the reasonableness, the power to satisfy human needs, and the beauty of the Christian message. Furthermore, this apologetic is addressed to the

22 See *ST*, I, pp. 72–74, 79–81.
23 See *ST*, III, pp. 406–7.

sophisticated modern mind, the product of today's colleges and universities.

As an apologete, Tillich must meet this sophisticated modern mind on its own grounds and go along with it as far as possible, in order eventually to win it over to the Christian message. Tillich is keenly aware of the caricature of meaning that some Christians, in the course of the centuries, have attached to the words of the Christian message, so that the modern mind justly finds their explanation of the Christian message unacceptable. He is very sensitive to the connotations of words for the modern mind. Many of the words which are so much a part of the Christian message have been so abused during the centuries of men's disputes about ultimate questions, that the true meaning of these words has been buried in a cloud of connotations which are false, or misleading, or charged with emotion. These words are more of an obstacle than a help in trying to convey the Christian message to the contemporary mind.

In order to reach the contemporary mind, Tillich is ready to cast aside words and phrases and formulas whose meanings have been twisted beyond repair and whose acquired connotations make them, for all practical purposes, false. As a result of this step, Tillich is compelled to find an entirely new way of expressing the traditional Christian message, a formidable pioneering attempt. If we wish to evaluate Tillich's theology perceptively, therefore, we must make a corresponding effort: we must not be content to compare his *expression* of the Christian message with ours; we must go beyond words; we must judge Tillich's theology on the basis of his intention, the *sense* of the totality of his words, and the correspondence of that sense with reality.

XVI

THOMAS F. O'MEARA, O.P.

Paul Tillich and the Problem of God

Paul Tillich combined the European interest in speculative theology with the American sense of the necessary practical import which a theology must have. Though Tillich's thought is profoundly European in its ontological horizon, he himself describes the not insignificant influence of America upon him.

American theology and philosophy have influenced my thinking in several respects. The spirit of the English language has demanded the clarification of many ambiguities of my thought which were covered by the mystical vagueness of the classic philosophical German; the interdependence of theory and practice in Anglo-Saxon culture, religious as well as secular, has freed me from the fascination of that kind of abstract idealism which enjoys the system for the system's sake; the cooperation with colleagues and students . . . has provided the experience of a type of Protestant religion and culture very different from that of Continental Europe; the world perspective, almost unavoidable on a bridge between the continents like New York and at a center of world Protestantism like Union Theological Seminary, has had a strong effect on my thinking about the situation of the church universal in our time.[1]

Dr. Jerald Brauer, in a memorial preface written after Tillich's death, described what Tillich's importance may be:

[1] PE, p. x.

Tillich's concern for the cultural and sociological consequences of the Christian faith has already made a profound impact on the American scene and provides the point of departure for a serious effort at a systematic ethics which is badly needed. One could point to Tillich's systematic effort to develop a theological method, to his concern for nature and its relation to grace, to his impact upon Roman Catholicism, to his abiding concern for his Jewish brethren, to his profound analysis of the interrelationship between psychiatry and religion, to his monumental effort to construct a genuinely dialectical theology, and to a variety of other contributions as a way of indicating why he is so widely read and accepted in America.[2]

Some Protestants would rank Tillich above Karl Barth; others would not. Nevertheless, the influence of both will extend at least to the limits of the twentieth century. Because of his rigorously logical and systematic theology, and his use of philosophy, because of his attempt to organize the various key concepts of four centuries of Protestantism into coherent unity, Tillich finds sympathy among Catholic readers. Despite nuances of faith without an object and Christ without Jesus, a Catholic theologian finds a familiar world in his order and conceptual precision. Like Barth, Tillich has placed himself in the camp of Augustine and Aquinas in constructing a theological edifice. He brings out first principles of Protestantism, analyzes them in dialogue with contemporary philosophy, and develops a system from both.

Systematic Theology

Tillich was not afraid to let reason, philosophy, systematic presentation, and theology explain the content of divine revelation. He felt that today's world needs a particular type of the theological treatise, the systematic form.

[2] Jerald C. Brauer, "Preface," In Memoriam Paul Tillich 1886–1965, The Journal of Religion, 46 (1968), 90–91.

System stands between *Summa* and essay. The *Summa* deals explicitly with all actual and many potential problems. The essay deals explicitly with one actual problem. The system deals with a group of actual problems which demand a solution in a special situation. In the Middle Ages the *Summa* was predominant, though by no means exclusively so. At the beginning of the modern period the essay became predominant, although the systematic trend never ceased to exist. Today a need for the systematic form has arisen in view of the chaos of our spiritual life and the impossibility of creating a *Summa*.[3]

The system deals with a special "situation," that is, with the particular environment, the special social pressures, the individual psychological drives and defects which life in one age and culture produces. The system "does not tell us what people have thought the Christian message to be in the past; rather, it tries to give us an interpretation of the Christian message which is relevant to the present situation."[4] Tillich's correlated theology joins revelation, telling us about God and existential philosophy explaining this revelation and making it relevant to twentieth-century man. Theology unites the data of revelation to organize it, to explain it and make it meaningful to the individual man on the street. There is ontology but no natural theology, for no metaphysics can begin with creatures and reach the true God. Revelation alone discloses God in human experiences. The Trinity is a correlation of man's psychoreligious drives with God's life outwardly manifest.

Tillich's philosophical background is existentialism. Where is the Protestant protest against the ability of human reason to explore the depths of revelation? The Reformers rejected the pretense of philosophy to explain God. Tillich does not accept, however, this tenet of past Protestantism. Philosophy does have a legitimate place in theology.

[3] *ST*, I, p. 59.
[4] *Ibid.*, p. 53. The application of this method to theological education and the pastoral ministry is described in T. F. O'Meara, "Where Is Theology Going?" *Thought*, 44 (1969).

It is unfortunate . . . that the reformers combined their rediscovery of the existential character of theology with a badly defined rejection of reason. If it is understood that reason received revelation and that it is an object of salvation like every other element of reality, a theology which uses theonomous reason may again be possible.[5]

It is not only bad theology but also a kind of ascetical arrogance when theologians—since Tertullian—indulge in nonsensical combinations of words, demanding of all true Christians that, in an act of intellectual destruction, they accept nonsense as divine sense. The "foolishness" of the cross has nothing to do with the assumedly good but actually demonic work of the sacrifice of reason.[6]

The Sources of Systematic Theology

We cannot understand Tillich's theology of God until we realize its paradoxical view of revelation. Tillich denies that any philosophy can prove or describe the "God beyond god." Yet, God is not made present only through the revelation of his words and deeds in the Bible. All human channels of religious experience point to an ultimate concern grounding our human existence, what we call God. "If groups of persons become transparent for the ground of being and meaning, revelation occurs."[7] In Christology, Tillich follows his former colleague, Rudolf Bultmann. Jesus, through an existential act of being at his death transparent to God, becomes (is

---

[5] *ST*, I, p. 155. "They [the Scholastics, especially the Franciscans] called theology a 'Practical' knowledge, pointing to what today is called 'Existential' knowledge. It is unfortunate that ever since the day of Thomas Aquinas this emphasis increasingly has been lost . . . and that the reformers combined their rediscovery of the existential character of theology with a badly defined rejection of reason." *Ibid.* St. Thomas speaks of theology being both speculative and practical (a reflection of the unity and extension of the divine knowledge), but *"magis speculativa." Summa theologiae*, I, q. 1, a. 4.

[6] *Ibid.*, p. 151.

[7] *ST*, I, p. 120.

adopted) as the Christ. His remarks on the Mother of Christ indicate the channeling of revelation through usually transitory media. Almost every religious symbol is a utilitarian religious symbol. Only Jesus who through his death rejected any heteronomy of the finite becomes the Christ and is the definitive revelatory event.

Original revelation is given to a group through an individual. Revelation can be received originally only in the depth of a personal life, in its struggles, decisions, and self-surrender. No individual receives revelation for himself. He receives it for his group, and implicitly for all groups, for mankind as a whole. . . . Since the correlation of revelation is transformed by every new group, and in an infinitesimal way by every new individual who enters it, the question must be asked whether this transformation can reach a point where the original revelation is exhausted and has been superseded. . . . Apollo has no revelatory significance for Christians; the Virgin Mother Mary reveals nothing to Protestants. Revelation through these two figures has come to an end.[8]

1. *The Bible.* Tillich has abandoned the Bible in the sense of orthodox Protestantism. The Bible is not a clear statement of truth and practice, but only one manifestation of God. It is filled with symbol, myth, legend, and indifference to history. "Biblical research in Protestantism has shown the many levels of biblical literature and the impossibility of considering the Bible as containing the infallible truth of faith."[9] The Bible is not the ultimate criterion of the content

---

[8] *Ibid.*, pp. 127–28. "Every revelation is mediated by one or several of the mediums of revelation. None of these mediums possesses revelatory power in itself; but under conditions of existence the mediums claim to have it. This claim makes them idols and the breakdown of this claim deprives them of their power. . . . [If] the revelation comes to an end, the idolatrous side is destroyed. That which was revelatory in it is preserved as an element in more embracing and more purified revelations, and everything revelatory is potentially present in the final revelation, which cannot come to an end because the bearer of it does not claim anything for himself." *ST*, I, p. 128.

[9] *DF*, p. 92.

of revelation, nor is it a unique medium of revelation in the traditional Protestant or Catholic sense; it is far too erroneous, too human for that role. When he begins to investigate the sources of a systematic theology, Tillich immediately asks whether the Bible is a source, a medium, a norm. He rejects the Bible as the *only* source.[10] First of all the meaning of the Scriptures depended upon the temporal culture and the believing Church. "The 'Word of God' is not limited to the words of a book and . . . the act of revelation is not the 'inspiring' of a 'book of revelations.' . . . The biblical message embraces more (and less) than the biblical books. Systematic theology, therefore, has additional sources beyond the Bible."[11] The Bible is the basic source because it is the original document about the founding events of Christianity. However, the Bible, in its very writing, was determined as much by the subjective acceptance of Jesus as the Christ by the writers as it was by objective facts and reality.

The norm of systematic theology is not the Bible, but its central content, "The New Being in Jesus as the Christ." The norm is the message of the Scriptures produced in an encounter between Bible and Church. After all, the history of the canon of the Scriptures indicates that there was another norm by which biblical books were judged; they were judged by the Spirit in the Church according to their reflection of Jesus as the Christ.[12] This "encounter between Bible and Church" is, perhaps, closer to the Catholic view of Scripture and tradition (seen as life of the Church) than to the fundamental Protestant insight.[13] Catholic theology emphasizes the incarnational—the presence and continuity (not the intermingling) of the human and the divine in Christ, Church, Christian, sacrament, authority. Tillich looks for a middle course avoiding absolute authority of hierarchy over book: "A way must be found which lies between the Roman Cath-

[10] See *ST*, I, p. 34.

[11] *Ibid.*

[12] *Ibid.*, p. 51.

[13] See Yves Congar, *Tradition and Traditions* (New York: Nelson, 1967).

olic practice of making ecclesiastical decisions not only a source but also the actual norm of systematic theology and the radical Protestant practice of depriving Church history not only of its normative character but also of its function as a source."[14]

2. *Church, Councils, Creeds.* The need for authority arose early in the Christian community. Tillich sees the response as creed and bishop: "On the material side the Church created a creed which . . . was supposed to contain the doctrinal norm. On the formal side the Church established a hierarchy of authorities—bishops, councils, the pope—who were supposed to guard the norm against heretical distortions."[15] Eventually in the Catholic Church the formal norm eliminated any need for the material one. This, Tillich says, is why Tradition became identified with papal teaching, and the Bible had so little influence on the dogmatic development of the Greek and Roman Churches.[16] The demands of this situation forced Luther to seek new norms of justification by faith and the Bible. Tillich's norm, as we have seen, is an encounter between the Bible and the Church which gives us the doctrine of the "New Being in Jesus as the Christ."[17] Tillich recognizes the Church as playing an important part in the creation and interpretation of the Bible. Unfortunately, the Church moved the norm of belief from Jesus as Christ to the Church. Creed, Canon of Scripture, dogma, bishop—all are the product of the Church, and none should be ultimate. Tillich emphasizes that it is individual conversion and individual response to revelation which should concern us, and not a Church.[18] "The Church very early forgot the word of our Gospel that He *is* the truth; and claimed that her doctrines about Him are the truth . . . [this] is the greatness of Protestantism: that it points be-

[14] *ST*, I, p. 51.
[15] *Ibid.*, p. 47.
[16] See *loc. cit.*
[17] *Ibid.*, pp. 49–51.
[18] See *NB*, p. 18.

yond the teachings of Jesus and beyond the doctrines of the
Church to the being of Him whose being is the truth."[19]

Tillich's attitude toward the dogmas of the councils is one
of demythologizing. The councils and their formulations
—dogmas—are only symbols pointing to the Christian message. These symbols were formulated into rational statements.
Although creeds are necessary, their truth lies not in the exact-
ness or perpetual substance of their message but in the ability of these symbols to express the unconditional. We must
not take their meaning literally, for then they become the in-
tellectually finite which is being defended as infinite.[20] Tradition has value only insofar as it records the various forms
of theonomy which have occurred in the history of Christianity. It offers numerous meaningful experiences and "symbols" to man. It contains the history of human acceptance
of the New Being; it does not contain a normative statement
about Jesus as the Christ. Tillich's interest in tradition is really
a study of Church history, of cultural tradition. Tradition is
necessary, nevertheless, because it is the link between the
Spiritual Community's foundation in Christ and each subsequent generation. The Protestant Reformation itself, Tillich observes, grew out of elements which were ultimately of
tradition—even the Bible. For Tillich, as for Bultmann, dogma
is a product of theology, a privileged but historically conditioned guideline. No revealed dogmas ever existed; there
was no deposit of faith, no list of truths and practices given
to the apostles and handed down. There are no revealed doctrines, but there are revelatory events which can be described
in changing terms.[21]

[19] *Ibid.*, p. 71.
[20] *ST*, III, pp. 174–76; *ST*, I, p. 32.
[21] On the general theology of authority see P. Tillich, "By What
Authority," *NB*, 79–91. "I call the Protestant principle the critical
element in the expression of the community of faith and consequently the element of doubt in the act of faith. . . . The criterion
of the truth of a symbol of faith is that it expresses the ultimate
which is really ultimate. This criterion contains a Yes—it does not
reject any truth of faith in whatever form it may appear in the history of faith—and it contains a No—it does not accept any truths

Background for a Theology of God

With some understanding of Tillich's use and critique of "theological" sources, we can now turn to the philosophical and cultural currents which were more influential in fashioning a theology of God. Tillich writes that he had the nineteenth century for his teacher during his university years from 1904 to 1907.[22] "The spirit of the nineteenth century still prevailed, and we hoped that the great synthesis between Christianity and humanism could be achieved with the tools of German classical philosophy."[23] Although he could not unlearn the impact of these formative years, Tillich saw that the First World War brought an end to this entire intellectual world. Tillich's early writings were his dissertations for the doctorate in philosophy and the licentiate in theology (both on Schelling)[24] and an interesting program for a philosophy

---

of faith as ultimate, except the one that no man possesses it. . . . The fact that this criterion is identical with the Protestant Principle and has become reality in the Cross of the Christ constitutes the superiority of Protestant Christianity." DF, pp. 29, 98.

[22] Paul Tillich, Ultimate Concern (New York: Harper and Row, 1965), p. 37. See Tillich's Perspectives on Nineteenth and Twentieth Century Protestant Theology (New York: Harper and Row, 1967); for a more detailed treatment of Tillich's relationship to Schelling and Heidegger, see T. F. O'Meara, "Tillich and Heidegger: A Structural Relationship," Harvard Theological Review, 61 (1968), 249–61.

[23] Tillich, "Autobiographical Reflections," The Theology of Paul Tillich, C. W. Kegley, R. W. Bretall, eds. (New York: Macmillan, 1952), p. 11; see Tillich, The Interpretation of History (New York: Scribner's, 1936), p. 60.

[24] Tillich's thesis for the doctorate in philosophy was: Die religionsgeschichtliche Konstruktion in Schellings positiver Philosophie, ihre Voraussetzungen und Prinzipien (Breslau: Fleischmann, 1910); for the licentiate in theology: Mystik und Schuldbewusstsein in Schellings philosophischer Entwicklung (Gutersloh: Bertelsmann, 1912); the licentiate thesis is reprinted in Frühe Hauptwerke, (Stuttgart: Evangelisches Verlagswerk, 1959), I, 11–108.

of religion.[25] All were written before Tillich's decisive years at Marburg. To study idealism's influence on Tillich in these works is quite different from understanding the influence of German philosophy on Tillich's mature works. Tillich in an autobiographical essay describes the entrance of Heidegger and existentialism.

In Marburg, in 1925, I began work on my Systematic Theology, the first volume of which appeared in 1951. At the same time that Heidegger was in Marburg as professor of philosophy, influencing some of the best students, existentialism in its twentieth-century form crossed my path. It took years before I became fully aware of the impact of this encounter on my own thinking. I resisted, I tried to learn, I accepted the new way of thinking more than the answer it gave.[26]

Two things here are important: first, it was through Heidegger (with whom during these years surrounding the appearance of *Being and Time* Tillich was in personal contact) that Tillich encountered existentialism; secondly, Tillich accepted the structure and the method of this philosophy more than its content. Although Tillich speaks of "existential philosophy," it is clear from his works that he appreciates the differences in existentialists, and that this means for him a German philosophy present today in Heidegger and Jaspers.[27] In *The Interpretation of History* Tillich gives us more details on Marburg and Heidegger.

---

[25] Tillich, "Religionsphilosophie," *Lehrbuch der Philosophie*, M. Dessoir, ed. (Berlin: Ullstein, 1925), II, 765-835, reprinted in *Frühe Hauptwerke, ed. cit.*, 295-366.

[26] "Autobiographical Reflections," *art. cit.*, 14.

[27] Tillich, "Existential Philosophy . . . ," *art. cit.*, 77. "The third and contemporary form of Existential philosophy has resulted from a combination of this Philosophy of Life with Husserl's shift of emphasis from existent objects to the mind that makes them its objects, and with the rediscovery of Kierkegaard and of the early developments of Marx, Heidegger, Jaspers, and the Existential interpretation of history found in German Religious Socialism are the main representatives of the third period of this philosophy of experienced Existence." *Ibid.*, 79.

By the appearance of the so-called "Existential Philosophy" in Germany, I was led to a new understanding of the relation between philosophy and theology. The lectures of M. Heidegger given at Marburg, the impression which some Marburg students and some of my colleagues experienced; then his writing, *Sein und Zeit* (*Being and Time*), also his interpretation of Kant, were of greater significance to followers and opponents of this philosophy than anything else since the appearance of Husserl's *Logische Untersuchungen* (*Logical Studies*).[28]

Tillich was prepared to accept this philosophy because of Schelling, Kierkegaard, and the philosophy of life.

These three elements, comprised and submerged into a sort of Augustinian-colored mysticism, produced that which fascinated people in Heidegger's philosophy. . . . By its very explanation of human existence it establishes a doctrine of man, though unintentionally, which is both the doctrine of human freedom and human finiteness; and which is so closely related with the Christian interpretation of human existence that one is forced to speak of a "theonomous philosophy," in spite of Heidegger's emphatic atheism. . . . The philosophy of existence asks the question in a new and radical manner, the answer to which is given in theology for faith.[29]

Heidegger's relationship to Tillich is a *structural* one, and as such is important. It enters into the very structure of theology as Tillich conceives and develops it; it offers the structural foundation for Tillich's theology of God, Ultimate Concern as Being-Itself. As an apologetic rather than kerygmatic theology, answering the contemporary situation, Tillich's theology must speak to man in both *existential* (from the ontological analysis of human existence related to being) and *existentiell* (what affects man personally in his concrete life) terms. Ontology may ask the questions, but it cannot answer them. Philosophy has an important role because the questions which revelation answers are existential-ontological,

---

[28] Tillich, *IH*, pp. 39-40.
[29] *Ibid.*

concerned with man's existence and being, and these questions will through correlation bring in the answers.[30]

Tillich bases his approach to God on "Heidegger's notion of 'Dasein' (being there) as the form of human existence and the entrance to ontology."[31] Tillich shows his accurate understanding of Heidegger when he relates his own use of the existential analysis of *Dasein* in these terms to a deeper ontological background. Meaninglessness, anxiety are not psychological terms but human forms of ontological finitude.[32] Tillich, referring again to Heidegger, affirms that the fundamental interpretation of human existence is finitude entering through non-being. "Both the basic ontological structure and the ontological elements imply finitude. . . . Finitude is experienced on the human level; non-being is experienced as the threat to being. . . . Finitude in awareness is anxiety." The question of God—or the human, existential questing for God (described by theologians as different as Schubert Ogden and Karl Rahner)—can be asked only after the questions of human existence and being are asked, just as Heidegger retrieves ontology through an existential analysis of man.[33]

Tillich's approach to God, oscillating between ontology and existentialism, between Aquinas and Heidegger, can be understood only in light of Heidegger's same approach in *Being*

[30] Tillich says the ontological question may not determine the answer, revelation; the question is precontained in the answer; *ST*, II, 14–18. "Faith includes the ontological question whether the question is asked explicitly or not." *BRSUR*, p. 59.

[31] *ST*, I, p. 62.

[32] *ST*, I, pp. 189, 190, 191; Tillich writes: "Anxiety is independent of any special object which might produce it; it is dependent only on the threat of non-being—which is identical with finitude. In this sense it has been said rightly that the object of anxiety is 'nothingness'—and nothingness is not an 'object.'" *ST*, I, 191. Heidegger had prepared this analysis: "*Angst* is always *Angst* about . . . but not before this or that. . . . *Angst* reveals nothingness. *Was ist Metaphysik?* (Frankfurt: Kostermann, 1960), p. 32. All translations of Heidegger are by the author.

[33] Heidegger, *Being and Time* (New York: Harper and Row, 1966), pp. 5–7, 14.

and Time, and Tillich's acknowledged debt to Aquinas, to Greek and medieval thought.[34] Tillich's use of Heidegger is different from Bultmann's. It does not limit itself to existential analysis of man and to an anthropocentric theological picture, but employs fundamental ontology in its widest scope, combining the existential analysis of man with ontology and historicity.

Today's Problem of God

The problem of God appeared in its present outlines (not independent of earlier formulations by Nietzsche, Schleiermacher, or Kierkegaard) at the end of World War II. The new writings of French and German existentialism, the questions smoldering in the ashes of old Europe, the new social and technological changes in America disclosed an absence of God. The Roman Catholic response concerned itself with a superficial, often Gallican confrontation with general existential ideas, or it entered into a sterile confrontation with what the scientific laboratory could or could not produce. Topics such as how magnetic fields, an expanding universe, and physical theories affected the possibility of God and his contact with creation were prevalent. This period faded away (it produced little that was important on either side), and a more mature period began, appreciating the nature and role of American social and economical structure, and appraising the value of secularization, personalism, existential-ontological analysis, linguistics, and communication theory. The theological dialogue is not so much with scientism but with the secular man who lives in the world today. Karl Rahner and Rudolf Bultmann saw relatively early that disbelief in its many forms was becoming a large movement. This

---

[34] On the influence and reinterpretation of the Middle Ages see P. Tillich, *A History of Christian Thought* (New York: Harper and Row, 1968). J. Heywood Thomas describes Tillich in brief as in the Augustinian tradition yet owing much to Schelling and Heidegger: *Paul Tillich, An Appraisal* (London: SCM, 1964), p. 174.

atheism is a consequence of the understanding of science prevalent in the past (joined to the optimism and the romanticism of the eighteenth and nineteenth centuries); it is a consequence, not the cause of the secularization of the world. Although Christianity helped man to master the world and science (here Bultmann agrees with Harvey Cox's analysis of secularism as a product of Christian culture), it moved later in its defensive periods to fight the world, becoming subjective, dogmatic, uncreative, fearful, anti-humanistic. Tillich appreciated the modern world as the only world there was, the world where Christianity would be heard or tuned out. He appreciated the study of philosophy, anthropology, psychology, and the social studies. He tried to understand the way sciences analyze man and his world as patterns to which the theologian must orientate revelation and Christ as the saving event.[35]

The Existence of God

Tillich's approach to the problem of the existence of God is one of the few attempts by a Protestant theologian to look positively at "natural theology." Tillich accepted Kant's reduction and critique of the traditional proofs, and of transcendental causality. Yet Tillich sees the proofs in a positive way, interpreting them in the context of man's existence (Heidegger). The basic ideas raised here, man's finitude and contingency, form a "pointer" to a being which must transcend the limits of man's ontological structure. Such a process is rooted in the real, external, ontological *existence* of man.

[35] On Tillich's theology of God, see C. Kiesling, "A Translation of Tillich's Idea of God," *Journal of Ecumenical Studies*, 4 (1967), 700–15; B. L. Clarkes, "God and the Symbolic in Tillich," *Anglican Theological Review*, 18 (1961), 302–11; D. Emmet, "The Ground of Being," *Journal of Theological Studies*, 15 (1964), 280–92; M. Fox, "Tillich's Ontology of God," *Anglican Theological Review*, 18 (1961), 260–67; D. H. Kelsey, *The Fabric of Paul Tillich's Theology* (New Haven: Yale University Press, 1967).

Finitude points to the unlimited, and this principle is behind all of the proofs (behind each specific form of the one illation): the insufficiency of the causal process is a form of finitude.

The traditional proofs in their many forms are statements for Tillich of the question-toward-God which is found in man's interpretation of his own existence.[36] The question of God stems from an awareness of the infinite disclosed in man's awareness of finitude. For Tillich this is not only an intellectual awareness of birth and death, not only an awareness of the limited ontological and physical nature of all created reality but a manifestation of the question transcending every finite category: the question of being-itself embracing and conquering finite being and existence. "Anxiety about meaninglessness is the characteristically human form of ontological anxiety."[37] Nothing is more important for man than to realize the truth which these arguments for God try to express: "The acknowledgement of the unconditional element in the structure of reason and reality."[38] Modern secularism, modern atheism is rooted in the idea that there are no "unconditionals." Atheism can mean only one thing: to be concerned about the meaning of our own existence.[39]

He [man] is aware of his potential infinite while being aware of his actual finitude. If he were what he essentially is, if his potentiality were identical with his actuality, the question of the infinite would not arise. . . . Man must ask about the infinite from which he is estranged, although it belongs to him; he must ask about that which gives him the courage to take his anxiety upon himself.[40]

The task of a theological treatment of the traditional arguments for the existence of God is twofold: to develop the question of God which they express and to expose the argu-

[36] *ST*, I, p. 232.
[37] *Ibid.*
[38] *Ibid.*, p. 231.
[39] *DF*, p. 45.
[40] *ST*, I, p. 229.

ments' inability to answer the question of God. These arguments bring the ontological analysis to a conclusion by disclosing that the question of God is implied in the finite structure of being. In performing this function they partially accept and also partially reject traditional natural theology. They drive reason to the quest for revelation. The proofs do not establish God, but rather because God is, the proofs state the question pointing to God in man's existence. This is similar to Max Scheler's views and those of many after him. "The proof for God's existence is not the foundation for religion—but religion is the foundation for the proof."[41] Tillich is writing theology; from *within* the context of Christian revelation-theology his estimation of the proofs are correct; the proofs cannot establish the God of faith.

God as Power and Being

The two basic aspects of the theology of God—God as Ultimate Concern and as Being-Itself—are the *formal* criteria of all theology. All theology must be correlated to what concerns us ultimately; this determines our being ultimately in existence and in meaning. Conversely, both criteria are God, for God is Being-Itself and our Ultimate Concern.[42]

1. Tillich's Phenomenological Term for God—Ultimate Concern

The first formal criterion for theology ("methodological guardians at the boundary line of theology") is "ultimate concern."[43] What is religious is ultimate and vice versa; it makes

---

[41] H. Fries, *Die katholische Religionsphilosophie der Gegenwart* (Heidelberg: Kerle, 1949), pp. 333; 85 f. Similarly H. Duméry, *The Problem of God in Philosophy of Religion* (Evanston: Northwestern, 1964).

[42] *ST*, I, pp. 11 ff.

[43] *Ibid.*

all other concerns secondary, limited, and preliminary. The unconditional concern is total—no part of the world or man, past or present, is excluded from relation to it. It is therefore not only ultimate, unconditional, and total, but infinite. Concern brings the ultimate into relation to the existential character of man and his religion. Tillich says that the ultimate concern, the unconditioned quality of the ultimate is not a thing.[44] What he means is that it is not an object, not some empirical thing, not a being as other created realities are. It is not an object for it is related existentially to man's concern. This is why Tillich, viewed uncritically, sometimes seems to deny the ultimate concern as an extramental reality.

Ultimate concern is a phenomenological term and a criterion of theology; as such it is necessarily introductory and propaedeutic.

[Ultimate Concern] is the correlate of an unconditional concern but not a "highest thing" called "the absolute" or "the unconditioned," about which we could argue in detached objectivity. It is the object of total surrender . . . it's a matter of infinite passion and interest [Kierkegaard], making us its object whenever we try to make it our object. For this reason we have avoided terms like "the ultimate," "the unconditioned," "the universal," "the infinite," and have spoken of ultimate, unconditional, total, infinite concern. Of course, in every concern there is something about which one is concerned; but this something should not appear as a separated object which could be known and handled without concern.[45]

Tillich emphasizes *something* and hence excludes the idea of a mental, object-less "concern." Ultimate concern, we might say, is the introductory yet existentially basic mode of how the object of revelation, religion and theology will be introduced to us, and how it will always transcend created structures of being, namely, how it will remain symbolic or ana-

---

[44] *ST*, I, p. 12.
[45] *Ibid.* "The concrete element in the idea of God cannot be destroyed." *ST*, I, p. 225.

logical. Tillich illustrates in a sermon why he has chosen this approach:

So we ask again, what is the one thing we need? And again it is difficult to answer. If we answer, "God," this will also be misunderstood. Even God can be made a finite concern, an object among other objects; in whose existence some people believe and some do not. Such a God, of course, cannot be our ultimate concern. Or we make him a person like other persons with whom it is useful to have a relationship. Such a person may support a finite concern but he certainly cannot be our ultimate concern.[46]

By "ultimate" Tillich wishes to make God the unconditional, free from peculiarities of objectivity, character, or circumstance, and to assert his total and infinite penetration of all places and times. By "concern" Tillich introduces the existential aspect of the divine as a matter of infinite, existential interest for the individual. From this phenomenological consideration, Tillich easily moves to the ontological perspective in which he conceives the divine as being itself.

God is the answer to the question implied in man's finitude; he is the name for that which concerns man ultimately. This does not mean that first there is a being called God and then the demand that man should be ultimately concerned about him. It means that whatever concerns a man ultimately becomes God for him. . . . Whenever infinite or unconditional power and meaning are attributed to the highest being, it has ceased to be a being and has become being-itself.[47]

Tillich's doctrine of ultimate concern raises the problem of whether man could not be ultimately concerned with what is not his real ultimate concern. This is a frequent criticism of Tillich, but it overlooks the fact that ultimate concern is a propaedeutic idea leading further, and that the true ultimate concern is discerned through a further relationship to questions of being and non-being. Since only the true ulti-

46 NB, p. 159.
47 ST, I, p. 234.

mate concern can concern our existence (this implies not necessarily saving us in this life and the next, but also rendering our existence meaningful), other false concerns cannot save us. Thus to choose a false ultimate concern is a matter of being or non-being for us. Sin, evil, non-existence, punishment, and the effects of sin are non-being. Tillich identifies the ultimate concern with the ground of being. "God is the power of being, resisting and conquering non-being. In relation to the creature, the divine power is expressed in the symbol of omnipotence . . . almighty God. . . . Only the almighty God can be man's ultimate concern. A very mighty God may claim to be of ultimate concern; but he is not, and his claim comes to naught, because he cannot resist non-being and therefore he cannot supply the ultimate courage which conquers anxiety."[48] The ultimate concern points out the mysterious and the holy. "Revelation is the manifestation of what concerns us ultimately. The mystery which is revealed is of ultimate concern to us because it is the ground of our being. . . . Revelation, as revelation of the mystery which is our ultimate concern, is invariably revelation for someone in a concrete situation of concern."[49]

2. God as Being-Itself

Does our ultimate concern inevitably relate to us?

Our ultimate concern is that which determines our being or non-being. Only those statements are theological which deal with their object in us insofar as it can become a matter of being or non-being for us. This is the second formal criterion of theology. Nothing can be of ultimate concern for us which does not have the power of threatening and saving our being.[50]

[48] ST, I, pp. 272–73.
[49] ST, I, p. 110; on false ultimate concerns, see *Ultimate Concern*, ed. cit., pp. 7–16.
[50] ST, I, p. 14.

Being is not only our metaphysical existence (Aristotle),
but the meaning and structure of this existence (Heidegger).
"The term 'being' means the whole of human reality, the
structure, the meaning and the aim of existence. All this is
threatened; it can be lost or saved. Man is ultimately concerned about his being and meaning."[51] Being is a dynamic
concept: the power of being. It is known when the ultimate
breaks into man's existence. Desperate man knowing his
plight and predicament reaches out for meaning and existence. For Tillich being-itself is not only the most accurate
name for God, but once it was the only "non-symbolic" term.

> The statement that God is being-itself is a non-symbolic
> statement. It does not point beyond itself. It means what it
> says directly and properly; if we speak of the actuality of God
> we first assert that he is not God if he is not being-itself.
> Other assertions about God can be made theologically only
> on this basis. Many confusions in the doctrine of God and
> many apologetic weaknesses could be avoided if God were
> understood first of all as being-itself or as the ground of
> being.[52]

Why is God best designated as being-itself? First, because
we object to God as *a* being, one among other. Tillich tried
to find a *nomen divinum* which transcends this univocal ontological individualism without reaching pantheism. This he
does with *being-itself defined as ground of being or power of
being.* (Being implies Heidegger's *Sein*—the reality, framework, disclosure—process beyond all beings.) The concept of
being as being-itself points to the power inherent in everything, the power of resisting non-being. Therefore, instead of
saying that God is first of all being-itself, it is possible to say
that He is the power of being in everything and above everything, the infinite power of being.[53]

The phrase "ground of being" could imply: a) conserva-
tion of being; or b) the foundation of the structure of being
in the sense that magnetic fields ground other phenomena

[51] *Ibid.*
[52] *ST*, I, pp. 235 f.
[53] *ST*, I, pp. 238, 235.

really, in models or mathematics; or c) a pantheistic element in all beings. The word *Grund* ("ground") has several meanings in German and a long history. This Germanic background is important for understanding Tillich's use of the word. "Ground" has not been so used in English until recent times and under the impact of German philosophy and theology. The English word "ground" tends to mean the earth, or a level of support in physical contact with what is supported. The German term looks more to an important subject which supports (*der tragende Grund*) and which is distinct from the reality grounded. The German word carries not only the meaning of real support and foundation but also that of reason, the Latin *ratio*.[54] Tillich writes that to convey the permanent creativity of God in all that is he uses the "ontological metaphor" ground of being.[55]

The second term, "power of being," implies the conserving, sustaining of being, an ultimate power of being in the sense that God's level of being is a power, an aspect of being (as in the power of mathematical number) determined to an infinite and transcendent degree.

These three terms yield one dominant single meaning defining what being-itself means for Tillich. Being-itself is

[54] It is common for German theologians, working from Aquinas or contemporary thought (e.g. Heidegger) to speak in terms similar to Tillich's, but it is not normal for American or English theologians (until recently and under the influence of Tillich and other German theologians) to use the word "ground." Heidegger writes: "That Being (*Sein*) is précised as Ground (*Grund*), everyone today takes that for granted." *Kants These über das Sein* (Frankfurt: Klostermann, 1962), p. 9. J. B. Lotz illustrates the use of *Grund* in theology in "Gott," HTHG, I, p. 573. See W. J. Richardson, *Heidegger: Through Phenomenology to Thought* (The Hague: Nijhof, 1963), pp. 161–62. English "ground" corresponds at first sight to *Boden*, the place where men and buildings stand and from which trees grow; consequently a pantheistic and materialistic tone can arise. Moreover, completely absent is the secondary meaning of reason (*ratio*) giving the German *Grund* a spiritual, intellectual, and separational meaning.

[55] Paul Tillich, BRSUR, p. 74.

"the power of resisting non-being," and "the infinite power of being."[56] Finiteness is not so much limitation but potentiality and direction toward non-being both in existence and meaning. From such a point of departure, Tillich determines his theology of God. God is: *the absolute, total power of resisting any form of non-being.*

The real meaning of almightiness is that God is the power of being in everything that is, transcending every special power infinitely but acting at the same time as its creative ground. In the religious experience the power of God provokes the feeling of being in the hand of a power which cannot be conquered by another power, in ontological terms, which is the infinite resistance against non-being and the eternal victory over it. To participate in this resistance and this victory is felt as the way to overcome the threat of non-being which is the destiny of everything finite.[57]

To understand Tillich's "ground" we must also be constantly aware of how in this passage he defines (and rejects) "cause" and "substance" as speaking of God.

The ground of revelation (God) is not its "cause" in the categorical sense of the word "cause." It is the "ground of being" manifest in existence. The revelation between the ground of being and its revelatory manifestations can be expressed only in terms of finite actions originating in a highest being and transforming the course of finite events. . . . In the same way the relation of the ground of revelation to those who receive revelation can be conceived only in personal categories for that which is the ultimate concern of a person cannot be less than a person, although it can be and must be more than personality. Under these circumstances, the theologian must emphasize the symbolic character of all concepts which are used to describe the divine act of self-revelation, and he must try to use terms which indicate that their meaning is not categorical.[58]

Is a ground of being pantheism? After the first volume of the *Systematic Theology*, Tillich wrote that the "ground of

---

[56] *ST*, I, p. 235.
[57] *LPJ*, p. 110.
[58] *ST*, I, pp. 155 f.

being" should not be seen as the cause or reason of things, for the ground of being is ultimate. "(It is) the creative source of everything that has being. And if this is the meaning of the phrase, sinister connotations in the sense of Schopenhauer are excluded. They are included, however, as a possibility in the metaphor 'abyss of being,' the depth in which everything finite disappears."[59] In 1956 Tillich answered his critics on the same point. Supranaturalism makes God univocal, one being among many in a "super-world," while "naturalism" identifies God with the universe.[60] Pantheism is more sophisticated than a crass identification of God with the world. "God is the name for the power and meaning of reality . . . he is a symbol of the unity, harmony, power of being; he is the dynamic and creative centre of reality."[61] Although this sounds like Tillich's own theology, pantheism is rejected. Pantheism denies the infinite distance between the whole of finite things and their infinite ground.[62] This calls for a third way, but this way is now new. Tillich says it was already recognized by Augustine, Thomas, Luther, Calvin, and Schleiermacher.

It agrees with the naturalistic view by asserting that God would not be God if he were not the creative ground of everything that has being, that, in fact, he is the infinite and unconditional power of being, or in the most radical abstraction, that he is being-itself.[63]

This, Tillich says, is thus far a refined naturalism, but . . .

At this point the terms "self-transcendent" and "ecstatic" which I use for the third way of understanding the term "God" become meaningful. The term "self-transcendent" has

[59] "Reply . . . ," K&B, p. 341. "I am not convinced by any of the criticisms of my use of the phrase *esse ipsum* as the first (certainly not the last) assertion about God, that it can be omitted or replaced by anything else. Being as the negation of possible non-being is the basic cognitive position, which precedes in logical dignity every characterization of being." "Reply . . . ," K&B, p. 339.

[60] ST, II, pp. 5–9.

[61] Ibid., p. 7.

[62] Ibid., p. 8.

[63] Ibid., p. 7.

two elements: "transcending" and "self." God as the ground of being infinitely transcends that of which he is the ground. He stands against the world . . . and he stands for the world. . . . To call God transcendent in this sense does not mean that one must establish a "superworld" of divine objects. It does mean that, within itself, the finite world points beyond itself. In other words, it is self-transcendent.[64]

Tillich's description of God in ontological rather than biblical terms, his asking whether there is one term which is non-symbolic and non-analogical to ground all the others, his vacillation on this point indicates that his theology of God involves deeply his own theory of symbol-analogy. That area is covered by other essays in this volume.

The importance of Tillich's theology of God is that it attempts to meet the underlying problem of increasing agnosticism and atheism; namely, the objectivization and univocalization of God by Christians. Tillich's theology is not the source of a Death-of-God theology; rather, it is the opposite. It is a theology born out of the prophetic voice of Nietzsche, out of the collapse of the nineteenth century during two world wars. It is an attempt to find the godly God (Heidegger) to which ontology and Scripture point, the God who is both beyond our greatest thought and yet intimately present to us in our existence, a God who has lived among us on earth and is now coming to us out of the future.

[64] *Ibid.*

PAUL TILLICH

An Afterword:
Appreciation and Reply

It is indeed a great honor for me that a book about my theology, consisting of contributions by a large group of outstanding Roman Catholic theologians is to be published. And it is an expression of generosity and openness that I have been asked to write an answer to some of the criticisms made by the contributors. I gladly accept this invitation, although I am aware of the limitations that a short reply to so many weighty papers necessarily has.

I want to start with a statement that refers to all of the articles in one way or another: A large part of the criticisms are an expression of the basic differences between the Roman Catholic and the Protestant understanding of Christianity, and even of the nature of religion. This is unavoidable. It is the consequence of that interaction between destiny and decision which determines the religious condition of every human being.

It seems to me that there are three main points in which this contrast appears directly: objectivity against subjectivity; authority against autonomy; analogy against symbol.

The understanding of my theology as subjectivistic is the most frequent one. I must restrict myself to a few of the more outspoken criticisms. A summary expression of it is Kenelm Foster's statement that my system could be considered as an "essay in theological anthropology" [p. 150]. Gustave Weigel relates subjectivity to existentialism, when he sees in my theology the objectivity of God dissolved into man's ultimate concern [see p. 43]. From another side the existentialist element is identified with emotion [see George McLean, p. 213]; and emotional participation is contrasted with cognitive participation, so that my theology is seen as alternating between subjective emotion and objective knowledge. In all cases, what is missed is objective knowledge of God. This is caused, one says, by my rejection of the validity of the classical arguments for the existence of God. For me, God can be known only in correlation with man, not "in himself," which is seen as especially manifest in my doctrine of the Trinity [see T. F. O'Meara, p. 347]. The same author extends the criticism of subjectivism also to my Mariological statements. Mary, he says, becomes a "utilitarian religious symbol" and value judgments replace statements of objective truth [see p. 349]. Finally the predominance of subjectivity leads to a subjectivistic concept of faith which does not include the belief in facts as they are reported, e.g., in Bible and tradition [see pp. 349–51]. Since these reports are subject to methodological historical criticism, they cannot be, for my thinking, a matter of faith which is an existential relation of the person to God.

These last words already contain a part of my answer to some accusations of subjectivism: With respect to historical beliefs, that strain of Protestantism which applies the methods of historical research to the Bible and tradition without dogmatic restriction is, I think, nearer to objectivity than both Catholicism and Protestant Orthodoxy. It is the objectivity of scholarly research, and not the objectivity of authority, exercised by a collective subject through its official representatives. One could answer that the historical method cannot exclude elements of subjectivity in every individual historian. This is true, but here there is the corrective of an international public discussion without limiting authorities, as in Catholicism, or a dogmatic predecision, as in Protestant Fundamentalism.

But the accusation of subjectivism against Protestantism generally and my theology particularly has more basic implications: It goes to the very depth of the problem of man in relation to God. In contemporary terminology, one could say that religion, as rediscovered by the Reformers, is an existential relation between God and man. This implies that God can be experienced only in terms of "ultimate concern" and never as an object which could be approached cognitively like other objects. Every knowledge of God, like every prayer, like every act of obedience, like every experience of awe and blessedness, is the work of the divine Spirit, i.e., God himself, present to our spirit. In these experiences the separation of the act of knowing from emotion and of both of them from will is impossible. Equally impossible is it to call such a relation to God subjectivistic, for the Spiritual Presence transcends the split between subject and object. This does not make the experience irrational, and in this sense subjective, but it is, like every act of faith, reason grasped ecstatically by the divine Spirit. Rather, it is irrational, and therefore subjectivistic, to believe in a supranatural disruption of the created structure of mind and reality as, for example, in the supranaturalistic interpretation of miracles as divine interference in the working of natural laws. This "rational irrationalism" remains subjectivistic even if it is supported by the authority of theologians and bishops. It may be subjective credulity, elevated to objective truth not by its intrinsic validity but by tradition and authority. For, after all, the acceptance of a particular system of authority is also the act of individual subjects. No religion can escape the point in which subjects are existentially involved and give witness to their experience. Therefore, I would suggest that, instead of making mutual accusations of objectivism and subjectivism, the Catholic-Protestant dialogue should center around the nature of that experience which I have called "ultimate concern" or "self-transcending reason" or "Spiritual Presence" or "Faith" (in contrast to "beliefs"). A hopeful step in this direction is the reference to the concept of "participation" by George McLean [see pp. 165–67]. He declares that this concept, which is much used by me, is not Protestant. He is right with respect to the main stream of Protestant thought. But since there is no religion which could exist without the experience of Spiritual Presence, Protestantism also has a strong line of thought in which the reality of participation is expressed, from the mystical elements of the early Luther on, to the doctrine of *unio mystica* in Protestant Orthodoxy, to Pietism, Schleiermacher, Rudolf Otto and the liturgical reform movements. In these cases "Catholic substance" reappeared under the control of the "Protestant principle."

The preceding discussion of objectivity against subjectivity has already touched upon the related problem of authority against autonomy. I turn now directly to it. The necessity of authority and the limitation of autonomy is most strongly expressed by George McLean [see pp. 106–7]. He demands the submission to authority as a religious duty, as a sacrifice which is humiliating and which has been loved by the saints just because it is humiliating. There is no salvation without going through "the lowly gates of submission." This is especially difficult for man's pride because it leads to the obligation "to give a kind of divine reverence to a human person" and because it implies not only submission with respect to acting but also to thinking. For this, "some of the autonomy" on which I insist must be sacrificed.

These statements are sharp formulations of what I would call "heteronomy," the subjection to a law which is not experienced as our own. It is a necessary consequence that as a Protestant theologian I cannot accept this "objectivation" of authority. But if authority is not embodied in human persons to whom "a kind of divine reverence" is to be given (bishops, councils, popes), a decisive element of autonomy is re-established, and then autonomy may become "theonomy," namely, directed, without being sacrificed, by the divine Spirit. It may or it may not become theonomy. If it does not, autonomy becomes empty and finally self-destructive. Then, often the longing for a new heteronomy appears, as in many of our contemporaries. Protestantism has experienced this whole dialectics: In declaring the Bible the only authority, the Reformers changed the meaning of authority. For a book cannot be a living authority like a person. It needs interpreters; and if there is no authoritative interpreter, autonomy has a wide field and is threatened by such dangers of pure autonomy as relativism, scepticism, cynicism. This is the "Protestant risk," inseparable from the Protestant principle. Protestant Orthodoxy partly and Fundamentalism completely reject this risk. But since they have no living authority, they fall into the absurdities of biblical literalism, and elevate, often unknowingly, the dogmatic theology of the late sixteenth and early seventeenth centuries to unconditioned authority, identifying this theology with the meaning of the Bible and, consequently, with the Word of God.

There are some other problems, dependent on the solution of the problem of authority. They refer to the concept of revelation. Revelation always combines a giving and a receiving side. It is the latter in which contradictions occur and even are unavoidable—e.g., in the relation of the New to the Old Testament. This seems to me to be implied in Avery Dulles' reference to the "patient pedagogy" of God [p. 175]. It is, of course, my conviction that this pedagogy is valid also for the history of the Church, for example, of the relation of Protestantism to the different forms of Catholicism and of the next stage of the history of the Church to the Protestant "era."

Christopher Kiesling [pp. 331–32] asks whether my doctrine of revelation does not undercut the Christian claim to be the true revelation in contrast to all others, thus introducing a religious relativism. To this I answer that the claim to final truth cannot be raised for the Christian churches or for Christianity as a religion, but only for the event on which Christianity is based, and which is both received and distorted by the Christian churches. Such understanding enables the Christian theologian to valuate the non-Christian religions in terms of a universal revelation very much in the sense of the early Christian doctrine of the *logos spermatikos*, the divine self-manifestation in all human history. But the criterion of every religion, including Christianity, is the appearance of Jesus as the Christ in the "center of history."

The accusation of subjectivism against my theology is in a very conspicuous way expressed in the discussion of my doctrine of symbols in the light of the Catholic doctrine of *analogia entis*. Naturally the criticism appears above all in a comparison of Thomas' and my own doctrine of the knowledge of God. After Gustave Weigel's [see p. 53] short evaluation of my theory of symbols as, so to speak, a Protestant "pointer" to Thomas' doctrine of the *analogia entis*, George McLean, in his article "Symbol and Analogy: Tillich and Thomas," develops the main argument. The difference, according to him, is that for Thomas reality itself is analogous, while for me reality is neither analogous nor symbolic. Therefore, Thomas is able to develop a rational and objective doctrine of God on the basis of the analogical character of reality, while for me symbols arise out of the changing existential relation of man to God. It is a further consequence of this difference that Thomas' rational method leads to a set of definite statements about God, while my existential method leads to the idea of changing expressions of the divine-human encounter and to the doctrine of the birth and death of symbols. It is, of course, the experience of the death of many Catholic symbols in Protestantism (especially that of the "Blessed Virgin"), which is the background of such a dynamic and existential understanding of symbols. But in spite of this basically Protestant analysis of the symbolic character of the religious language, I would reject the criticism that for me "reality is neither analogous nor symbolic." I have often emphasized that all dimensions of reality can provide for symbolic material, because they are rooted in that which they are supposed to symbolize, the divine Ground of Being. But, because I gave this justification for the use of symbols in our speaking about God, the accusation of a strong pantheistic element appeared [see p. 235]—which I shall return to later. Here I want to discuss one other criticism by George McLean, namely that symbols, "in my sense," do not give "objective information" about God [see pp. 235–36]—as conclusions from analogy assumedly do. "Objective information about God" is indeed a phrase which I must radically reject because it sounds to me almost blasphemous: It makes God into an object about which "informations" are possible. Against this I would say that symbols of the divine can appear only for the existential situation of ultimate concern; and they are meaningless outside the situation.

After having discussed differences which necessarily follow from the basic Catholic-Protestant conflict, I now turn to particular problems which transcend this conflict, although even here the confessional difference influences the respective formulations. The first problem in point is the doctrine of God. I could agree with Gustave Weigel's statement that God, for my thought, is the "matrix of reality" [p. 43], if matrix means that in which everything that is has its being. The term "Ground of Being" points to the same truth (which is also implied in the symbol of *creatio continua*). God is the source of all meaning and certainly not meaningless without man (as I am accused of saying). We experience meaning as meaning, since we are human, and we experience the Ground of Meaning not by detached analysis and conclusions, but by a breakthrough of the ultimate into preliminary meaning; and ultimate meaning can be received only in a state of being ultimately concerned about what is ultimate. I do not believe that one could call such theology "purest naturalism" [p. 47]. Categories like ultimacy, its breakthrough into the preliminary, existential concern about "Being and Meaning Itself" cannot appear within a naturalistic system. And if, in my system, "we never leave the realm of human concern" [p. 48] this concern transcends the merely human because it is ultimate. It is easy to call a theology which rejects supranaturalism naturalistic. It is more difficult but very necessary to find adequate expressions for what inadequately could be called "self-transcending" or, even bolder, "ecstatic" naturalism.

A very serious and extremely difficult problem is raised by Kenelm Foster [see pp. 142–45]. He defends Thomas against my criticism that Thomas speaks of the existence of God in a double sense: one, God in himself; and one, God for us. He refers to Thomas' doctrine of the double meaning of the copula "is": the first, designating reality in itself; the second, designating our judgment about it. While in the first sense God is beyond that contrast between essence and existence which characterizes finite being, in the second sense he can become an object of our judgment. We can affirm that he is (exists), and can find objective arguments for his existence. But the question is whether this double use of the copula can be applied to our speaking about God. In the second use (judgment of existence), he would be considered as an object besides others (though the most eminent one) which may or may not exist. But the possibility of such an objectifying question about God is dependent on a preceding awareness of God by him who asks. In every serious question about God, God asks the question of himself through man; man could not ask this question if he did not know in an immediate way what he wants to know discursively. This means that the nature of God itself prohibits objective arguments for his existence. This agrees with the classical doctrine that God's being is above essence and existence. I believe that Thomas, in this point (as well as, e.g., in his psychology), was split between the Platonic tradition and the rediscovery of Aristotle. And I believe that the Platonic (Augustinian-Franciscan) tradition is more fundamental for the understanding of our knowledge of God. With Kant I believe that the ontological argument (which should appear not as an argument, but as a description) precedes and enables the cosmological arguments (which should not appear as arguments either, but as analyses of finitude and questions beyond it). This is the reason why I think George McLean is right when he accuses me of admitting only "immediacy of knowledge" with respect to God; and he is right when he points to my preference for the term "awareness" over against "knowledge" in this connection. "Immediacy" and "awareness" stand against the possibility of an argumentative knowledge of God. Awareness of God precedes discursive knowledge of him.

A point, often appearing in the articles, is the question of a pantheistic trend in my thought. I myself have spoken of a "pantheistic element" in every adequate doctrine of God. This, of course, has been said against the half-deistic theism of much Protestant theology. It should not have been criticized by Catholic theologians whose tradition implies the doctrine that God is *ipsum esse*. But since the question has been raised I want to reply. First, I must sharply reject the assertion that I call God "the essence of all things" [p. 120]. In many places I emphasize that this dissolves God into the essence of the world and removes his qualitative transcendence. It is an essentialistic (formerly called idealistic) form of naturalism and it would indeed deny freedom and individuality both to God and to creatures [p. 149]. But after this has been said, the so-called "pantheistic element" must be used as corrective: If we attribute freedom to God we must also attribute necessity (or as I prefer to call it: destiny) to him. And if we attribute individuality or self-hood to God, we must also attribute universality to him; and in both cases we must say: God transcends the polarities, as he transcends essence and existence.

George McLean notices a preponderance of the *via negativa* in my doctrine of God [see p. 113]. This is correct; it is rooted in the present situation, in which theologians as well as nontheologians turn away from a "God-language"—as it is called—in which a large amount of positive statements can be made about God, his nature, and his actions, without the negative corrective. This is one of the reasons for the sympathy of many contemporaries for the Eastern religions and of others for the purely secular language even within theology. A deep feeling for the riddle of existence and for the mystery of being makes it impossible for these people to accept a too "well-informed" speaking of God.

The last point I want to discuss is the criticism of my Christology, adding some remarks about Mariology and ecclesiology. The basic accusation by several of the contributors is the same which I am used to receiving from my Protestant and some humanist critics, namely that I have "a Christ without Jesus" [p. 346]. Even a superficial reading of the chapters of the second volume of *Systematic Theology* which deal with the "historical Jesus" should silence this criticism. My question was and is: How can the methodological scepticism which is an essential element in all historical research be united with the assertion of faith that Jesus of Nazareth is the Christ. My thesis is that the uninhibited scientific approach to the biblical records about Jesus cannot undercut the assertion of faith concerning him, nor can it deliver a biographical picture of the man Jesus as the basis for faith and Christological doctrine, whether the particular results of the research are more conservative or more sceptical. Faith alone can guarantee the historical character of that event on which faith is based; it can guarantee that something has happened in history which is sufficient to explain what has happened to him who has faith, namely, the transformation of his estranged existence. But faith cannot guarantee the reliability of historical records about the event, and faith (whether that of an individual or of a community) never can and never should try to determine the results of historical research. Therefore, neither the authority of the Bible in terms of the doctrine of verbal inspiration nor the authority of the Church in terms of its infallibility has the right to interfere with honest historical criticism. Under this presupposition I have tried to ask the question of faith and historical research and have attempted to give both of them what they have a right to demand.

The second criticism of my Christology is directly dogmatic. It calls my Christology Nestorian [see pp. 134–35] and Adoptianistic [see pp. 348–49]. My task in answering these accusations cannot be an attempt to deny them. From the point of view of the accepted dogma they may correct. But, theologically, ideas rejected by the ancient theologians and their successors may contain a truth which must be expressed in contemporary categories and concepts. I have tried to do so in the third volume of the *Systematic Theology* under the heading, "A Spirit Christology." This chapter restates decisive elements of the synoptic image of Jesus, elements which got lost by the complete victory of the Logos-Christology in the later dogmatic development. I do not reject the Logos-Christology, especially because of the universalistic element it brings into the assertion that Jesus is the Christ. I always defended it against Karl Barth's rejection of it. But I believe (with the great historians of the dogma, Harnack, Loofs, etc., to whom, surprisingly, George Tavard never refers) that the Logos-Christology was largely spoiled by the partly official (Second Council of Constantinople), partly popular removal of the human image of the Christ. It is the hidden Monophysitism of the Catholic Church (and of many Protestant groups) against which my Christology stands.

On the basis of these considerations, I can also answer the question, whether for my thought "This man Jesus also was God" [see pp. 283, 295–96]. I certainly would not use such a phrase nor do I believe the formulators of the Christological dogma would have used it. They were rightly afraid of making the Christ into a person "with two heads" (the Antiochean school was accused of this) or of making him into a transformation of God himself (as the monarchianists tried to do). I believe that we need a completely different terminology, and that this terminology must be determined by an existentialistic approach, by the question: What does Jesus, who was called the Christ, mean for us?

It is hard for me to speak about Mariology. In any case I would maintain that the dogma has not developed out of the few historical indications in the Gospel records (whose legendary character is a highly probable critical proposition), but, as T. F. O'Meara rightly emphasizes, as a logical consequence of the dogma of incarnation (especially in its Cyrillian interpretation) and, as I would add, out of the increasing valuation of the ideal of virginity under monastic influence, and beyond this out of the strong need of popular piety (and the human heart) for a powerful symbol of the protecting, motherly loving, embracing side of the actual relation of the divine to the human. The tremendous significance of the figure of Mary for contemporary Catholic piety confirms this analysis.

Only a few words about the doctrine of the Church: The basic difference has been discussed in the first part of this article, especially in the section on authority. Yet, there is an interesting remark in Maurice Schepers' chapter on my doctrine of the Church: He says [see p. 318] that I have neglected the horizontal dimension of the Church. Something similar is expressed by T. F. O'Meara, when he says [see p. 351] that God's power is more manifest in the historical development of the Church than in particular breakthroughs of revelatory character. Only in the third part of the system have I discussed this problem. There, however, the function of the Church, in its latent as well as in its manifest form, is fully discussed. The Church, represented by the churches, is the fighting side of the Kingdom of God in history. And the objective of the fight (priestly as well as prophetic) is always the creation of faith and love, that is, reunion with God and man and world.

I want to repeat that I did this reply with the same joy about a fruitful dialogue with which I read the articles. One thing I learned in doing so is the necessity that we learn more about each other's thought, the classical as well as the contemporary. Much misunderstanding on both sides could be prevented by such better information. But fundamental differences cannot be removed and must be acknowledged. Only the divine Spirit and historical providence can overcome the splits amongst those representing the Spiritual Community which transcends every particular church and every particular religious group. A dialogue, done in "listening love," can be a tool of providence and a channel of the divine Spirit.

General Index

OTHER IMAGE BOOKS

ST. JOAN OF ARC – John Beevers (D131) – 75¢

A HISTORY OF PHILOSOPHY: VOLUME 1 – GREECE AND ROME (2 Volumes) – Frederick Copleston, S.J. (D134a, D134b) – $1.25 ea.

A HISTORY OF PHILOSOPHY: VOLUME 2 – MEDIAEVAL PHILOSOPHY (2 Volumes) – Frederick Copleston, S.J. Part I – Augustine to Bonaventure. Part II – Albert the Great to Duns Scotus (D135a, D135b) – $1.25 ea.

A HISTORY OF PHILOSOPHY: VOLUME 3 – LATE MEDIAEVAL AND RENAISSANCE PHILOSOPHY (2 Volumes) – Frederick Copleston, S.J. Part I – Ockham to the Speculative Mystics. Part II – The Revival of Platonism to Suárez (D136a, D136b) – $1.25 ea.

A HISTORY OF PHILOSOPHY: VOLUME 4 – MODERN PHILOSOPHY: Descartes to Leibniz – Frederick Copleston, S.J. (D137) – $1.45

A HISTORY OF PHILOSOPHY: VOLUME 5 – MODERN PHILOSOPHY: The British Philosophers, Hobbes to Hume (2 Volumes) – Frederick Copleston, S.J. Part I – Hobbes to Paley. Part II – Berkeley to Hume (D138a, D138b) – $1.25 ea.

A HISTORY OF PHILOSOPHY: VOLUME 6 – MODERN PHILOSOPHY (2 Volumes) – Frederick Copleston, S.J. Part I – The French Enlightenment to Kant (D139a) – 95¢. Part II – Kant (D139b) – $1.25

A HISTORY OF PHILOSOPHY: VOLUME 7 – MODERN PHILOSOPHY (2 Volumes) – Frederick Copleston, S.J. Part I – Fichte to Hegel. Part II – Schopenhauer to Nietzsche (D140a, D140b) – $1.25 ea.

A HISTORY OF PHILOSOPHY: VOLUME 8 – MODERN PHILOSOPHY: Bentham to Russell (2 Volumes) – Frederick Copleston, S.J. Part I – British Empiricism and the Idealist Movement in Great Britain. Part II – Idealism in America, the Pragmatist Movement, the Revolt against Idealism (D141a, D141b) – $1.25 ea.

THE WATERS OF SILOE – Thomas Merton. Account of the Trappists (D144) – $1.25

WE WORK WHILE THE LIGHT LASTS – Dom Hubert van Zeller, O.S.B. Meditations on contemporary problems (D146) – 75¢

MARY MOTHER OF FAITH – Joseph Weiger. A beautiful meditation on Our Lady (D148) – 85¢

TRANSFORMATION IN CHRIST – Dietrich von Hildebrand. Analysis of the Christian experience (D152) – $1.45

CATHEDRAL AND CRUSADE (2 Volumes) – Henri Daniel-Rops. A history of the Church between the eleventh and fourteenth centuries (D154a, D154b) – $1.35 ea.

OTHER IMAGE BOOKS

FAITH AND FREEDOM – Barbara Ward (D73) – 95¢

THE IDEA OF A UNIVERSITY – John Henry Cardinal Newman. Introduction by G. N. Shuster (D75) – $1.45

DARK NIGHT OF THE SOUL – St. John of the Cross. Edited and translated by E. Allison Peers (D78) – 85¢

TERESA OF AVILA – Marcelle Auclair. Translated by Kathleen Pond (D79) – $1.45

WOMAN OF THE PHARISEES – François Mauriac (D82) – 95¢

THE PILLAR OF FIRE – Karl Stern. A psychiatrist's spiritual journey from Judaism to Catholicism (D83) – 95¢

THE LONG LONELINESS – Dorothy Day. An Autobiography (D89) – 85¢

A POPULAR HISTORY OF THE REFORMATION – Philip Hughes (D92) – $1.25

THE CATHOLIC CHURCH IN THE MODERN WORLD – E. E. Y. Hales (D95) – 95¢

THE LIFE OF TERESA OF JESUS: The Autobiography of Teresa of Avila – Translated by E. Allison Peers (D96) – $1.25

SCHOLASTICISM AND POLITICS – Jacques Maritain (D98) – 95¢

THE SON OF GOD – Karl Adam. A dissertation on the humanity and divinity of Christ (D99) – 95¢

THE CONFESSIONS OF ST. AUGUSTINE – Translated with an Introduction by John K. Ryan (D101) – $1.45

THE HEART OF MAN – Gerald Vann, O.P. Unique and compassionate insight into man's nature (D103) – 75¢

SPIRITUAL CANTICLE – St. John of the Cross. Translated with an Introduction and Notes by E. Allison Peers (D110) – $1.45

THE THIRD REVOLUTION: A Study of Psychiatry and Religion – Dr. Karl Stern (D113) – 95¢

WE HAVE BEEN FRIENDS TOGETHER and ADVENTURES IN GRACE – Raissa Maritain (D114) – $1.25

WE DIE STANDING UP – Dom Hubert van Zeller, O.S.B. (D115) – 85¢

INTERIOR CASTLE – St. Teresa of Avila. Translated with an Introduction and Notes by E. Allison Peers (D120) – 95¢

THE MEANING OF MAN – Jean Mouroux. The significance of man and his relation to God (D122) – $1.25

SOUL OF THE APOSTOLATE – Jean-Baptiste Chautard, O.C.S.D. (D124) – 85¢

THE SONG AT THE SCAFFOLD – Gertrud von Le Fort. A novel of faith during the French revolution (D126) – 65¢

THE CHURCH OF APOSTLES AND MARTYRS (2 Volumes) – Henri Daniel-Rops (D128a, D128b) – $1.35 ea.

LATE HAVE I LOVED THEE – Ethel Mannin. A deeply moving novel of spiritual regeneration (D130) – $1.25

OTHER IMAGE BOOKS

PRAYER IN PRACTICE – Romano Guardini (D157) – 85¢

THE PROTESTANT REFORMATION (2 Volumes) – Henri Daniel-Rops (D159a, D159b) – $1.35 ea.

ON THE LOVE OF GOD (2 Volumes) – St. Francis de Sales. Translated and with an Introduction by John K. Ryan (D164a, D164b) – 95¢ ea.

THE CHURCH IN CRISIS: A History of the General Councils, 325–1870 – Philip Hughes (D168) – $1.25

ISRAEL AND THE ANCIENT WORLD – Henri Daniel-Rops (D169) – $1.55

THE SPIRITUAL EXERCISES OF ST. IGNATIUS – Translated by Anthony Mottola, Ph.D. Introduction by Robert W. Gleason, S.J. (D170) – 85¢

A NEWMAN READER: An Anthology of the Writings of John Henry Cardinal Newman – Edited with an Introduction by Francis X. Connolly (D171) – $1.45

THE GOLDEN STRING – Bede Griffiths, O.S.B. (D173) – 75¢

THE WAY OF PERFECTION – St. Teresa of Avila. Translated and edited by E. Allison Peers (D176) – 85¢

REFLECTIONS ON AMERICA – Jacques Maritain (D177) – 75¢

THE CATHOLIC REFORMATION (2 Volumes) – Henri Daniel-Rops (D179a, D179b) – $1.25 ea.

WE HOLD THESE TRUTHS: Catholic Reflections on the American Proposition – John Courtney Murray, S.J. (D181) – $1.25

LETTERS FROM VATICAN CITY – Xavier Rynne (D182) – 95¢

LIFE AND HOLINESS – Thomas Merton. Exposition of the principles of the spiritual life (D183) – 75¢

THE EMERGING LAYMAN: The Role of the Catholic Layman in America – Donald J. Thorman (D186) – 85¢

THE SOCIAL AND POLITICAL PHILOSOPHY OF JACQUES MARITAIN – Selected Readings – Edited by Joseph W. Evans and Leo R. Ward (D188) – $1.45

AMERICAN CATHOLICISM – John Tracy Ellis. A comprehensive survey of the American Church (D190) – 85¢

THE CHURCH IN THE SEVENTEENTH CENTURY (2 Volumes) – Henri Daniel-Rops (D191a, D191b) – $1.25 ea.

THE WORLD'S GREAT CATHOLIC LITERATURE – Edited by George N. Shuster (D192) – $1.45

THE CRISIS OF WESTERN EDUCATION – Christopher Dawson (D194) – 95¢

SOCIETY AND SANITY – F. J. Sheed. An explanation of Christian sociology and ethics (D195) – 95¢

THE COUNCIL, REFORM AND REUNION – with a new Introduction by Fr. Hans Kung (D198) – 95¢

OTHER IMAGE BOOKS

WITH GOD IN RUSSIA – Walter J. Ciszek, S.J., with Daniel L. Flaherty, S.J. (D200) – $1.25

THE CHURCH IN THE EIGHTEENTH CENTURY – Henri Daniel-Rops (D201) – $1.45

CURRENT TRENDS IN THEOLOGY – Edited by Donald J. Wolf, S.J., and James V. Schall, S.J. (D202) – 95¢

A HOPKINS READER, Revised and Enlarged Edition – Edited with an Introduction by John Pick (D203) – $1.45

MODERN PSYCHIATRY: A Handbook for Believers – Francis J. Braceland, M.D., and Michael Stock, O.P. (D204) – $1.25

THE STORY OF THE CHURCH, Revised Edition – Domenico Grandi and Antonio Galli. Translated by John Chapin (D206) – $1.25

THE CUNNING OF THE DOVE – Alfred Duggan. The story of St. Edward the Confessor (D208) – 85¢

A MARITAIN READER – Selected Writings of Jacques Maritain – Edited with an Introduction by Donald and Idella Gallagher (D210) – $1.45

POPE JOHN AND HIS REVOLUTION – E. E. Y. Hales (D213) – 85¢

THE TWO-EDGED SWORD – John L. McKenzie, S.J. Outstanding interpretation of the Old Testament (D215) – $1.35

THE CHURCH IN AN AGE OF REVOLUTION: 1789–1870 (2 Volumes) – Henri Daniel-Rops (D217a, D217b) – $1.35 ea.

MORTE D'URBAN – J. F. Powers. A brilliant, poignantly satiric portrait of a worldly priest (D218) – 95¢

STRANGERS IN THE HOUSE: Catholic Youth in America – Andrew M. Greeley (D221) – 95¢

THE DEPTHS OF THE SOUL: A Christian Approach to Psychoanalysis – Ignace Lepp (D222) – 95¢

COUNT BOHEMOND – Alfred Duggan. Preface by Evelyn Waugh. A novel of the First Crusade (D223) – 95¢

A FIGHT FOR GOD (2 Volumes) – Henri Daniel-Rops. This ninth volume of the *History of the Church of Christ* covers the period from 1870 to 1939 (D224a, D224b) – $1.45 ea.

CHRIST AND THE CHRISTIAN – Robert W. Gleason, S.J. (D227) – 95¢

THE DIVIDING OF CHRISTENDOM – Christopher Dawson (D229) – 95¢

OUR CHANGING LITURGY – C. J. McNaspy, S.J. (D230) – 95¢

NO MAN IS AN ISLAND – Thomas Merton (D231) – 95¢

ROAD TO RENEWAL – Bernard Häring, C.SS.R. (D233) – 95¢

CONJECTURES OF A GUILTY BYSTANDER – Thomas Merton. A collection of notes, opinions, reflections (D234) – $1.25

OTHER IMAGE BOOKS

THE NOONDAY DEVIL: Spiritual Support in Middle Age – Bernard Basset, S.J. A funny-serious book of spiritual direction (D237) – 95¢

UNDERSTAND THE BIBLE – J. Holland Smith (D238) – $1.25

HEALTH OF MIND AND SOUL – Ignace Lepp (D239) – 95¢

RELIGION AND PERSONALITY – Adrian van Kaam, C.S.Sp. (D240) – 95¢

RELIGIONS OF THE WORLD (2 Volumes) – John A. Hardon, S.J. An account of the history, beliefs, and practices of the major religions of the world (D241a, D241b) – $1.25 ea.

THE RELIGION OF TEILHARD DE CHARDIN – Henri de Lubac, S.J. (D242) – $1.65

CHRISTIAN RENEWAL IN A CHANGING WORLD – Bernard Häring, C.SS.R. (D244) – $1.45

CHRISTIAN SACRAMENTS AND CHRISTIAN PERSONALITY – Bernard J. Cooke, S.J. (D246) – $1.25

THOUGHTS IN SOLITUDE – Thomas Merton (D247) – 85¢

WHAT IS THE BIBLE? Revised Edition – Henri Daniel-Rops (D250) – 95¢

NEW TESTAMENT ESSAYS – Raymond E. Brown, S.S. (D251) – $1.35

TEILHARD DE CHARDIN AND THE MYSTERY OF CHRIST – Christopher Mooney, S.J. (D252) – $1.35